Group Processes in the Classroom

Sixth Edition

Richard A. Schmuck
University of Oregon, Eugene

Patricia A. Schmuck
Lewis and Clark College

 Wm. C. Brown Publishers

Book Team

Editor *Paul L. Tavenner*
Developmental Editor *Sue Pulvermacher-Alt*
Production Coordinator *Carla D. Arnold*

Wm. C. Brown Publishers

President *G. Franklin Lewis*
Vice President, Publisher *Thomas E. Doran*
Vice President, Operations and Production *Beverly Kolz*
National Sales Manager *Virginia S. Moffat*
Group Sales Manager *Eric Ziegler*
Executive Editor *Edgar J. Laube*
Director of Marketing *Kathy Law Laube*
Marketing Manager *Pamela S. Cooper*
Managing Editor, Production *Colleen A. Yonda*
Manager of Visuals and Design *Faye M. Schilling*
Production Editorial Manager *Julie A. Kennedy*
Production Editorial Manager *Ann Fuerste*
Publishing Services Manager *Karen J. Slaght*

 WCB Group

President and Chief Executive Officer *Mark C. Falb*
Chairman of the Board *Wm. C. Brown*

CHAPTER OPENING PHOTO CREDITS

*One: © Mark Antman/The Image Works, Inc.; Two: © James Shaffer;
Three: © Steve Takatsuno; Four: © Steve Takatsuno; Five: © Jean-
Claude Lejeune; Six: © Steve Takatsuno; Seven: © Jean-Claude
Lejeune; Eight: © Rollin Kocsis; Nine: © Michael Siluk; Ten: © James
Shaffer.*

Cover design by Edwin Harris

Interior design by Edwin Harris

Copyedited by Mary I. Waddell

Photo research by Kathy Husemann

TO CELEBRATE THE LIFE OF
RON LIPPITT (1914–1986)

Contents

Figures, Instruments, and Tables

Preface

This sixth edition is being issued when educators' interests in group processes have never been higher. Group concepts and skills undergird most innovations that have come recently to the forefront, including cooperative learning, students as conflict managers, peer tutoring and peer coaching, strategic planning, site-based management, restructuring for excellence, and interdisciplinary curricula in middle schools.

This edition will be useful for teachers, administrators, counselors, curriculum specialists, psychologists, and staff developers who want to make schools more collaborative climates for academic learning. The book's straightforward theory and down-to-earth descriptions of teachers' practices can also help parents and concerned citizens to better understand the relevance of interpersonal aspects of student learning.

Each successive edition of *Group Processes in the Classroom* has been different from the last one. Since the fifth edition appeared in 1988, we have altered all ten chapters of this sixth edition in accord with feedback from our students and with recent developments in the field. Our students have

helped us reduce the length of some laborious sections on theory and increase the length of overly brief accounts of practical application. They also have offered tips on sentences and paragraphs to highlight with italics.

Because action research on cooperative learning has grown immensely during the last decade, we give much more space to it. We aim to help teachers choose among the several schools of thought and specialized techniques in the cooperative learning movement. In the face of so many different articles and books on cooperative learning, we thought it helpful to present an overview of them so that the reader might learn about both the benefits and the limitations of cooperative learning. We have also attended more in this sixth edition to such popular topics of the 90s as using students as conflict managers, developing effective classroom discussions, restructuring schools and site-based management, debriefing how the class is going, and engaging students in new forms of classroom and school governance.

Unlike previous editions which reviewed primarily urban-based research and practice, this sixth edition introduces information about group processes from small town schools as well. During the first half of 1989, we drove almost 10,000 miles to visit 25 school districts of isolated small towns in 21 states. We went in search of democratic participation, i.e., citizen involvement, administrators and teachers sharing influence, teacher collaboration, student voice, and cooperative learning in classrooms. Many of the exemplary practices we found are described in this edition.

Along with our regular teaching duties at the University of Oregon and Lewis and Clark College, our thinking about this edition was also influenced by three events: (1) a study of 15 Oregon teachers who were nominated for their exemplary use of group-process techniques by their administrators; (2) a seminar on "the cooperative classroom" with 86 teachers and administrators from Alberta, Canada, each of whom evaluated a personal attempt at using group-process designs in the classroom and school; and (3) a series of lectures and seminars at Hebei Normal University in China under the auspices of the World Bank. On Thanksgiving day, with nearly 100 students, we had a poignant experience of transforming an ill-at-ease audience of passive listeners into 25 enthusiastic groups of active participants. Results from each of the three projects are included in this sixth edition.

Our experiences during the last four years have included more than teaching and special projects with educators. We have also learned about the culture of small firms in the communications industry that are taking the place of a fading timber business in the northwest. Managers of such small firms have told us that teamwork is absolutely essential to productivity in their firms.

They predict, moreover, that their task forces and work units will be working on problems and products within six months that are completely unknown to them today. In other words, the managers believe that rapid changes in problems and products will be routine. Their new employees will have to be flexible, creative, and cooperative. They will have to have communication skills in order to cope with the continual group problem solving that will be integral to their work. Many of those managers believe that our schools should be doing more to prepare workers of the future in group-process skills, and that teachers should know more than they do now about teaching students how to communicate effectively in teams.

We intend this sixth edition to answer the demands of a changing American culture. It should be especially valuable to teachers in preservice training programs who are learning a repertoire of ideas and actions that they will eventually use in the classroom. They might read the book in their curriculum, instruction or educational psychology courses. In addition, we trust that experienced teachers, counselors, psychologists, and administrators will find here a multitude of concepts that will broaden and deepen their views of the classroom and that they will make use of this sixth edition in inservice training meetings.

In this sixth edition, chapter 1 presents a detailed history of the group-processes movement in American education. Chapter 2 presents a social-psychological framework for analyzing the complexities of classroom life. It summarizes important variables and group dynamics theory. Chapter 3 describes important aspects of classroom climate by showing how students typically react at different phases of group development. It helps teachers see how to realize teambuilding and teamwork with their students. Chapter 4 deals with how interpersonal expectations, especially expectations of achievement, become influential in the classroom. In chapter 5, we examine how leadership is exerted and investigate power as an integral feature of classroom climate. Chapter 6 discusses how friendship patterns affect classroom interaction and how the cohesive classroom group is created and maintained. In chapter 7, we focus on how group norms work for or against academic goals and how norms for cooperative learning can be fostered. Chapter 8 describes how communication patterns occur in the classroom and how the different patterns relate to supportive and unsupportive climates. Chapter 9 deals with conflict—the conditions in which it arises, the variety of forms it takes, and how teachers can help students to handle it openly and constructively. Chapter 10 deals with relationships, linking the climate of the school with the climate of its classrooms. We show how classroom climate can be influenced by the interactions and norms of professional staff members

All ten chapters include a statement of objectives, theory, and research, diagnostic instruments, and a large number of action ideas designed and implemented by teachers. Although we have added some new practical action ideas (primarily from small town teachers in Canada and the United States), we have continued our reporting of research results and new theory. The college textbook market has an expanding number of specialized books and monographs on cooperative learning and only a few practical texts on classroom group dynamics in general. We have taken these books into consideration in this revision. This sixth edition of *Group Processes in the Classroom* is the only comprehensive text on the market that combines the latest theory and research with the tested, practical ideas of teachers. We don't intend to give up that balance.

We would like to acknowledge the reviewers who worked with us on this edition:

Kep Keoppel
Southern Nazarene University

Robert Shaw
Brown University

Marlene LaCounte
Eastern Montana College

Ethel Migra
National Louis University

Peterann Siehl
Bowling Green State University

R.A.S. and P.A.S.

Group Processes
in the Classroom:
An Historical Perspective

1

The study of classroom group processes, a subdiscipline of modern social psychology, grew irregularly during four explicit eras of the 20th century. From 1920 to World War II the writings of John Dewey, Kurt Lewin, and Jacob Moreno gave the empirical basis of small group research and presented a practical foundation for democracy in education; the post-war period, 1945 to 1965, exploded with experimental research on group dynamics and its application to classroom settings; then, from 1965 to 1980 there arose a serious concern for individual freedom, humanized interpersonal relationships, and the attainment of civil rights for minorities and women. Finally, in the 1980s, we saw educational research turning to the characteristics of effective school organizations and a political agenda for educational reform and higher academic standards. Although the public sentiment of the 80s stressed "excellence" for a few to regain America's place in world markets, concern still lingered on among educators and social scientists for democracy, the rights of the individual, and a nation free of discrimination and prejudice. Those humanistic sentiments are best portrayed in the concern of the 1990s for cooperative learning in the classroom.

Objectives of this Chapter

This chapter presents an historical perspective on classroom group processes. In it, we strive to help students understand the historical and social context of classroom group dynamics from the 1920s to the present. Over the past seventy years, there have been many changes in the social agenda for schooling and research on teaching and learning. Enlightened educators have an understanding and appreciation for the continuously changing reality of schools and educational research.

Despite the many changes, however, we argue in this chapter that school improvement often does *not* occur because the interpersonal relationships and group processes within schools are too much ignored. To us, school improvement requires changes in the ways administrators, teachers, and students work together. We believe that understanding the history of schooling with a focus on group processes will help today's educators find their place in the improvement tradition. We end this chapter with a concise overview of the history of classroom group processes, showing four historical periods, important ideas, and key people.

Democracy in Education: 1920–1945

Much of the current thinking and research about group processes has grown out of three separate but interrelated historical movements. One of these stems from the influences of John Dewey, who emphasized the social aspects of learning and the role of schooling for training students in problem solving and democratic, rational living. The second historical movement stems from the action research of Kurt Lewin and the subsequent development of scholars and practitioners of group dynamics. The third grows out of the active and productive life of Jacob Moreno whose eighty-four years of effort touched many arenas of thought in education. Moreno's most significant contributions to the classroom are the development of methods of sociometry and role playing. Both Lewin and Moreno stressed the collection of scientific data to undergird the philosophical pragmatism of Dewey, and both introduced the practical action techniques, still much in contemporary practice, for improving classroom group processes.

Dewey, Lewin, and Moreno shared a common interest in taking action to bring about social improvement. Although some social psychologists have taken the stance that classroom improvement can be brought about only by waiting passively for the day when the scientific enterprise has completed its task of understanding classroom group processes, Dewey, Lewin, and Moreno took quite a different course. Their work emphasized taking the risks involved in working for classroom improvement by initiating action research, even in the face of insufficient scientific data. Their pioneering spirit in acting to improve social interaction patterns in schools lives on in this book.

Dewey's primary contribution developed from his focus on the process of learning rather than its content (see Archambault 1964, Dykhuizen 1973, and Coughlan 1976). For Dewey, the aim of education is to develop socially responsible citizens who can work together to solve social problems. If students are to become socially responsible adults, they will have to participate in planning and evaluating their learning experiences in school. He argued that if children are to learn to live democratically, they will have to experience the living process of democracy itself in the classroom. Life in the classroom, according to Dewey (1930), should be a democracy in microcosm. The classroom should represent democracy, not only in the ways that students learn to make choices and carry out projects collaboratively, but also in how they learn to relate to the people around them. That entails being directly taught to empathize with others, to respect the rights of others, and to work together rationally.

The social psychologist, Gordon Allport, once said, "Although Lewin never met John Dewey, there was a community of spirit between the German-born psychologist and the American-born philosopher. Both were deeply concerned with the workings of democracy. Both recognized that each generation must learn democracy anew; both saw the importance to social science of freedom of inquiry, freedom that only a democratic environment could assure. If Dewey could be termed the outstanding philosopher of democracy, Lewin was surely the major theoretician and researcher of democracy among the psychologists."

Kurt Lewin and Jacob Moreno spearheaded practical, scientific group dynamics work on different fronts. While they did not work collaboratively, they helped to set in motion two streams of social psychology that undergird many of the concepts and action ideas of this book. In order to comprehend their conceptions of group dynamics, it is necessary to understand that their professional self-concepts entailed much more than those of "scientist" as defined in conventional contemporary terms. For Lewin and Moreno, group dynamics was a complex combination of science, therapy, social reconstruction, and morality. For them, the validity of a group exercise, a sociometric inventory, or a role-playing episode depended, in the final analysis, on its usefulness for restructuring social relationships. If a recorded response had no implication whatsoever for social improvement, then collecting and analyzing it would take on very little value.

Group Research into Practice: 1945–1965

One of the keys to unlocking Dewey's contributions to democratic practices in the classroom and to the practical application of the ideas of Lewin and Moreno lies in the development of group dynamics as a sub-discipline of social psychology. Group dynamics, which began with the contributions of Lewin and Moreno, developed into a viable and legitimate domain of study after World War II. It embellished Dewey's democratic philosophy by gathering evidence on the functions, operations, and processes of small, face-to-face groups. The group movement always had a social action element; the beginning of the National Training Laboratories in 1948 with Lippitt, Bradford, and Benne, for example, focused on some of the intergroup social problems facing communities and institutions in the United States. While Lewin's contributions to psychology ranged from basic research on cognition to action research in communities, it was primarily the techniques of action research applied to face-to-face groups that influenced educators' views of classrooms. One of Lewin's students, Ronald Lippitt, applied those ideas of action research in the classroom and spawned a host of projects on the topic.

Another of Lewin's students, Jack Kounin, applied those ideas to classroom management and discipline, while a third, Morton Deutsch, made pathbreaking contributions to educators' understanding of cooperation and competition in the classroom. Indeed, there is a generation of applied researchers who have followed the Lewin tradition, including the two of us, who worked with Lippitt: Barker, Wright, Gump, and Sherman, who were influenced by Kounin; the Johnson brothers, who were influenced by Deutsch; and Aronson, who worked closely with Festinger, another of Lewin's students. (See Marrow, 1969, for historical details.)

The National Training Laboratory and the T-Group

Lippitt, Leland Bradford, and Ken Benne, were co-founders of The National Training Laboratories (now titled NTL: The Institute for Applied Behavioral Science). NTL focused on the direct application of group research to improve personal learning and organizational processes and was significant in the changing trends of public education in the late 60s and early 70s. A notable invention emanating directly from the creative work of Lewin, Lippitt, Bradford, and Benne was the training group—or T-Group as it became popularly labeled. During the 70s and continuing today in most communities, people have been engaged in some kind of "group experience." The popularization of such groups in the 1970s, however, emphasized individual and personal growth goals rather than the understanding of interpersonal relations or the application of the concepts to social change.

Important works relevant to the T-group are Bradford et al. (1964); Schein and Bennis (1965); Dyer (1972, 1976); Lieberman, Yalom, and Miles (1973); Benne et al. (1975); Golembiewski and Blumberg (1970, 1977); Porter (1979); and Smith (1980). A number of contributions on organizational group processes that included applied studies were also related to the development of T-group technology (March and Simon 1958; Likert 1961; Katz and Kahn 1966; Argyris 1972; Likert and Likert 1976; and Dyer 1977).

Action Research

Until the mid 50s, much of the pragmatic, action research in social psychology—the sort inspired by Lewin, Lippitt, and Moreno—was carried out primarily in industry, social agencies, and government. However, the empirical work of Miel, Withall, Thelen, Miles, and Gronlund offered notable exceptions. Alice Miel (1952) presented descriptions of action research with more than 75 teachers at the Horace-Mann-Lincoln Institute of School Experimentation. Her study aimed to help teachers promote cooperative learning experiences for students and served as a precursor to the contemporary interest in cooperative learning. Withall's technique for measuring social-emotional climate, first published in 1949, had a major influence on the application of group dynamics to classroom life for the next 35 years (1949a, 1949b, 1951, 1963, 1977). Other published works on group dynamics in the classroom and school settings, which brought Lewin's practical theory to life, included Herb Thelen's, *Education for the Human Quest* (1960), Matt Miles' 1959 version of *Learning to Work in Groups* (revised, 1981), and Norman Gronlund's 1959 publication, *Sociometry in the Classroom,* which also made heavy use of Moreno's ideas.

These books helped build a bridge between social-psychological theory and classroom practice. An article by Trow et al. (1950), compared to one by Getzels (1969), and another by Crist (1972), clearly reveals the large number of studies on classroom groups carried out during the decades of the fifties and sixties. The differ-

ence among those three review articles is striking. The 1950 article consisted mostly, if not solely, of theoretical propositions. The 1969 article, in contrast, presented substantial empirical evidence from research done directly with classroom groups and school organizations. The 1972 article went one step further by reporting on the success or lack of success of numerous group dynamics interventions being attempted in real classrooms.

In general, research on group processes proliferated during the 50s and 60s. In 1953, Horowitz summarized knowledge about group dynamics for educators, referring mostly to studies published during the post World War II period. In 1955, Hare and others annotated a bibliography of 584 items on small groups. By 1959, Raven had collected 1,445 references related to group processes. In 1962, Hare published his first *Handbook of Small Group Research* consisting of 1,385 items; and by 1966, McGrath and Altman had presented a bibliography of 2,699 items. In 1969, Raven updated his references with 5,156 items divided into 67 categories; and by 1977, Hare's second *Handbook of Small Group Research* took up 320 pages to list 6,037 references. During the same period, the number of relevant journals in research and training on small groups increased fourfold.

Also during that time, classical books on small groups were continually being brought up-to-date. Cartwright and Zander's 1953 edition was revised in 1960 and again in 1969. A compendium by Hare et al. (1955) was considerably altered with twenty additional articles in 1965.

Other analyses continued to be published over the next decades indicating both the magnitude and interest in group processes (Golembiewski 1961; Luft 1963, 1970; Napier and Gershenfeld, 1963; Olmstead 1959; Shephard, 1964; Argyris, 1976; Shaw, 1971, 1976; Nixon, 1979; McGrath and Kravitz, 1982).

A Focus on Education

Although research done within classrooms and school settings continued to be underplayed compared with group research in other settings, increased emphasis was placed on the application of group processes to educational settings in the early 60s. The *59th Yearbook of the National Society for the Study of Education* (Henry, 1960), for example, presented social-psychological theory about classroom groups and proposed ways of using research findings to improve instruction. Ned Flanders provided systematic ways to study teacher-student interaction in the classroom (1960, 1963, 1964, and 1970). At that same time, short articles on classroom groups were beginning to appear in the journals (e.g. Bradford, 1960a and 1960b; Menlo, 1960; and Lippitt and Gold, 1959). A year later, in the fall of 1961, the American Educational Research Association sponsored a conference on the topic, "Effects on Mental Health of Interaction Within the Classroom." The conference was attended by Ned Flanders, Ron Lippitt, Herb Thelen, and John Withall, and had significant effect on their subsequent work, as well as on the work of their students.

A considerable list of texts published after that AERA conference attest to the growing maturity of knowledge in applying social psychology to the study of education (Backman and Secord, 1968; Deutsch and Hornstein, 1970; Guskin and Guskin, 1970; Johnson, 1970; Lesser, 1971; Bany and Johnson, 1975; and Glidewell, 1976). A common theme in all of these books was the idea that a vital hidden curriculum in education is the interaction of teacher and student, of teacher and class, and of student and student. In addition to the first five editions of this book, other publications have offered considerable empirical data about group processes in the classroom and the school (Glidewell et al., 1966; Jackson, 1968; Getzels, 1969; Miles and Charters, 1970; Schmuck and Miles, 1971; and Glidewell, 1976). And, many other publications have marshalled data to make recommendations for improving teaching and classroom group processes (Schmuck, Chesler, and Lippitt, 1966; Fox, Luszki, and Schmuck, 1966; Chesler and Fox, 1966; Amidon and Hunter, 1966; Poirier, 1970; Schmuck and Schmuck, 1974; Good, Biddle, and Brophy, 1975; Rivers, 1976; Sharan and Sharan, 1976; Vacha, McDonald, Coburn, and Black, 1977; Stanford, 1977, and McMillan, 1980).

The continually increasing number of studies on public education were due, in part, to increased federal funds and foundation grants. From 1950 to 1960, federal funds for educational research and development increased tenfold. Funds for educational researchers continued to increase at an even more rapid rate during the early sixties, with the United States Office of Education taking the lead in encouraging and steering the national research and development effort in education. The convergence of several forces during that period cleared the way for federal involvement in the school; among them, a big rise in the school-age population, concern about Soviet scientific gains, the civil rights movement, and the "war on poverty."

Civil Rights and Individual Freedom: 1965–1980

This decade and a half, fraught with dramatic and wrenching tensions in American society, witnessed two educational movements, each urging teachers to work self-consciously on the group processes of their classrooms. Those separate but interrelated movements had to do with equal educational opportunity and humanizing the dehumanized school.

Equal Educational Opportunity: Race

During the late sixties and most of the seventies, after the assassinations of Martin Luther King and the Kennedys and during the Vietnam War, American society was torn apart by racial disturbances in many of its major urban centers. Civil rights advocates targeted the schools for significant social change. While the Supreme Court called for "all deliberate speed" in the desegregation of public schools and ordered racial balance in schools throughout the nation, interracial tensions were raging in many urban schools. Many of them were closed; some remained open, even as students boycotted or picketed. The public schools were in crisis. Private schools were established overnight as the evening news presented visual reminders of the difficulties the schools were facing. Television pictures of students, parents, police, and school administrators in violent confrontations were presented continually. Freedom schools, established in storefronts, churches, and homes, primarily in the south, to provide educational continuity for displaced students, were run by civil rights workers—

Blacks and Whites, often from the north—who were organized by Students for a Democratic Society, the Student Non-Violent Coordinating Committee, and the Congress for Racial Equality. It was many of those college students, "the new left," who called for an end both to racial segregation and dehumanizing relationships between teachers and students in public schools. Freedom schools, not part of a hierarchical, formal organization, were run autonomously and locally. There were no bureaucratic rules directing the teachers on what could or could not be taught or done with the students. What began as a reaction to a critical social need to provide safe education for youngsters with no place to go ended as a movement to create "alternative schools" or "free schools" within the public and the private sectors. And the emphasis in the alternative schools was on the affective quality of human interaction in schools; the focus was on the freedom, spirit, and self-esteem of the individual.

While many of the proponents of freedom schools argued that schools were damaging the spirit of all students, they had a particular concern for poor children, primarily Blacks, whom they saw as the principal victims of a society gone bad. Not only was school damaging to their self-esteem as black people, but it also provided little hope for escaping the inevitable cycle of poverty in American society. After the Civil Rights Act of 1964, James Coleman was commissioned by the federal government to do a study of schooling. The publication in 1966 of his *Equality of Educational Opportunity* confirmed the view that schools were, indeed, discriminatory. It concluded that since race and social class were the primary predictors of student success in school, classroom instruction was essentially maintaining, even reinforcing the status quo in the society (see Jencks, 1972; Bowles and Gintis, 1976, for more about that point of view).

Equal Educational Opportunity: Gender

Civil rights legislation, directed toward racial minority groups in America, led the way for other powerless and disenfranchised groups to seek litigation for their own plights. The women's movement, in particular, was concerned about the equal educational opportunities available for girls. Feminist advocates, who were also Washington, D.C. bureaucrats, actively lobbied Congress, until in 1972 Congress passed Title IX, disallowing sex discrimination in schools. Throughout the 70s and early 80s, books and articles were published about sex bias in classroom interactions and instructional materials (Guttentag and Bray, 1976; Fischel and Pottker, 1977; Sadker and Sadker, 1982), about the exclusion of women from educational history and philosophy (Martin, 1982; Burstyn, 1983), and about sex-segregated employment patterns in schools, notably the absence of women in educational administration (Schmuck, P. 1976, 1980; Shakeshaft, 1987).

The Womens' Educational Equity Act Program, begun in 1976, provided federal funds for model projects for eliminating bias and discrimination. The Technical Assistance Centers established under the Civil Rights Act of 1964 provided training for school personnel to provide equal educational opportunity and to implement equity policies and practices (see Schmuck, P. et al., 1985). In the seventies there was an explosion of research and development to enable schools to more adequately provide equal educational opportunity. The 1985 publication of *The Handbook on Sex Equity Through Education,* sponsored by the Research on Women in Education of the American Educational Research Association, was a culminating compendium representing the work of over 50 different authors and a decade of work in sex equity and schooling (Klein, 1985).

Equal Educational Opportunity: Handicapped

Public Law 94–142, commonly referred to as the "mainstreaming" legislation, was passed in 1973 to protect the rights of handicapped students to be educated in the "least restricted environment." In some jurisdictions, for example, handicapped children were barred from attending school because of their special needs. The aim of the law was to ensure a free public education for all children, including those with handicaps. This legislation has profoundly altered the schools and classrooms in America. Each child is to have an individualized educational plan (referred to as an IEP) to be developed in concert with the regular classroom teacher, the parents, and the special education teacher, as well as other appropriate specialists. Thus the goal of providing appropriate education for special needs children is met through collaboration of all concerned parties.

In all arenas—race, ethnicity, gender, and special needs children—the schools are increasingly being held accountable for reducing discrimination that exists in the society at large.

Humanizing the Dehumanized School

Arguments for the humanizing of interpersonal aspects of school life became more and more prevalent in the professional literature of the seventies. In his seminal work of 1969, *Freedom to Learn,* Carl Rogers called for a relaxation of authoritarian direction and control in schools. At the same time, Ivan Illich's 1970 treatise, *Deschooling Society,* proposed a restructuring of educational programs and change in the inhumane norms of school life. Both books were widely read, reviewed, and discussed; both added fuel to young people's rebellion against the traditional authoritarianism of public education. They gave intellectual support to the San Francisco "flower children" who viewed schools as institutions which were destructive and damaging to students. The writers of that period, often referred to as "educational romantics," criticized neither curriculum materials nor teaching methods. Instead they focused on the dehumanizing and demeaning interpersonal relationships—for faculty as well as for students—that typified public education. The works of Kozol (1967), Kohl (1969), Herndon (1971), Hentoff (1966), Postman and Weingartner (1971) and Ashton–Warner (1972) represent the writings of the "educational romantics." They described the damaging and dehumanizing outcomes of public education with clear and shocking prose. Consider, for example, the poignant titles of Kozol's, *Death at an Early Age,* Hentoff's *Our Children Are Dying,* and Herndon's *How to Survive in Your Native Land.*

A similar critique of the schools was also presented by more dispassionate observers. The three-year Carnegie study by Silberman (1970), *Crisis in the Classroom,* presented a detailed description of schools and portrayed well the same themes of psychological decay and stagnation in public schools. And our own *Humanistic Psychology of Education: Making the School Everybody's House,* published in 1974,

elucidated a systematic plan for schools to pay attention to the affective needs of students, teachers, administrators, parents, and, indeed, everyone in the school.

A literature also developed on the alternative schools that were being created (Barth, 1972; Kozol, 1972; Render, Moon, and Treffinger, 1973; Duke, 1978). Often that literature pointed to the failure of schools to create favorable changes for students because of organizational inefficiency, ineffective relationships between teachers and administrators, or failure to change the existing norms and procedures that support a more humanized working environment (see, for example, Smith and Geoffry, 1971; Gross, Giacquinta and Bernstein, 1971). In addition, there were advocates of innovative teaching methods and procedures with a focus on the human side of interaction in school settings and a concern for emotion and self-concept in the classroom. George Brown organized a curriculum called "Confluent Education for Elementary Students" (1971), Glasser provided a classroom procedure called "The Magic Circle" to discuss the human and feeling side of the classroom (1969), and some British educators wrote about the Infant Schools as a model for early childhood education, stressing individual diversity and active participation in learning (Brown and Precious, 1968).

Most alternative schools lasted for only a few years, but some continue to exist even today. In 1992, for instance, Eastside Elementary School, an alternative school created in 1973 within the Eugene Public Schools, continues to thrive. We were active in its creation and took part in its governance during the years our children were elementary students. During its 19 years of existence, Eastside has changed location, much of its staff, and its curriculum and procedures. Still it remains a viable alternative for parents and children who want an educational program that relies on teacher-student-parent cooperation and the idea of school as a community with democratic decision making.

The Effective School and Educational Reform: 1980–1990

During the 1980s there was a noticeable leveling off of federal funding for school improvement as well as a marked decline in the federal government's appetite to enforce the civil rights legislation written a decade earlier. In addition, the research focus shifted; a concern for the needs and rights of individuals changed to a concern for an "effective" school. The public agenda for education became focused more and more on the competitiveness of the United States in the world marketplace. The Committee on Educational Excellence, appointed by the President of the United States, argued our nation is "at risk" because of the mediocrity of its educational system (Committee Report, 1984); that report was only the beginning of a plethora of demands for reform.

The Effective Schools Movement

Coleman and Jencks, two decades earlier, argued that schools did not make a difference and that the best predictor of student academic success was students' socioeconomic status. Rutter (1979) in England and the late Ron Edmonds (1979) in the United States questioned those conclusions, emphasizing the great variability in the quality of different schools. They argued that the academic qualities of schools were different one from another, and that dif-ferent schools had different student outcomes when controlling for social class differences. They further claimed that the social climate for academic learning varied among schools and that different school cultures resulted in different student achievement levels. In some schools, for example, they found that social class was not a predictor of student achievement. Edmonds wrote that the instructionally effective school "brings the children of the poor to those minimal masteries of basic school skills that now describe minimally successful pupil performance for the children of the middle class" (1979, p. 16). The variables making up the culture of a school included social climate factors such as degree of academic emphasis by the staff, the amount of supportive, interpersonal relations among staff, and staff morale. Additional research by Brookover (1979, 1981), and subsequent reviews, summaries, and critiques of that research by Purkey (1983), and Leithwood (1982), led to the common use among educators of "the effective schools research."

The Northwest Regional Educational Laboratory, for instance, developed a program to apply the results of effective schools research to the improvement goals of individual, local schools (see Blum, 1984, for details). The report by Blum refers to 250 citations on effective schools that are used to construct 30 categories of school effectiveness. Those 30 categories are meant to cover all the classroom, school, and district-wide variables that are correlated with favorable student outcomes, particularly focused on academic achievement.

Ideas in the effective school research were paralleled by ideas in contemporary organizational literature from business and industry. Organizational theorists Kanter (1983) and Schein (1985), as well as the popular writers Peters and Waterman (1982), studied profit-making organizations that were highly "effective" in achieving outcomes, i.e., they had high profit margins and were comfortable places to work. Like the school effectiveness researchers, they found that the quality of the organizational cultures of businesses are associated with their profitability and morale. Moreover, those high quality business cultures are characterized by supportive social climates where the workers are experiencing social support, positive reinforcement, and feelings of power and achievement. The concept of social climate, developed by Withall and published in 1949, was being revisited in the name of "effectiveness."

The Reform Agenda

In the 1980s the "effectiveness" research, coupled with the national "drive for excellence," dominated national politics. After the report of the Educational Commission for Excellence was published in 1984, virtually all state departments of education in the USA took on the task of making their schools more excellent. The literature on educational reform tended to agree in its criticism of public schooling; the focus was on raising standards of education and called for the renewed efforts of schools to focus on upgrading the academic enterprise (Adler, 1983; Goodlad, 1984; Lightfoot, 1983; and Sizer, 1984).

What's Wrong with the Reform Agenda?

Critics have noted, however, that those reports called for universal treatment of all students and ignored the legislation on equal education (see Tetreault and Schmuck, P.,

1985). The many reform reports listed above did not cover the concerns for equal educational opportunity and alternative choices within schools. They emphasized the cognitive processes and deemphasized the affective processes; they emphasized academic achievement and deemphasized prosocial interpersonal relationships. The reform reports of the 80s echoed past times in our educational history when we decried our decreased academic standards and called for increased rigor and similar treatment for all students in our schools, despite differences in backgrounds, skills, aptitudes, and interests. The historian, C. H. Edson, likened the reform movement of the 1980s to the Committee of Ten's report at the turn of the 20th century and to the educational response to the Sputnik scare in the 1950s, when Americans were fearful of their lack of progress against the Russians in the race to the moon (see Edson, 1984). Each time in history we called for increased academic standards, each time we ignored the affective side of the educational enterprise, and each time we returned to an ethic of Social Darwinism where only the best and the strongest survive.

The cry for increased academic standards has also led to criticism of teachers and teacher preparation programs. The concern that the profession does not attract the "best and the brightest" has not led, however, to incentives to attract competent people to the field, but rather to a national certification process emphasizing minimum competencies. Recommendations for improving teacher training coming from The Holmes Group, an organization of Deans of Education, have called for an emphasis on subject matter specialization and the creation of post baccalaureate education programs, therefore decreasing specialized training for teachers.

While we heartily support efforts to attract competent people to the education profession and improvements in teacher education, we are fearful these efforts are misplaced. Instead of increasing the bureaucracy for certification, we need mechanisms to reward and respect good teaching. Instead of decreasing emphasis on the educational process of teaching and learning, we need programs available in universities and school districts for continued professional development for new and practiced teachers.

Whereas the federal government has been calling for excellence in education, there has actually been a decrease of federal funding for educational research and improvement. The critics of increased funds for schooling claim that educational institutions have not improved, despite massive spending during the last few decades. We agree that spending does not automatically lead to school improvement. Indeed, the premise of this book is the concept that substantial school improvement has not occurred because the interpersonal relationships and collaborative working relationships within schools remain ignored. That view continues to be valid, despite the work on effective schooling. Even though educators have learned a good deal about organizational effectiveness and can describe the factors comprising an effective school, there remains the problem of achieving such a state of organizational effectiveness in practice (see Leithwood, 1983). What do principals and teachers do during the daily life of a school to convert a less effective school into a more effective one? How do they behave? Where do they start? How should supervision and evaluation be changed if most of the teachers are ineffective and incompetent? How will we

involve parents if they don't care about schooling? How will staff development and improvement occur if the central office provides little financial or moral support? How will we create a safe and pleasant place for academic learning when the school is being vandalized? How will we maximize student learning when students are fearful and anxious?

The answers lie, at least in part, in facing the fact that schools are human institutions. It is what teachers DO in their classrooms, it is what HAPPENS in the teachers' lounge, it is HOW the process of supervision and evaluation occurs, it is HOW problems are identified and solved, and it is the FEELINGS, SKILLS, AND ATTRIBUTES of people which make up effective schools. It is adult people, their skills, values and interactions that make up professional staffs. The effective schools research teaches us to improve the human condition for *everyone* in our schools as a means to reaching higher levels of cognitive development.

An Optimistic Future

Even in the face of the return to Social Darwinism, we continue to be optimistic about the future of schools and the progress of group dynamics as a critical influence on classroom processes. We are optimistic for several reasons. First, there continues to be an increasing number of books, both in the United States and abroad, which focus on the interpersonal setting of classroom life. In 1976 we found no less than fifty books concerning humanistic education (Schmuck and Schmuck, 1976) and that number continues to grow. Those books are written by educators throughout the western world (see, for example, Mulford, 1977 and Vandenberghe, 1984). Second, with the increased emphasis on organizational excellence, the theory of group dynamics is being applied more and more to classroom and organizational settings. Finally, we see a continuously growing interest in cooperative learning. The philosophical roots of cooperative learning extend back to the ideas of John Dewey and the work of one of Kurt Lewin's students, Morton Deutsch, who wrote classic articles about competition and cooperation in 1949. The work of Morton Deutsch is being carried on currently by his student, David Johnson, at the University of Minnesota.

Indeed such a high, world-wide interest in the study of cooperative behavior has emerged, especially by Israeli researchers faced with issues of intergroup cooperation and competition, that The International Association for the Study of Cooperation in Education was organized and met for the first time in Tel Aviv, Israel, in 1979. It met again in Provo, Utah, in 1982, in Regina, Saskatchewan, in 1985, back in Israel in 1988, and in Baltimore in 1990. Several research publications have been produced from those conferences (Sharan, Kagan, Hertz-Lazarowitz, Webb, and Schmuck, 1983, and Slavin, Sharan, Kagan, Hertz-Lazarowitz, Webb, and Schmuck, R., 1985). The newsletter of that association also has been excellent; it is full of information about cooperation in education. See, for example, the newsletter (Vol. 8, No. 1) issued in March, 1987, for information about the roots of cooperative learning. It featured information about John Dewey, Alice Miel, Kurt Lewin, and Morton Deutsch, to name a few. In 1989 the newsletter was transformed into a magazine entitled *Cooperative Learning*. It is being edited by Ted and Nan Graves and can be ordered by writing to them at 136 Liberty Street, Santa Cruz, CA 95060.

The research and development on classroom cooperation, covered in detail in chapter 7, has relied heavily on the work of David and Roger Johnson (1975, 1982, 1983, and 1989), Robert Slavin (1983 and 1990), Spencer Kagan (1980), and Shlomo Sharan and Rachel Hertz-Lazarowitz (1984), Elizabeth Cohen (1986), and Shlomo Sharan and Hanna Shacher (1988). The most comprehensive work was published by Sharan in 1990. The strategies for teaching cooperative learning, developed in that research, focus on the structure and process of teacher initiatives. Teachers can choose to promote competition, individual separateness, or cooperation in their classes. The choice they make determines different cognitive and affective outcomes for students. Whereas there is a time and place for competition and for individual work, the current research proclaims in bold letters that *cooperative learning can encourage both academic excellence and healthy affective development*. On balance, more teachers should be using cooperative learning procedures more of the time.

In conclusion, as we move through the last decade of the 20th century, it appears that the ideas and procedures for emphasizing group processes in the classroom have gained legitimacy and acceptance among researchers. And educational practitioners, now, much more than in the past, seem to be basing their analyses and action recommendations on the findings of the behavioral sciences. Social psychology, in particular, offers many new intellectual rubrics for understanding how classrooms and school organizations operate. In

Table 1.1 An Overview of Classroom Group Processes: Historical Periods, Important Ideas, and Key People

	1920–1945 Democracy in Education	1945–1965 Group Research into Practice	1965–1980 Civil Rights and Individual Freedom	1980–Present Effective Schools and Educational Reform
Important Ideas	Social improvement Process as content Sociometry Living democracy Learning by doing	Group dynamics Action research The T-Group Classroom group dynamics	Equal educational opportunity Humanizing schools Alternative schools	Effective schools National Reform Agenda Reform as Social Darwinism Cooperative learning Organization development
Key People	John Dewey Kurt Lewin Jacob Moreno	Ronald Lippitt Morton Deutsch Jacob Kounin Alice Miel	Martin Luther King James Coleman Jonathon Kozol Charles Silberman	Ron Edmonds David and Roger Johnson Shlomo and Yael Sharan Pat and Dick Schmuck

addition, social psychology continues to provide the means for effectively adapting the knowledge to the contemporary student within the framework of the values set forth by Dewey, Lewin, and Moreno. What follows in chapter 2 are some concepts and findings from social psychology that teachers and school administrators have found useful.

Group Processes in the Classroom: A Social-Psychological Perspective

2

During the 1980s the National Commission on Excellence in Education reported that our schools were being threatened by a "rising tide of mediocrity" and recommended increased attention to individual excellence in academic subject matter. The imperative for school reform, spearheaded by important educators, politicians, and policymakers has already had a profound influence on schools. Most states have responded to the national pleas for upgrading standards by increasing academic requirements and attention paid to test scores. In response to the Commission, a group of twenty-seven, well-known educators rejected the Social Darwinism implied in the Commission's report and called for an increased concern for the schools' social responsibility in helping to develop the character of our youth (see *Developing Character. . . ,* 1984). Those educators realized that school is not only responsible for individual excellence in subject matter but also for the development of a social conscience; students need to be taught to have concern and care for other members of our society and to learn to live successfully with other people. They recommended, "students, at all grade levels, should be more frequently assigned group responsibilities for academic and school-related activities" (*Developing Character. . . ,* p. 7).

This book explores how the processes of group interaction combine to facilitate or restrain cognitive and affective learning in the classroom. While studies from industry, government, and the military have been helpful in generating insights and perspectives in group living, they provide only a partial picture. In order to understand classroom group processes, one must go into the classroom. There is no substitute for research done directly in public schools. This book is about the dynamics of real classrooms, studied under natural conditions, within real schools.

We believe that what actually happens in classrooms involves interpersonal complexities and subjective depths of meaning that challenge any teacher's imagination. Because classrooms are replete with so many facets of social life, no narrow theory of teaching or of learning to account for all the dynamics involved is feasible. Instead, we will offer numerous concepts of social interaction in the classroom, coupled with the available research expressed in practical terms with living examples.

Objectives of this Chapter

This chapter presents a theoretical foundation for the book by offering details of a social-psychological perspective on classroom group processes. We strive to help students understand this perspective by summarizing the theory concerning the relationship of small groups to classroom life. We also aim to give a research basis to the practical concepts and action ideas that are presented in subsequent chapters. The academic perspective taken in this chapter not only aims at enhancing students' breadth and depth of knowledge but also strives to build a conceptual bridge between theory and practice.

The Importance of Group Processes

Group processes in the classroom continue to be of primary concern to many educators for several reasons. The increasing complexity of social conditions and the large concentrations of people have brought to the forefront the need for and the importance of learning to work effectively in groups. Contemporary life places a premium on citizens' abilities to relate well to others. The future will hold an even more compelling need to deal with interpersonal tensions and conflicts. Look, for example, at the relationships between the races, ethnic groups, and the sexes that became of paramount concern in the seventies and eighties. They reflect merely the proverbial tip of the iceberg. People cannot learn simply to avoid these problems; they must learn to handle them constructively and creatively if we are to live and work well together.

Parents want the best for their children at school. They want a safe, secure environment; they want teachers who provide a personal interest in their children. They want to be kept informed about their children's progress and they expect teachers to help their children develop constructive friendships and hope that the administrators will provide opportunities for their children to engage in satisfying, extracurricular activities. Above all, parents want their youngsters to feel good about school and to develop healthy self concepts as students (Epstein, 1989).

There are many troublesome societal challenges for students and teachers. Divorce, child abuse, teen-age pregnancy, and increased drug use are among the realities facing many of today's children. Hodgkinson's (1985) briefing on current demographic trends tells us that 12% of children are born out of wedlock and often to a teenage girl, 40% will face divorced parents, at least four million are "latch-key" children and think of home as a dangerous and frightening place, and there is a rapid increase in the number of poor households

headed by a female. Although two out of three poor children are Caucasian, the percentage of Black and Hispanic children living with a single parent in poverty is much higher than for Whites. For many of these children who are "at risk" in developing a healthy, secure future, school is their only hope. School can help ameliorate some of the difficulties these children face in their growing years. Since peers can help troubled students adjust to school, teachers are strongly advised to facilitate cohesive support structures within their classrooms. Indeed, friendships can buttress an otherwise weak psychological foundation for many youngsters (Kurdek and Siesky, 1979, 1980; Pett, 1982; Wallerstein and Kelly, 1980).

As a result of social changes during the past several decades and the contemporary tensions within the cities, schools have an increased responsibility for helping students learn behavioral skills that will equip them to fill responsible and useful roles in society and contribute maximally to the productivity of groups. As viewed here, this means that concurrent with the academic curriculum, schools must concern themselves with developing interpersonal skills in their students as well. They must become aware of the adequacy of the students' relationships to classmates, regardless of sex, ethnicity, handicap, and race, as well as relationships to teachers and to each other. Helping youngsters cope with life has become a major challenge of our schools everywhere in America.

Another dimension of group life is the important part it plays in the developing self-concept of individuals, as indicated by the authors of *Developing Character* (1984). Healthy self-esteem is enhanced when key people in a person's environment respond toward that person in supportive ways. This appears to be true for very young infants, children, and adolescents, as well as for adults of all ages. People rely on others for the gratification and rewards that help them to feel worthwhile and esteemed, or for the punishment and disapproval which lead them to feel inadequate and worthless. It is primarily other people—in person or in the images held of them—who are able to make individuals feel secure and happy or alienated and unhappy. Students' concepts of themselves are formed primarily through the accumulated bits of feedback that they receive from those with whom they come in contact in school.

At the same time, persons are not passive receptacles or "tabula rasa" being pushed and pulled into narrow behaviors by social influences. Babies, even at birth, differ significantly from one another in their behavioral patterns (see Thomas et. al., 1963, Horowitz, 1982; Lipsitt, 1981). Some are very active in their squirming and kicking; others lie more or less passively in a very relaxed manner within their bassinets. Some have strong tendencies to approach physical objects; others withdraw from physical stimuli or avoid them. And some appear to manifest generalized moods of happiness, while others appear to be unhappy much of the time. Even attention spans differ significantly for babies just after birth. Moreover, some babies show unique ways of either reaching out or holding back in relation to others. Such active striving or censoring influences the ways in which others respond to the infant. Similarly, just as babies respond in unique ways, students will react differently to the same teacher's directives, praise, or punishment. A teacher's frown or smile directed at students generally will be received differently by each student.

Unique interactions occur in classrooms between student and teacher and between peers. The individual's internalized concepts and skills guide and direct exploratory behaviors that elicit responses from the others. In turn, the perceived responses of teachers and peers modify the individual's concepts and skills, which undergo subsequent accommodations during classroom interactions. Thus modified, the individual's slightly changed concepts and skills direct further exploration, readying the student for still more diverse responses from others. After the student experiences several interactions, he or she develops patterns of psychological reactions and achievement.

Although each person experiences unique social influences and responds to them in unique ways, there are some developmental stages which all persons go through as they mature. In a classic theory of personality development, Erikson (1950) conceived of a sequence of eight stages that depict the developmental challenges faced by everyone throughout life. The developing child from infancy through adolescence passes through stages of: (1) trust vs. mistrust, (2) autonomy vs. shame, (3) initiative vs. guilt, (4) industry vs. inferiority. Then the emerging adult passes through: (5) identity vs. confusion, (6) intimacy vs. isolation, (7) generativity vs. stagnation, and (8) integrity vs. despair.

How the problems posed at each of these stages are resolved by any individual depends, in part, on what has happened to that individual previously. For instance, a person who has not successfully developed trust and identity in the early stages may have difficulty facing intimacy in adult relationships.

People contine to grow psychologically; their developing personalities emerge out of a past which itself shapes the growth process. Even though all persons face similar developmental challenges, each one seems to solve them in very special, individualistic ways. The dynamics of the group processes of the family, the peer group, and the school provide powerful environments in which each developmental challenge will be faced.

Five-year-old children have already developed varying degrees of trust or distrust in others (see Charlesworth and Hartup, 1967). Infants are more likely, for example, to share a toy with a peer rather than with an adult stranger, and they prefer to interact with a friend rather than with a strange peer. They have a sense of independence or dependence in relation to others, and their feelings of personal competency are based on their own past achievements and failures. They arrive at school with concerns about being accepted, being influential, and being competent. These three motivational domains play a significant role in how individual students cope with the group processes in which they become involved.

In turn, the social climates of the school, in general, and the classroom, in particular, influence how the students will behaviorally execute their needs for affiliation, power, and achievement. Unless children's early experiences have been unduly harsh, they also come to school with curiosity, interest in learning, and strong drives to understand their immediate environment. Most children are curious, eager, and exploratory, taking pleasure in discovery and problem solving. Thus, the school receives active, highly motivated children, and over a number of years is hopefully instrumental in helping to point these children toward salutary goals.

Classroom Life

"More than a quarter of my class comes from single-parent or divorced homes. Some days you just have to forget about math and talk about getting along with each other and about values. We are doing a tough, frustrating, and lonely job; we have become the adult society's last alternative to abandoning millions of its heirs to the streets." (a fifth-grade teacher from a small town in California).

This strong statement was made by a very sensitive teacher, but it does not depict an unusual circumstance. It could have been uttered by the majority of public school teachers in this country. Classrooms, whether in large cities or small towns, are certainly not depersonalized settings. On the contrary, they typically abound with emotion between teachers and students and their peers. It is primarily members of the peer group who respond empathetically to a student's affective needs. A close friend can help a student to overcome anxiety and loneliness in a large and complex school. The combination of teachers' responses to students' personal needs and the peer group's interaction with them constitute the core of group processes in the classroom.

In a descriptive study of a junior high school, Everhart (1979) demonstrated the very different preoccupations of teachers and students. The teachers saw their role as dispensing knowledge, delivering the curriculum, and arranging instruction so that students would learn. The students summed up what the teacher wanted with one word: *work*. They saw teachers as directing and controlling their behavior and giving them work to do. The students were preoccupied not only with work but also with their place in the peer group. Indeed, social relationships with peers were an important aspect of the daily routine described by both students and teachers, although students thought of their relationships with peers as much more important than did teachers.

After giving questionnaires to 11,767 secondary students in seven states, Benham, Giesen, and Oakes reported what the students said when asked to tell the "one best thing" about their schools (1980). The top four choices were: "My friends," "Sports," "Good School Spirit," and "Particular Classes." Seldom did they mention teachers or administrators. At the same time in its "Report to Parents" in 1988, the National Association of Elementary School Principals asserted that between 10% and 15% of students are regularly picked on or attacked by bullies.

Peers can be particularly influential, whether that influence is positive, benign, or malignant, in shaping the group processes of a classroom. Peers provide emotional support as students attempt to break loose from dependency on their families and other adult figures. They can also threaten each other, making classroom life uncomfortable. Peers directly influence information about attitudes toward others. As children give and take from one another, they learn ways of relating to persons of all ages with some degree of empathy and reciprocity or with some degree of hostility and social distance. Peers also help shape some of the students' own attitudes, values, aspirations, and social behaviors.

A real-life anecdote involving our son, Allen, illustrates how the emotional dynamics of peer group life can go hand-in-hand with academic learning. When he was in the second grade, Allen struggled haltingly to expand his very small number of friends to include a few slightly older buddies interested in participating in competitive sports. At the same time, he was confronted with the frustrations associated with learning to read. For several months, he failed in both endeavors, and his actions both at school and home often were intolerable. He retreated to the television set, he repeatedly expressed his feelings of loneliness, incompetence, and powerlessness, and rarely did he make it through the family dinner hour without being banished to his room. He wanted to be removed from interpersonal contact, and yet he still hoped for success in both his peer relationships and in learning to read.

In cooperation with several teachers, we began to focus a part of each day on tutoring Allen in reading. Gradually we made progress; the mystical reading code was being cracked. At the same time, we noticed that more youngsters—both older and the same age—were accompanying Allen home after school. The ping-pong table was set up, baseball games were organized, and four-square tournaments were formed. Allen began reading signs, cereal boxes, and books. The television stayed off for days, and Allen took a younger student under his wing to give advice about "why people don't like you and what you can do about it."

Allen's experiences are not atypical. The formal school curriculum and the instructional procedures aimed at teaching academic knowledge and skills can never really be separated from the informal relationships of the peer group and the existential place of oneself in relation to others. How students arrange their relationships with one another and what they learn from and, in turn, teach to one another are connected to academic learning and vice versa.

Although the peer group is very important, the classroom is made up of much more. It is a meeting ground for the peer group taken collectively, the teacher, the individual students, and the academic curriculum. Teaching and learning are complementary acts that involve a host of interpersonal processes. When the learning process takes place in the classroom, it is complicated and affected by the relationships among students and between the students and the teacher. In some classrooms the learning process is enhanced by peer relations that strongly support a productive learning atmosphere; in others, it is inhibited by unsupportive peer relations. Several major elements combine to influence the teaching-learning process: the teacher's instructional style, affective orientations, and the curriculum; the students' feelings about themselves and their academic abilities; and the nature of the interpersonal relations in the classroom.

In a study we did recently of 212 working and middle-class teenagers, ranging in age from 13 to 18, we asked them about good and bad teaching (see Schmuck and Schmuck, 1991, for details). The rank order of the most frequently occurring answers for good teaching were:

1. Gives students respect, is patient, and easy to get along with.

2. Makes the subject interesting and fun by involving students in activities and demonstrations.

3. Tells jokes and smiles a lot. Good sense of humor.

4. Listens to student questions and makes changes in class to help students learn.

The rank order of the most frequently occurring answers for bad teaching were:

1. Low respect for students, lacks patience, and treats you like you are stupid.

2. Seldom smiles, very serious and stern, and issues either too harsh or too permissive discipline.

3. Doesn't explain well, lazy, hands out work sheets and tests; you have to learn everything on your own.

4. Doesn't care about or pay attention to individuals; not helpful.

5. Has favorites; favors the smart students or one sex over the other.

It was fascinating to find that instead of being concerned about the curriculum, homework, and tests, the adolescents thought more about their affective relationships with teachers. They wanted their teachers to respect them, to engage them in joyful activities in the classroom, to have fun with them, and to respond flexibly in helping them learn.

The adolescents' views have not been taken into consideration in the literature of the school reform movement of the 1980s. These reports focus on the intellectual competence and the academic performance of teachers, not on their compassion, empathy, respect, and love of young people. The reform reports emphasize teachers' intelligence, academic achievement, course work within the liberal arts, and years of college education. They do not focus on the social-emotional characteristics of teachers with which the adolescents themselves emphasize. The adolescents we interviewed were not concerned with their teachers' subject-matter competence, breadth of knowledge, or ability to do well in college classrooms. Rather, they wanted teachers to be human beings who show trust, respect, and understanding of youth.

Each member of a classroom group brings to it a special, unique set of characteristics, and since the classroom is only one part of the lives of its members, it is vulnerable to the influences of social forces surrounding it. The classroom group is influenced both directly and indirectly by the organization of the school staff and the social-psychological characteristics of the district in which both the local school and the larger district are located. The different sociological environments of social class, race, sex, and rural-urban settings create variances in the classroom's constitution. To implement identical classroom programs in large city schools and small rural schools would be unwise, if not impossible, because of these important differences.

Even though these sociological factors can play a significant role in what happens in any classroom, this book will not focus on them, except to show how the organizational processes of the local school can influence the group processes of the classrooms within that school (see chapter 10). We are primarily interested in describing and explaining the classroom group processes themselves, whatever the varying inputs from the sociological surroundings might be. We understand that students and teachers bring to the classroom many personal characteristics which set the stage for the group processes that are played out. But what goes on in the classroom is more than the simple summing up of the individuals' characteristics. The group processes and the many reciprocal interactions that consti-

tute classroom life assume a unique life of their own over time. We therefore give the major share of this book to descriptions, analyses, and action ideas concerning the classroom processes themselves.

Perhaps the most useful point of view the teacher can adopt is the concept that all members interacting in the classroom are, at the same time, different and similar. Naturally, individuals differ one from the other. They have had different experiences, they have acquired different skills and abilities, and their attitudes and personalities have developed differently. At the same time, all school participants, whether students, teachers, or administrators, have certain intrapersonal and interpersonal needs and desires that must be gratified. Each of the classroom members wants to feel included, influential, and loved, and each wants respect and a feeling of personal importance and relevance. Each student also must spend considerable time concentrating on academic subjects if he or she is to grow into a well-informed and well-rounded citizen. An accommodation, thus, must be made for every student between interpersonal time and academic time. One without the other results in ineffective classroom life.

The Class as a Group

Even with increased interest in group processes, the role they play in the classroom still lacks clarity. Classrooms are not necessarily groups in the social-psychological sense. Each classroom should be conceived of as being placed from high to low on a dimension of "groupness." The closer it lies to the high end of such a dimension, the better it can be understood with group dynamics theory, research, and the action ideas presented at the end of each chapter.

To illustrate the "groupness" of a classroom, let us describe two very different classes which are being taught a foreign language. One class uses an individualized, programmed procedure in which students are allowed to proceed at their own rate and in their own unique fashion. Each student is seated in a separate booth, lowering the opportunities for face-to-face contact among them. Assignments are presented to each student by a teacher or an aide, and all students use an audiotape for their lessons and are finished with each tape as they correctly answer questions presented to them. There is no formal group discussion; indeed, peer group interaction is discouraged.

The second class varies significantly and contrastingly from the first. Small groups of students gather to discuss a topic in the foreign language they are learning. Exchanges of information, paraphrasing, and some repetitive practice in the language are attempted in the discussion. At planned intervals, the teacher asks students to divide into groups of three or four to help one another with new words and pronunciation. After such interchanges, students return to the larger groups to discuss what they have learned, with the teacher leading the group discussion. In the second class, interpersonal contacts are paramount and group processes are pervasive.

A third, and perhaps even more typical classroom would combine both procedures at one time or another. In such a class, the same collection of persons could be doing programmed instruction part of the time and group discussion at other times. Indeed,

programmed instruction and group discussion need not be antithetical to each other. Whether the more individuated format is in a separate class or the same class as the more group-oriented format is irrelevant to our discussion. While the latter is proceeding, it represents more "groupness" than the programmed instruction class, and therefore what goes on in it can be better understood by applying knowledge of group dynamics. Let us now look at some of the properties of groups that we have in mind when we speak of the classroom as a *group*.

Interaction and Interdependence of Persons

A group may be defined, in part, as a collection of interacting persons with some degree of reciprocal influence over one another. Thus, we would not consider as groups prople who are in mere physical proximity, such as persons at a football game or in a lecture hall, or collections of people with something in common, such as redheads or all of the citizens of the U.S.A.

The group-oriented class described above featured more interaction and interdependence of students than the programmed instruction class. This is not to argue that the programmed instruction class did not have some interaction between the students. As we will see later in this chapter, the mere presence of others, not to speak of informal interactions, can have a significant impact on intellectual performance. We know, too, that even the physically separated cubicles allow for noises, giggles, whispers, and note passing. We should also keep in mind that students carry within themselves images of others in the class and concepts about themselves. And it is primarily these images of other persons which influence students' feelings about the classroom and the curriculum. Nevertheless, the second class, described above, because of its formal features involving small group discussions, was more interdependent and had more interpersonal interaction and reciprocal influence.

Interdependence has been the central theme of group dynamics since its inception. The words written in 1947 in a eulogy to Kurt Lewin hold as much truth today as they did forty years ago. "Although his (Lewin's) life line could be analyzed in terms of many themes, the most persistent and central was his continuous study of the mysteries of interdependence in the successful functioning of individual personality, of group life, and of science. . . . To Kurt Lewin, the American culture ideal of the 'self-made-man,' of everyone 'standing on his own feet' seemed as tragic as the initiative destroying dependence on a benevolent despot. He felt and perceived clearly that we all need continuous help from each other, and that this type of interdependence is the greatest challenge to maturity of individual and group functioning" (Lippitt, 1947, p. 87, 92).

Several theoretical approaches to characterizing the interdependence of persons in groups are useful for understanding the classroom as a group. Let us review the work of Thompson, Parsons, and Schutz.

The Ideas of Thompson

First, the three forms of interdependence discussed by the organizational theorist (Thompson, 1967) can be useful in understanding classrooms. The one he referred to as *pooled interdependence* describes a social situation in which two or more members of the group render a discrete contribution to the whole, while not directly interacting with one another. Each member is interdependent in the sense that unless each performs adequately, the total group is jeopardized. Failure of any one can threaten the whole and thus the other parts. Examples of pooled interdependence occur when students clean and maintain the classroom and subgroups of youngsters take charge of different tasks and execute them separately such as watering plants, cleaning chalkboards, putting away learning games, and returning books to the library.

Sequential interdependence, the second form, describes a social situation in which the work of one member of the group must be carried out before the work done by another member of the group can be executed. Here there is also a pooled aspect to the members' interdependence. In addition, direct interdependence can be pinpointed beween them, and the object of that interdependence can be specified. Sequential interdependence may take place as a class performs a play or skit. The writers of the drama must carry out their work before the stagehands begin to make costumes and sets and they, in turn, must execute their tasks before the actors can put on a polished performance. Finally, the third form described by Thompson is *reciprocal interdependence* referring to the circumstance in which the work of each member of the group directly penetrates the work of all other members. This is the sort of interdependence that occurs in project teams and occurs each time a subgroup in the classroom works together on a complex task from start to finish. Classrooms may at one time or another be characterized by these three types of interdependence.

The Ideas of Parsons

A second and very different way of viewing interdependence originated with the sociologist Parsons (1951), who suggested that there are five dimensions of basic interaction modes for describing groups:

1. *Affective-Nonaffective*—focuses on the emotions involved in interaction. For example, in some classes, expressions of feeling are welcomed and supported, but in many others, students are encouraged to keep feelings of happiness and displeasure to themselves.

2. *Self-Collective*—describes whether the interaction is aimed at satisfying personal motives or at achieving group goals. For example, some classes are self-oriented, focusing upon individuated, programmed learning. Other classes enter into many group tasks and focus on the collective well being of the classroom by setting rules together.

3. *Universalism-Particularism*— describes how consistently and uniformly persons in similar roles are defined by one another in the interaction. In some classes the teacher treats all students alike, sometimes supporting an expectation for uniform performances and behaviors.

4. *Achievement-Ascription*—refers to whether persons gain status by performance or by some inherent characteristics. In many American classrooms, one's status with the teacher is achieved by dint of personal effort. In others, however, one's status upon entering class—as manifested, for example, by sex, social class, and skin color—can influence the status eventually arrived at in the classroom group.

5. *Specificity-Diffuseness*—refers to the degree to which the interaction in a content domain is focused. For example, many teachers think class discussions must be highly focused on the proper content of the curriculum. For others, a broader array of topics, including very personal ones, are legitimate and seized upon as valid experiences for learning.

The Ideas of Schutz

A third theoretical scheme for describing modes of interaction in groups was developed by Schutz (1958). His psychological theory assumed that group activities can be predicted by coupling knowledge of the person's interpersonal needs with the principles governing person-to-person interaction. He computed compatibility scores for pairs of persons in terms of their needs for *inclusion, control,* and *affection.* Scores on these three motives are derived in two ways: the person's expression of these needs and the amount of each kind of need he or she desires. Classroom compatibility can be gauged by estimating whether or not each of these needs is expressed in a sufficient amount. Involvement problems arise if inclusion responses are lacking. Power problems arise if students are either competitive or apathetic about exerting influence. And problems dealing with the adequacy of emotional support surface if too little warmth and love are expressed.

The Importance of Understanding Peer Interaction

An important empirical study of third-grade classrooms offered data on the importance of peer group interaction and interdependence (Calonico and Calonico, 1972). The study showed that the more frequently third-graders interacted with one another, the stronger were their feelings of friendship for one another. The research also corroborated the common hypothesis that friendly people receive supportive feedback and unfriendly people receive negative responses. Calonico and Calonico showed that the friendly third-graders received support from their peers, while those third-graders who expressed a great deal of unfriendly aggression received rejecting responses from their peers. The authors also presented data to show that the higher the sociometric status of a third-grader, the more likely that student was to conform to the norms of the peer group.

These findings illustrate the relevance and importance of student interaction and interdependence in the classroom. The teacher who discourages peer interaction is neglecting one of the main resources of classroom learning; however, it must also be remembered that sheer interaction time is not bound to be effective in itself. The teacher should seek to use different forms of group interdependence. In this way, the benefits of peer group interaction will facilitate academic learning. The major implication of Calonico and Calonico's study is that teachers should encourage, rather than discourage, interaction and interdependence among students in their academic learning. We concur and believe that a teacher who constructively uses the inevitable chatter and sharing among students can accomplish more educationally than the teacher who sets rules that discourage interaction. The latter teacher spends too much time and energy striving to get students to refrain from talking with one another.

Interaction Toward Common Goals

Groups pull and tug. They pull between tasks to accomplish and work to produce, but they also tug to maintain cohesiveness and an optimal level of morale. There also exists in all groups the persistent pull between group goals and the tug of individuals' motives. Group goals describe a preferred or desired state that guides the behaviors of group members. The learning of required, academic subject matter could be an example of a group goal in the classroom, while development of some social skills could represent individual goals. Various dimensions for describing goals have been advanced, but the dichotomies of task and social-emotional, along with group and individual, have been most popular.

When these continua are used to construct a matrix, four categories emerge: task-group, task-individual, social-emotional-group, and social-emotional-individual. Industrial work groups in which completion of tasks requires concerted effort and in which the persons who work are viewed as interchangeable are examples of groups featured by task-group goals. Classroom groups have learning tasks to accomplish and, typically, the focus is on individual students' skill development. Therefore, much of the time classes are in the task-individual goal category. T-groups or group dynamics seminars that concentrate on the emotional processes of groups are in the social-emotional-group category, while group therapy, with its focus on personal mental health, is illustrative of the social-emotional-individual category.

Groups can become more effective as they are able to pursue more than one of these goal categories simultaneously. A project in which an industrial work group analyzes its social-emotional processes can enable the group to produce higher economic gains (Kuriloff and Atkins, 1966). In classrooms, an individual's interest in learning the academic curriculum can be strengthened by the teacher's helping the class to set group tasks to perform (Schmuck, 1971). At the same time, classroom group processes can be improved by satisfying the social-emotional needs of individuals (Schmuck, 1966). Students who are liked by at least a few other classmates typically feel more secure and are better able to expend energy on the task-group and task-individual goals.

In theory, the classroom with the highest degree of "groupness" in its goals would have small groups of students working on subject-matter projects (task-group); individuals working alone, but in parallel situations, on skill development (task-individual); discussions in which group expectations and feelings were made public (social-emotional-group); and informal relationships of warmth and security that are satisfying to the individual students (social-emotional-individual). (See Figure 2.1.)

Interaction through a Structure

Groups also can be described by their social structures. Patterns of interaction that are repetitive, and to some extent expected and predicted by the participants, are what we mean by structure. Getzels and Thelen (1960) have proposed two fundamental structural patterns for the classroom: *nomothetic* roles, which are formalized and institutionalized; and *idiographic* aspects of structure, which bear on personal dimensions. For Getzels and Thelen, the nomothetic structure is characterized by persons in roles carrying out the functions of a social system. Examples would be teachers and students carrying out their responsibilities and duties apart from any consideration of their personal characteristics as individuals. From this perspective, it is possible to make an abstract analysis of what goes on in a classroom and to predict, in general, the behaviors of members without ever really knowing the individual persons. The idiographic dimension also must be included in such an analysis before a complete view of the living classroom can be understood. In actuality, no two roles are carried out identically; a personal component is always present.

Walberg (1968, 1969) and Walberg and Anderson (1968) have executed a series of empirical studies using the conceptual framework of Getzels and Thelen. Their research has shown some of the blends that can occur in classrooms between the idiographic and the nomothetic aspects of structure. For instance, background interests and peer group norms (nomothetic) of students are important in determining the general climate of the classroom, while the personality characteristics (idiographic) of teachers can make a difference in how daily routines proceed and in how formal or informal the climate of the group is. Anderson (1970) also showed how the normative climate of the classroom, in turn, affects the academic learning patterns of individual students.

The salient analytic feature of using nomothetic and idiographic aspects of structure lies in the proportion of each in the classroom. If the class maximizes the nomothetic, it will tend to emphasize the

FIGURE 2.1   Examples of Goal-Related Activities

	Task	Social-Emotional
Group	Group Projects Content Discussions Setting Learning Goals with the Class	Discussions about Classroom Procedures Making Group Agreements about Classroom Roles
Individual	Programmed Instruction Independent Assignments Reading Alone	Supportiveness Acceptance Helpfulness

academic tasks and the disciplinary rules of the school. Classrooms with a high nomothetic emphasis do not offer much freedom for the unique and varied expressions of individuals. Emphasis on the idiographic assumes that students will seek what is relevant and meaningful to them. It will emphasize individuality and variation. From the group process point of view, both dimensions are inevitably a part of the classroom. The classroom group is part of a formal institution with certain prescribed goals, while at the same time it is made up of different personalities. Effective group processes are those that work through to a balanced blend of the nomothetic and the idiographic in the classroom.

Unfortunately, many schools have become so formally structured and are characterized by so much nomothetic impersonality that they do not leave much room for individuals to relate authentically and closely to one another. Indeed, the foremost impetus for the contemporary growth of alternative schools has been rejection of formally structured schools that dehumanize and devalue many of the individual participants. In most of the alternative schools we have observed, the individual is proclaimed to be of supreme importance. Often formal, nonhuman aspects of the school structure, such as curriculum materials and specified times for classes and meetings, are very much underplayed and sometimes avoided entirely. Of course, those innovative school structures that have survived beyond their first year of existence do develop some formal rules and routine procedures. No organization, even the most humanized school, can remain viable without some division of labor—in the form of differentiated role taking, some formal rules and regulations, and some routines that are expected of everyone.

Group Dynamics Theory

Our theory of classroom group processes is based on ideas and research findings from six historical traditions in social psychology. The social-psychological perspectives of these six traditions are summarized with some attention to relating them to the classroom.

Perspective 1: Systemic Nature of Groups

The initial perspective that sheds light on classroom group processes grows out of the sociological analyses of Durkheim, Simmel, and Parsons, and was significantly elaborated and formalized by J. G. Miller (1965). It focuses on the interrelated nature of a living system. This perspective's flexibility allows for analyses of widely different levels of life, from an amoeba to the Library of Congress. Systems theory has been used to conceptualize the processes and interactions of individuals, classroom groups, school organizations, entire school districts, and even their community environments. Indeed, as a multileveled orientation to analyzing what occurs in schools, it is a useful perspective for viewing the relevance of group processes to student learning.

According to systems theory, a classroom group is an open system contained within a school, constantly influencing and being influenced by its members and the surrounding organization. It is primarily oriented to the attainment of specific goals—for example, the intellectual and emotional development of students. Any goal that the classroom group does attain, especially in the form of modified thoughts, feelings, and behaviors of its members, constitutes output that becomes input for another interdependent system—for example, students' families or other groups in the school.

Similarly, each group within the school district, whether it is a classroom, an administrative council, a curriculum committee, or a student club, constitutes an interdependent subsystem. Indeed, the school district itself, as a social system, has a relationship interdependent with its internal subsystems as well as the larger community and regional environments. The resources for achieving the objective of educating useful citizens in our schools come from other systems: teachers from colleges or other schools, an ever-changing array of students from families, and curriculum materials from publishing houses. Out of a combination and interaction of these resources, learning experiences produced in classrooms develop students who enter other classrooms, change families, colleges, the armed services, jobs, and so forth.

The term "system" refers to any organized part of an educational institution that is working to achieve certain goals and that has a large amount of internal interaction and interdependence. Examples of educational systems at different levels include tutoring pairs, project groups, committees, staffs, districts, and, of course, classrooms.

"System" is used to refer to the particular focus of analysis, regardless of its size; the word "subsystem" refers to small systems within a larger system. Focus on a classroom as a system might lead to an analysis of such subsystems as friendship cliques or influence hierarchies among students. Analogously, the investigation of a school staff could lead to a focus on its subsystems—staff friendships and influence relationships.

Although the individual student is the focus of the learning process, we should remember that individual behavior and psychological experiences arise out of a cultural context and are based on interpersonal relations. The systems theory alerts us to the systemic nature of classroom life and turns us away from a narrow psychological focus. Classroom groups are more than collections of individuals. They achieve a stable existence and identifiable culture even as individual students come and go.

Perspective 2: Informal and Formal Aspects of Groups

The second perspective also originated in classical sociological theory, but in a different school of thought from that of systems theory. C. H. Cooley's *Human Nature and the Social Order* offered the intellectual foundation of this perspective (see Cooley, 1965, for historical background). This perspective emphasizes the reciprocal influences between the intimate, informal aspects of a group on the one hand and the formal role requirements, performances, and goals of the encompassing organization on the other. Classroom groups, like other groups, have both formal and informal aspects. The formal aspects have to do with the ways in which any youngster performs the nomothetic role of academic student, as defined by the teacher, school district, and adult community at large. The informal aspects of a group involve the idiographic ways in which each member relates to other members as persons.

In the classroom, an informal feature would be the way affection, or students' friendship for one another, is distributed. These informal relationships often have an important bearing on the way in which the formal processes are carried out. Many of them, such as the amount of friendship members have for one another or their willingness to help and encourage one another, may be thought of as emotionally supportive and enhancing classroom group processes.

Early Research on Informal Aspects of Groups

Early sociological research on industrial organizations established the importance of informal relationships in small work groups for accomplishing the goals of production (Mayo, 1933; Roethlisberger and Dickson, 1939; and Roethlisberger, 1977). In this research, employees in industry were not viewed primarily as being motivated by wages, but rather as striving for self-esteem and self-actualization. What the employees hoped for, above all else, was credit for work done well, interesting and stimulating tasks, appreciation, approval, and congenial relations with their fellow workers. Industrial administrators were encouraged to look at the informal, person-to-person relations on the job, because the emotional lives of the employees were seen as being importantly related to the production goals of the organization.

While some of the findings of the classical research by Mayo, Roethlisberger, and

Dickson have been criticized on methodological grounds (see Franke and Kaul, 1978), it is an accepted concept that there is a connection between formal and informal group processes (see Wilson 1978).

In his classic book, *Who Shall Survive?*, Moreno (1934) vigorously exhorted organizational managers to take into consideration the feelings and informal interpersonal relations of the organization's members. He argued that affective relations between persons are inevitable in any formal organization. He stressed, furthermore, that if the structure of the formal organization does not take such informal relations into consideration and nurture them, then discord, strife, and conflict will appear at the formal level of organizational functioning. Moreno argued that too little concern for interpersonal relations and human feelings will be the downfall of our bureaucracies. And the group processes that arise in many classrooms and school staffs support Moreno's argument. When the informal group processes, in the form of peer relations and norms, are not supportive, considerable interpersonal tension can occur, and the learning of the formal curriculum can be hindered. Much energy is spent on just maintaining the peace, leaving little reserve for skillful teaching, academic learning, and personal creativity.

A Philosophical Discourse on Human Nature

The forces between the formal and informal aspects of group life are reflected in a philosophical debate concerning people's rational and emotional natures. In sociology, as well as economics, rationality has been seen as the key to understanding how organizations are able to make the best adjustments to the social environment. In eco- nomics, the concept of the "rational man" has prevailed. Emotionality has not been viewed as important in solving problems in the external environment, but rather thought of as the medium through which groups maintain their internal viability with a minimum of strain and tension. Emotionality has been viewed as an internal (or informal) dynamic, while rationality has been viewed as the external (or formal) structure of organizations. This dichotomy is shown through the terms that typify the literature on group dynamics; terms such as *secondary* and *primary, instrumental* and *expressive, task* and *social–emotional*.

We think this is a false dichotomy between rational and the emotional, between the formal and the informal. Within the last decade, the argument has been addressed by feminist scholars in a new way. The argument is the idea that our past preference for rationality (a stereotyped male characteristic) has subsumed the role of emotionality (a stereotyped female characteristic). Gilligan (1982), and Belenky et. al. (1989) argue that we have placed too major a role on rationality, and too minor a role on emotionality. These researchers have given a new voice to the importance of emotionality as they emphasize the importance of relationships and connections in people's lives. Although their research has focused primarily on women, we believe they offer new insights for changing the direction of the study of humans in organizational life. In school organizations and in classrooms, administrators, teachers, and students come to find, or not find, meaning in their relationships and connections with others.

The Current Understanding

There has been a resurgence of the importance of the informal aspects of organizational life in the business sector of the society. The recent organizational literature, some of it making its way onto the best-seller lists and into television programs, emphasizes the informal aspects of organizational life as separating the effective, or high performing companies, from the ineffective companies (Peters and Waterman, 1982, Kanter, 1980, 1989; Deal and Kennedy, 1985). High performing companies, such as Disneyland, McDonalds, Apple Computer, and the 3M Company have received national attention because they pay attention to the human ambience of the work place as well as their products. Employees feel they belong because there is a recognition by management that people need to feel included, respected for what they know, and valued for being contributors to the organization's goals. Indeed, the current popular organizational literature preaches that to be effective and profitable, a company should pay attention to the informal dynamics of the workplace.

This is also true for classrooms. Classroom groups with supportive friendship patterns enhance academic learning, while more hostile classroom environments reduce learning (Schmuck 1966). The data indicate that student academic performances are conditioned by emotional contents associated with their self-concepts as peers and students, and these self-concepts are influenced, in part, by the students' friendships and influence relations with their classmates. Informal group processes in the classroom can and do make a difference in the accomplishment of the formal goals of the school.

Perspective 3: Emotional Aspects of Small Groups

The third perspective, which is complementary to and overlapping the first two, grew out of the tradition of psychoanalytic theory and emphasizes the deeply emotional nature of face-to-face relations in small groups. Bion (1948), Thelen (1954), and Rice (1965) best express this perspective via their stress on the unavoidable affective nature of interpersonal relationships. Much of the early theory-building and research on this perspective was carried out at the Tavistock Institute of Human Relations in London—particularly at its Centre for Applied Research. The work of Margaret Rioch (1970s and 1970b) at the Washington School of Psychiatry lead to the practical application of the Tavistock work within the United States. She, with a few associates, introduced Group Relations Conferences to North America (Colman and Beston, 1975).

Using a psychoanalytic perspective as a starting point, these social scientists assume that emotionally laden, interpersonal reactions will be inevitable within a group of people who meet regularly. They argue that the initial interpersonal relationships a person experiences in the family are saturated with feelings, and that it is from the emotional intimacy of the family setting that a person learns basic ways of relating to other people. People who are involved in prolonged daily contact with others will tend to relate in ways similar to the emotional styles they have learned in their families. Thus, within small groups there will exist a number of covert processes having to do with infant fantasies, unconscious wishes, and defense mechanisms that will impact on how the group performs. Group Relations Conferences offer intensive interpersonal encounters through which the participants can learn about the impact of such covert dynamics on the groups in which they carry out their work.

Other aspects of family life are also related to the experiences that the student will have in the classroom, such as special roles the child takes regularly in relation to the parents or the types of interactions the child has with siblings. In relation to parents, the child's degree of compliance or defiance can transfer to the classroom in the form of the expectations the child has for teacher reactions. Moreover, wishes and aspirations that the parents project onto their child can influence the child's level of self-esteem or self-doubt in relation to the teacher. Significant in relation to the student's adaptation to the classroom peer group is how cooperative or competitive relations are among siblings in the family. All of these family processes can be relived and reenacted in the classroom.

The classroom clearly offers a setting in which high levels of feeling exist daily and wherein covert psychological dynamics often come into play. As students interact, and as students and teachers relate, they communicate—however indirectly—their feelings about one another. Such gestures of affect influence how students view themselves, their abilities, their likability, and their general worth. Moreover, feelings, evaluations, or defenses make up students' self-esteem and have impact on the degree to which they use their intelligence and the manner in which they form their current educational aspirations.

In addition to having difficulties in academic performance, youngsters with poor self-images tend to dislike and be disliked by other students and to perpetuate uncomfortable interpersonal relations. Students engaged in these unproductive relationships often are unable to work on their academic subjects with concentrated effort, vigor, and insight. Their perceptions sometimes become so distorted or their defenses become so salient that they are unable to study and learn effectively. The greater the threat students feel in the presence of their peers, the more pronounced the restricting and distorting effect on how they perceive their academic work. Classroom disturbances tend to proliferate when students have poor self-images and, at times, teachers unwittingly exacerbate such tensions by scolding or punishing, thereby perpetuating negative self-images and unacceptable classroom behavior.

Perspective 4: Group Effects on the Self-Concept

Some social psychologists have argued convincingly that people's self-concepts develop through their interactions with other persons. According to Mead (1934), Cooley (1956), and Sullivan (1948), human beings develop in a sequential and systematic manner. They grow intellectually and emotionally, not because of the gradual unfolding of instinctual tendencies, but because they experience a regular sequence of interpersonal interactions in their lives. The family, the peer group, close friends, brief and prolonged formal and informal contacts, marriage, parenthood, and an ever-changing array of people are grist from which the self is formed and reformed. For preschoolers, play and games are situations in which important informal learning takes place. In the development of a self-concept, communication with others makes possible taking the role of the other by providing a set of common meanings and being able to see oneself through the eyes of the other person. This learning process initially involves one person imagining how he or she looks to a second person. This is followed by the first person's estimate of how the second reacts. In the final step, the first person internalizes a new view of self, based on his or her view of the second person's reactions.

Mannheim (1957) tested this theory about the development of the self-concept by analyzing extensive data collected through questionnaires from college students. She concluded that students' self-images tended to be similar to the self-image reflected to them by members of their dominant reference group, which, in most cases, were the people of their living unit. Her analysis also revealed that changes in reference groups were associated with changes in students' self-concepts, both positive and negative.

Because of their position of low status in relation to the adults or to older students, elementary and secondary students may be particularly vulnerable to a lowering of their self-esteem as they proceed through school. Both the symbolic-interactionist (Mead 1934) and the psychological-success (Coopersmith 1967) theories suggest that the low-status position of students may lower their self-esteem. Studies by Zander and Cohen (1955), French (1963), and Berger, Cohen, and Zelditch (1966) reveal that people occupying low-status positions are believed to have modest competencies; that negative attributes are associated with the people who hold these positions; and that negative evaluations are communicated to such low-status persons. Both negative

feedback and neglect of persons in low positions are likely to increase the high-power and status person's self-esteem. Prolonged membership in a high-power or low-power status position has been found to affect self-esteem through the reflected appraisals and feedback received from others (see Heiss and Owens, 1972; Maykovich, 1972; Yancy, Rigsby, and McCarthy, 1972, for data).

Students with low status both in their peer group and in relation to adults are also likely to suffer a loss of self-esteem because they have so few opportunities for psychological success and so many for psychological failure. According to Argyris (1970), psychological-success experiences become the bases for a person concluding that he or she is capable. The opportunities for psychological success increase (and for psychological failure decrease) as (1) people are able to define their own goals; (2) goals are relevant to their central needs; (3) activities require their important abilities; and (4) goals represent a challenging level of aspiration.

High-status persons in an organization generally have more opportunities for psychological success than do low-status persons. In addition, low-power persons must often determine their activities and goals according to the wishes of the high-power persons. Low-power and status persons, like students, are apt to experience frequent psychological failure that lowers self-esteem.

Low self-esteem is likely to undermine academic performance as well as psychological well-being (Johnson, 1970; Johnson and Johnson, 1984) in at least three ways. First, a fear of failure can cause students to avoid academic challenges and to feel defensive about grades. Second, feeling worthless in comparison to one's peers produces depression which can inhibit the desire to work hard on the schools's curriculum. Third, continuous academic failure is, of course, discouraging and it is unlikely that discouraged students will want to spend time studying.

Students' self-concepts are influenced strongly by the reflections they garner from the reactions of their teachers and their classmates. Unfortunately, students who receive unfriendly reactions from these others develop a poor view of themselves, and such a negative self-concept can have a couple of debilitating effects. First, the way students feel about themselves is an important determinant of their behavior toward others. Thus, students who have negative feelings about themselves tend also to hold negative feelings toward others. Their aggressive reactions toward the others merely support the others in turn reacting negatively. Second, students with low levels of self-esteem in the classroom are apt to slip into daydreams or misbehave when they are in school. They are also prone to drop out of school as soon as possible. Thus, students whose self-esteem in school is low, or for whom self-esteem is unrelated to school achievement, should be prime targets for corrective interventions by creative teachers. The alternative is an ever increasing student alienation and a higher and higher dropout rate.

Perspective 5: Human Motivation in Social Contexts

Motivational theories and research have played predominant roles in the development of psychology as a science of human behavior. Early in the history of psychology, concepts such as "instincts" and other inborn human attributes dominated scientific thought about humans' striving. Next, the pleasure and pain principle of hedonistic philosophy replaced the earlier concepts, and human beings were viewed as acting to increase pleasure and to avoid or decrease pain. Later, Freud's psychoanalytic theory focused on the centrality of sex and aggression in human motivation, but for most American psychologists of the 1920s, Freud's ideas were considered prescientific.

A number of notable experimental psychologists, such as Guthrie, Hull, and Tolman, attempted to provide more concise and measurable ideas about motivation and learning that could be tested within the animal laboratory. Although these ideas were precise and objective, they were so narrowly conceived that they were generally not applicable to understanding complex human situations. It was primarily Henry Murray (1938) and Gordon Allport (1937, 1955) working side by side at Harvard University who offered both concepts and research relevant to understanding human motivation in social contexts. The theory development and research by McClelland and his associates (1953) posited this conceptual scheme about human motivation. The three domains are: 1) striving for achievement, 2) striving for affiliation, and 3) striving for power (see White, 1959; Atkinson and Feather, 1966; Maslow, 1967; Berscheid and Walter, 1969, McClelland, 1975 and Fyans, 1980).

But much of this theory and research has come under recent criticism because the theories of human development have primarily centered on male subjects. Feminist researchers have pointed out the sex bias evident in much of the research on human motivation; women were presumed to be moderate in achievement motivation, high in affiliation motivation and have no power motivation. These biases, along with the absence of women subjects, has led to a theory about male motivation which may or may not be true for women (Horner, 1972; Denmark et al., 1986, Miller, 1984). Certainly the stereotypes about being male and female influence differently the motivational states of boy and girl students in school. While we cannot answer whether there is or is not a sex differential in human motivation, we caution teachers to be aware of bringing biased interactions to their male and female students.

We think all students will ponder these issues for themselves. What can I accomplish? How can I feel competent instead of incompetent. Who will like me? What will I do when people don't like me? How can I exert my will? How can I influence others? Will people listen to me? The motives for achievement, affiliation, and power can be recognized in the behavior of students in all classrooms. For example, in relation to achievement, students may express a feeling of incompetence leading to behaviors of inattention or inactivity in classroom learning. Listlessness, day dreaming, and lack of interest in learning may indicate a frustration over the motive for achievement. The motive for affiliation and liking can often be seen in overt aggressiveness or withdrawal; feelings of loneliness, alienation, and even betrayal are indicators of needs for affiliation not being met. In relation to power, we often see behaviors of putting people down or ignoring others that may lead to aggressive behavior or a heightened anxiety when called on to perform. Incompetence, rejection, and powerlessness are perhaps the most serious motivational problems within classrooms.

Perspective 6: Group Effects on Intellectual Performance

The mere presence of other persons who are working on a similar task has been shown to have significant effects on the intellectual and motor performances of an individual. This tradition of psychological research, referred to as the "psychology of social facilitation," is best represented by F. Allport (1924) and Dashiell (1935), who gave attention to the effects of groups of people upon the individual person. They compared the achievement of individuals performing with other persons physically present to those of individuals working on the same tasks alone.

Most of this research showed that the mere presence of other coacting persons had a detrimental effect on intellectual functioning and a facilitating effect on the performance of simple motor tasks. One important dimension in this research was the psychological complexity of the task to be performed. The presence of other persons had more negative impact on the individual as the task became more complex; in particular, when it became cognitively more complex. The point in time when the presence of other persons become detrimental is still unclear. However, the research is convincing in pointing out that the intellectual activity of individuals can be influenced negatively by the presence of others doing similar tasks.

Subsequent research by Sharan and Sharan (1976) showed that the presence of others during learning can have a significant facilitating and enhancing effect on the individual. When students are taught to work interdependently and cooperatively on learning tasks, they can learn the material faster and retain it longer than when they are given mass instruction with no attention to collaboration and helping. This research revealed the limitations of over generalizing from the earlier work of F. Allport. We must understand the nature and quality of the interpersonal relationships within a learning setting to tell whether they will facilitate or restrain academic learning.

A theory about the psychological impact of feeling uncomfortable in the presence of others can be helpful in understanding the contrasting findings of Allport and Sharan and Sharan. Snygg and Combs (1949) argued that when people feel anxious or fearful in the presence of another, they have difficulty in accurately perceiving the world. The greater the threat people feel from others, the more pronounced the restricting and distorting effect on how they view their surroundings. People's perceptions may become so distorted that they are unable to behave efficiently. An experiment performed by Combs and Taylor (1952) illustrates this phenomenon. Belligerent examiners introduced mild degrees of personal threat while students were performing a task requiring intellectual functioning. The researchers predicted that this personal threat would result in an increase in time required to complete the task, as well as an increase in errors in performance. The fifty participants in this experiment were given the task of translating sentences into a simple code. With only one exception, the students required longer time periods to complete the coding procedures when they were working under threatening conditions, and they also made a greater number of errors of translation than in a comparable, nonthreatening situation.

It is not difficult to predict what might happen to students who are presented over and over again with interpersonal situations that are threatening to them. One of the possible effects of having others working in near proximity, especially others with whom students feel insecure, is a reduced level of performance on complex, cognitive learning activities. The extent to which such students use their intelligence is likely to be considerably reduced when working in such a threatening classroom situation.

Group Dynamics Theory and Classroom Climate

These six historical perspectives from social psychology in general, and group dynamics in particular, help us to build a rudimentary understanding of the role of group processes in the classroom. The students in a classroom are more than a collection of individuals. They form a living social system in which they experience interdependence, interaction, and common goal-striving with peers. In the social system of the classroom, there are many subsystems that have impact on how the larger system works and how individuals relate to one another. The students interact with the teacher and with one another, both informally and formally. Informal relationships often go unnoticed, even though they can be extremely important for classroom life. The students perform academic tasks in the physical presence of one another in order to develop themselves intellectually and emotionally. Their informal relationships of friendship, influence, prestige, and respect can have decided effects on the manner in which the more formal requirements of the student role are accomplished by the individual youngsters. At the same time, informal relationships in the peer group are often fraught with emotion and involvement, and some sort of an interpersonal underworld is inevitable for every student.

As these informal peer relations increase in power and salience, the individual student's definition and evaluation of self become more and more vulnerable to peer group influence. Each student's self-concept is on the line within the classroom setting, where the quality of informal relationships can be either threatening and debilitating, or supportive and enhancing to the development of self-esteem. In particular, the motives of achievement, power, and affiliation must be satisfied to some extent for an individual student to feel comfortable in the classroom. The negative feelings of incompetence, powerlessness, and rejection arise when these motives are not satisfied. The more threatening or supportive the interpersonal relationships in the classroom are in relation to satisfying these motives and in raising or lowering the self-esteem, the more likely the student's academic learning and classroom behavior will be affected. In short, emotion-laden interpersonal relationships that occur informally can affect the student's self-concept which, in turn, can influence his or her intellectual performance.

The term *classroom climate* can be applied to the interpersonal feeling tones associated with informal interaction patterns, emotional responses to the group, and to both the self-concepts of students and their motivational satisfactions and frustrations. Classroom climate can be informally diagnosed by observing physical movement, bodily gestures, seating arrangements, and patterns of verbal interaction. How do students move toward the teachers? Do they stand close or far away? Are they physically at ease or tight and tense? How often is affection indicated by smiles, winks, or pats on the back? Do the students move quietly and unobtrusively with measured steps through the hallways or do they walk freely and easily in ways that indicate the school is truly their own? Are students reluctant to approach clusters of teachers? How do students relate to one another? Are they quiet, distant, and formal, or do they walk easily and laugh spontaneously? How

often does hostility erupt into fighting between students? How is fighting handled by other students when it does occur? Are the classrooms neatly organized and run primarily by the teachers? Do students sit in rows facing the teachers, or are the seats arranged in seminar style or in small groups? Do the seating arrangements shift from time to time, or do they remain the same regardless of the learning activity? Are students intent on what they are doing? Are they working together within a spirit of cooperation?

Classrooms that have a climate of competitiveness, hostility, and alienation cause anxiety and discomfort and do not facilitate the intellectual development of many students. Classrooms in which students and teachers support one another facilitate the development of self-esteem and the satisfaction of fundamental motives. They also provide the opportunity for students to use their intellectual capacities to their fullest.

In an analysis of 116 junior high science classrooms in Australia, Fraser and Fisher (1982) demonstrated sizable relationships between classroom climate and students' academic abilities. Measures of the degree to which students were encouraged to participate in classroom discussions, to assist each other and work together, to interact with the teacher in a personal way, to be treated differently according to skills and learning styles, and the clarity of the learning tasks and student behaviors were positively related to classroom achievement in science. The educational environment has profound implications for academic achievement.

The interpersonal power that students feel in relation to their classmates, and the levels of skill and competence students see in themselves, also encourage positive feelings about school and increased involvement in classroom tasks. The relevance of positive classroom climates for optimal school adjustment of students is now commonplace for most educational practitioners.

Even though there is a general agreement about the significance of social climate, there is not a general agreement about how it can be measured (see Fraser and Fisher, 1982; Walberg, 1979). For us, *a positive classroom climate is one where the students support one another; where the students share high amounts of potential influence—both with one another and with the teacher; where high levels of attraction exist for the group as a whole and between classmates; where norms are supportive for getting academic work done, as well as for maximizing individual differences; where communication is open and featured by dialogue; where conflict is dealt with openly and constructively; and where the processes of working and developing together as a group are considered relevant in themselves for study.* In such classrooms, we would expect to find students and teachers collaborating in attempting to accomplish common goals, feelings of positive self-esteem, feelings of security, high involvement in academic learning, feelings of being influential with the teacher and other students, and a high degree of attraction to one's classmates, class, and school.

Although each separate property of climate is important by itself, the climate of a classroom is more than the sum of its parts. The term "climate" describes how each of the properties is integrated and working in relation to one another. The concept of climate summarizes the group processes that are worked out by a teacher in interaction with students, and between the students in the classroom. Climate is *what* the classroom activity *is* in carrying out ed-

ucational goals; it is *how* the curriculum and learning materials *are actually used* through the human exchange; and it is the *styles of relating among members of the classroom group.*

Overview of Chapters 3–10

This book deals primarily with research on the social climate of the classroom—the group dynamics of classrooms. Most of the concepts presented have been derived from empirical research on interpersonal relations, group dynamics, and organizational psychology. Some of this research has not been carried out in public school settings. Some of the material that will be presented represents strong hunches, extrapolated from other settings but not yet directly empirically tested in classrooms. At the same time, liberal use will be made of research on classroom settings from an emerging and rapidly growing number of social psychologists in education. Each step of the way we attempt to clarify the distinction between empirically tested findings and our tentative conclusions based on theory.

Chapter 3 serves to summarize the key aspects of classroom climate by showing how class members might be expected to react at different stages of the group's development. The core content of the book lays out what empirical research indicates are the essential properties of classroom climate. Chapter 4 deals with how interpersonal expectations—especially expectations for achievement—become patterned and influential in the classroom. In chapter 5, we examine how leadership or interpersonal influence is exerted and look at power as a feature of classroom climate. Chapter 6 deals with the manner in which friendship patterns affect the classroom and with attraction and hostility as features of classroom climate. Chapter 6 also is concerned with the cohesive classroom group and how it is created and maintained. Cohesiveness as a central feature of classroom climate is fully examined. In chapter 7 we focus on how group norms work for or against educational goals and look at the effects of interpersonal expectations and pressures on the social climate of the classroom. In chapter 8, we describe how communication patterns occur in the classroom and how the different patterns relate to positive and negative climates. Chapter 9 discusses conflict in the classroom, under what conditions it arises, the variety of forms it takes, and how the teacher and students can handle it openly and constructively. Chapter 10, the final chapter, deals with the relationships that exist between the organizational processes of the school and the classroom group. We will show how the classroom climate can be affected by the interpersonal relationships and norms of the professional staff. Each chapter includes a statement of objectives, theory, and research, diagnostic instruments or tactics, and a number of practical plans for action designed by teachers to implement specific instructional activities, plans that are based on group dynamics principles.

Phases of Group Development

3

Most learning in school takes place in classroom groups, but the principles of individual development still dominate educational thinking. In this chapter we focus on group development in the classroom. A classroom group, like an individual, passes through phases during a school year. We have specified and analyzed four phases. Classes with healthy climates pay attention to where they are developmentally and what they must do to move to the next, more mature phase.

Objectives of this Chapter

In this chapter we review the theory and research on group development and provide concrete plans for teachers. We aim to help the reader recognize four different phases of classroom group development which include: (1) membership, (2) shared influence, (3) the pursuit of academic goals, and (4) self-renewal. We review the theory and research about group development, diagnose a classroom group's phase of current development, and design effective interventions for facilitating mature group development in the classroom. We strive to make the abstract ideas of researchers useful to teachers and to help teachers appreciate the potential of seeing their classes in an historical-developmental perspective.

Overview of Group Development

Erikson's theory (1950) of psychological development offers some helpful analogies for understanding the growth of classroom groups. He argues that individuals face a sequence of psychological problems during their lifetimes—problems that must be resolved before they can move on successfully to the next stage. As Erikson views it, psychological development is sequential and successive; each stage follows another in time, and solutions to problems at all later stages are dependent upon the resolutions that were made during prior stages.

Classroom groups similarly pass through sequential and successive phases in developing their formal and informal social patterns. Moreover, resolutions to current interpersonal problems in the classroom are dependent on solutions to prior problems. As in the case of individuals, classroom growth can also be arrested at any developmental phase. For example, a classroom group would have difficulty carrying out an activity requiring group cooperation and a flexible division of labor if it had not previously developed trust and openness of communication among the members. Indeed, if the members of a class never developed a foundation of basic interpersonal trust and closeness, they would have difficulty proceeding to more advanced phases of group interdependence.

Most teachers report a difference in their classes from the beginning to the end of the school year. This difference is partly due to the maturing of individual students; however, the way the individual's psychology develops is also influenced by the social context of the group. Consider for instance, the contrasting opportunities available to individuals for learning about responsibility in the following classrooms described by Wilson et al. (1979), as related by a teacher.

> Kids are responsible for the way that they are seated and for the way the group runs. After a while, a trial run, it

works out that the kids are seated in a place where they feel happy. Also on the notice-boards around the room they have a little area, so they sit fairly close to that so at the end of the lesson they can pin up things that they've done or something they want me to look at, and that's the way I check their work (p. 52).

And in contrast, another teacher reported quite a different climate concerning responsibility.

We didn't set any class rules up. I'm reasonably autocratic on a few things. One is kids preventing others from working—I would ask them to leave. There are degrees. First they are separated, put up near the door. The next step is out, they vanish for the lesson. That's it. I don't care where they go. The other one is homework. If they can't do their homework, I expect a note from Mum and Dad (p. 42).

These two teachers were part of a well-designed study in South Australia, one of the few empirical studies of developmental processes in the literature. The authors gave particular attention to reciprocating influences between the individuals and the group. Thus, the development of the classroom group was viewed as being dependent on the maturation level of the individuals comprising the group. And, at the same time, the individual's maturation was seen as depending on the developmental maturity of the classroom group.

While individual and group development are both sequential and successive, they are also cyclical, with very similar developmental issues coming up again and again. In other words, even though certain psychological problems and group process issues seem to accrue with more specificity at certain times than others, individuals and groups continually face similar challenges as they mature. For example, Erikson argued that establishing interpersonal trust is the first significant problem faced by the infant. At the same time, the psychodynamics of trust are confronted again when the child begins to have friends, again when adolescent dating takes place, and again after the marriage vows are made. Yet, to some degree, the interpersonal trust learned during infancy always remains with each person as he or she enters new relationships. In an analogous fashion, group development is cyclical: issues of trust and accurate communication continually arise as the group copes with the dynamics of leadership, attraction, and norms. At the same time, the reservoir of trust that is established early in the group's developmental history will reap subsequent benefits as the group is confronted with challenges.

Of all the class members, the teacher's influence on the group's developing climate is most critical. And of all the times during the year that the teacher is influential, the first day of class is most critical. Teachers deliberately or unwittingly guide and direct the development of group processes in the classroom from that day on. In the South Australian study described by Wilson, for example, those classes that reached higher stages of group development had teachers who exhibited different behaviors than classes that remained at lower stages of development. The teachers of the former classes intervened right from the start to stimulate and encourage open communication, group work, and discussion about how the class was going. In the more mature classes the teachers used their legitimate power to facilitate greater student choice, more teacher-student feedback, and constructive group work among the students. The teachers of the less mature class groups were much less likely to encourage group work, and, when they did, tended to maintain high control over how the students were allowed to work together.

Thus, although the teachers with developmentally mature classes actively intervened in the students' group work, they did not dominate the group's choices. Wilson indicated that well-meaning teachers frequently cannot separate active intervention and domination; they try to stimulate student choice, but unwittingly control the students, perhaps out of a fear of losing control. In classes where teachers do not provide opportunities for student choice and responsibility, where much of the formal talk and academic information come from the teachers, and where students infrequently hear one another's ideas, the students do not get the opportunity to develop interpersonal trust or to engage effectively in decision making about classroom activities. Such a "collection" of students will not be socially capable of carrying out learning tasks that require student planning, cooperation, and interdependence.

At the same time, the teacher's power can be reduced significantly if the group's developmental history is at odds with the teacher's style. Ron Lippitt was fond of telling a story about his own experiences as a teacher-trainer in relation to the strength of the classroom group. Early in his teaching career in the early 1940s, Ron was in charge of preparing college students to teach in rural Illinois. He learned quickly that his ideas about shared decision making, the democratic classroom, and equality between teachers and students did not take hold once the neophyte teachers took jobs.

Even though his trainees could behave democratically in the role playing that he organized in the college classroom, they seemed unable to follow through with these behaviors in their actual teaching.

As Lippitt saw it, these neophyte teachers were taking over classroom groups in which levels of trust and openness were low, and in which the students shared firm expectations that the teacher was the sole authority and organizer. Faced with schools of this type, the new teachers soon reverted to traditional, authoritarian practices. Subsequently, Lippitt revised his preservice training program to include practicing "how to be a humane authoritarian teacher" and "how to move a group from autocracy to democracy," so that the prospective teachers would be able to cope wisely and effectively with the classes they would face.

Classroom groups begin at different stages, depending on the students' past experiences in school. Classroom members who have previously experienced primarily authoritarian teachers will be at different skill levels from classroom members who have had ample experiences in communicating with one another and in collaboratively working on improving their classroom dynamics. A recent real-life occurrence will help to elaborate this point.

A friend of ours returned to teaching sixth grade after a twenty-year hiatus from classroom teaching. His most recent work had included a fair amount of administrative activity: he consulted with schools and taught teachers about group processes in the classroom. He became tired and disgruntled in dealing with the "politics of administrative trivia" and returned to what he then considered the "less demanding job" of classroom teacher. His dreams and hopes for what he would do in the classroom were not unlike those of a novice teacher who leaves the "hallowed halls of ivy" to set the educational world on fire. The first day he asked students to form into work groups. There was chaos. He tried again and again, with unsettling results, and found himself becoming both the evaluator and the controller of student behavior. The "less demanding" job of sixth-grade teacher was resulting in similar headaches to those incurred in his administrative position. Finally, after several weeks of struggle, like Ron Lippitt with his teachers in rural Illinois, our friend pulled in the reins and began using skill training and group activities in small doses. Although his students had achieved feelings of inclusion and membership—because they felt free to publicly express their concerns, needs, fears, and ideas—they had not acquired the skills for joint goal-setting and collaborative work. He had not accurately diagnosed their skill levels and learned by directly experiencing what *didn't* work. He realized that he would have to respect the developmental phase of the youngsters he was working with and proceed from there.

We often work with neophyte teachers who are "turned on" to the idea of democratic teaching or cooperative learning, or who wish to make frequent use of small-group instruction. Sometimes such teachers will hand over the reins of leadership totally to students, who themselves are unprepared and unskilled in assuming initiatory roles. When the class falls into disunity and disarray, the teacher pulls back the reins of control and explains, "I tried it and it didn't work." But, as all teachers come to see, students cannot change their expectations, behaviors, and skills simply by administrative fiat—behavioral changes

in student groups require understanding, planning, and practice over a sustained period.

Teachers who understand the sequential nature of the developing classroom group and can accurately diagnose the skills of the members, can influence growth in planned and productive ways. Conversely, teachers who do not consider the need for the gradual development of skills and behaviors in attaining effective group performance will have classes that are thwarted or stilted in their development and do not become optimal environments for individual development. A book by Mick Rivers (1976), a classroom teacher, nicely capitalizes on the importance of group development in its title, "Manipulating Freedom in Groups: Two Months Hell and Ten Months Heaven." Rivers noted that "hell is the first few months of any new system in the classroom" while "heaven is the excitement, change of attitudes, the interest and involvement shown by students, together with the new depth of communication . . ." once they have had a chance to develop as a supportive learning group.

Theories of Group Development

Classroom groups have academic tasks to accomplish. The way these tasks are carried out is due, in part, to the emotional processes established in a group's life. Both sets of social dynamics—the task and the emotional aspects of group life—develop simultaneously. In a comprehensive review of the literature about small group development, Shambaugh (1978) notes that "group development follows a fluctuating stepwise course" (see also Bradford, 1978).

Among the several theories describing group development, four models are especially useful for understanding classroom life. Each deals with task and emotional issues but emphasizes different aspects.

The *Interpersonal Composition Model* is illustrated best by the work of Schutz (1958, 1966), who maintained that the task orientation of groups is based on members' needs for inclusion, control, and affection. Schutz's Interpersonal Composition Model focuses on the personality dynamics of individuals. The *Cooperative Learning Model* (Johnson, 1981, Johnson and Johnson, 1982, Slavin, 1980, 1983, Webb, 1982) emphasizes the individual skills needed to perform effective task and emotional goals of groups; these authors argue that effective group work depends on instructional context and individual skill. The *Role-Function Model,* on the other hand, tends to underplay the skill or personality characteristics of individuals, putting emphasis on the roles or functions that members must carry out if problem-solving groups are to perform effectively. Parsons and Bale's (1955) work is useful for understanding the activities members must perform in order for learning to occur in a group setting. Finally the *Individual-Group Maturation Model* contains both elements of emotionality of members and group problem-solving functions. Jack Gibb's (1964) theory of individual and group development is useful for our understanding and practical orientation toward the development of classroom learning groups.

We must note, however, that only the Cooperative Learning Model has been used directly in research on learning groups in school. Schutz's studies included some teacher-student, two-person units and several sensitivity groups with educators, but were not carried out directly in public schools. Parsons and Bales made use of simulated problem-solving groups and real families, none of which was in a school setting. Gibb conducted his experimental and field studies in several industrial and noneducational organizational settings.

The Interpersonal Composition Model

According to Schutz, individuals naturally express the three interpersonal needs of *inclusion, control,* and *affection* to different degrees and in different social settings. In the beginning of a group's development, the most dominant domain of interpersonal interaction focuses upon inclusion. This is followed later by more interactions involving control, which, in turn, are followed by interactions of affection. This sequence may recur in the form of a cycle several times prior to the termination of a group's life. The final three stages prior to a group's demise occur in just the reverse order, with affection preceding control and ending with inclusion. While these stages of group development are sequential, they are also overlapping and continually intertwining and are never completely exclusive of one another.

Issues concerned with interpersonal inclusion clearly seem to characterize the beginning of group life in the classroom. On the first day of school, the students and teacher confront one another's presence and raise questions such as: "How will I fit in here? Who will accept me? Who will reject me? What do I have to do to be accepted?" Academic work cannot easily be accomplished until questions such as these are answered satisfactorily. All people—students or teachers—cautiously reveal aspects of themselves, while at the same time, gathering information about others. Schutz labeled the content discussed during the initial meeting as "goblet issues," because he visualized persons figuratively picking up goblets and gazing through them to size up others without, at the same time, revealing themselves. Becoming included in, and therefore a member of, a peer group may revolve around many factors: having friends in common; where one lives; what one's hobbies are; or clues about one's nature—whether one is pleasant and considerate. Students reveal themselves bit-by-bit and issue-by-issue until each one considers himself or herself in or out of the class in terms of psychological membership. Unfortunately, some students never achieve a feeling of membership, and their attendant anxiety can interfere significantly with their academic achievement.

After group membership has been achieved by most of the members, Schutz views groups as having struggles with control and influence, struggles that typically entail the development of decision-making norms and the sharing of responsibility. He calls this the "stage of control." It appears inevitable in classrooms that students will test their degree of influence with the teacher as well as with other students. This period of testing for one's degree of influence, discussed extensively in chapter 5 on "Leadership," finds all class members attempting to establish a comfortable level of influence for themselves within the group.

Following the interpersonal struggles for influence, group members begin to confront the emotional issues of interpersonal affection and psychological closeness. "Who will like me?" and "Whom do I like?" are characteristic questions of this third stage of development. During this stage of group growth, discussed in chapter 6 on "Attraction," all members strive for optimal degrees of intimacy with others to suit their personal needs.

Fundamental to Schutz's theory of group development is the variable of interpersonal compatibility, discussed also in chapter 6. He defines compatibility as "the amount of comfort that exists between two or more persons by virtue of their satisfying each other's expressed and wanted needs." Compatible groups are composed of some members who want inclusion, control, and affection, and other members who express these same interpersonal needs in an exchange fashion. Members who want inclusion, control, or affection behave differently from members who express these characteristics. According to the theory, groups tend to develop optimally when members complement one another's' psychological needs. In contrast, incompatible groups are comprised of members who do not complement each other; for instance, a project group composed of students who want affection and those who express control probably will not work effectively.

Educators have found some practical usefulness in Schutz's Interpersonal Composition Model. Many teachers, for example, have seen that simply grouping students according to such characteristics as ability or achievement will not necessarily result in effective work groups. *Psychological compatibility in many instances is the most useful criterion to use in small group work.* Letting students organize their own ad hoc task groups is one straightforward way to group students according to their personal compatibilities. In some cases, students are the best judges of whom they can work with and who in the peer group will satisfy their needs.

The Cooperative Learning Model

The Johnsons assert that successful group development rests on the effectiveness of individual social skills in learning to work *cooperatively* (1984). They argue that the context of classroom instruction can be organized *competitively* (where students work against each other to attain scarce resources, such as grading on a curve where only some students can obtain their goals, if and only if the other members of the class fail to obtain their goals), the classroom can be organized *individualistically* (where students work on assigned individual work, such as a language program, and their progress is unrelated to the progress of other students), and classrooms may be organized *cooperatively* (where students work together to accomplish shared goals, such as presenting a group report or preparing a class event). They argue that the structure of classroom learning is inordinately skewed toward the competitive or individualistic structures; and this, they argue, is dysfunctional for several reasons.

First, individual achievement is hampered when students do not effectively use the resources of their peers. Second, the processes of individual development are hampered when students are not psychologically connected to each other; they cite isolation, loneliness, and meaninglessness as the outcomes of school processes which do not build on the connectedness or the feelings of social empowerment of students. Finally a fact of life is the reality that most individuals will work most of their lives in organizations which often require group decision making and the resolution of human conflict. For these reasons the Johnsons argue that classroom instruction should include all three learning structures.

Cooperative learning skills, however, require training and the opportunity to develop. The skills emphasized include learning communication, building trust, providing leadership and managing conflicts. The Johnsons also assert that cooperative, interpersonal skills can only be developed within a cooperative context. Thus, students cannot be taught to communicate effectively if they are expected to work alone without interacting with each other; students cannot be expected to join together in collaborative work if the context requires individual work and evaluation is competitively determined. The current work on cooperative learning echoes Dewey's themes that the classroom is the microcosm of the society; we cannot expect students to learn about democracy except through experiencing democratic relationships. Thus the context of the learning environment, which is controlled in great part by the teacher, plays an important theme in building individual cooperative skills.

The Johnsons' work at the Cooperative Learning Center of the University of Minnesota consists of research and training for educators in teaching cooperative skills (see also Dishon and O'Leary, 1986). They suggest four steps of individual skills to be taught:

1. *Forming:* The bottom-line skills needed to establish a functioning cooperative group.

2. *Functioning:* The skills needed to manage to accomplish a group task and maintain effective work relationships.

3. *Formulating:* The skills needed to build a deeper level understanding of the material studied; to stimulate reasoning strategies and to maximize mastery of the material.

4. *Fermenting:* The skills needed to stimulate reconceptualization of the material covered, search for new information and to communicate the rationale behind one's conclusions (Johnson and Johnson, 1984, p. 45).

The Johnsons use the development of group skills to enhance individual learning.

The Role-Function Model

Parsons and Bales specify that members must perform certain roles before the group can solve its problems and remain viable. The two fundamental clusters of roles they designate entail *task* and *maintenance* functions. The essential argument is the idea that if both functions are not performed, the group will not be effective. Any member potentially can perform task or maintenance functions, but in most real groups, particular individuals engage in specific behaviors to a greater degree than others. In addition, interpersonal expectations involving who will or who should perform which of the functions are usually established. In contrast to the thinking of Schutz, Parsons and Bales view personality characteristics as important determinants of group life only insofar as they explain why particular persons might take particular roles. Their theory specifies that groups develop in a sociologically predictable fashion, regardless of the personalities within them.

Research on the Parsons-Bales theory of group development has been carried out on four to eight person groups faced with specific problems to solve (see Bales and Slater, 1955, for detailed data). The research shows both the development of a group over several meetings and its mini-development during one meeting. In relation to the latter, three stages, labeled *phase movements,* were shown to occur within a single meeting. The idea that there are a number of small phases that recur and follow a definite sequence is a theme in current research on small group development (Shambaugh 1978). Generally the pattern runs as follows:

The first phase entails giving and receiving information about the problem itself, background to the problem, and potential solutions that are tentative and not well developed. The middle phase is characterized, for the most part, by an exchange of opinions and a period of evaluation. Members test out solutions, criticize one another's solutions, and jointly develop new solutions. Decision making about what actions to take also tends to occur during this phase. During the final phase, there is a definite increase in the exchange of pleasant feelings and a decrease in the amount of criticism expressed. Joking, the release of tension, and jovial laughter are typical during this period. Members seemingly are trying to increase their solidarity and turn their attention to the effective support of one another.

Particular groups will go through different phases in one session and different stages over a period of time. A single meeting is, in some ways, a microcosm of total group development. *For learning groups to gain strength and momentum, they should be allowed and encouraged to move through all phases during a single meeting.* Lippitt (1940), for example, showed an instance in which a group of youngsters failed to reach the final phase of group development, but remained instead at the stage of criticizing one another. The students were floundering without direction; decisions were hard to make in the face of interpersonal conflict; and the leader attempted to intervene with controlling and dominating behaviors. The meeting ended on a note of divisiveness with many negative feelings being expressed. Perhaps the meeting ended that way because the leader intervened in a controlling manner during the middle stages of the group's development. Perhaps the students could have achieved some agreements had the leader merely pointed out the time remaining and proposed a scheme for making decisions. Similarly, high amounts of negativism can occur in classrooms when the teacher initially gives the group freedom to solve a problem but steps in too soon to control and alter the decisions.

In many classrooms, the first few days or even weeks are fraught with ambiguity and unclear directions from the students' points of view. How the resulting frustrations and insecure feelings get resolved can be critical for determining the extent of student involvement in the subsequent life of the group. Teachers who do not allow the students' ideas and feelings to emerge early, and who take over in a highly controlling fashion, may retard the development of the group and be cutting off important emotional support for learning within the peer group.

Systematic patterns of group development have been shown to arise over the duration of a series of classroom sessions. In one careful study, Runkel et al. (1971) documented the key developmental stages of task activities within a college class. The primary requirement of this undergraduate course was for groups of students to complete an independent research project collaboratively. The developmental processes of these research groups were documented by observers using Tuckman's model (1965) of group development. Following Tuckman's concepts, the observers discovered

four distinct phases of development: (1) time during which members defined the task and set limitations on it; (2) emotional responses to the task, usually in the form of resistance to carrying out the task; (3) the open exchange of information, feelings, and opinions; and (4) the generation of solutions and plans for work.

Heinicke and Bales (1953) found that over a span of four meetings, members gradually spent less time doing work and more time carrying out social-emotional functions. Although the first meeting was characterized in large part by cautious and polite behaviors, a great deal of negativism arose during the second meeting. The researchers labeled this observed negativism "status struggles," parallel to what Tuckman had termed "emotional resistance to the task," and what Schutz had labeled the "control phase." Heinicke and Bales noted that interpersonal conflicts arose mostly when the group was faced with making decisions. *The groups that did not resolve their status struggles did not move on to become effective in problem solving, nor were the members very happy with their group experience.* Groups that did proceed successfully through this stage and then moved on to make plans for action developed favorable feelings and supported one another strongly.

One of the most consistent results filtering through all of this research on group development is the tendency of groups to alternate in a cyclical fashion between emphasizing task pursuits and social-emotional concerns. When groups of students are asked to work together on classroom projects, it is realistic to expect that they will spend nearly half of their available time dealing with the emotional aspects of their interpersonal relationships.

Indeed, teachers must expect days when it appears everyone in the class has gotten out of bed on the wrong side. A knowledgeable teacher will expect such days, trying to use them constructively in helping students and work groups to develop toward maturity. All groups, including student and adult groups, spend considerable time on emotional issues that require energy and hard work. Indeed, *if learning groups do not discuss and attempt to solve their emotional problems, there is a high probability that they will have difficulty in accomplishing academic learning tasks.*

The Individual-Group Maturation Model

Gibb's ideas (1964) are relevant to the development of classroom groups. His major themes note that groups grow into maturity only after they develop interpersonal trust and that groups in which trust is not established do not help individual members to develop self-esteem. The theory proposes four basic concerns of members while their group is developing.

The first concern is for interpersonal acceptance and the formation of trust and confidence in the self and the group. On the personal side, one's feelings of adequacy and self-esteem are at stake. For the group, concerns of membership and trust in others are most prominent. The second concern is for what Gibb refers to as "data-flow." During this stage, individuals think less about themselves and more about the group and their task. They become aware of the ways in which the group is functioning and begin to evaluate whether they like what the group is doing. Norms begin to form in relation to how the group will make decisions. If some degree of acceptance and trust has not already been established, decision

making will be hampered by closed and guarded communication, and decisions will get made without deep commitment and psychological ownership of the members.

The third concern is for the achievement of goals for the individuals and the group. Individuals want to achieve something that helps them feel successful and competent. They will become independent and autonomous, provided that earlier concerns have been successfully resolved. Within the group, norms will be established about goals and procedures. If there is open communication, goals can be determined to complement the individuals, and the group will develop a comfortable and flexible task structure.

The final concern is for the amount of freedom and control experienced by the members. Individuals feel independent and autonomous, provided that earlier problems have been resolved successfully. For the group, norms are formalized, interpersonal behaviors are agreed upon, and the group is able to change itself when the members choose to do so.

These four developmental concerns nicely describe what goes on in the interpersonal underworld of many classroom groups. Students do not directly express their own ideas and opinions publicly until they have learned that their peers and the teacher will not reject them. Those students who do not feel accepted and included will tend to withhold their ideas from discussion. They will feel alienated from academic learning, be without direction and poorly motivated, suppress their feelings, and not abide by the academic norms of the school. Students who learn to trust their peers will become more involved in pursuing their own goals in the learning group and will tend to abide by the primary norms of the group.

Classroom groups naturally differ considerably in how these developmental concerns are handled. In one class, the group may not be able to "work through" the phases of development, and the interpersonal relationships may become formalized and distant. Students will not become very well acquainted with one another in such classes because they are not communicating openly and personally. Indeed, some of the students will feel afraid to express their ideas; discussions, when they do occur, will tend to be awkward and lack spontaneity. The learning goals that are presented to the students by the teacher are not owned by the students. Moreover, the rewards for conforming to classroom rules are extrinsic, and the direction of the group will be determined more and more by the evaluations of the teacher. The classroom organization will, for the most part, become routinized, norms will be characterized by a narrow range of tolerable behavior, and the teacher will be obliged to enforce classroom rules. This picture, unfortunately, represents the lion's share of public school classrooms that we have observed during the past thirty years.

In a classroom with a healthier climate, the same developmental concerns may be involved; but, because of different ways of working with them, the group develops differently. As the students cautiously reveal parts of themselves, the teacher accepts a variety of student behaviors. The students learn that their peers are also afraid to reveal themselves, but gradually imitate the teacher's behaviors of acceptance. The students begin to reward one another for the expression of ideas, information is freely exchanged, and collaborative decision making begins to occur. Later the students start to direct their own behavior and to establish things they want the class to accomplish. Norms are discussed and changed jointly by the teacher and students as they prove to be no longer helpful to what everyone wishes to accomplish.

The Social Context of Group Development

There are many important variations in the development of a classroom group. The behavior of the teacher is one important factor in accounting for such variations. The development of classroom groups is strongly influenced by teacher behavior. For example, Gibb identified two clusters of leadership behaviors, which he labeled as "persuasive" and "participative," that could influence groups to cope with developmental issues in different ways. Behaviors of the *persuasive teacher* tend to emanate from an orientation of distrust; such teachers lack confidence in their students. They consider students to be immature or not wise enough to make decisions for themselves. These persuasive teachers see their role as setting goals for learning and convincing students that these are worthy goals to pursue. Their authority is clear; academic learning is formal and routine; and they set the norms for appropriate classroom behavior and enforce the norms.

In contrast, *participative teachers* begin by trusting and accepting their students. They place themselves in an equalitarian position in relation to their students by often functioning as one of the class members. They expect to be listened to just as they expect to listen carefully to the students. They encourage students to make decisions for themselves, to express themselves, and to participate in determining the policies and procedures for learning and behavior. Participative teachers typically encourage a classroom climate that is informal, relaxed, and supportive.

The Johnsons note that teachers can develop different contexts for learning; the competitive, individualistic, and cooperative contexts. Different materials, teaching purposes, and learning goals require different contexts. The competent teacher can provide these differing contexts for instruction.

Shambaugh (1978) also pointed to the importance of the leader in a review of research on small group development. He traced the historical roots of an emphasis on the leader to Freud who postulated that group members identify strongly with their leader, leading to strong love-hate relationships similar to relationships between children and parents. Thus, students may be seen to alternate between dependence and independence in relation to their teacher. As members decrease their dependence upon the leader, the leader becomes less central and members begin to focus on each other to resolve their developmental problems as a group and to articulate their own individuality. Teachers who remain centrally authoritarian in all classroom matters present an omniscient front, thereby denying the potential of individuals and the group to develop toward more advanced and complex stages of growth.

Classroom groups also change in membership during a school year; in some schools there is a high turnover of students. Moreland and Levine (1984) showed how individuals pass through groups where people are at different stages of membership. A new student comes to class and must be assimilated into the ongoing group processes; this student passes through phases of membership and belonging and the group must alter its self definition.

Social situations also present different issues for learning and group development. Consider, for example, the different developmental challenges that face groups of all boys or all girls in contrast to the issues facing a mixed-sex group. The sex composition of a group alters the behavior of individuals in the group. Race is also a social variable that often carries important social meaning in group development; students who are a racially integrated class may have different group issues than those in racially homogenous groups. In American society our expectations and behaviors are often influenced by the sex and race of the person with whom we are interacting. Lockheed and Hall (1976) found, for instance, that the sex composition of a group influences an individual's behavior in task-oriented groups. They investigated the differences in behavior of males and females in mixed-sex and single-sex groups. High school students were instructed to play a decision-making game which required them to agree on a series of paths to move a token from one side of a game board to another in following a maze. They investigated activity level, attempts at influence, and task orientation. In the single-sex groups there was no difference in the behaviors of males and females; whereas, in the mixed-sex groups, males were seven times as likely to emerge as leaders as females.

The progress of classroom group development will be affected by the skills and competencies of the individuals; furthermore, the role people take within the classroom will be influenced by their gender socialization. Females have learned to be less initiatory and active in relation to tasks and to defer to the male's leadership. Males and females are influenced more strongly by a male than a female.

Similarly, the racial composition of a group can be related to certain group processes. For example, Lewis and St. John (1974) showed that blacks are most popular with whites in majority-black classrooms and that whites are more popular with blacks in majority-white classrooms. While the outcomes of research on attitudes and group processes in desegregated schools is generally yet unclear and inconclusive (Schofield 1978, 1982), racial mixing is one important aspect of classroom group development.

The cultural meaning given to one's sex, race, and ethnic origins are issues for individual and group development. Equality-inequality is the social issue at hand and students must cope with this in one way or another. *The ultimate purpose of a teacher's guiding a group of students through the different stages of development is to maximize the learning ability of the individuals by developing group norms and procedures that encourage all students to do their very best.* Certainly a student's sex, race, and ethnic identification have direct and profound implications for how he or she learns subject matter and copes with interpersonal relations in the class. Understanding and recognizing the informal messages of the stereotypes of sex, race, and ethnicity can free teachers and students from many social restraints on their learning together.

A Practical Guide to Group Development—Action-Ideas for Change

The necessary ingredients for the development of a positive climate for learning involve the skills and abilities of members to resolve interpersonal problems and personal concerns at different stages of group development. Because understanding the member's skills and abilities is so crucial for systematically planning group activities, we have included a section on diagnosis of classroom climate. This is followed by a description of the four developmental stages of learning groups, including the exercises and procedures that can be used to highlight the issues of group development at each stage.

An exercise (or simulation) is a structured game-like activity. It is designed to produce group processes that participants can easily understand because they experience these processes firsthand through the game. Each exercise is designed to highlight a certain aspect of group process, thereby making lessons about group life easily comprehensible. No exercise is intended to match the complexity of the group's full reality, but rather to enable members to learn the advantages of specific forms of group behavior. In brief, each exercise has a specific content and product.

A procedure, on the other hand, refers to group activity that does not, in itself, entail learning a specific content. Rather, it enables a group to accomplish its work more effectively. A procedure can be used for a variety of tasks or purposes. For example, the use of a certain form of decision making such as majority vote, or the use of a problem solving sequence are typical procedures. Whereas exercises are usually carried out only once or twice by a learning group, procedures can and should be used regularly throughout the life of the group. Although our ideas are presented in a sequential format, we wish to emphasize again that group development is also cyclical. Thus, exercises that are used at the beginning of a group's existence to resolve membership concerns, for instance, may be appropriate at a later time because questions about belonging inevitably will come up over and over again during the life of a group.

Our primary criteria for including the following sample of useful activities are three. First, the techniques primarily emphasize ongoing group processes and development, in contrast to abstract or theoretical items about social behavior that are in established curricula. Second, the techniques may be used by anyone—administrator, teacher, or student—with a small amount of previous experience in working with classroom groups, and a modicum of time and energy. Finally, the techniques do not require special materials that cannot be found in most schools. All of our suggestions are presented in a general manner so that they can be altered and tailored to fit classes of all ages.

Diagnosis of Classroom Climate

The way students feel about their peers, about their studies, and about their teachers plays an important part in the emotional underworld of classroom life. In addition, students' behavioral skills and capabilities are critical in determining the sorts of learning situations that should be provided for groups. Students who have never had experience in sharing responsibility for their own learning will be at different skill levels than students with experience in setting classroom and individual learning goals. We have developed two diagnostic questionnaires which will help to determine these various skill levels. Instruments 3.1 and 3.2 may be used to measure both the learning atmosphere and the behavioral competence of students.

How to Administer the Instruments:

For older students, depending on reading ability, the forms can be self-administered. For students in the lower elementary grades who do not have sufficient reading skills, an adaptation of this form is required. Teachers must use fewer and simpler words in administering diagnostic tools. One technique is for the teacher to read selected items from the instrument (we recommend only six to eight items) using an answer sheet with smiling and frowning faces (Figure 3.1). The teacher asks students to put an X under the face which best shows the answer to the question.

An alternative answer sheet to the smiling and frowning faces has Snoopy, the dog, drawn in various poses of happiness and unhappiness. On the far left, Snoopy is drawn jumping for joy; next he is smiling, but not jumping quite so gleefully; in the middle he is lying on the top of his doghouse on his back sleeping (to show indifference); just to the right he is sitting with his head bowed over in depression; and on the far right, he is growling angrily with his mouth wide open.

How to Use the Data:

Survey feedback, a technique of compiling data anonymously and presenting it to the group, can be a powerful means of relaying information about the current situation and using the data to begin group problem solving. In Instruments 3.1 and 3.2, the discrepancies between the students' views of "How the Students in This Class Think" and "How I Think about My Class" may also be interesting information. For instance, if a large majority of students check on Instrument 3.1 that the class thinks only

FIGURE 3.1   Instrument Answer Sheet for Students without Sufficient Reading Skills

a few believe "it is good to help others with their schoolwork, except on tests," yet almost everyone checks on Instrument 3.2 he or she "agrees almost always" that "it is good to help others with their schoolwork, except on tests," there is important discrepant information that could be useful for class discussion.

INSTRUMENT 3.1
How the Students in This Class Think

How do you think your classmates feel about the following things? Under "How Many People Think This Way?", put a check in one of the boxes for each item, 1–12. There are no right or wrong answers.

How Many People Think This Way?

	Almost All	Many	About Half	Some	Only a Few
1. It is good to help others with their schoolwork, except on tests.					
2. Only a few students cooperate with the teacher.					
3. The girls only do things for a very few others.					
4. The boys only do things for a very few others.					
5. It is good to get along with others in this class.					
6. It is good to be a high achiever.					

INSTRUMENT 3.1 (Continued)
How the Students in This Class Think

How do you think your classmates feel about the following things? Under "How Many People Think this Way?", put a check in one of the boxes for each item, 1–12. There are no right or wrong answers.

How Many People Think This Way?

	Almost All	Many	About Half	Some	Only a Few
7. Working together with your classmates is a good thing to do.					
8. It is good to do what the teacher wants you to do.					
9. There are some cliques within this school.					
10. Quite a few students often go against the teacher.					
11. It is good to be able to work on your own in this class.					
12. Only a few students can get others to do things.					

Diagnostic Observations

The observation forms in Instruments 3.3 and 3.4, or parts of them, can be used as part of an ongoing system of diagnosis for work-related activities in the classroom. (Form 1 is designed for the older student, Form 2, for the younger student with less advanced verbal skills.) For instance, student observers could be trained to fill out the form for perhaps just one lesson a day, every other day or weekly. After the study is complete, observers would report their findings to the entire class. The form could be used either when the students work together as a total classroom group or when they work in small task groups. If used regularly and in the context of academic activities, such observations and discussions about the group processes of the class can be easily integrated into the daily life and work of the class and not become isolated

INSTRUMENT 3.2 (Continued)
How I Think about My Class

Put a check in the box that tells what you think about each of the statements below. There are no right or wrong answers.

What Do You Think?

	I agree almost always.	I agree more than disagree.	I agree as often as I disagree.	I disagree more than I agree.	I disagree almost always.
1. It is good to help others with their schoolwork, except on tests.					
2. Only a few students cooperate with the teacher.					
3. The girls only do things for a very few others.					
4. The boys only do things for a very few others.					
5. It is good to get along with others in this class.					
6. It is good to be a high achiever.					
7. Working together with your classmates is a good thing to do.					
8. It is good to do what the teacher wants you to do.					
9. There are some cliques within this school.					

INSTRUMENT 3.2
How I Think about My Class

Put a check in the box that tells what you think about each of the statements below. There are no right or wrong answers.

What Do You Think?

	I agree almost always.	I agree more than disagree.	I agree as often as I disagree.	I disagree more than I agree.	I disagree almost always.
10. Quite a few students often go against the teacher.					
11. It is good to be able to work on your own in this class.					
12. Only a few students can get others to do things.					

---

into a special curriculum. By so doing, students will learn that interpersonal interactions occur during math, reading, and recess, and not only at "group process" time.

One elementary teacher assigned two student observers for every day of the week. The pairs observed one specific activity each, but the activities observed changed daily (i.e., a total class math lesson, work groups on a class play, an art class, etc.). Each day after the observation took place, the class spent about ten minutes listening to the observer's report, analyzing what happened, and suggesting improvements in the class's operations. Used in this way, all students can become active observers of their own classroom group behavior.

Stage I: Action Ideas for Facilitating Psychological Membership

During the first few days of a class, the students, in seeking a secure niche within the group, are reticent and, to some extent, fearful of presenting a weak image of themselves. Students often try to be on their best behavior, presenting ideal images to one another and working earnestly on what the teacher requires. It is at this point, by virtue of his or her legitimate position of authority, that the teacher takes on extraordinary power in setting the tenor of the group's future.

INSTRUMENT 3.3
Observing Work in Our Class: Form 1

Direction to Observers: Write down a specific example that you saw of the following behaviors.

1. Showing they are listening   _____

_____

2. Describing a feeling   _____

_____

3. Giving ideas   _____

_____

4. Suggesting how to do something   _____

_____

5. Asking someone for his or her ideas   _____
    or feelings
_____

6. Building on someone else's ideas or   _____
    feelings
_____

Questions for Observers:

1. Did everyone talk?

2. Which students participated the most?

3. Did everyone understand what he or she was supposed to do?

4. How would you rate the group's work?

    A. Very good

    B. Good

    C. O.K.

    D. Not so good

    E. Poor

5. Give a *reason* for your rating.

Instrument 3.4

Observing Work in Our Class: Form 2

For younger students the following simple observation form could be used. Initials of the students could be placed in the "What I Saw" area, and the observation should last only ten to fifteen minutes so students can remember the evidence.

What I Saw!

1. Who listened?

2. Who talked?

3. Who gave an idea?

4. I think this group was:

5. Why I think the group was like that.

_____

_____

_____

During the period of group growth, the teacher is already influencing the students either to move toward formal, routine, and impersonal relationships or toward more intimate, challenging, and supportive relationships. Not until later in the group's development have the students gathered sufficient information and built up sufficient emotion to decide whether the teacher's behaviors are worth following, ignoring, or rejecting. What is crucial at this early stage, because of the teacher's significant influence, is that he or she take the initiative to help the members of the learning group move toward establishing feelings of psychological membership.

During this time, questions such as, "Will they accept me? Will they like me? Who are they?" and "Can I get close to them?" are asked implicitly and preconsciously by all students. Many classrooms, unfortunately, do not develop past this early phase because needs for inclusion and membership are never met. Questions such as the ones listed above remain unanswered throughout the life of such groups. Indeed, there are some classrooms in which students have spent a whole term working next to one another without learning the names of many of their peers.

Ideally, after a few weeks or less in class, every student will strongly agree with the following statements about the class: "Everyone has a good chance to get to know everyone else in this class. Many members of the class have become friends. All students know one another quite well; and, finally, each student knows all the other students in the class by their first names."

We cannot be exact about the length of time it takes for students to achieve feelings of inclusion and membership in most classrooms. The intensity of the human striving for inclusion and its eventual resolution will depend on several factors, among them: the amount of time the students spend together; the previous relationships among them; the ages of the students; and students' previous experiences in working out some of the developmental issues that every group faces. However, it is apparent that every classroom group will first have to resolve the basic issues of belongingness and membership in some way, even though the ways in which these issues get resolved will take on very diverse forms and patterns.

The following action ideas provide what Schutz refers to as the "Goblets" through which teacher and students can constructively size up one another and, perhaps, cautiously reveal parts of themselves. These exercises and procedures emphasize the sorts of interaction between teacher and students that we believe will help a class move to a more mature stage of development. The activities described herein should be tried during the first few weeks of a new class, or during the time when new students first meet one another, to facilitate more rapid inclusion, involvement, and rapport among the students.

1. Who Are They? Students are asked to mill at random around the room, or to form two circles, one inside the other, and to walk in reverse directions so that they pass one another. The teacher gives the following series of directions at two-minute intervals:

"Greet others without words or elaborate physical gestures. Say a brief word of greeting to all the people you see. Find another student with whom you believe you may have something in common and talk for a few minutes about what you might have in common. Find a person whom you do not know very well and find out a few things about that person. Find someone about whom you are curious and ask him or her questions about himself or herself." Finally, "Find someone with whom you would like to work and talk about why you've chosen that person."

A more structured procedure for this activity is for every student to wear a number and for the teacher to give instructions for different pairs of numbers. For example, the teacher might say number 1 find number 11, number 2 find number 12, etc. until the students are paired. Next, the teacher would give an instruction, such as: Ask each other about your favorite hobbies or tell each other about something special you did last summer. The objective is to get students to know one another better and to be able to answer the query: "Who are my peers in this class?" or "Who are they?"

2. What Makes Us Comfortable in Groups? Students are asked to mill around the center of the room. Without verbal communication among them, they are asked to divide up into groups of four people each. The rule of four-to-a-group is very useful unless the number in the group does not allow for this kind of division. As a subgroup becomes too large, members are asked without words to leave it to form another one. The teacher should not talk or suggest where students are to move, but simply remind them of the rule of four-to-a-group. After the groups have been formed, the students are asked to discuss how this entire process felt. They are asked to share how they felt when they had to leave one group and join another, and, in general, their reactions to forming and reforming groups. The teacher might say, "Was it easier to move toward some groups and not others? What were the nonverbal

messages of acceptance or rejection that were given? What were they like?"

After the subgroups have had an opportunity to discuss each person's experience, the class should then discuss as an entire group what the exercise means for all of them insofar as the class will be working together for long time. The students should be encouraged to construct a list of behaviors that communicate acceptance of others and another list of behaviors that communicate rejection. The group might also construct a list of feelings they have when they are not accepted or when they do not feel part of a learning group. Finally, the students can discuss activities that they might carry out to help new student members feel more at ease and to become an integral part of the group.

3. Human Resource Hunt Each student is given a list of human experiences, attributes, and hobbies and is supposed to match that list with the others in the group. For example, the list might include the following: (a) plays a musical instrument, (b) has helped cook a meal at home, (c) understands some words in a foreign language, (d) likes to watch nature programs on television, (e) traveled outside the state last summer, (f) likes to do math, (g) has a pet at home, or (h) has a birthday during the summer.

The students mill around the group trying to match names with attributes by interviewing one another. The teacher then goes down the list with the entire class orally, perhaps printing on large pieces of butcher paper the students' names under each attribute. The main point of the activity is to facilitate the formation of friendships and to raise the students' awareness about the many resources in the group.

4. The Blind Walk   Each student is paired with another student. One member of the pair is blindfolded and is silently guided by the other through, over, or around things. After five minutes the roles are reversed, but during this second phase, talking is allowed. When the walk is completed, students share their mutual reactions about the two ways of communicating in trying to build trust. The teacher leads the class in a discussion, asking for specific examples of people's behavior that have led to trust.

5. Encouraging Acceptance of New Members   The goal of this activity is to increase interaction among students in order to facilitate the formation of friendships for many students. The teacher tells the class that each student will be expected to prepare a biography of another student. Then, the whole class works together on preparing an interview format to collect personal data from everyone. Next, each student is paired off with another student. Interviews are carried out, and the biographies are prepared. Then a booklet of class biographies is put together. (In one primary class they used the booklet for one hour during their reading period.) The practice helps facilitate a rapid acquaintance process, especially for students new to the class and especially for classrooms with high student turnover.

After the biographies have been written, the teacher might ask the students to write down the names of those students they'd like to work with in the future in small learning groups. Encourage each student to jot down as many names as he or she wishes. The sheer quantity of choices will be a positive experience.

6. Billy Goat   This playful activity is useful for getting everyone involved on an equal basis. A group of about 6 to 8 stands in a close circle; the teacher steps into the center of the circle and says, "When I point to someone and say, "Billy Goat," that student must place his or her hand beneath the chin to resemble a goat's beard and bleat *baa*. The students to the "goat's" immediate left and right must, at the same time, form a goat's horns by each holding an index finger to the head of the "goat." The last student of the three to do this must then step to the center of the circle and choose the next Billy Goat. After a few rounds, the teacher may introduce variations, such as Elephant (middle student makes a trunk by holding two fists to his nose while neighbors form floppy ears), or Kangaroo (middle person makes a pouch by cupping hands while neighbors hop up and down). There are endless variations, and the students should be encouraged to create a few.

7. The Tire Challenge   This physical activity works best with an old truck tire and about 12 to 15 students. The objective is to get all students on the tire at the same time for three seconds without touching the ground. The students are encouraged to talk about how to do it and to make certain that everyone is included. Most groups figure out a way to accomplish the task and feel a sense of pulling together as a result.

8. The Tinkertoy Procedure   The students are divided into groups of about five, and each group is instructed to use Tinkertoys to produce a symbolic representation of what it hopes the class will be like within a few weeks. When all groups have completed their constructions, all students gather round one of them. For five or ten minutes, those who did not build that particular model comment on the sort of class the symbolic structure suggests to them, while those who actually built it reply and explain. The same procedure is repeated with all other constructions. Eventually the class as a whole summarizes its group agreements about what it would like to be in a few weeks.

Stage II: Action Ideas for Establishing Shared Influence

After the teacher and students become well acquainted, build some security, and begin to feel that they belong with one another, two sorts of "power struggles" typically become prominent. One entails testing the limits of the teacher's power and, typically, has to do with the psychodynamics of dependency and counterdependency. The other concerns the pecking order of the student peer group and involves the psychodynamics of domination and autonomy.

The traditional teacher attempts to maintain all authority over the students and, consequently, most classroom groups remain at an unresolved stage of control and influence throughout most of the school year. Underneath the surface of a controlled classroom, interpersonal conflicts and tensions exist between the teacher and students, and also within the student peer group. Teachers have been warned, "Don't smile before Christmas." This means that if they can maintain their formal control of the students during the first four months of school, they have a good chance of not having to face many disruptions or attempts to gain control.

Those teachers who manage to "keep the lid on" not only waste a great deal of energy in policing students' interactions but also tend to miss the excitement—as well as the pain—of getting genuinely close to their students. It is very natural that conflict will arise over how things will operate and who will make those decisions. After all, such conflicts arise in all of the human sectors of life. They occur between child and parent, between friends, between spouses, between groups within a community, and between nation-states.

Attempts to control the behavior of others can be seen clearly at certain phases of child development. There are, for example, the invincible and incorrigible two and three-year-olds who struggle with their parents as they try out ways of becoming autonomous and independent. "I do it myself," they say, as they persistently but incapably try to button a shirt; or "You go away," as they touch a forbidden object. Children hear the word NO over and over again as they attempt to establish their independent position in the world. Of course, a child's attempts to gain autonomy and influence are mixed simultaneously with wishes for love, acceptance, and security. Part of the issue of control for youngsters concerns the testing of limits of love and acceptance. Similar developmental phenomena can be seen in classroom groups. Just as young children learn about autonomy and power through the way parents handle their authority, so will students in the classroom learn about influence relationships from the leadership behaviors of the teacher. The teacher who has successfully maintained all power by "not smiling before Christmas" most likely will produce a well-ordered, formal (possibly even a pleasant) classroom in which no student will make any obvious attempt to gain power. Such classrooms also tend to have students who are alienated from the school and do not consider themselves an integral part of the classroom life; they are classrooms in which there will be few public influence struggles, save for two or three isolated bursts of anger.

We do not intend to imply that teachers who have encouraged closeness, belonging, and shared leadership in the beginning phase of the learning group's life will have an easy time during this second stage. After all, since the norms built during the first stage supported public discussions of conflict, movement toward collaborative decision making and shared influence will also carry considerable tension and stress. But teachers who are genuinely committed to a classroom environment in which learning is viewed as part of the process of living, and not limited to reciting the multiplication tables by rote, will endure the stress and strain in exchange for the joy of educating. Indeed, it gets easier and easier, although not less joyful, once the teacher has experienced several groups of students who have become a healthy and productive learning group.

Ideally, after a month or so in class, every student will strongly agree with the following statements about the class: "Students can cooperate effectively with all others in the class, class decisions tend to be made by all the students, decisions affecting the class tend to be made democratically, and each member of the class has as much influence as any other member."

Classroom groups that have achieved a sense of belonging for all members are, typically, active and rather noisy places. Most members feel comfortable and secure in sharing their own points of view. Consequently, discussions often become disorderly when people are so intent on giving their own ideas that they forget to listen to

others. For this reason, the procedures described here emphasize the right to talk as well as the right to be heard.

1.   Rotating   Leadership   Committees During the first week of class, each student reaches into a large bowl to pull out a small piece of paper on which is printed a number from one to the number of students in the class. The teacher announces that students numbered 1–4 will be the class leadership committee for the first week, students numbered 5–8 will be leaders for the second week, etc. until everyone in the class has had a chance to serve. The role of the leadership committee is to help the teacher run an efficient and an effective class. Members help pass out papers, get supplies for activities, help change the desk arrangements, and the like. More importantly, the leadership committee meets once, typically on Thursday at lunch, with the teacher to discuss things that are going well in the class, and things which are not going so well. On Friday, the teacher and the leadership committee lead the class in a discussion about how to improve itself.

2.   The Chance to Listen   Although discussion in a class can allow everyone to have his or her say, often there is too little regard for whether what was said was understood or not. One procedure that can facilitate clearer communication and even more participation is to require the student wishing to speak to paraphrase what the previous speaker has said. The same rule should apply, of course, to the teacher. Moreover, before a proposal for action is decided upon, several students should paraphrase the terms of the proposal so that everyone is clear about what is being decided. The teacher or a student might be charged with insuring that each participant, along with the right to be heard, is granted the right to listen and to be clear about communication within the group. This procedure might be tried first as part of an exercise for practicing communication skills, later attempted as a procedure within the leadership committee, and finally employed during discussions among the entire class.

3. Tokens for Talking This procedure, as well as the one which follows, can be employed to help all students participate in discussions and decision making. For instance, when only a few students talk during discussion, it might be suggested that time tokens be used to ensure wider participation. Each student is allotted the same number of tokens. At the point of making a verbal contribution, the students must give up one of their tokens to a spot in the middle of the group. They can speak only as long as their tokens last.

4. High-Talker Tap-Out Another method for preventing domination by only a few students is the "high-talker tap-out." A coordinator (either the teacher or a student) monitors the group to see if any student seems to be dominating the interaction. Names of talkers may be listed on the board. If one or two are dominating, then the coordinator hands instructions to them asking that they refrain from further commenting. However, the instructions might permit comment on the group processes. In this way, the remainder of the participation can be balanced out more evenly.

5. Buzz Groups Another procedure that can be used to spread participation in a large class is the "buzz group." The class meeting is temporarily interrupted while subgroups of four or so students form to discuss an issue for a short time. This can be done to best advantage when important decisions have to be made and some students hesitate to express their contrary views in front of the entire class. When feelings are difficult to bring out into the open, the buzz groups might have reporters summarize the ideas and feelings of their group without indicating which students expressed them. Summaries also make it difficult for any one group of students to dominate the flow of interaction.

6. Numbered Students Another procedure for buzz groups is to have each student per group count off from one to four so that each individual has a number. Then all members of a group are responsible for listening and being able to summarize the group's ideas because the teacher will randomly select a number from each group for reporting out to the entire class.

7. Helping Trios The class is divided into groups of three. Each of the trios has three roles: *student, helper,* and *observer.* The role of the student is to ask for help with some academic assignment. The role of the helper is to coach the student to figure out the academic problem by himself or herself. The role of the observer is to reflect on what was helpful and what was not so helpful in the helping relationship. During a single period, the roles within a trio rotate so that each student performs all three.

8. Fishbowl Since the problems of participation in a large class are much more complex than those in a small one, time tokens and tap-outs might not be very useful and practical. One procedure that uses some of the advantages of the small group discussion, within the setting of the large meeting, is the "fishbowl" or "theater-in-the-round." In a fishbowl arrangement, a small group is formed within a circle made by a larger group. Chairs are arranged in the middle of the room, while the rest of the class sits around in a larger circle. The small group (which could be the steering committee, for instance) discusses whatever is on the agenda, while the other students observe. Empty chairs can be provided in the fishbowl so that any observing student can come in and join the discussion with the understanding that his or her seating will be temporary, thus assuring wider participation.

Stage III: Action Ideas for Pursuing Academic Goals

Classroom groups qua groups are not ready to work effectively and productively on academic learning until they have settled, to some degree, issues related to group membership and interpersonal influence. This does not mean that classes have merely to "sit and rap" for their first few months of existence. Some academic work, of course, does get done during the earliest phase of the group's development, but not with the same social support that it received during this third stage of the group's life.

A fourth-grade teacher put the case very nicely when she described her multi-staged design for the year. The first stage generally lasted from the beginning of school until November. Students carried out the usual tasks of skill development and reading, but her primary goals involved helping the students to feel comfortable with one another, to work independently, to make collaborative decisions, and to learn how to behave cooperatively. She visualized December through May as the period of highest academic productivity. During these

months students set their own goals and developed many projects that emphasized various academic skills, and more academic work was accomplished during this time period than any other time during the school year. May and June were primarily given over to evaluating the students' work, setting goals for the students' next academic year, and getting the students ready to work effectively with their fifth-grade teachers.

One frequent complaint expressed by teachers is the lament that they waste too much time policing interactions within the class. Complaints about unruly and undisciplined students indicate that the first two stages of group development have not been resolved to a sufficient extent to allow academic work and personal growth to become predominant themes. In our experience, students who have achieved feelings of membership, along with the skills of shared influence and collaborative decision making in their classes, do not have the large number of discipline problems that plague traditional classroom groups. A book by Long and Frye (1977) entitled *Making It Till Friday* recommends very much the same sort of multi-stage strategy for establishing effects of classroom management and student discipline.

The third phase of group development is a high production period. It is during this time that the norms and procedures established during the first two phases come to fruition in the form of attainment of academic and personal goals. This stage is most clearly visible in a class coming together for a short period of time to fulfill a specific function, such as a special learning project. By the third stage the students know one another well and have an understanding of one another's resources. They have settled some of the leadership questions and are ready to set clear goals, divide tasks, and agree on deadlines for completing their tasks.

During this phase of classroom life, antagonistic pulls between the production goals of the group and the students' feelings about themselves as learners will become obvious and persist. As indicated earlier in this chapter, research by Bales and Parsons suggests that groups tend to swing back and forth between a focus on the task and a focus on the social-emotional issues. Some meetings are almost totally given over to individuals' feelings, while others are directed toward production and performance. Discussions having to do with students' preferences and feelings should take up a good deal of time in classes. The time taken will not be wasted in terms of academic learning. Indeed, it is imperative that social-emotional issues are handled if classes are to work productively. Classes that ignore the basic pulls and tugs of students' personal goals in conflict with academic goals will not be successful in their production efforts and will be missing the personal growth aspect of education.

The third phase is by no means all "sweetness and light," with students diligently and efficiently working on academic goals. Group development is cyclical as well as successive. Predominant during this phase is a constant oscillation between fulfilling the formal academic demands as defined by the school and the emotional needs of the students. Some hours or days, even at the height of productivity, will be filled with conflicts about students not participating properly or doing their jobs completely. This will also be the time when the conflict between the individual student and the class as a whole can occur with inten-

sity. Class members may come to a collective decision, but there will often be a minority of students who do not agree with that decision, causing conflicts which should, of course, be publicly discussed. And, it must be borne in mind that small ad hoc groups which are part of the more stable classroom groups will themselves represent in microcosm the developmental sequence of the larger group.

Ideally, after a few months or so in class, every student will strongly agree with the following statements about the class: "The students enjoy their academic work. The class has students with many different interests, but still they work together well. After the class is over, the students have a sense of satisfaction, and there is enough room in this class for both individual and group work."

For students who have developed some trust and skill in communication and group decision making, the key problems of the first two phases can be resolved quickly and easily. Unfortunately, too many teachers do not provide opportunities for their students to learn about group development. Consequently, those teachers who do have an interest in group processes will have to spend considerable time developing in their students the skills and competencies that are necessary for arriving at effective interaction patterns within the classroom.

The third phase of group development focuses upon the pursuit of academic goals as well as the student's personal growth. The following procedures can be used by students and teacher to reach both personal and academic goals.

1.   Tutoring Pairs Pairs of students might work together on a variety of academic activities, e.g., checking homework, correcting math assignments, reviewing foreign language terms, preparing for tests, and critiquing each others' papers. With regard to the last, the teacher sets up guidelines on how to criticize a written product. The students in a pair exchange papers, each one silently reading the other's paper. Next, one student tells another about the ideas he or she intended to communicate in the paper. The listener strives to figure out if there is a clear parallelism between what his or her mate intended to write and what really comes across in the paper. After a helpful exchange, members of each pair change roles so that everyone in the class receives help on his or her paper.

2. *Working Trios*   Another grouping for pursuing academic goals is the working trio in which each student takes one academic role at a time. The roles in the trio are information giver, summarizer, and recorder. The information giver is responsible for researching the topic prior to the trio's meeting. At the meeting the information giver reports on his or her research. The summarizer is responsible for paraphrasing and summarizing the key points made by the information giver. The recorder writes down what the three participants agree to be the key points in the research. Typically, such trios stay together for several weeks so that each person gets ample opportunity to take all three roles in relation to some particular academic subject matter.

3. *Cooperating Fours*   A group of four students is a good number for working cooperatively on a study project. After the group is clear about what its project is to focus on, each member takes one-fourth of the academic content and is responsible for learning it well enough to teach it to the other three. Once the group members have taught and mastered all four parts, they decide on how they will teach what they've learned to the rest of the class, or perhaps to another small group of four, or perhaps to another class of younger students. Group interaction variables related to learning are giving and receiving explanations, receiving responses to questions, and verbalizing ideas aloud, while also listening to others' ideas.

4. *A Problem-Solving Procedure*   This generic procedure can help individuals, pairs, trios, fours, or larger classroom groups work out new avenues for reaching their academic goals.

In this procedure, a problem is defined as a discrepancy between a goal stated and present reality—between what ought to be and what is. The procedure emphasizes making clear statements about goals, diagnosing the situation as it is now, and establishing plans and commitments for future action. The formal sequence involves several rather detailed steps: (1) specifying the problem; (2) analyzing the problem; (3) generating multiple solutions; (4) designing plans for action; (5) forecasting consequences of intended actions; (6) taking action; and (7) evaluating the actions.

Step 1. State where you are (the situation) and where you would like to be (the target), precisely and specifically. Discuss with others their views of the two positions and then confirm their perceptions by restating.

Step 2. Think of all the forces that are keeping the group from moving closer to its target, and think of all the forces that are helping the group to move toward its target. Ask all group members to think about those things which are helping and those which are hindering. List the forces in order of importance.

Step 3. Think of the ways in which the forces holding the group from its target might be reduced. It is usually more efficient to reduce hindering forces than to intensify helping forces. This is one proper stage in problem solving into which one should bring an expert who knows a lot about the substance of the problem.

Step 4. Make a concrete and specific plan of action. Be sure to get the help of the people who will implement the plan.

Step 5. Anticipate the barriers to carrying out the plan effectively. Simulate part of the plan and get feedback from others. Revise the plan if necessary.

Step 6. Put the plan into action. Make the first move and then alter the plan according to how it works.

Step 7. Evaluate the effects of the group's working together in terms of both the problem-solving effort and its interpersonal processes. Assess the changes that have occurred in the problems. If necessary, return to Step 1 and start all over again.

Teachers can use this problem-solving procedure to help the classroom group come to grips with deficiencies in its operation. Healthy classes, like healthy students, eventually reach a condition of adaptive maturity in which problem solving is expected to be a regular and continuous procedure.

Stage IV: Action Ideas for Self-Renewal

For the healthy student and classroom group, reaching maturity is not an end but rather a state of readiness for continuous growth and for the broadening of competence, skill, and interest. Adaptive maturity involves the confrontation of the options in one's life, the ability to respond with choices, and the courage to accept the consequences of one's decisions. John Gardner (1963) applied the term "self-renewal" to this condition in a group, organization, or society. Self-renewing groups can continue to set up new purposes and procedures out of their own internal resources and wherewithal, and they have the competence to adopt new processes when the old ones are no longer functional. They are called "mature" because the members accept the responsibility for their group-life and are continuously striving to improve it.

Although this description may sound appealing, self-renewing learning groups are not easy to maintain. They contain a continuous array of human problems, such as intermittent feelings of exclusion and alienation, power struggles and resentments, and frustrated goals achievement. While they afford much satisfaction and comfort to the members, they do not allow for complacency. While they support individual growth and insight, they are also confrontative and challenging. An adaptive classroom group will be continually stimulating and challenging to its members.

A constructive step for the teacher to take is to lead the class in evaluations of how the class is going, particularly with regard to feelings of membership and involvement, feelings of power and influence, and feelings of competence and achievement with academic matters. One method is to have a class discussion about the high points and the low points of the last few days. Students might commence such discussions in pairs or trios, followed by a recorder from each group reporting out to the entire class. Another method is to ask each student to write his or her evaluation of the class, and then for the teacher to summarize the data and report it back to the class for a problem-solving discussion. Still another method is to have the "rotating leadership committee" take responsibility for leading the class in an evaluation of itself.

The questionnaire, entitled "Clues About Classroom Life," can be used to assess the classroom situation on a regular basis. If it were used early in September, again in December, and again in April, it could provide comparative developmental data as well as clues for what problems need to be solved immediately. Self-renewing groups, similar to growing individuals, continually struggle toward new forms of group structure and cooperation.

Implications for Teachers

In the main, we have been arguing that teachers should be sensitive to the reality of a classroom group's developmental maturity. It is not easy to diagnose a classroom group's phase of development, nor is it readily apparent as to what interventions the teacher should make to facilitate a class's development. Teachers too often get caught in the ebb and flow of daily events to be accurate observers, and therefore need to assess consciously and systematically where they are, how they got here, and where they need to go next. The questions in table 3.1 provide some benchmarks to assist teachers in using the key concepts of this chapter. Answers to these questions serve as indicators of group effectiveness and should help teachers to cope more effectively with the complexities of group development in the classroom.

A Practical Guide to Improve Classroom Climate

The core content of this book (chapters 4 through 9) lays out what empirical research indicates are the fundamental properties of the developing classroom group. The six variables we focus upon are expectations, leadership, attraction-cohesiveness, norms, communication, and conflict. As we have already noted, each of these complex variables constitutes an ingredient of classroom climate and can be used to assess the health of any classroom group. Moreover, each variable constitutes a category for planned interventions that a teacher can use to improve the classroom climate. As such, chapters 4 through 9 serve as "A Practical Guide to Improve Classroom Climate."

But there are two additional guides to classroom improvement about which teachers should be knowledgeable. Improving Classroom Social Climate (1979, for the upper primary grades or middle school) and Classroom Learning to Attain Social Skills (for lower elementary grades) were developed by teachers in the Orcutt Union School District in California (P.O. Box 2310, Orcutt, CA 93455). These two packages provide a series of classroom activities based on the concepts of this book. Through a federally funded Title IV-C activity, Vacha, McDonald, Coburn, and Black (1979) created curriculum materials to be disseminated throughout California. Based on the contents of *Group Processes in the Classroom,* the teaching strategies were taught to teachers in districts throughout California, Oregon, and Washington. Although by 1987 funds were no longer available for dissemination and

INSTRUMENT 3.5

Clues about Classroom Life

So that we may get some ideas about how to make life more interesting and important for everybody in this class, each of us needs to contribute ideas about what should be improved. What things happen that shouldn't happen? What ought to happen that does not? Imagine you are a detective looking for clues to a "good day" and a "bad day" in this class. Jot down what you might look for or might see to answer these questions.

What are some clues to a good day in this class? What things happen that are signs of a good day?

1. _____

2. _____

3. _____

4. _____

What are some clues to a bad day in this class? What things happen that are clues that this class is not going the way it should, or the way that you would like it to?

1. _____

2. _____

3. _____

4. _____

What are some things that should happen a lot more than they do to make this class a better place for learning?

1. _____

2. _____

3. _____

4. _____

Table 3.1 Important Questions about Group Development and Group Effectiveness

Stage 1: Facilitating Psychological Membership	Stage 2: Establishing Shared Influence	Stage 3: Pursuing Academic Goals	Stage 4: Recognizing Conditions of Self-Renewal
Are there procedures to get to know everyone? Is it all right for students to express their fears, concerns, and ideas?			
Do students and the teacher listen to one another?	Can the students take constructive leadership?		
Do students interact with a variety of classmates?	Can leadership be shared and rotated?	Are individual differences respected? Are students motivated to study?	
Is there sensitivity to and appreciation of the different needs and styles of others?	Are new and different ideas listened to and evaluated?	Can the group set some long-range goals?	
	Are conflicts openly recognized and discussed?	Do students support one another in learning?	
		Is there a balance between group and individual accountablity?	Can the group evaluate its own effectiveness?
	Are the skills of all members being used?	Can problems be specified and resolved?	Can the group solve its own problems?
		Can conflict be used creatively?	Can individuals evaluate themselves and set goals for personal improvement?

training, many school districts still are using the materials which focus on the development of the classroom as a group, rather than a focus on individuals. The materials are designed to be implemented by either a counselor serving several classrooms or by teachers working within their own classes.

Assumptions undergirding these materials include the ideas that learning occurs most effectively with active involvement, offering variety and alternatives in learning activities elicits more teacher participation, providing sequential, age-graded experiences facilitates student learning, and presenting detailed lesson plans is crucial for successful implementation.

Improving Classroom Social Climate consists of:

1. Core lessons—a year-long program of sequential, weekly, one-hour lessons

2. Supplementary lessons—to be used when diagnoses indicate the class has particularly severe problems

3. Sound filmstrips—a classroom introduction to each of the six variables

4. Diagnostic techniques—to assess strengths, weaknesses, and changes in the six variables

5. Classroom management techniques—necessary to support and reinforce the lessons

6. Leadership and role-playing cards—materials to help students learn to perform leadership roles

7. Teacher's handbook—a guide containing an introduction to the six variables, core and supplementary lessons, classroom-management techniques, and diagnostic procedures.

We have used these supplementary materials successfully working with teacher-trainees at the college level and in staff development programs with teachers. They provide a practical, hands-on, useful set of teacher-developed materials that bring to life many of the theories discussed in this book. Lessons are developed which may be used independently or in conjunction with other subjects. They can be used by consultants working with teachers, used independently by a group of teachers engaged in their own staff development, or by college professors to supplement the regular teacher training curriculum.

Expectations

4

At the heart of classroom group processes are the expectations that each participant—teacher and student—holds for the ebb and flow of interaction with others. An interpersonal expectation is a prediction of how another person will behave in a particular social setting. The impetus for many behaviors comes not only from the motivation and intent of the acting individual, but also from that person's expectations about how others in the immediate social environment will react in return. Interpersonal expectations may grow out of the individual's own personality structure, out of his or her generalized images of what the other person is like, or out of specific reactions perceived to be coming from the other. All students and teachers develop expectations of themselves as well as the primary people with whom they interact over a sustained period.

To illustrate, Suzie, a fifth-grader, may see another student, Judy, struggling with a problem that she, Suzie, has already solved. Suzie is pleased with her success and wishes to be helpful to Judy. Her act of helping Judy attests to her own firm feelings of self-regard. Suzie might make a rather neutral comment to Judy such as, "I see you're having trouble with this problem; maybe I can help you." Judy's response depends in great measure on the expectations she holds for Suzie. If Judy sees Suzie as a "show-off" who enjoys building herself up at the expense of others, Judy will most likely refuse the offer of help. However, if Judy views Suzie as supportive and friendly, she most likely will accept the offer.

Objectives of this Chapter

In this chapter we review the psychological theory and research that shows that each of us strives for a sense of competence, achievement, and self-esteem. These motives are common to each human being, although they may be realized in different ways. We also show how individuals develop certain working predictions, or expectations, in order to cope effectively and competently with a complex, interpersonal world. Such expectations are normal and are created in part from past associations, from information, and from social stereotypes. We show that a special sort of expectation, called *attribution,* assigns a cause to behavior, either that of another or our own. Furthermore, those expectations and attributions are communicated to others, thereby influencing their behavior. This is called the "circular interpersonal model of interaction." We strive to demonstrate how teachers themselves unwittingly create and perpetuate some student behaviors and we review the educational research on the self-fulfilling prophecy, a concept popularly known as the "Pygmalion effect." Finally, we offer concrete ideas on how to apply the theoretical ideas presented in this chapter.

The Striving for Competence

In an insightful essay, White (1959) developed a theory of motivation that we find especially useful and sensible in relation to group processes and the achievement motive. White referred to a master motive for humans as the "motive for competency," arguing that people exert behavioral energy in large amounts when they feel effective in accommodating to the social environment, i.e., when they are adapting successfully to reality. Moreover, he viewed human behavior as fundamentally social-psychological, insofar as the human striving for achievement exists primarily in relation to someone, some group, or some environmental circumstance. Such striving for competence does not emanate merely from an inborn attribute, but develops through social learning and through coping with interpersonal challenges. This coping, in turn, brings social rewards. Basically, the theory argues that if the environment responds well, it feels good inside because we have behaved competently.

To act competently requires the individual to have a realistic and objective view of the environment. Pepitone (1964) referred to the search for accurate knowledge about the immediate external world as the need for *cognitive validation.* The need for cognitive validation develops along with the striving for competence. The individual learns how to attend to particular environmental cues and how to "read the world" in relation to his or her own knowledge and skills. The psychodynamics of cognitive validation commence at a very early age when the infant establishes mental pictures and unconscious predictions about the environment. Through simple conditioning, footsteps come to be associated with food, arms with caring, and heartbeats with warmth and security.

Later, more complex cognitive pictures are developed about the parents' feelings—about affection and anger. As life experiences mount in complexity and difficulty, it becomes necessary for children to rely more on their memories of the social environment during previous experiences. Indeed, people would not exist very long—at least not in a mentally healthy state—if every social situation were completely new and totally unpredictable. The experience of traveling to a new country illustrates the phenomenon of familiar memories. The pre-trip anxiety experienced by many travelers originates from unclear expectations. Coping with

mundane activities such as eating, shopping, finding a place to sleep, and doing laundry can require a great deal of psychological energy until new norms and procedures become familiar. To attain maturity means, in part, that we have a variety of psychological and social skills for coping competently with a changing environment.

But the six-year-old child, of course, has not attained such a reservoir of competencies. Consider a child's initial experience with school. It is like traveling to a foreign country.

For many children, especially those who have had very few complex experiences outside their nuclear families, the unknown nature of the classroom environment and the unpredictability of its interpersonal relationships can be frightening and even traumatic. For some children, the anxiety about the first few days at school is so great that a syndrome known as "school phobia" has been noted by psychologists as a fairly common phenomenon.

Of course, most youngsters who manifest school phobia during the initial days of the first grade are able to cope with classroom interactions after they have developed clear expectations of their own about what life will be like in school, with the teacher, and with classmates. Even some teachers experience a certain amount of anxiety and stress when faced with a new class in a new neighborhood. In fact, it is often quite disconcerting, and at times frightening, for any of us to think of entering unpredictable social situations where past experiences may not hold true. Under such circumstances, the human striving for competence is heightened, and the behaviors we see reveal how the individual has learned to act competently in strange and new circumstances.

Expectations and Interpersonal Relations

The complexities that arise in relating competently with the physical world seem minor compared to the web of meaning and deep feelings that arise out of our interpersonal relationships with others. Expectations are such a natural part of interpersonal relations that for our own security and cognitive clarity, we normally make subconscious predictions about how a particular interpersonal interchange will transpire. Indeed, a large number of anyone's relationships with others take on an almost game-like quality. There are rules to follow, and it is typical to establish regularized routines quickly in many of these relationships. Most people follow the rules and put themselves into the regularized routines most of the time.

Indeed, we have tended to establish so many interpersonal games and to follow routinely so many rules that a major dilemma for our bureaucratic society is the erosion of genuine interpersonal closeness, intimacy, and authenticity. We interact too often as partners in role configuration—as wife, husband, child, teacher, and administrator—leaving out of our relationships the fact that we are all basically individuals with some of the same human motives and feelings. In so doing, we have made it increasingly difficult to establish interpersonal closeness and empathy.

In most formal role relationships, we typically play out the rules of the game. We expect particular behaviors from the supermarket clerk, other behaviors from the carpenter, the plumber, and still others from the physician or the airline pilot. Moreover, generally we expect these different role-takers to carry out their functions in a consistent fashion from day-to-day. Of course, as we get to know each of them as individuals, we gradually expand our pool of expectations about them, adding some of their unique personality characteristics to our cognitive map. We come to expect a joke from the clerk at the corner store, a big smile from the carpenter, a sour face from the plumber who fixed our shower, a special kind of greeting from the family doctor, or a particular kind of exchange from the pilot. And we might become mildly upset if we notice they do not behave in the expected ways.

There also are formal role relationships within the school, and particular behaviors are expected from the persons playing the various roles. The secretary in the office performs functions and behaves differently from the principal, and the custodian differs from the aides, etc. Even on the first meeting of a class in which the teacher and students are strangers to one another, certain expectations already exist because the social context itself carries meanings for all of the participants, even without interpersonal interaction. The societal norms associated with classroom life soon give way, however, as the teacher and students interact more and more with one another. The teacher learns to count on certain students for the correct answers; students learn which of their peers will be helpful to them and which ones will stay away from them; and all members will begin to establish expectations about the students who will create trouble, those who will study hard, and those who will help the group to laugh. Thus, the development of both generic and idosyncratic expectations about interpersonal behavior in the classroom is natural and inevitable.

Some social psychologists regard the school as consisting of various *behavior settings,* e.g., the hallways, the lunch room, discussion circles, classroom seating, and the gymnasium. Kounin (1976) has shown that discipline problems arise more often in some behavior settings than others, e.g., the lunch room vs. discussion circles. Moreover, how the teacher handles the situation can make a difference from one behavior setting to the other. Kounin found, for example, that student behavior was influenced differently by the very same teacher behavior, depending on the behavior setting. During seatwork a teacher's varying the task from time to time decreased discipline problems, while the very same teacher behavior during recitation increased discipline problems. Apparently, students develop different expectations for different behavior settings; behavior settings take on a power of their own over time. Teachers will need to search for a fit between their behavior and the expectations of students in different behavior settings.

Expectations Include an Assessment

Expectations about interpersonal relations entail making both cognitive predictions about how others will behave and attributions of other people along evaluative dimensions. In other words, interpersonal expectations are made up of both thoughts and feelings. Obviously, the teacher assesses the student who is expected to be a troublemaker. Likewise, students will assess peers they expect to be congenial differently from those they expect to be moody or aggressive.

Evaluation as a part of interpersonal expectations emerges in bold relief when expectations are not met. The parents who expect their child to act with good manners at a restaurant are disappointed when the child does not live up to their expectations. And a teacher who expects students to work independently will become upset when students act in a disorderly fashion during a study period. The student will feel rejected and angry when a trusted friend puts him or her down publicly by revealing something confidential.

Colloquially, the term "expect" often is used to mean "holding hopes or aspirations." When parents say, "We expect you to have good table manners," they may, in fact, be hoping the child will have good manners but actually and covertly be predicting that the child won't. If they simply predicted good table manners, they would not be so likely to communicate a reminder to the child. The teacher who "expects" students to study independently may also appoint a monitor to watch over the students during study time. The presence of a monitor communicates to at least some of the students that the teacher expects them to goof off. Thus, the presence of a monitor demonstrates, just by that person's walking up and down the aisles, that the teacher predicts that students will have trouble with independent study.

Interpersonal predictions can often have an even stronger effect on classroom group processes than interpersonal hopes and aspirations. In this chapter, we will not use the concept of expectations to mean hopes or aspirations. Instead, we will use it to mean those *working predictions* that are used in relating to others in the classroom. When such expectations are not supported, feelings will inevitably interact with the cognitive predictions.

Expectations are Communicated

Expectations as interpersonal predictions are communicated in a multitude of direct and indirect ways. Consider, for example, a student who has seriously broken a school rule for the first time and is called to the principal's office for a conference about the misbehavior. If the principal says something like, "I'm surprised and disappointed in your behavior; explain to me how this happened," a much different interpersonal stage is being set between the two, than if the principal were to say, "This is intolerable, but I'm not surprised. I'm going to make sure that you are not in a position to do this again." The first statement made by the principal indicated that she did *not* predict that the student would have behaved as he did, while the second statement established that the principal did, indeed, predict that the student's misbehavior would continue unless strong measures were taken.

There are other more indirect ways of communicating one's predictions about the behavior of others. For example, when an important visitor is observing in the classroom, teachers may choose to call on those students whom they predict will be able to perform well. The teacher's interest in showing off a bright and capable class will not be missed by the students, even if the observer does not fully grasp it. In another example, students making choices for a baseball team will convey their assessments of another student's baseball skills to the entire group. In still another case, students indirectly communicate their predictions about interpersonal rapport by asking one classmate for academic help rather than another.

How teachers' expectations are communicated to students are influenced by what the teachers assign as the cause of the students' behavior. Research on the communication of expectations has focused on what is called *attribution theory* (see Weiner, 1979). An attribution entails a belief in the origin of behavior. Typically, when teachers see the origin of a student's

disturbing behavior as lying outside the student's psyche, they will not blame the student for misbehaving, nor will they communicate a prediction of bad behavior in the future. In contrast, when teachers view the origin of misbehavior as emanating from within the student's motivational field, they will hold the student responsible for that misbehavior and communicate a prediction that it will continue.

It is important to point out that interpersonal predictions and attributions of student behavior are often incorrect. The teacher may actually call on the wrong students to get the correct answers; students may not choose the best baseball players first; and the student may not choose the most knowledgeable helper in a particular academic area. Nevertheless, these behaviors communicate interpersonal expectations that can have impact in creating the social-psychological reality they predict.

Finn (1972) has defined expectations usefully in his statement that expectations are evaluations—whether conscious or unconscious—that one person forms of another (or of the self) which lead the evaluator to treat the person being evaluated as though the assessment were valid. The person doing the expecting typically anticipates or predicts that the other person will act in a manner consistent with the assessment.

Self-Expectations

No less crucial to an understanding of group processes within the classroom are the expectations that each student or the teacher has for his or her own behavior. Although self-expectations develop within specific social situations, they also are influenced strongly by the general picture of self that the individual brings into the new situation. We all make predictions of how well or poorly we will do in a given social situation, based in part on our personal security and self-confidence in general, but also on the sorts of behavioral cues about ourselves that we pick up from others in that situation.

Consider the youngster who was called to the principal's office because of some sort of misbehavior. If the student held a self-image as a troublemaker, before entering the office, even though the student never had broken a serious school rule, he or she might have thought without saying it, "Here I go again!" On the other hand, students who view themselves as conscientious, rule-abiding members of the school will tend to view interactions with the principal quite differently. Likewise, students who know that they are skilled in baseball may not care if they are chosen near the end, just as students who have many friends may not be frustrated by not being chosen as an academic helper.

Sometimes the images we hold of ourselves are so firmly fixed that our self-expectations are realized, even though the objective facts may be quite divergent. Eric Berne (1972), as part of his research and writing on *transactional analysis,* has developed the concept of the "life-script" to explain the power of interconnected clusters of self-expectations. Life-scripts are firmly grounded in self-expectations, as, for example, in the case of the "born-loser" who confirms his or her lack of effectiveness again and again with each new challenge. This person always loses, or at least perceives a loss, even when he or she is actually on the winning side. For most people, feedback can be used to reassess competencies and to move to a new level of self-expectation. For persons living through a "loser" script, however, favorable feedback can be twisted and tangled until it fits the negative image they have of themselves.

Among the findings of attribution theory (see Weiner, 1979, 1985), is the observation that students are different in how they assign responsibility for their successes and failures. Two sorts of students have been classified as internally oriented (accepting responsibility for their behavior) and externally oriented (attributing successes or failures to circumstances over which they have no control). Differences between the two are apparent in the classroom. Internally oriented students attribute their academic performance to ability, or effort, while externally oriented students attribute their academic performance to luck or the difficulty of the task.

Self-Expectations and Achievement

Students, for the most part, strive to be competent, and the ways in which they will behave to prove their competency are influenced significantly by their self-expectations for personal success. Students with low confidence in their own abilities will behave differently from students who have high self-confidence. The classroom group is used often as a testing ground for the student's self-expectations. Students who believe that they have done an excellent job on an assignment, and who receive a similar evaluation from the teacher, will feel bolstered by the feedback and the academic learning experience. When students receive a low evaluation, on the other hand, the dissonance often motivates them to reassess their capabilities and to expect a lower level of personal performance when facing similar challenges in the future.

Research by Benjamin (1950) has shown that classroom performances can be altered by changes in students' self-images. Benjamin first asked forty-eight senior high school students to rank themselves on their own intelligence level. Next, he administered an intelligence test, after which he presented false information to each student about his or her performance. For half of the students, Benjamin presented scores that were one level above what the students expected, and for the other half, scores below actual student predictions were presented. Finally, Benjamin administered another form of the same intelligence test. A majority of scores for the second test changed in the direction of the falsely reported ranks. Students who thought they did better than expected performed better on the second test, and students who thought they did less well than they had expected did less well on the second test.

But how do such expectations get communicated in a classroom? Means et al. (1979) argued that teachers communicate two messages to students about their performance. First, they communicate expectations for performance, such as "I think you will do very well on this lesson," or, "I think you will have difficulty doing this." And second, teachers appraise student performance and give feedback, such as, "You did very well," or, "You did very poorly." These are typical phrases teachers use before and after the completion of an assignment. Working with eleventh graders in a remedial reading program, Means et al. found that incongruent combinations (i.e., "I think you will do well," and "You did very poorly,") resulted in students' higher achievement on a reading assignment than congruent combinations. The authors explain how these incongruent

messages may serve to spur on students. Students may say, "It was an easy task. I did poorly. I need to work harder," or, "It was a hard task. I did well, so I must have worked hard. If I work hard, I will continue to do well." Although psychologists do not agree on the precise mechanisms by which teacher expectancies and feedback affect student self-appraisals and consequently their performance, it is very clear that these factors influence student outcomes.

In other research, Sears (1940) presented data to show that students' levels of aspiration are influenced by their past experiences with success and failure within the classroom. Sears tested a sample of upper-elementary students on their arithmetic and reading performance, making estimates of the time each student took to complete a page of work. Those students who experienced failure on these tests set their levels of aspiration at unrealistically high or unrealistically low levels, and they also manifested a high fear of failure, low self-confidence, and self-perception as losers. Either they set up each situation so that they would most certainly succeed and be able to dismiss their success to themselves by saying, "Anyone can do that!" or they would set goals that they could not possibly achieve, once again proving to themselves that they were incompetent. On the other hand, those students who set realistic goals typically had experienced successes in the past. They chose levels of aspiration that were challenging but also offered high probabilities of success.

In other research, DeCharms (1976, 1977) theorized that students differ according to the degree to which they act as a "pawn" and to what extent they act as an "origin." Pawns are students who possess very little self-confidence and who feel that someone or something else is in control of them. They have difficulty making deliberate choices about the directions of their lives. Origins, on the other hand, are students who direct their own lives, showing confidence that they can make choices on their own and can plan for and pursue their own interests. Compare, for example, a person with a pawn-like orientation and a person with an origin-like orientation toward a homework assignment. A pawn tends to be controlled by others; thus homework may remain undone if there is interference from others—parents took the student visiting, a friend called and didn't stop talking, or the student had to baby-sit. The external circumstances tend to control the pawn's behavior. An origin, on the other hand, will act upon the environment. The origin will react to the interference from others by claiming homework must be done or at least understand he or she is ultimately responsible for whether the homework is completed.

DeCharms' origins and pawns are similar to Weiner's internally and externally oriented students. There are several interesting findings from research concerning internally and externally oriented student. One study shows that the former are more achievement oriented than the latter (Thomas, 1980 and Uguroglu and Walberg, 1979). A second is the concept that the former deal with failure better than the latter. Externally oriented students tend to view failure as confirming their self-concept of helplessness; they are unable to rebound from failure because the failure confirms how vulnerable they are to defeat. Seligman (1975) has referred to that condition as *learned helplessness.*

Of course to pigeon-hole students as internally or externally oriented or as origins and pawns oversimplifies the way the per-

sonality works; we all behave as pawns in some situations and we all behave as origins in other situations. DeCharms argues that people have different basic orientations; each of us is more or less a pawn or an origin. DeCharms has applied these theoretical notions to classroom situations. He looked at two key hypotheses derived from his theory about students as pawns and origins (1971, 1972). First, he posited that student pawns and origins are created out of the expectations that other key people hold for them. Second, he hypothesized that a relationship exists between origin-like student behavior and successful academic achievement. He conducted a three-year intervention and evaluation program in an urban district to test these hypotheses, collecting data from fifth-graders and following those same students during their sixth and seventh grades.

As he was collecting data from fifth-graders about their pawn-origin orientations, DeCharms was simultaneously training sixth and seventh-grade teachers in how to help students develop more origin-like behavior. The teachers were trained to use exercises for bolstering self-concept and procedures for stimulating achievement striving and concepts bearing on the pawn-origin orientation.

Essentially the teachers were taught that enhancing motivation by raising self-confidence calls neither for forcing children to do something nor for allowing them free rein. Rather, the most fundamental principle for origin behavior stresses the point that making a choice gives a student some feeling of personal influence and self-esteem. *Learning to make choices in the classroom leads to commitment and to responsibility for the results of the choice.* However, teachers were trained to give small but real choices, at least in the beginning, since being given too many choices might make a student feel just as much a pawn as not having any choices whatsoever.

DeCharms's evaluation showed that in the experimental groups the teachers did change their classroom behaviors, and that the students in those same groups gained in academic achievement and in origin-like behaviors as compared with control groups. DeCharms thus demonstrated that students' expectations about their own behavior can be crucial to what happens in their striving for academic achievement, and that a teacher can have significant influence on the expectations that students develop about themselves.

How Expectations Develop

Developing expectations about how other people will behave in particular circumstances is a natural, human phenomenon. Without predictions and assessments of others, in fact, life would be overly complex and seemingly random. We have attempted to show that the most obvious and direct way of obtaining expectations of others is through repetitive interaction with them. At the same time, there are other more indirect avenues for developing interpersonal expectations as, for example, when the others take on such jobs as clerk, carpenter, plumber, physician, or pilot. In schools, teachers and students employ many means to develop assessments and to make predictions of others' behavior. In particular, four means of developing interpersonal expectations are used most frequently in classroom and school settings: the formal gathering of information about others; the stereotypes of social class, minority group membership, and gender; the force of a social situation in which others find them-

selves; and the ways people are assumed to act because of their role in a group. Let us explore each of these.

Expectations Through Gathered Information

Many teachers routinely receive or actively seek formal diagnostic information about their students. School records typically portray each student's psychological history with lists of grades, I.Q. scores, and achievement test scores. Some cumulative school records also include scores on personality inventories, results of self-concept questionnaires, and notes of anecdotes or impressions that have been prepared by former teachers. Conscientious teachers seek out such data, using them both to plan their instructional program and to counsel certain students. The reason for such deliberate planning should be obvious, especially in special skill courses involving reading and math. Students who are performing below an expected standard for their chronological age will, of course, require special attention and innovative instruction.

Some teachers also use other diagnostic techniques to obtain information about the social-emotional lives of their students. These include attitude inventories, sociometric tests, student essays, discussions about goals and aspirations, or special diagnostic inventories focused on specific academic areas. Such attempts at diagnosing classroom learning environments and the attitudes of the students can help move teacher and students closer together and can facilitate collaboration and emotional support in the peer group.

Unfortunately, data about students are often misused by teachers. Information about students' previous intellectual performances and their personality characteristics can predispose teachers to expect such students to continue to perform as they have in the past. And those teacher expectations, in turn, can influence the sorts of interactions that the teachers initiate with the students. There are teachers, for example, who use reading achievement scores to form permanent reading groups, thus building psychological boundaries and distance between students. Frequently, such grouping is implemented on the basis of a single test. Even some first-grade teachers who have very little data on children at their disposal still use informal and intuitive means to estimate their students' I.Q.s before any testing takes place.

Doyle, Hancock, and Kifer (1971) asked first-grade teachers to estimate their students' I.Q.s before formal testing. Then, later in the school year, they found that those students whose I.Q.s had been overestimated by the teacher had achieved more in reading than would have been predicted from the student's actual I.Q. score. Conversely, those students who had been underestimated achieved less. Furthermore, the research showed that teachers who generally underestimated the I.Q.s for their entire class had more students who were achieving less at the end of the school year compared to the students of teachers who had been prone to do more overestimating.

Students who have been labeled troublemakers or behavior problems carry such labels with them from teacher to teacher. The ostensibly "bad" students are often confronted on the very first day of class with a statement from the teacher such as, "You can rest assured I will not allow you to get away with any misbehavior here!" Or, the teacher might comment, "I've heard about you; for starters, you can sit right here by my desk so I can keep my eye on you." Typically, such troublemakers are boys, thus giving rise to the stereotype many teachers harbor which suggests that boys will require more control than girls. Some boys indeed do begin to act out primarily because the teachers expect them to create some disturbances.

In a more informal manner, students gather information about teachers from which they develop expectations. Information about teachers usually gets passed on through the "grapevine" of the peer group. It has been our experience that teachers seem reluctant to acknowledge that students pass expectations and feelings on about the teachers, and that students very quickly form favorable predictations about particular teachers. But the act of sharing expectations about teachers within the student peer group is very real. Students say to one another, "He's hard," "She's strict," "He's nice," "She's interesting." "He's having trouble at home, so he doesn't demand much"; and "She dislikes the principal," etc.

In open-space, alternative schools in which we have observed, information about teachers has been organized and disseminated formally. It is viewed as legitimate and useful to talk about the attributes of the staff and, in particular, to describe the strengths of each staff member. Some of these schools have booklets that describe courses and teachers. Other schools, described by Shaw (1973), have built formal procedures for channeling student evaluations of teachers as a means of improving instruction. Information about teachers or students can be valuable and useful, provided it is descriptive and not just evaluative.

Some evidence from research on student-to-teacher feedback shows how powerful it can be. Tuckman and Oliver (1968) found that student appraisals of teacher performance constitute much more powerful feedback—as measured by the amount of subsequent teacher change—than the appraisals of supervisors or principals. The teachers were more affected by the reactions of their students than by the reactions of higher-status personnel. Margaret Nelson (1972) showed a parallel phenomenon in a study of change among substitute teachers. She supplied the substitutes with systematic, questionnaire feedback from students about the teachers' classroom behavior and subsequently showed major behavioral changes among the substitutes.

Expectations Through Cultural Stereotypes

Like each of us, students and teachers are bombarded continually by images of the sociological categories which exist in the larger culture. Such images are transmitted through television, newspapers, radio, and books, as well as through discussions of social events with family and friends and through participation in the neighborhood with civic groups and other organizations. This transmission, often referred to as acculturation or socialization, culminates, in part, in the internalization of stereotypes. A stereotype consists of assumptions and beliefs assigned to every member of a particular social category. So, for example, "Redheads have tempers," "Electricians are skinny," "Plumbers are fat," or "Southerners are bigots." Such nonscientific thinking is natural. It becomes detrimental, however, when we do not allow new information to change the stereotypes. Three kinds of cultural stereotypes in our society that are prominent, and often present obstacles to achieving healthy classroom interaction, involve the categories of social class, minority-group membership, and gender.

Frequently, teachers establish firm expectations about a group of students because of the socio-economic level of the neighborhood in which the children live. In one study, Rist (1970) documented how first-grade teachers perpetuated a social class hierarchy within their classrooms by assigning students to reading groups according to their socio-economic background. Unwittingly, the teachers placed middle-class children in higher level reading groups than the lower-class children. Research conducted by Finn (1972) revealed that teachers in suburban schools held higher expectations for the academic performance of their students than teachers in urban schools.

Finn asked 300 fifth-grade teachers to evaluate some essays written by students. The essays were accompanied by fictional data on the sex, race, intelligence level, and achievement test scores of the individuals. The urban teachers paid special attention to the fictional information on intelligence and achievement in evaluating the quality of the essays. The suburban teachers, in contrast, were less influenced by the fictional data. Finn concluded, "In the urban school, the expectations held by the teachers for pupils of differing ability and achievement were so strong as to pervade their evaluations of the pupil's actual performance" (p. 403). His supposition was the concept that the urban teachers had built an image of urban students as being socio-economically deprived and expected them to have low intelligence and achievement.

In research on 49 self-contained elementary classrooms and their teachers, Haller (1985) could find no evidence that the teachers either consciously or unconsciously were racially biased in their ability groups for reading. At the same time, the fact that those teachers believed in ability grouping for reading instruction meant that black students were much more likely than white students to be placed in the lowest reading groups. The social problem, according to Haller, is not with teacher racism, but rather with the lack of an effective pedagogy for teaching high and low ability youngsters to work together on learning to read.

In another study focusing on the problem of social class and discrimination in the schools, Martell (1971) discussed a legal brief that had been prepared by a community group in Toronto which maintained that the Toronto school district had discriminated against students with low-income families. Apparently with good intentions, students of low-income families were being placed in "opportunity classes" which were seen by all of the participants as the "bottom stream of the educational ladder." The community group's analytic survey (included within the legal brief) showed that "if . . . you're classified . . . 'sheet metal worker' . . . your child has 18.5 times the chance of ending up in one of these bottom streams compared with the child of an accountant, engineer, or lawyer! The figure jumps to 40 times the chance if you are on workman's compensation or retired, to 43.5 for the unemployed, and 67 times the chance for welfare or mother's allowance" (p. 11). Acknowledging the fact that lower-class children did, indeed, have more severe academic problems than their middle-class counterparts, the community group asked that their children be granted

adequate educational facilities and resources without the cultural stigma of being "dumb" and "deprived." The group exhorted the school to emphasize the strengths, both cognitive and emotional, of children from lower-class and minority-group backgrounds and to measure success and resourcefulness in the school more broadly than before.

Of all the cultural stereotypes that pervade American society, none is so destructive as that of racial and ethnic group differences. In our society the visible minority groups—Afro-Americans, Mexican-Americans, Native-Americans, and Asian-Americans—are continually faced with and must cope with pervasive stereotypes about themselves. Along with long-term discrimination in jobs, housing, and education, the damage of cultural stereotyping is heightened by informal relationships in organizations, particularly in our schools. And, of course, the sort of social phenomenon described by Finn in which teachers hold different expectations for minority-group youngsters is too often true.

Interaction in the peer group can also exacerbate expectations being communicated by teachers. In an observation by Sagar and Schofield (1983) of sixth graders in an urban desegregated school, students interacted primarily with others of their own race. While no race effect was observed in the students' own task orientations, peer behaviors were more likely to be task-related when directed toward white rather than black interactants. A parallel study of sociometric choices (with whom do you interact most frequently and to whom do you go in the class for help on academic subjects?) confirmed both conclusions.

Black students are frequently labeled "culturally deprived." The label of the "culturally deprived child," communicating the lack of a proper culture, ignores the strengths inherent in the minority member's culture and can stigmatize the child. The assumption of deficit can undergird a strong expectation that the minority youngster is doomed to failure, leading the teacher to behave in condescending and overly sensitive ways toward the youngster. Instead of viewing the minority child as developing within his or her own culture, which has its own resources and strengths, the deficit model of cultural deprivation tends to stress the weaknesses and the deficiencies of the child.

Thorne (1983), while studying the games students play in elementary schools, observed that boys and girls have even more difficulty working together than do blacks and whites. Children seem to be learning, she concluded, that "members of the other sex are alien beings." Her observations in California and Michigan indicated that girls and boys live in separate worlds and that teachers frequently reinforced that by pitting the sexes against one another in spelling bees and in the lunchroom. Boys who choose to sit at the same cafeteria table with girls are likely to be taunted by peers and teachers alike. Chasing games on the playground, both formal and informal, also pit girls against boys. Thorne suggests that distance between the sexes can be reduced through cooperative activities in mixed-sex groups, but that teachers and parents must take initiative for that to happen.

During the past decade, awareness has been raised about the detrimental impact of stereotyping the sexes. In one study of first-grade teachers, Palardy (1969) asked the teachers to indicate whether boys could learn to read as fast as girls in the first grade. For those teachers who did not expect a difference in reading performance between the sexes, there was no difference by

the end of the year. Conversely, those teachers who expected the girls to learn to read faster than the boys did typically fulfill their predictions. In another study of seventh-grade classrooms, McCandless, Roberts, and Starnes (1971) found that boys received much lower grades than girls, even though the boys' scores on standardized achievement tests were only insignificantly lower than the girls' scores.

Even though girls tend to receive higher grades than boys throughout school, many studies support the contention that low self-confidence is a problem among females. Some examples from research have indicated that girls in the fifth grade expected to do less well than boys of the same age at a novel marble-dropping game (Motanelli and Hill, 1969); girls in the seventh and ninth grades expected to do less well than their male counterparts in their English classes (Battle, 1966); and female college students anticipated doing less well than their male peers at anagrams tasks (House and Perney, 1974).

According to the highly regarded review on gender differences by Maccoby and Jacklin (1969), the primary psychological reason for females expecting to do less well than males on an assortment of diverse tasks is their relatively lower levels of self-confidence. Indeed, Maccoby and Jacklin suggested that women are lower in self-confidence than men in almost all achievement situations However, Lenney's comprehensive review of the available research up until 1977 indicated that females do not display low self-confidence in all achievement situations.

Lenney (1977) found that there are three kinds of situations which influence the self-confidence of females compared to that of males. Each of these situations can be associated with classroom group processes.

The first situation involves the nature of the specific task. Both boys and girls expect to do well on those challenges that are presented as being most appropriate for their sex (see Stein, Pohly, and Mueller, 1971, for details). Second, the nature of the sex difference in self-confidence depends upon the availability of clear, unambiguous feedback. When externally provided information on specific task abilities is unequivocal and immediately available, girls do not make lower ability estimates than boys (see Hill and Dusek, 1969). However, according to McMahon (1973) and Nicholls (1975), when such feedback is absent or ambiguous, girls seem to have lower opinions of their abilities and often do underestimate their abilities in relation to those of the boys.

Third, research by Jacobson, Berger, and Millham (1970) and House and Perney (1974) has shown that when girls work alone or in situations in which they do not expect their performances to be compared to those of others, their ability estimates are not likely to be lower than those of the boys. However, according to studies by Benton (1973) and House (1974), when girls work in classroom situations in which competitive aspects of the environment are strongly emphasized, their estimates are usually lower than those of the boys.

Expectations Through Social Situations

Cultural meanings associated with particular social situations are also important for the development of interpersonal expectations. Such differences in expectations exist between countries as well as between settings within the same country.

One example that was experienced by our family illustrates the variation in expectancies of people from different countries. As our family prepared for living in Belgium, our children were eagerly anticipating the chance to improve their soccer skills since that is such an established sport in Europe. (Soccer, the national sport in Belgium, is referred to as "football.") Upon arrival, we contacted the schools where we expected such sports would be organized as they are in most American schools. We were surprised on two counts. First, the schools offered virtually no sports or other extra-curricular activities. And second, people were surprised that our daughter wished to play "football." We were told, "Nice girls don't play football." Although we found a club that provided football for Allen, Julie was not able to play. Whereas soccer in the USA is relatively new and considered a coed sport, in Belgium (and most of Europe) it was a well-established sport and clearly defined as a male-only activity.

Institutions also shape the expectations people hold for each other. In a cross-national study, Finn (1980) found little student achievement differences when he compared fourteen-year-old male and female students in the United States, Sweden, and England. Generally, girls had better attitudes toward reading than boys and boys out-performed girls in certain areas of science. Finn found that there were exceptions to this case when studying the students in an all-girls' school; those girls out-performed boys in reading and several science subjects. Similar findings are reported by Dale (1969) in a comprehensive review on mixed or single-sex schooling. Perhaps coed and single-sex institutions encourage a different set of expectations. In the girls' school, with primarily female teachers and an all-girl student body, perhaps the traditional expectations, or stereotypes, governing male-appropriate and female-appropriate behaviors are underplayed. In single-sex schools, girls see females performing all the roles, even those that may be more commonly played by males in a coeducational setting. Consequently, girls come to have different expectations for how they perform in different areas, depending on whether they attend coeducational or single-sex schools.

Another example of how institutions shape the expectations that the participants hold for each other was presented by Rosenhan (1973). In an ingenious research project, eight "stooges" were admitted to a mental hospital after feigning the hearing of voices. After being formally admitted, all eight behaved naturally, presenting accurate stories about their backgrounds, personal interests, and social concerns. All eight were admitted with the diagnosis of schizophrenia and released subsequently with the label of schizophrenia in remission. While in the hospital, perfectly normal behaviors and interests on the part of the eight healthy stooges were interpreted by the hospital staff as part of the schizophrenic syndrome. Although the staff remained detached and impersonal, and sometimes acted even cruel toward the eight, all of the stooges believed that staff members were not operating out of malice or incompetence.

Rosenhan concluded that the staff's perceptions and behaviors were influenced more by the culture of the hospital than by malicious dispositions. In a different, more benign environment, the staff members' reactions no doubt would have been more emotionally supportive. The main theme of the research was that the labeling of someone as schizophrenic within a hospital over-determines others' reactions toward that person.

Professional personnel within schools often interact with students in particular social situations that give rise to interpersonal expectations. The vice-principal for discipline may assume immediately that a student walking into the administrative offices has done something wrong. School psychologists who are asked to test a child may unwittingly assume that the child has a serious problem for which they must find an appropriate diagnostic label. And remedial reading teachers may expect the students they receive to have serious reading disabilities. In all of those social situations, expectations can significantly bias the sorts of interaction that would subsequently take place between the professional educator and the student.

We knew a teacher who taught a special classroom of mentally retarded students within a junior high school. Although most of the students had been in the special class for several years, she had reason to believe that many of them could perform quite well in a regular class. Upon her insistence for careful mental testing, she discovered that, in fact, less than half of the children were retarded. Many of the youngsters needed special help; many were from lower-class and minority-group backgrounds. Most of the children were not, however, technically retarded. The teacher experienced great difficulty in trying to persuade the school's administrators that new alternatives were called for. She had even more difficulty in convincing the students that they were not mentally retarded.

During the past decade, mainstreaming regulations have been adopted, obligating schools to integrate mentally retarded, emotionally disturbed, and physically handicapped students into regular classrooms. One psychological rationale for mainstreaming is the idea that youngsters with special educational deficiencies often suffer even greater harm by being set apart from "normal youngsters," thereby suffering combined stigmas of stereotyping, social rejection, and unsupportive interpersonal expectations. Integrating such youngsters into regular classrooms is, of course, only one step toward eliminating the negative impact of unsupportive expectations. Ways in which teachers relate to these students during regular classroom routines could serve to maintain stereotypes or gradually to eliminate them.

Expectations Through Taking A Role

The plight of the "at-risk" youngster within the regular classroom can be understood in light of the variety of roles that get played out in all social situations. Over time, all groups—including families and classrooms—develop a regular pattern of interpersonal behavior. This regularized interpersonal pattern can be referred to as the group's informal role-structure. One study carried out with sixth-grade boys showed how the informal structure of a classroom influenced students' views of each other and their expectations for performance. Mozdzierz et al. (1968) found that students with high sociometric status were seen as performing better than they actually did and students with low sociometric status were seen as performing worse than they actually did. Expectations become so ingrained that they may distort our perceptions of objective data. In some families, for example, one child may take on the role of mediator while another performs more often as the scapegoat. Indeed, some learning problems that students have can be traced to a role they are playing out within their families. In many classrooms,

student roles emerge early and remain the same throughout the year. Some students are pegged early as helpers, clowns, wise guys, and troublemakers. Often interpersonal expectations become so firmly shared and consensual for the members that individual students find it difficult to get the social support needed for making changes in their behaviors.

The Circular Interpersonal Process

In interpersonal exchanges between two people, expectations about the other person interact with one's self-expectations, and both give rise to one's interpersonal behavior. Expectations about another and about the self grow from two sources. They grow from previous encounters with a given individual, and they develop through indirect avenues such as information, cultural stereotypes, social situations, and expected role functions.

Two examples of common interpersonal exchanges in classrooms may be instructive. Students who view themselves as competent, secure, and helpful typically will behave in friendly, supportive, and interpersonally enhancing ways. Other students will perceive this friendliness and helpfulness and, in turn, convey their own satisfaction with the others' behaviors. The first students are reinforced for their behavior. Later if they do not behave in those expected ways, there may be surprise and even disappointment shown toward them, i.e., "I wonder what's wrong with so-and-so today?"

Conversely, trouble-making students become engaged in a much different sort of behavioral cycle. Teachers often have self-defined ideas about who the troublemakers

FIGURE 4.1   Circular Interpersonal Process

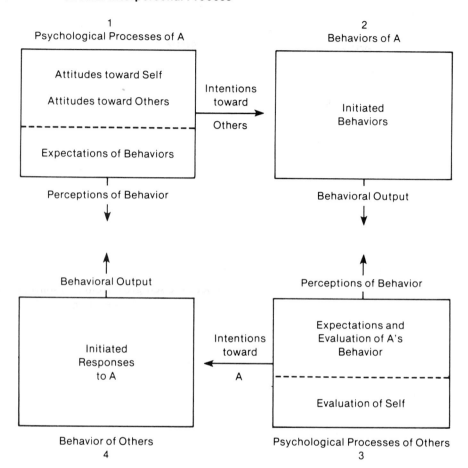

are and quickly curtail behaviors from the targeted students which would normally be allowed from others. The teachers usually argue that "the troublemaker doesn't know when to stop, so I have to do it." Yet, trouble-making students come to rely on the teacher to control their behavior and come to expect to be controlled.

When two people interact over a long period, their relationship becomes rather stable and predictable. Lippitt (1962) referred to this stable and predictable inter-personal exchange as the "circular interpersonal process." As you can see in Figure 4.1, the two most important features of initiating any behavior are the attitudes and expectations one holds about the self and the attitudes and expectations one holds for the other.

Figure 4.1 shows the psychological processes and behaviors of person A, in boxes 1 and 2. Attitudes about the self and others, as well as the expectations that A holds for the behaviors of others, influence

FIGURE 4.2 **Supportive Cycle of Interpersonal Relations**

```
                1                                          2
   Psychological Processes of A                     Behaviors of A

  ┌──────────────────────────┐                ┌──────────────────────────┐
  │      Accepts Self:       │                │                          │
  │  Feels Competent and     │   Intends      │  Helpful, Open, Pleasant,│
  │        Secure            │   Pleasant,    │     Nonthreatening       │
  │     Accepts Others       │  ──────────▶   │       Behaviors          │
  │- - - - - - - - - - - - - │  Reciprocal    │                          │
  │                          │  Interaction   │                          │
  │ Receives Positive        │                │                          │
  │    Reflections           │                │                          │
  └──────────────────────────┘                └──────────────────────────┘
   Perceptions of Behavior                       Behavioral Output
            ▲                                           │
            │                                           ▼

   Behavioral Output                          Perceptions of Behavior
            │                                           ▲
            ▼                                           │
  ┌──────────────────────────┐                ┌──────────────────────────┐
  │                          │   Intends      │   Expects Friendly,      │
  │   Accepting, Helpful,    │   to Be        │   Helpful Behaviors;     │
  │  Sharing, Dialogue       │  ◀──────────   │     Feels Positive       │
  │     Behaviors            │  Helpful, to   │- - - - - - - - - - - - - │
  │                          │  Reciprocate   │                          │
  │                          │                │  Feels Good about Self   │
  └──────────────────────────┘                └──────────────────────────┘
     Behavior of Others                  Psychological Processes of Others
            4                                          3
```

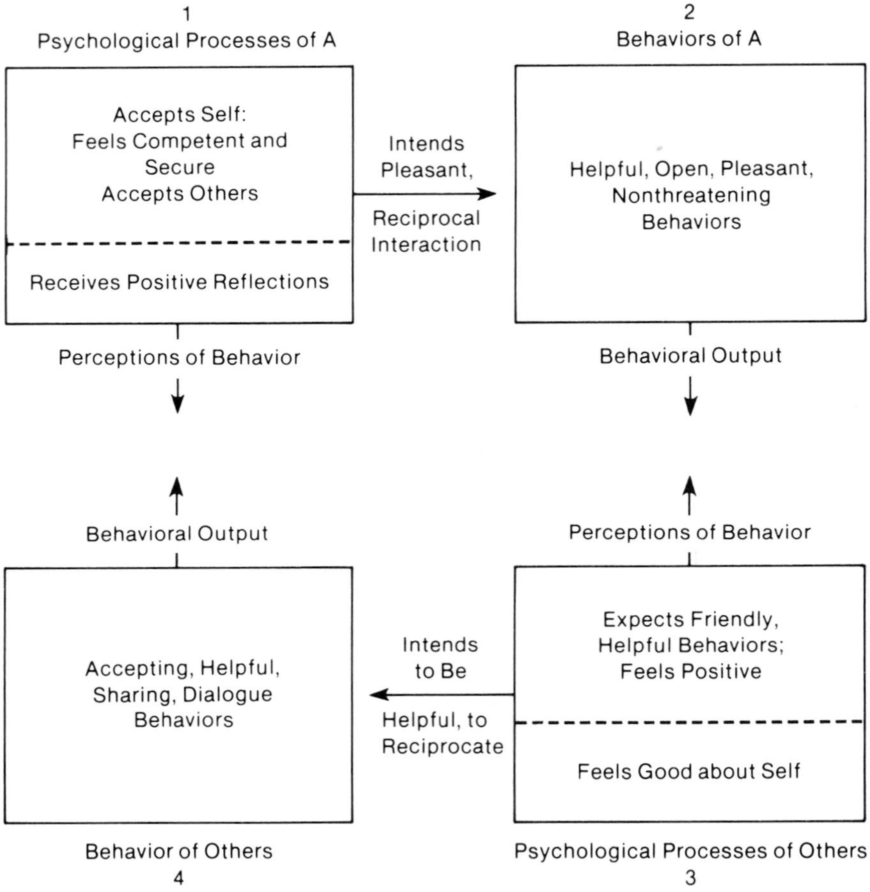

A's intent to act. These three variables—attitude, expectation, and intent—in turn, influence the way in which A behaves toward others. Each aspect of A's behavior is shown as being directly associated with or as arising out of those psychological processes.

To complete the circle, psychological processes and behaviors of others are depicted in boxes 3 and 4. The others' perceptions of A's behavior influence their expectations and assessments of A and themselves. Those help to shape the other's intentions which, in turn, become actualized in their own behaviors. A perceives those behaviors, and the circle is completed.

An example of a supportive cycle of interpersonal relations is shown in Figure 4.2. Student A holds a favorable feeling about self and about others. A has received friendly responses from others and feels secure in their presence. A's behaviors toward others represent a blend of open-

FIGURE 4.3   Unsupportive Cycle of Interpersonal Relations

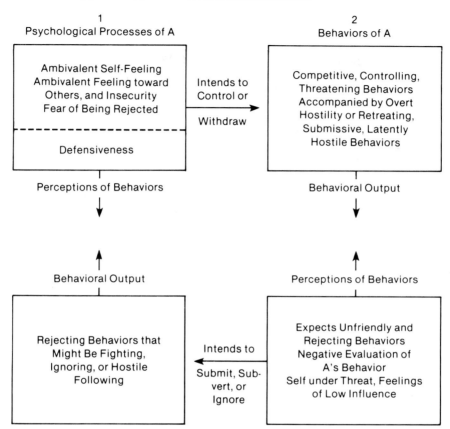

ness, helpfulness, and congeniality. As others perceive A's behaviors, their expectations of A as a warm and supportive person are confirmed: A is viewed as nonthreatening and friendly, and as enhancing others' favorable views of themselves. Others are thereby free to interact with A without fear of losing security or self-esteem. Their responses are positive and supportive toward A, and A, in turn, receives reinforcing evidence of personal likability. Thus, person A and his or her associates support one another in a mutually friendly and respectful interchange.

Figure 4.3 describes an unsupportive cycle of interpersonal relations, one which is significantly more negative than the one shown in Figure 4.2. Student A has ambivalent feelings about self and about others. Student A has adopted a defensive, interpersonal orientation because of rejection or isolation in the past. "At-risk" students with a psychological pattern characterized by low self-esteem, insecurity, and feelings of incompetence might behave in at least two very different ways. One person could attempt to control others in order to establish self as being worthy—an absence of affiliation for such persons can lead to a grab for power. Another person might withdraw from others and become an isolate so as not to face his or her rejection. Such people often retreat submissively, accepting others' attempts to influence them while still harboring latent hostility toward those others. Both patterns of behavior—domination and withdrawal—are likely to be viewed as unfriendly and unhelpful, and the communication of these perceptions will confirm A's self-expectation of being unfriendly, unhelpful, and a rejectee.

We must point out, however, that the pattern is cyclical. That is, we have begun to discuss the cycle at the point of "psychological processes of A." We do not mean to imply that this point is the primary cause of behavior nor the primary target for intervention. As in any cycle, causes are at several points and intervention can occur at multiple places.

The interpersonal expectations that eventually are formed about a student's behavior can become so firm that even as that individual attempts behavioral changes, others may not notice the changes. Expectations can influence perceptions to such an extent that the incoming information becomes biased and distorted as it is psychologically processed. Thus, the student who is working within an unsupportive, interpersonal cycle might attempt to change by acting in a friendly fashion. The student might, for example, tap another student softly on the shoulder to indicate a reaching out for friendship or to indicate nonverbal agreement. Unfortunately, such physical behavior, in itself, might be perceived as hostile—as striking out, hitting, acting smart, or as trying to start an argument. Unsupportive cycles of interpersonal relations can become especially vicious when even neutral and benign behaviors are viewed as negative and as confirming original expectations.

A family example illustrates the strength of the expectations of others. In this case it was solved by making a drastic move—by changing social environments. Our son, when he was in the sixth grade at a public alternative school that was loosely structured, continued a negative behavioral pattern. His sometimes destructive behavior had its roots in the first grade—his first year in the school and the school's first year of existence. You might say the school and Allen grew up together. They also grew in different directions. Yearly he devalued academic skills whereas the school staff increasingly emphasized the basic skills. Yearly he became more and more of a student leader and the school was placing more emphasis on adult leadership. It was clearly a problem of changing expectations and a negative cycle for both Allen and the school staff. Whereas we and the staff had tried many times, with Allen's help, to change his behaviors, the attempts were unsuccessful. Things would go smoothly for a few months and then another small crisis would occur. At one point he explained his behavior by saying, "But I've got a reputation to live up to." In a painful and traumatic decision we, with the full cooperation of the school, decided to change the environment and create a whole new set of interpersonal expectations. We moved him to a new school, a new group of peers, a new teacher, and a new set of expectations. Agreements were clear and rules rigidly enforced at school and at home. In the new setting he had no "reputation to live up to" and he was dissatisfied enough with his own behavior to use the opportunity to mold new behaviors, interpersonally and academically. In fact his new teacher commented that in his classroom he saw none of the behaviors that had inspired the move. This experience, coupled with his following year's experience in a strictly controlled, Catholic, Flemish-speaking school and an increasing maturity, changed that unsupportive cycle of interpersonal relations; what was destructive in the cycle changed to a healthy and constructive pattern.

Although classroom teachers do not usually have the opportunity to move a student into a totally new environment, careful diagnosis of the problems and creative interventions at one or two points in the cycle of interpersonal relations can result in some positive changes.

Teacher Expectations and Student Performance

Through circular interpersonal processes such as those described above, teachers' expectations for students' behaviors affect teachers' interactions with students as well as the psychological reactions of the students. Studies on the social psychology of classroom interaction have sought to establish the validity of parts of this theory. They seek, further, to make practical applications of it by pinpointing how the teacher's expectations relate to the quality of the circular interpersonal process, and how different qualities of interpersonal interaction relate to student academic performance. Nash (1976) has fully delineated both the theory and related research in his text, *Teacher Expectations and Pupil Learning,* and Finn et al. (1975) described how those expectations work in a naturalistic study of the classroom.

The Self-Fulfilling Prophecy

An early pioneer in American sociology, W. I. Thomas, set forth a postulate basic to social psychology: "If men define situations as real, they are real in their consequences." Thomas's famous statement provides a useful reminder that human beings respond not merely to objective features of a situation, but also to the meaning the situation has for them. Later, Robert Merton (1949) elaborated on Thomas's postulate in his classic text, *Social Theory and Social Structure,* by introducing the "self-fulfilling prophecy." Merton argued that public predictions or prophecies of a situation can become an integral part of the situation and thus affect subsequent developments.

The self-fulfilling prophecy is, at the outset, an invalid definition of the situation, evoking a new cluster of behaviors which makes the originally false conception come true. In a subsequent text, Merton (1957) wrote that "the self-fulfilling prophecy is, in the beginning, a 'false' conception come 'true.' This specious validity of the self-fulfilling prophecy perpetuates a reign of error. For the prophet will cite the actual course of events as proof that he was right from the very beginning."

In 1968, Rosenthal and Jacobson attempted to show how the self-fulfilling prophecy may work in the classroom. The title of their book, *Pygmalion in the Classroom,* made reference to George Bernard Shaw's story of how an unschooled young woman from the slums is transformed into a "fair lady." A real-life counterpart occurred when F. Scott Fitzgerald designed and implemented a college curriculum for the unschooled Sheilah Graham (Graham,

1967). In their research, Rosenthal and Jacobson presented false information about
their students to a sample of teachers. The
experimenters told the experimental
teachers that some of their youngsters were
assessed to be "academic spurters"; that is,
these spurters would show great progress in
their academic achievement during the
school year. Other youngsters were given
no special designation by the experimenters. In actuality, tests of academic potential were never really administered and
the students who were described as
"spurters" were chosen randomly. Data
collected after the year of schooling showed
that the "spurters" made more significant
gains in intelligence test scores, reading test
scores, and in teachers' ratings about their
personal and social adjustment than their
nonlabeled peers.

Several reviews of *Pygmalion in the
Classroom* severely criticized the research
methods employed in the study (Jensen,
1969). For example, Thorndike (1968) and
Snow (1969) questioned the presumed re-
liability of the I.Q. measures, pointing out
that some of the premeasures of intelligence were incredibly low. These and other
critics also questioned the use of teachers
as data collectors and the accuracy of the
data analyses. Critics pointed out, too, that
the data as presented in the tables and ap-
pendices raised questions as to the interpretations made by Rosenthal and Jacobson.
Rosenthal (1973) himself responded to the
critics by arguing that as many as 84 out of
a possible 242 studies had replicated aspects of the original Pygmalion research,
giving substantial corroboration to the
original findings. Rosenthal argued that
only twelve studies, not eighty-four, would
be expected to support the Pygmalion hypotheses by chance alone.

Finn (1972) and Brophy and Good
(1972) offered very useful and reasonable
reviews of the Pygmalion studies, pointing
to the many methodological problems inherent in this sort of research on the circular interpersonal process. Both reviews
concluded that the research on the self-
fulfilling prophecy in the classroom leaves
little doubt that the expectations of teachers
have important and real effects on students.
However, both reviewers also concluded that
the effects of interpersonal expectations in
the classroom probably are not so strong as
the Pygmalion zealots would have us believe. Nevertheless, one must conclude that
the making of a "fair lady" is observable
and measurable in the classroom.

The Quality of
Teacher-Student Interaction

In the Rosenthal-Jacobson study no data
was collected on interpersonal interaction
between the teacher and the spurters. The
Pygmalion effects were established by
noting statistical variations between what
the experimental teachers were told about
their students (analogous to teachers'
reading cumulative student records) and
how the students changed in their later performances on mental tests. What might actually have occurred within the
interpersonal exchanges associated with
teacher expectations and student academic
performance was studied by Brophy and
Good (1970). Indeed, they established a
new and improved methodology for research on the self-fulfilling prophecy within
the classroom.

Brophy and Good put emphasis on the
quality of teacher-student interaction within
the context of studying Pygmalion effects.
They did not investigate mental test scores,

nor did they attempt to manipulate the teachers' expectations. Instead, they asked four teachers about their current expectations for different students—expectations that were formed naturally—and then studied very carefully the circular interpersonal processes themselves.

Brophy and Good asked the teachers to rank all of their current students according to intellectual ability. Then observers plotted the sorts of circular interpersonal processes that occurred in the four classrooms. The data indicated that those students whom the teachers labeled as having very high ability received more praise, more coaching and help in forming ideas, and more time in answering questions than those who were labeled as low-ability youngsters. In interacting with the students who were designated as having low ability, the teachers were more critical, accepted poorer quality answers, and were less likely to praise good performance, even when quality performance did occur. The research showed that the teachers waited longer for the "high-ability" students to answer difficult questions than for those labeled "low-ability," just the reverse of what most teachers would argue to be sound pedagogy.

Following Brophy and Good's work, a series of research studies has emerged attempting to identify the covert and overt processes of communicating expectations. In a partial replication of the Brophy-Good research, Rubovits and Maehr (1971) studied neophyte student teachers. Those practice teachers were told that their students were either from the "gifted track" or the "regular track" of the schools they attended. Just as in the Brophy and Good study, the teachers paid attention to and

praised the "gifted students" more than they did the "regular students." Rothbart (1971) also showed that teachers were more attentive to students for whom they had high expectations, and Weinstein (1980) focused on how students perceived this different treatment.

Rosenthal (1973) discussed four social-psychological mechanisms by which teachers communicate expectations for student performance: *climate, feedback, input, and output.* Within the first mechanism, high expectations for another's behavior give rise to a climate of warmth, attention, and emotional support. In the second area of feedback, teachers tend to give more encouragement and praise to students for whom they have high expectations. The third mechanism deals with the sorts of input teachers give to students for whom they have high expectations. Teachers rephrase questions, give helpful hints to answers, and give more information to students whom they believe know an answer than they do to "low-ability" students. Finally, the fourth social-psychological mechanism involves the teacher's encouragement for the output of student responses. Teachers wait longer for answers from "high-ability" students than from their "low-ability" peers.

Cooper (1979) wrote an outstanding summary of research on the self-fulfilling prophecy and did a nice job of setting a new research direction. Cooper developed a model for how teachers communicate performance expectations. He specified six steps of causation showing how and why teachers give feedback differently to students for whom they have high expectations (referred to here as high expectation students) and those "at-risk" students for whom they have low expectations (referred to here as low expectation students). The model is as follows:

1. Teachers develop different expectations.

2. Teachers have more concern for *control* of low expectation students and praise efforts of high expectation students.

3. In giving feedback, teachers emphasize control over low expectation students and praise efforts of high expectation students. Thus interaction with low expectation students is not as concerned with student *performance* as it is with controlling behavior.

4. Low expectation students thus receive less praise for performance and they decrease performance initiations, which, in turn, increases the teacher's attempted control. This is how "at-risk" students can become more "at-risk."

5. Low expectation students do not feel as personally in control of the situation; they feel more like "pawns" than "origins," and they exhibit lower achievement motivation than high expectation students. In addition, low expectation students exert less effort than high expectation students toward academic performance.

6. Finally, students' self-esteem and predictions about their performance, which varies with teacher feedback, influences their performance.

Although competent teaching entails helping students move a step beyond their present position, the Pygmalion research indicates that many teachers follow this rule of thumb only for the students for whom they have high expectations. Many teachers do not encourage or demand high performance from "at-risk" students whom they believe have low ability. Apparently for many teachers, their bias in favor of high-ability youngsters is unconscious. And most research on teacher expectation has assumed that teachers are unwitting culprits in a cycle of interpersonal relations. Cooper's article is the first to recognize teacher variability in awareness of how their expectations may affect student behavior. After all, the self-fulfilling prophecy is a concept that has been around for some years and we know many teachers are aware of its implications. Research such as Cooper's can help to specify the concrete behaviors that teachers can change. It is up to teachers to use this research to help improve student performance and to work more effectively with "at-risk" youngsters.

We know from our own experience that giving appropriate and equitable support to all students is not easy. We know, too, that as parents we often have influenced our daughter and son to behave in favorable and unfavorable ways because of our expectations for their behavior. We know that as teachers we often have behaved inappropriately because of our expectations. And we have been sobered indeed by some of our recent observations in classrooms where teachers have said things like, "I don't know why I trouble with you, you'll never get it anyway,"; or "Don't start putting numbers on your papers yet; you'll probably do it all wrong anyway,"; or, "Is everyone ready to move on? Well, those of you who aren't, I don't expect you to ever be ready anyway!"; or, "Each day you get into trouble, and I expect you to get into trouble again today and tomorrow. You'll never amount to anything!"

In writing about the cruelty of negative instances of the self-fulfilling prophecy, and in recalling our own frustrations in trying to conquer the subtle power of interpersonal expectations, we are reminded of a very successful teaching experience Pat had while working with a group of "at-risk" boys with severe learning disabilities. Her initial impression was how unlovable the boys were. They had been academic failures and their self-concepts were very negative. They were often boisterous, uncooperative, and just plain obnoxious. While Pat found it easy to see their faults, she found it very difficult to find their redeeming attributes. Needless to say, she started the school year by not expecting much academic performance and by anticipating a great deal of difficulty.

In attempting to overcome her own negative expectations, we decided that she should try to discover at least one attribute of each boy that was likeable and, hopefully, resourceful. She did find strengths and admirable qualities in each boy that were hidden under many layers of defensiveness and aggressiveness. She employed some of the action ideas found at the end of this chapter and several which are described in later chapters of this book. Her eye was on developing a comfortable climate, on using as much supportive feedback as was feasible and realistic, on attending to any nonverbal cues of confusion from the boys, and on sticking with them to clarify questions, procedures, and assignments. That year and that class of partially disturbed boys turned out to be one of her most satisfying teaching experiences and added existential reality to what we are writing about here.

Once Pat had discovered something favorable about each student, she was liberated from a tendency to coddle or apologize or make allowances for the boys. She felt free to expect and demand adequate academic performances. In her own mind (and stomach), she felt free to say honestly to each youngster, "You will do this assignment because I know that you can do it."

The power of the self-fulfilling prophecy is very real to us. It is a concept that makes a lot of sense. We question its simplicity and are aware of some of the technical difficulties in the research methods. We believe—and some research and considerable experience support our belief—that teachers do influence achievement, sociometric position, self-esteem, and satisfaction of students.

At the same time, not all teachers have such power, and even very powerful teachers do not influence all their students in the same ways. Certainly, we cannot discount the influence of students' families and their neighborhood peer groups. Even in the classroom, the teacher's expectations and resulting behaviors are mediated by the interpersonal norms and relationships in the peer group. We believe, therefore, that student performance is influenced simultaneously by the teacher, by the peer group, and by the family. Teachers' expectations for student achievement are very important, but they represent only one phase of the multiple circular interpersonal processes that are occurring in the lives of the students.

Implications for Teachers

The following summary statements capture the key implications this chapter holds for teachers:

It is natural and psychologically functional to develop expectations, in the form of predictions, for the behaviors of students. Those interpersonal expectations are reciprocal in that both teachers and students hold them, and they usually include both cognitive elements and an evaluative assessment.

It is important, both for the achievement of instructional objectives and for the development of a supportive social climate, to be aware of the expectations held by each member of the class, including ourselves as teachers.

Our expectations for how each student might behave in the future influence the ways in which we ourselves behave toward the student.

It is important to engage in introspection and to diagnose one's own beliefs about those expectations, as well as to obtain feedback about the ways in which we are behaving toward each student. It is also important to use many diverse sources of information in seeking to understand what makes each student behave as he or she does. In particular, be aware of your expectations and attributions toward blacks and whites, girls and boys, and students of different social classes.

Our relationships and patterns of interaction with students often become stable and regularized over time.

It is important to be open to modifying our expectations and behaviors toward students upon receiving new information. At times we will have to seek new information about students deliberately in order to free ourselves of stereotypes.

Our continual treatment of students in particular ways can influence those

students to behave in the manner we expect them to behave.

It is crucial, given this state of affairs, to know about and to have the skills to implement action plans for breaking into negative circular interpersonal processes.

Action Ideas for Improving Climate

The following classroom practices were carried out by teachers who were attempting to reduce the detrimental effects of interpersonal expectations in the classroom.

Confronting Negative Cycles With "At-Risk" Youngsters

A junior high teacher, working with a noisy and inattentive class, introduced a simplified version of the diagram of circular interpersonal processes (shown in Figure 4.1) as an instructional device. She discussed how all people can become involved in negative cycles, drawing some examples from Figure 4.3. Next, the teacher asked the students to enact some dramatic vignettes which she had developed to depict the ways in which negative cycles get going. She developed several scripts, using ideas from a book on role playing by Chesler and Fox (1966) in which each character's intentions and expectations were made clear to the students. It was up to the students to behave as they imagined the characters would have behaved. After about three weeks, and when the students had become accustomed to discussing interpersonal difficulties, the teacher used actual classroom events, from both planned lessons and spontaneous behavior. All of the negative and disruptive behaviors were not eliminated, but they typically were ended rather quickly as a consequence of this curriculum. Although the teacher worked with this kind of curriculum for only the last four months of school, she planned to implement it from the very beginning of the next school year.

Role Playing

Role playing is a specialized technique that has been used in a variety of professions and settings (see especially Chesler and Fox, 1966, and Shaftel and Shaftel, 1967). Role playing permits open investigation of areas that often stay hidden; it demonstrates the dynamics of human exchange. The novice to directive role playing should begin with simple scripts and, with increasing skill, move into scripts with more complex emotion.

The sequence in using role playing entails: (1) selecting the problem; (2) warming up; (3) setting the stage by explaining the situation, describing participant roles, and explaining audience roles; (4) enactment; (5) analysis and discussion; (6) evaluation; (7) re-enactment of the role play; and (8) generalizing to the daily life of the classroom.

Role Playing The Self-Fulfilling Prophecy

To demonstrate the power of the self-fulfilling prophecy, one teacher created an experiment using stooges. A word of caution is in order: creating a script with stooges takes some personal risk. There are usually only one or two people uninformed about what happens—they should be carefully selected and the event should be fully revealed to them as soon as possible.

A fictitious discipline problem was being discussed by a 7th-grade class. After the problems were made clear, four student consultants were chosen to make a plan of action—what to do about the discipline problem. They had ten planning minutes in a different room and then were to report to the class. The class was informed that everything two of the consultants said was to be praised and accepted, whereas everything the other two consultants said was to be criticized and rejected. The consultants presented the plan; discussion lasted ten to fifteen minutes; then the stooges were fully informed of the plan. The discussion focused then on the feelings and subsequent behaviors of praise and acceptance, criticism, and rejection.

Understanding Self-Expectations

One teacher used the model of research reported earlier in this chapter on self-expectations. As a routine part of tests, students were asked to estimate their performance. After the test, they were given feedback. Finally they discussed why they were accurate or inaccurate in their self-assessments. The objective was to make students more accurate in their self-estimates and to help them to think about how they could improve.

Class Expectations and Pluralistic Ignorance

Pluralistic ignorance is a group phenomenon; each individual believes he or she knows what others think about an issue, but their thoughts are incorrect. For example, if several people are asked the question, "Would you object to living next door to a person from the Middle East?" and all respond, "No, I would not mind, but my neighbors would," this is a case of pluralistic ignorance. Everyone incorrectly assumes what other people think. The following list of questions in Instrument 4.1 helps check the pervasiveness of pluralistic ignorance; each person not only answers for himself or herself but also makes estimates of what others think. The questions are samples; teachers should make up questions that are pertinent to their classes.

Expectations and Stereotypes: Sex Roles

An expectation is a working prediction about the world. Expectations can be accurate or inaccurate and they are easily changed. We all have them; they are normal. A stereotype is an expectation—or a working prediction—about a category of people, such as meeting an individual from

---

INSTRUMENT 4.1
Class Expectation Survey

	What I would say, do, or think	What others would say, do, or think
When a teacher says or does something that I don't like, I will tell the teacher about it in private.	Yes ___ No ___	Yes ___ No ___
When I do something a teacher does not like, I want the teacher to tell me about it in private.	Yes ___ No ___	Yes ___ No ___
When another student does something I don't like, I will tell the person about it in private.	Yes ___ No ___	Yes ___ No ___
When I do something another student does not like, I want the student to tell me about it in private.	Yes ___ No ___	Yes ___ No ___
When I disagree with someone, I will tell that person.	Yes ___ No ___	Yes ___ No ___
When someone disagrees with me, I want that person to tell me.	Yes ___ No ___	Yes ___ No ___
I think cheating in class is wrong.	Yes ___ No ___	Yes ___ No ___
I like school.	Yes ___ No ___	Yes ___ No ___
This is a good class.	Yes ___ No ___	Yes ___ No ___

a particular category and assuming the individual, too, has the characteristic expected of the category. Stereotypes are often false but they do not change easily. Examples of stereotypes are: red heads have tempers, football players are dumb, girls can't do math, people who wear glasses are smart, fat people are happy.

A junior high school teacher in a discussion about stereotypes used the following exercise. The class was broken up into same-sex groups of about four to seven students. They were asked to answer four questions; each group had a large sheet of newsprint to write answers large enough to be visible to the whole class. Students took a fifty-minute period to answer the questions in small groups and another fifty-minute period to present and discuss the ideas. The questions were:

For Boys' Groups:

1. What I like about being a boy.

2. What I don't like about being a boy.

3. What I like about girls.

4. What I don't like about girls.

For Girls' Groups:

1. What I like about being a girl.

2. What I don't like about being a girl.

3. What I like about boys.

4. What I don't like about boys.

Another time the teacher varied the exercise to check male and female pluralistic ignorance and asked the questions this way.

1. What I like about my sex.

2. What the other sex likes about my sex.

3. What I don't like about my sex.

4. What the other sex doesn't like about my sex.

Recognizing Individual Differences: The Animal School

A third-grade teacher introduced us to a vignette about "The Animal School," which apparently has been passed down in various forms through the generations with the originator being unknown. The teacher would read the story to his students, and then hold a discussion with the students about its implications for their class and for themselves. The teacher's goal was to help students develop appreciation for the individual differences in the class. The story is as follows:

One time the animals had a school. The curriculum consisted of running, climbing, diving, and swimming. All the animals took all the subjects.

The duck was good in swimming, better, in fact, than his instructor, and he made passing grades in flying, but he was practically hopeless in running. Because he was low in this subject, he was made to stay after school and drop his swimming class to practice running. He kept this up until he was only average in swimming. But average is acceptable, so nobody worried about that except the duck.

The eagle was considered a problem pupil and was disciplined severely. She beat all the others to the top of the tree in climbing class, but she had her own way of getting there.

The rabbit started at the top of the class in running, but he had a nervous breakdown and he had to drop out of school on account of so much make-up work in swimming.

The squirrel led the climbing class, but her flying teacher made her start her flying lessons from the ground instead of the top of the tree down and she developed charley horses from the overexertion at the take-off and began getting C's in climbing and D's in running.

The practical prairie dogs apprenticed their offspring to a badger when the school authorities refused to add digging to the curriculum.

At the end of the year, an abnormal eel that could swim well, run, climb, and fly a little was made Valedictorian.

Raising Peers' Expectations of Isolated, "At-Risk" Students

A sixth-grade teacher wanted to bring several isolated youngsters more squarely into the classroom peer group. After corroborating her suspicions of their isolation through a sociometric inventory, the teacher asked one of her colleagues to collaborate in finding ways of integrating the three isolates into the group. Because all three students were generally successful at schoolwork, they were asked to serve as tutors in the other teacher's class for one hour every other day. Along with these three, several other less isolated children were also asked to serve as tutors. The fact that a total of six students were granted preferential treatment could hardly go unnoticed by their classroom peers. The teacher also went to special lengths to praise and encourage the three isolates during regular class time. It should be noted, parenthetically, that these isolates did not display overt behavior problems, but were simply being ignored by their peers. After five months, the teacher administered another sociometric inventory from which she discovered that the isolates were being chosen by several classmates.

They had not become "stars," but they had made headway in gaining some acceptance from classmates.

Combining Student and Teacher Expectations for Learning: The Learning Contract

The expectations of students and teachers for academic learning can be integrated and brought into increased agreement by their cooperatively building contracts for learning. Through collaborative discussions about learning goals and instructional procedures, students and teachers can reach some agreement about what is to be learned, how it will be learned, and how long the learning process will take. We will illustrate such "contract-building" with two actual cases: one plan was designed and implemented by a high school math teacher; the second was developed by the teacher of a self-contained, third-grade class.

The high school math teacher decided upon the basic concepts and skills which he enumerated for the students as the competency requirements. He then stipulated a particular period of time (usually two to three weeks) and a system of accountability (most often a written test, but sometimes an oral exam or a project). Thus, he offered several alternative paths which the students could take in learning to perform the tasks in the allotted time. Some options included working cooperatively with several peers, using old workbooks and ditto sheets (new programmed materials were not available), working with a student-teacher in a small group, or working through a large lecture-discussion with the teacher.

At the beginning of each work period, the teacher would present the tasks to be mastered, and the students were asked to decide how they would attempt to master the lessons, ultimately presenting a written contract (indicating the means and schedule) to the teacher. The teacher offered conferences for those students whom he thought could not handle the contract-building. Competency tests could be taken at any time and no limits were placed on how many times they could be repeated. Many students would finish the competency requirements early, and a supply of learning games were available for these youngsters. In fact, one war game lasted so long that a previously underachieving student worked for long periods of time outside of class to complete his competency requirements so that he could return to the game.

A third-grade teacher used learning contracts in a more general way. Each day students were asked to write down how they would spend their time on the next day. At the very beginning of the year, the students planned for only one hour, then for half a day, and finally for the whole day. By the end of the year, many students were preparing week-long plans. The teacher also asked the students to put down one new major learning objective for themselves every week. Those objectives were as varied as learning the multiplication tables, learning not to interrupt, making a new friend, finishing a report, or making a spaceship. On each Friday the students met in small groups to review their progress. Those discussions with peers were especially helpful in giving new ideas to students who were experiencing confusion about how to design and write up their contracts.

Leadership

5

The human striving to wield influence over important others is basic. It enters into classroom life whenever both formal and informal leadership are executed by the teacher or by students. Leadership essentially means influence or power over other people, and influence over others enables teachers or students to do things, to get things, and to accomplish objectives that, by themselves, are unattainable. The teacher has the greatest potential for leadership in the classroom, but in being a leader the teacher must bring the student leaders along. Thus, to limit leadership functions in the classroom solely to the teacher would not present an accurate picture of classroom group processes. Most teachers have faced some active or passive resistance by students and realize that power does not reside solely in the ascribed role of the formal leader. Indeed, influence over others implies their consent. And in the classroom, leadership is actually performed by many members of the group, for students influence other students in many significant ways.

Some students' influence can be in opposition to the goals of the school. A classroom with a favorable social climate has leadership performed by many students and the teacher. The potential for influencing another person is an important facet of students' feelings of self-worth and satisfies the basic striving for power. In classrooms where only a few students are able to influence others, powerlessness and negative feelings about self and school are often the resulting responses of those who have no power.

Objectives of this Chapter

In this chapter, we aim to help you, the reader, understand concepts and research on leadership in the classroom. It is particularly important to note the actual power that students can wield and how student leadership interacts with teacher leadership. It is also important to note what a teacher can do to act as an effective leader. The chapter summarizes the functions, psychological and social bases, and dynamics of leadership. It goes on to draw implications for the teacher, both in terms of diagnostic schemes to understand how leadership is functioning in the classroom and in terms of action ideas for improving the class's leadership dynamics.

Leadership Conceptualized

Leadership has been conceptualized from two very different perspectives—as a property of an individual or as that of a group. The former perspective conceptualizes leadership as the psychological traits of the individual exerting influence, while the latter perspective views leadership as interpersonal exchanges and as social-psychological properties of a group.

From the individual point of view, leadership is analyzed in terms of the personality traits or social background characteristics of the leader. Historically, this position has been emphasized more by behavioral scientists than has the social-psychological perspective, but it has had definite limitations. In general, the research has not led to consistent results about the traits or behaviors of effective leaders. After summarizing studies on leadership traits carried out between 1948 and 1970, Stoghill (1974) concluded that for the most part, personality measures have not proved to be predictive or useful for the selection of leaders. Similar conclusions were reached in the reviews of Fielder (1971) and Burns (1978).

While certain clusters of personality characteristics, such as a drive for responsibility, vigor, persistence in pursuit of goals, initiative, self-confidence, and willingness to deal with stress, often seem to typify successful leaders, there are many other effective leaders who have other combinations of traits. Indeed, the ability to lead successfully appears to entail much more than a single set of personality characteristics. Ryan (1960) has confirmed this view in showing that research on the personality traits of successful teachers has not led to any consistent findings. In fact, according to Ryan's thorough review of research, effective teachers appear to have a full array of traits with no particular personality pattern standing out. The contemporary point of view is the idea that teachers can learn to be more effective leaders, not by executing a set plan of action, but by sizing up the class and by using appropriate interventions. Flexibility and insight are more important than particular personality traits.

The second perspective emphasizes interaction within a group and appears to be more useful for understanding how influence works within the classroom. Here leadership entails such variables as social prestige, the holding of legitimate authority, the performance of duties in a role, and the emotional relationship between leader and followers. A significant point about this perspective is its emphasis on the transactional interchanges between the person exerting leadership and those who accept the influence. This view includes the social structures of the group and leadership as an interpersonal event that occurs within those structures. Leadership is not simply a personal style, intent, or skills of an individual.

We believe that a combination of those two perspectives offers a fruitful way of thinking about leadership in the classroom. Leadership starts with the teacher taking action, and therefore how the teacher thinks about leadership and executes it will make a difference in how students react. Still, groups and situations differ and a teacher who holds fast to a single leadership strategy is doomed to failure over the long run. The social nature of leadership must be paramount in the teacher's mind.

Leadership is an interpersonal influence process; it is at least dyadic rather than an attribute of a single person. It is a verb rather than a noun. In those senses, leadership is viewed as behaviors, some desirable and some undesirable, that help the group move toward particular objectives. Desirable leadership consists of actions that aid in setting academic goals, moving the group toward its academic goals, improving the quality of the interactions among the members, building the cohesiveness of the group, or making individual competencies available to the group.

Functional Leadership

The desirable influences we referred to in the preceding section may be conceptualized according to what theorists of group dynamics—in the traditions of both Lewin and Moreno—have labeled "functional leadership." Leadership behaviors are interpersonal influences which help a group carry out its needed group functions so that its group goals will be reached. Leadership is viewed as the performance of acts which help a group achieve its preferred outcomes, and it is a dynamic process which exists between members of the classroom group. Such a view frees us from the concept that only teachers exert leadership in the classroom. Students also perform group functions; sometimes their behaviors facilitate classroom learning and at other times they impede it. In fact, it appears that students wield great amounts of classroom leadership. This becomes obvious when students are victorious in a struggle with the authorities of the school. How functional student leadership can be for achieving desirable goals is, of course, problematic.

We have observed the following sorts of leadership behaviors on the part of students in the classroom: students stating out loud that another student has done a good or a poor job on an academic task; teachers asking students to help one another when working on difficult assignments; students comforting a peer who has been hurt; students copying the defiant behavior of another student; and students reminding one another of work that is due or classroom behavior that is expected.

Thus, as we analyze classroom leadership, it is useful to step beyond the view that functional leadership is wielded only by the teacher and to look at leadership as influence occurring within a classroom group. Emphasis is on interpersonal influence within the group—whether or not it is about academic concerns. *Leadership is behavior which influences others in the classroom group to follow. Sometimes such behaviors are employed by the teacher; at other times they are executed by students. Sometimes they may facilitate reaching educational goals; on other occasions they may impede the achievement of those goals.* Of course, our major concern is with promoting leadership behaviors which facilitate academic objectives.

Task and Social-Emotional Functions

Class members can influence one another in many different ways, but two general categories of group functions, *task* and *social-emotional,* have been described as necessary for group effectiveness (for details, see the classic article by Benne and Sheats, 1948, and the work of Parsons and Bales that was summarized in chapter 3). *Task functions help accomplish the work-oriented, subject matter requirements of the classroom, while social-emotional functions help the group maintain its internal cohesion and favorable interpersonal feelings.* Examples of task functions are activities such as initiating ideas, seeking information, giving information, clarifying or elaborating, summarizing, or checking to see if others in the class understand the content that is being taught. Task functions in the classroom include presenting an outline of what is to be learned, lecturing on a substantive topic, asking questions to get information about a topic, explaining why a phenomenon works the way it does, testing to see if material is being learned, and evaluating performances in the class to give feedback about progress in learning a particular topic.

Examples of social-emotional functions are such activities as encouraging others, expressing feelings in the class, harmonizing, compromising, seeing that silent members get a chance to speak, and applying previously agreed upon standards to the class's functioning. Social-emotional functions that take place in the classroom include giving pats on the back because of a good performance, calming down those who are frustrated or angry, asking questions of silent members to encourage them to speak, reminding group members of previous group agreements, tracking progress on an assignment, smiling and joking to communicate good feelings, and expressing concern about the way another person feels. Ideally, most, if not all, students should be able to perform both task and social-emotional functions, but generally they do not. The teacher, in most classrooms, typically performs both sets of functions. Furthermore, in most classes, a few students perform only a very few of the group functions, and quite often the functions that the students do perform are from the social-emotional side rather than the task functions.

The perspective of functional leadership emphasizes the transactional nature of group processes in the classroom. The meaning of any particular leadership act or the execution of any one of the group functions arises within the social context of interpersonal relationships between class members and takes place at a particular time in relation to a certain task. Thus class members who are disliked or viewed as incompetent typically will not be successful in executing a group function, even if their behaviors are appropriate, timely, and competent. Similarly, students who are well-liked may also be ineffective in their influence if they choose to perform a group function at the wrong time, or if they fail to perform the function competently.

Executing classroom leadership entails both interpersonal relationships and behavioral skills. It requires competent behaviors toward others, and the meaning of any behavior will depend, in part, on the nature of the relationship between the members. Teachers who have the objective of helping students improve their performance of the task and social-emotional functions need to be concerned with two factors. They must be aware of the students' behavioral repertoires for performing such acts and of the quality of the interpersonal relations and norms within the classroom group that determine the meaning and impact of such leadership behaviors.

Psychological Bases of Influence

An analysis of the bases of interpersonal influence can be helpful for understanding how leadership works in the classroom. French and Raven (1959) have developed five concepts about the bases of interpersonal influence. Their set of categories includes:

1.   Expert power—the extent of relevant knowledge and skill that a person is viewed as possessing, e.g., teachers' knowing a lot about their specialty, a student's knowing a lot about a subject, or a student's having had experience with a teacher or a school for several years.

2.   Referent power—the extent of identification or closeness that others feel toward the target person, e.g., students' thinking of their teacher as a great person, a student's wishing to have the skills or knowledge of another student, and teachers' viewing students as growing up in families similar to their own.

3.   Legitimate power—stemming from the internalized values that others hold toward the accepted right of a person to be influential, e.g., students' believing that their teacher should have the right to boss them around, students' giving a peer special status after the latter has been elected to a position of influence, and teachers' viewing students as having certain rights that limit the influence methods the teachers can rightfully use in the classroom.

4. *Reward power*—the extent to which a person is viewed as having ability to mete out rewards, e.g., students' watching the teacher for supportive comments, smiles, and pats on the back, teachers' listening to favorable comments from parents about their youngsters' experiences in the classroom, and students' observing which of their peers say nice things about them.

5. *Coercive power*—the extent to which a person is viewed as being able to punish others, e.g., students' fearing that their teacher will evaluate them negatively, teachers' feeling anxious about the critical comments of some students or their parents, and students' avoiding getting near another student who is perceived as a bully.

According to research by Hornstein et al. (1968), teachers prefer to work more with a principal who employs expert or referent power than with one who imposes legitimate or coercive power. We suspect, moreover, that much the same would be true for students in relation to their teachers.

Subsequent to the classical article by French and Raven, Raven and Kruglanski (1975) added a sixth base of influence, i.e, *informational power,* and Hersey and Goldsmith (cited in Hersey, 1984) introduced a seventh, i.e, *connection power.* They were defined as follows:

6. *Informational power*—the amount of insider information a person has about the history, culture, and customs of the group, e.g., teachers having taught in the same classroom and school for many years, and students' knowing a lot of personal infor-

mation about other students. Informational power may be categorized as a special kind of expert power.

7. *Connection power*—the number of close relationships that a person has with other key members of the group, e.g., teachers' communicating with key staff members within the school or with influential citizens outside the school, and student's communicating with influential peers within the school or with influential adults outside the school.

Those seven bases of influence can be observed within the classroom by looking at how both *teacher authority* and *student power* are executed. A teacher's legitimate power is not achieved by dint of personal effort. A teacher has authority because of values communicated to the students and their parents by the larger community. The school, as a formal organization, and the community, through its elected school board, indirectly designate the teacher as the legitimate and official authority in the classroom. Moreover, state laws usually grant the teacher power to wield control and often place duties of a custodial nature upon the teacher. For two useful analyses on how teacher authority is rooted in community values see Thelen (1954) and Jenkins (1960).

The position of legitimate authority held by the teacher has three bases of interpersonal influence: legitimate, reward, and coercive. Research indicates that these three are the least effective of the seven bases of power for exerting interpersonal influence, yet we cannot deny that teachers have power in the classroom. The major question for understanding leadership in the classroom is *not* that teachers have authority invested in their position, but rather *how* their authority is exerted interpersonally. Several studies support the supposition that successfully influential teachers develop *referent, expert, informational,* and *connection* bases of power with their students.

One relevant research project on the bases of influence within the classroom was done by Kounin and Gump (1958), who analyzed several hundred videotapes on classroom interaction to study ways in which teachers use their authority to discipline students. They were concerned with effects on the rest of the class of a teacher's use of coercive power over one misbehaving student. They called the resulting current of social activity emanating through the peer group the "ripple effect." The research indicated that the most effective way for a teacher to use coercive power was to be quite specific and clear in giving instructions or in making a disciplinary intervention. For example, when a teacher demanded, "Eric, put down the truck and go to the painting table," in contrast to simply, "Eric, stop that," the probabilities were much better that Eric would conform and that other students who observed the more specific command would be more conforming to subsequent teacher requests.

Conversely, Kounin and Gump found that while harsh, punitive, and non-specific techniques usually led to immediate changes in the behaviors of the misbehaving student, those disciplinary tactics backfired because observing students would be subsequently more disruptive. Using the concepts of the bases of influence, Kounin and Gump's research showed that teachers' coercive power can be increased when they also hold referent and connection power. Indeed, teachers who are attempting to discipline students have greatest leverage when the students are attracted to them and, in some sense, identify with them (see Kounin 1979, for details).

All teachers enter their classrooms with legitimate power ascribed to them, power which also includes both the reward and the coercive variety. The leadership of teachers in terms of real influence appears to be enhanced if they distribute group functions to the students, encourage independence, stimulate open communication, and attempt to become attractive to the students. Holding on tightly to authority and only occasionally allowing students to influence what happens in the classroom often leads to high dependency, as well as to resistance and interpersonal tension and friction. In short, teachers should attempt to establish influence, based on referent, expert, informational, and connection power to supplement the legitimate, reward, and coercive bases of power that they already hold.

According to Jenkins (1960), the teacher who strives to accent expert and informational power has two essential functions as leader: the first is creating physical and psychological conditions in the classroom that facilitate academic work, and the second is organizing study activities so that appropriate learning may be achieved. How well those two teacher responsibilities are carried out becomes the chief criteria of effective leadership for teachers.

The students, too, are important agents of influence. Even though students do not hold legitimate authority, they do have significant power in the classroom. They can get their peers to do things by rewarding them with smiles, gifts, or other inducements. They can also wield influence by coercing peers through threats of physical punishment or exclusion. Some students are influential because they are charismatic, i.e., others find them attractive and can identify with them. Still others are able to get their peers to follow them because they are viewed as experts, because they have important information, and because they are connected to key peers and adults.

Several empirical studies have systematically explored the characteristics of students with high power in formal group or classroom settings (see Polansky, Lippitt, and Redl 1950 and Gold 1958, as examples). That research has generally shown that influential students possess attributes that are valued by members of the peer group. Students who hold positions of high power are good at doing things (expert power) and have a cluster of highly valued personal characteristics (referent power) such as strength, good looks, friendliness, and helpfulness in interpersonal relations. Moreover, the actions of powerful students are typically observed more closely by their peers than the actions of others in the classroom. Thus, powerful students can either measurably enhance or inhibit effective classroom group processes by their actions.

The teacher who can help influential students feel involved in the classroom will have an easier time influencing the entire group than a teacher who is in conflict with the high-power students. Additional research on the "ripple effect" by Kounin, Gump, and Ryan (1961) indicated that the ripples of disturbance in the class were greatest when students with high power were the targets of the teacher's disciplinary actions. The entire class showed interpersonal tension and behavioral disturbances when the high-power students showed defiance toward the teacher's requests. Conversely, detrimental and disturbing ripple effects were barely discernible when low-power students were the targets of a teacher's disciplinary actions.

The bases of teacher power can be significantly undermined when overt conflict occurs frequently with high-power students. Since quite often the power of students is based on their being identification figures who are attractive (referent and connection power), and teacher power is based primarily on legitimacy, high-power students have more influence over the peer group than the teacher does. When teachers face overt conflict with students in the classroom, they cannot achieve influence and increase student learning by simply resorting to their legitimate authority or by using punishment. Coercion may gain short-term, overt compliance, but punitive behaviors will reduce the students' longer term interest and lessen the likelihood of the students' reaching important academic goals. Direct, open encounters between students and teacher—those which recognize the *right* of students to have some power over their own classroom procedures—can be used as a means for developing plans and procedures acceptable to both parties. The teacher who learns the skill of sharing decision making with students will generally achieve some referent and connection power and will, in fact, have fewer instances of overt power struggles.

The issues of power in the classroom—who has power and how it is used—are relevant to an understanding of classroom climate. Students who feel powerful and influential tend also to be happy, effective, and curious. Teachers who feel influential with their students can relate closely to students while also providing clear and direct leadership in pursuit of academic subjects.

Class members with some influence feel secure and useful in the classroom. But students who feel powerlessness also tend to possess poor images of themselves. They feel negative about school and do not perform at levels consonant with their abilities. Powerlessness also induces anxiety; the classroom becomes a threatening and insecure place. *A classroom with a favorable social climate is one in which all students see themselves as having some influence.* Although shared power and influence are difficult to establish, a teacher can begin by distributing part of the legitimate power to students and by arranging for students to participate actively in classroom leadership positions.

In their classic study of leadership (under the guidance of Kurt Lewin), White and Lippitt (1960) studied three types of leader behavior in boys' clubs. Each leader's authority was rooted in legitimate influence, but there was a difference in the way each power position was played out in interaction with the boys. The autocratic leader's power was based mostly in legitimacy and coercion, and, to some extent, in his rewarding the students. He made virtually all of the group's decisions. He gave specific directions as to what the work was supposed to be and how it would be accomplished. The autocratic leader kept and used all of the legitimate power that was given to him.

The democratic leader, in contrast, based his power more on the boys' identifying with him, and, to some extent, on his expertise. He distributed more power throughout the group by asking the boys to perform many of the group's functions. He asked the students to decide among alternatives, and he informed them of the various materials that they might use as they set out to work. In short, the democratic leader used his authority to distribute influence among the younger members of the group. The "laissez-faire" leader abdicated his authority and performed very little leadership behavior. The only basis of power that he retained was that of legitimacy, which eroded because he did not exert his legitimate power.

It is interesting to note that the designation of laissez-faire leader occurred after the research was under way. In their design with Lewin, Lippitt and White originally had set out to contrast the effects of democratic and authoritarian leadership, but during the research they found that some of the leaders who were labeled democratic did not attempt very much leadership, nor did they provide mechanisms to disperse the influence among group members. The effects on the group climate were evident, and the behaviors of the students were strikingly different under the three types of leadership. Boys with the laissez-faire leaders, for example, experienced the most stress. They were disorganized, frustrated, and produced little, if any, work. Groups with autocratic leaders produced quantitatively more work, but the democratic groups were qualitatively better in their performance. The most outstanding difference between the autocratic and democratic groups, however, was not in their productivity, but rather in the interpersonal relations between the leader and members, and among the members. Hostility, competitiveness, and high dependency marked the autocratic group, while openness, friendly communication, and independence typified the democratically led group.

Social Status as a Basis of Power

While the famous studies by Lewin, Lippitt, and White (1939), Anderson (1939), and Withall (1951) all tended to show that democratically collaborative and student-centered teachers encouraged the best peer group climates, later reviews by Stern (1962) and McKeachie (1963) suggest that for some academic goals, authoritarian, teacher-centered leadership can be superior. For example, whereas democratic leadership may be better for the development of favorable attitudes as well as group skills, autocratic methods may be superior for the acquisition of facts and concepts. Moreover, the early studies on democratic leadership focused almost entirely on teacher behaviors rather than on the possible effects of the sociological power differential that exists between "adult teachers" and "minor students."

Indeed, objectively unequal power relationships, such as those involving teachers and students, may very well induce powerlessness. The pitfalls of student powerlessness were delineated very well by Kozol (1967), Herndon (1965), Kohl (1967), and Silberman (1970). And the alternative school movement represents a response on a large scale to the desire of students to have more of a say in classroom procedures and their own learning goals.

In a critical review of the literature on power in public schools, Tjosvold (1976) summarized some ways in which the authority hierarchy of administrators and teachers can pose problems for group processes in the classroom. Tjosvold points out several factors: (1) School personnel often use their status to control unilaterally many student behaviors that are unrelated to academic achievement, and, by so doing, fail to facilitate the objective of creating skillful, self-directed, responsible adults. (2) Confronted with students they believe are uncommitted to classroom procedures and academic goals, educators may use their power in ways that may backfire. So, for example, the use of isolation or expulsion may enhance educator power, but usually won't encourage academic learning. (3) People who occupy unequal social status usually have interpersonal relationships characterized by inaccurate communication, deception, competition, and ineffective conflict resolution. For example, students in trouble will not seek the advice or assistance of educational authorities. Tjosvold concluded his summary by arguing for the need for structural change in schools, along with the behavioral changes pointed to in the democratic leadership studies. He suggested cooperative structures to decrease the inevitably superior social status of school administrators and teachers and to increase student participation in school-related problem solving and decision making.

It is not just the students who suffer because of social status differentials in our schools, but also the teachers, counselors, and administrators. Unequal status and power can have negative effects on the superordinate and subordinate persons and their relationships as well. Lord Acton wrote in 1887 that "Power tends to corrupt and absolute power corrupts absolutely." Paulo Freire (1970) in his *Pedagogy of the Oppressed* explained similarly how unplanned collusion between the oppressors and those who are oppressed is to the disadvantage of both of their educations. Many contemporary feminists point to the inevitable negative consequences of sex stereotyping which affect both men and women and the relationships they have with one another. According to Boocock (1973), social status inequities and their attendant consequences are recurrent themes not only in the social sciences but in philosophy and literature as well.

Even in the face of all of the theory and research which indicate the benefits to be gained by decreasing status differentials between students and teachers, we all know of many teachers who are highly valued and revered, even though they hold despotic control over students. These despotic teachers always seem to hold high-expert and informational power, but at the same time they use a considerable amount of coercion and negative criticism to intimidate their students. One college student we knew consistently complained about the horrible remarks her professor would utter in class and at work, yet she continued to look forward to classes with him and to working near him. When questioned as to why she continued those associations without being required to, her response was, "I know he's a bastard and that I'm afraid of him, but he knows so very much!"

Universities may have some "bastards who know a lot," but there are typically only a very few superior students who can benefit from them. In our elementary and secondary schools we can't afford very many grouchy, cantankerous experts. Perhaps in very stable communities it is possible for "bastards" to gain expert status over time and to become acceptable, but in rapidly changing, pluralistic communities the case for insensitive interpersonal relations and a punitive style is hard to build for the teacher and the administrator. And, as we have argued previously, an educator's leadership will be significantly impaired as students come to reject that educator's expertise and legitimacy.

Sex Roles as Bases of Influence

In our society there is a definite absence of women in leadership roles in government, business, medicine, law, industry, religious life, and education. Even in the field of public education where women have predominated since the Civil War, 98 percent of the district superintendents and about 80 percent of the principals are men. The reasons for women's lack of representation in leadership positions are, of course, multifaceted. Discriminatory laws, formal institutional practices governing admission and advancement, and community customs regarding what is appropriate behavior for men and women all serve as sociological explanations for male-female leadership differences in our society. Moreover, through their family and classroom socialization experiences, girls and boys learn to internalize the idea that it is a man's job to be in charge. Michael Apple (1983), for instance, argues that the sex segregation of the educational work force, where women teach and men manage, replicates power relationships in the family and society in general. The expanding research on sex inequities in education is summarized and reviewed in Stockard and Schmuck et al. (1980), and in Schmuck (1987).

Paula Johnson (1976) provides specific examples of how the bases of social power are used differently by males and females. Johnson hypothesizes that expert, reward, and coercive power are used differently by males and females because of their different experiences during early socialization. With regard to expert power, girls learn early that they should not display their expertise and knowledge openly—especially when in the company of boys. The classic bind girls face is, "If I do too well in school, who will ask me to the senior prom?"

The stereotypic female orientation toward males is one of helplessness. Girls who behave as helpless toward boys eventually come to believe they are less competent than boys. In Patricia Schmuck's 1976 studies of public school women administrators, the "Who, me?" question of wonder was illustrated several times. Adult women, when asked to take on a task of influence and responsibility, often responded, "Who, me?" implying both their own sense of incompetence and their self-perception of low worth toward others.

The reward and coercive bases of power are also used differently by males and females. Females tend to use them more indirectly than males, i.e., with threats of anger, tears, or ingratiation, while males use each of those bases of power more directly. In fact, the direct uses of rewards and coercion have been designated as stereotyped masculine behavior—females who use rewards and coercion overtly and directly are considered to be masculine, and boys who execute rewards and coercion indirectly are labeled "feminine" or "sissy."

Legitimate power, according to Johnson, is complex because it relies heavily on the personality style of the individual and on prior experiences during early socialization. People who use legitimate power must believe they have the right and responsibility to influence others, and the persons being influenced must feel obligated to comply. Women do not hold many legitimate power positions in our society, except in the field of public education. Their le-

gitimate power in education, however, is typically toward students—not toward adult professionals, as evidenced by the small number of women in public school administrative positions. According to an analysis by Eagly and Wood (1985), the widely held belief that women are easily influenced is the idea that in western society, men tend to hold higher status positions than women and therefore possess more legitimate authority.

In an effort to see if female and male teachers differed in the ways they behaved toward girls and boys, Brophy and Good (1970) investigated and summarized a large number of relevant studies. They were unable to uncover any significant differences between teachers of the two sexes. Men and women teachers alike treated boys and girls differently, and consistently so. Boys were more active, interacted with teachers more frequently, and the interactions tended to be more negative compared with interactions between teachers and girls. Torrance (1965) observed similar sex differences in his studies of creativity. Regardless of the sex of the teachers, they tended to recognize the creative behavior of boys more often and rewarded the boys for creativity, whereas teachers communicated to girls the demand for conformity. These and other studies suggest that male and female teachers reward boys for one set of behaviors and girls for another. In addition, peer group members themselves are strong reinforcers of the sex-stereotyped behaviors that are expected by the teachers. Thus, classroom behaviors of both the teacher and the students consciously or unconsciously, wittingly or unwittingly, perpetuate sex-stereotyped behavior.

Throughout the history of sociology, social status has been designated as a very important variable for understanding social interaction. As early as 1908, Simmel wrote, "The first condition of having to deal with somebody is to know with *whom* one has to deal." The sex of an individual is a significant status characteristic in our society. Indeed, being male or female communicates certain status characteristics, not only symbolically, but also behaviorally.

In reviewing the literature on leadership in mixed-sex groups, Lockheed (1976), for example, came up with three generalizations. (1) Men are more active than women; that is, men initiate more verbal acts than women. (2) Men are more influential than women; that is, women are more likely to yield to men's opinions than men are to women's. (3) Men are more task-oriented and women are more social-emotional; that is, men make more suggestions that move groups toward the completion of a task, whereas women initiate a higher proportion of responses relating to the emotional support of members. We should hasten to add that according to Eagly and Wood's (1985) review, Lockheed's generalizations are based on laboratory research, not observations in natural settings.

Still there are some important implications for teaching about Lockheed's research. For in her efforts to replicate the findings of some previous research on leadership in mixed-sex groups, Lockheed developed a game that could be used by high school students. When the students played the game the first time in mixed-sex groups, the males tended to dominate the group, but when the same groups played the game over again, there was a balance of activity, influence, and status manifested between boys and girls. Thus, the possibility exists that, with practice, feedback, and debriefing, mixed-sex groups of students can learn to get rid of stereotyped behaviors and to achieve more equality of leadership between boys and girls. Also, as we've noted in our own teaching in America, Belgium, Guam, and China, the teacher can go a long way toward balancing the contributions of female and male students during class discussions. Indeed, as we will show later in this chapter, the planned and deliberate actions of classroom teachers can provide latitude to both boys and girls, freeing them from the limitations of sex stereotyping.

Individual Attempts at Leadership

A theory of motivation which grew out of the thinking of Kurt Lewin, one that was clearly explicated by Atkinson and Feather (1966), can be useful for organizing some of the psychological facts that are involved in an individual's attempting leadership in the classroom. Atkinson and Feather proposed that the tendency to act in a certain way is determined by a motive force, an expectancy factor, and an incentive value of acting, all combined in a multiplicative relationship. According to this equation, the tendency to attempt leadership would be a function of a person's motive for power, multiplied by an expectation of success in leading, multiplied by an incentive for accomplishment.

The motive force for power is viewed as a drive to influence others, a drive which stems from a relatively stable aspect of the personality. It is related psychodynamically to such personality needs as control, achievement, and affiliation. Of course, individuals clearly will differ in their drives for control or power, and consequently will differ in how much they attempt leadership. In general, we would expect students with strong needs for control, achievement, and affiliation to make bids for leadership. That is, provided they expect, at least to some extent, that they will succeed, and provided that some sort of external incentives exist for gaining leadership.

Hemphill (1961) reviewed four studies which supported the expectancy-of-success and incentive-value parts of the Atkinson-Feather theory. Expectancy entails the belief that one can be successful when attempting leadership. Hemphill showed that persons who previously had been successful in influencing others were subsequently more likely to attempt leadership than they were before. He also demonstrated that persons who viewed themselves as being experts in the content being discussed attempted leadership more often than did those who saw themselves as being less expert. Incentive value constitutes a reward for actually being successful in leading. In another experiment, Hemphill varied the amounts of reward received for completing a group task and found that members of groups with high incentive attempted more leadership than persons in low-incentive groups.

In the classroom we would expect that students who previously have been influential in the peer group or with the teacher would continue to attempt leadership again and again. Moreover, the confident students who think of themselves as knowing a great deal about a topic will attempt more leadership than less confident students, even though the former students' perceptions of their own expertise may be quite inaccurate. When rewards are available for exerting influence such as being laughed with, applauded, followed, or even elected to an office, students will be more likely to attempt to influence their peers.

Students' tendencies to attempt leadership can also be influenced by interpersonal and situational factors. Hemphill showed, for example, that support and acceptance of a person's ideas encouraged that person to attempt leadership more often. Moreover, Hamblin (1958) found that situations in which all group members face a common crisis induce more leadership attempts, and that developing or changing groups show higher incidences of attempted leadership than static groups. These findings have direct implications for classrooms.

All students at one time or another have psychological fantasies about making attempts to influence others. For instance, perhaps Susan wants the class to take a field trip to a museum and she believes it is a good idea. Will she speak out? Will she attempt to sway others in the group? Will she try to exert leadership? It depends on her motives, her expectations, and her perceptions of the incentives. Her motives may include a strong desire to travel and to visit the museum in hopes of learning something new (achievement). She may simply want to be near a girl friend (affiliation). Or, she may wish to exert her influence over the teacher or others in the group (control).

Her talking out and attempting influence will depend on the activation of some of those motives along with her expectations and perceptions of incentives. If her previous group experiences in making suggestions were favorable, she will desire to attempt influence. And, if she perceives the teacher as wanting to go to the museum and feels that the teacher will like her suggestion, she will have some incentive to attempt leadership. However, if her suggestions have been met with a teacher's negative responses, or if she sees valued peers as being opposed to the museum trip, she may hesitate in stating her wishes. She would have little desire to "stick her neck out" and risk being rejected and rebuffed by her peers, particularly if her affiliation needs are strong.

Even if Susan's expectation of success and incentive value for attempting influence were low, she might try in any case, provided certain group circumstances prevail. If there is a general climate in the class for accepting ideas from many people, Susan might speak out. If the group's membership had recently changed and if expectations were still unclear, she might risk making the suggestion. If the group's decision-making procedures are open and there are norms in support of hearing from everyone before making decisions, she would probably speak out. In brief, Susan will attempt to influence the group: (1) if encouragement for such influence is high by her most valued peers and the teacher; (2) if she has some motive to satisfy; (3) if she expects to be successful; and (4) if she sees some reward forthcoming for trying.

Students such as Susan usually find their way into some niche in the classroom power structure. The power structures of most classrooms tend to take shape early in the school year and to remain stable throughout the rest of the year (see Lippitt and Gold, 1959). Moreover, Glidewell (1964) has shown that one can accurately predict a particular student's power position in the classroom from year to year.

Even though change in a stabilized power structure is not typical, it is, of course, possible, and it does happen in many classrooms. However, as shown in studies by both Bonney (1971) and Lilly (1971), planned efforts at modifying peer group power structures are very difficult to launch and also very difficult to maintain so that the changes become self-sustaining. Bonney focused on the efforts of teachers to aid students who were rejected by their classmates. Those teachers gave special attention, special assignments, and special roles to rejected students. Although a few students made some gains in their status among their peers, those gains lasted for only a few days to a week.

Lilly experimented with ways of improving the interpersonal acceptance of unpopular, powerless, low-achieving elementary students by having them participate in a special movie-making project. They worked closely with highly popular peers and were given permission to leave the regular classroom to engage in this highly valued project. The treatment was successful in improving the acceptance of the low-status peers—but again, as in Bonney's results, for only a short time. On the same measures, given six weeks after the treatment, Lilly found that the gains did not endure.

The reasons that peer power structures are so stable appear to lie in the expectations among the peers as to what particular students will be like. Also, students hold their own internalized expectancy structure which regulates their own behavior within the group. The dual force of the social structure and the individual's psychological make-up account for a great deal of the stability of power structures in the classroom.

Changing the power structure of a classroom group requires keen diagnosis, constructive action, and continual and persistent efforts at structural changes over a long period of time. The teacher should be aware that such changes cannot be brought about by simply attempting to modify personal characteristics of some of the individual students. Attempts at helping low-power students learn skills in trying to wield interpersonal influence may meet with some short-term success, but only normative and structural changes in the day-to-day group life in the classroom would assure major changes in classroom leadership patterns.

A teacher wishing to improve the leadership capabilities of individual students should observe several aspects of a student's behavior to diagnose whether he or she feels powerful and secure enough to attempt leadership. When classroom work is going on, the teacher might see (1) who gives ideas and suggestions in classroom discussions; (2) who voices opinions that are different from the teacher and other students; and (3) who takes the initiative or performs his or her own work independently without checking with the teacher.

When peers are in formal interaction on classroom work, and especially when they are working in small groups, the teacher might observe (1) who tries to put ideas across to get them implemented; (2) who suggests things to study or how to do work; (3) who suggests ways of presenting the products of the group to the teacher or class; and (4) who offers help and advice to other students.

When there is informal interaction among several peers, the teacher might make observations on (1) who tells others of good movies, records, or things to do outside of school that other students would enjoy; (2) who organizes activities, either in subgroups or with individuals, at recess or lunch; and (3) who offers to help other students with problems they are facing, either in or out of school.

Such observations can be made in a variety of ways and in a myriad of settings. They can be carried out when students are doing academic work, when they are in formal interaction with peers in the classroom, and when they are relating informally with peers outside the classroom. They can be executed periodically whenever the teacher has time and interest. They do not have to be carried out regularly or routinely.

Still, some teachers may choose to set up brief periods of five or ten minutes of observation during different parts of the day. Such observation periods would ideally be carried out during different activities, e.g., classroom discussions, highly structured individual work time, or more loosely structured work in small groups. The teacher might also make use of a student teacher, aide, parent, or small group of students to collect larger amounts of relevant data over larger blocks of time. Finally, the teacher might concentrate on just a very few students at one time to observe their leadership attempts in particular.

Many behaviors might be observed. The important point is to look beneath superficial events to interpersonal influence in all areas of the school. Peer group influence is subtle and often hidden. Teachers interested in understanding the power structure of the classroom peer group will have to use formal tools to sharpen their observations and to focus their listening.

Interpersonal Influence

Interpersonal influence entails directing a class's actions toward either constructive or destructive ends. It may emerge informally, as it typically does in the peer group; or it may be imposed formally, as when the teacher wields leadership. Emergent influence occurs when the acceptance of power is based on the consent of the followers. Imposed influence is based more on superior authority as defined by group roles and norms. *In most classrooms, teachers have imposed influence through their legitimate authority, while students, if they are to acquire power, generally gain emergent influence.*

Hollander (1961) has described the essential bases of a person's emerging with interpersonal influence within a group as being twofold—both adhering to group norms and being seen by others as competent and approachable. In the classroom, the students who emerge as influential initially behave in ways that confirm other students' expectations about how class members ought to behave. Then the influential student accumulates what Hollander refers to as "idiosyncracy credits." Idiosyncracy credits are gained by acting in ways that are seen as contributing to the group's task while also living up to the interpersonal expectations of the group members. The accumulation of psychological credits requires that the student accurately estimate opinions of other students in the class.

In other research on emergent influence, Bugental and Lehner (1958) found that emergent leaders are superior to others in judging the group's opinions on familiar and relevant issues. Moreover, Hamblin (1958) showed that persons who initially achieve some influence may lose it if they are unable to maintain attractiveness for others and to continue to be seen as competent. Hamblin's research leads to the conclusion that the basis of emergent influence in the classroom peer group will often entail a mixture of connection, expert, and referent power. Kirscht and others (1959) discovered that emergent leaders reinforce and maintain their power positions by giving and asking for suggestions, as well as by summing up and integrating the comments of others.

Research indicates a number of characteristics of persons who wield imposed influence that shed light on teacher behaviors likely to be influential with students. Persons who have imposed influence seem to differ, but only slightly, from those who emerge as leaders. For instance, both types of leaders wield influence successfully, especially when they possess empathic ability. Empathic ability, the ability to understand what others are feeling, is a skill of very great importance to the classroom teacher. Imposed leaders influence successfully when they reward members actively (Spector and Suttell 1959), when those rewards are given frequently (Bennis et al. 1958), and when they allow members of the group to participate actively (Hare 1953). Sometimes even dominating, authoritarian leadership can be influential. Berkowitz (1953), for example, showed that some members of groups did not object to dominating leaders when they knew that as members they could also participate and, at times, take the initiative.

Stoghill (1974) summarized thirty-eight studies on the relationships between participative or authoritarian leadership on the one hand, and group productivity, satisfaction, and cohesiveness on the other. While he indicated that the results showed a tendency for group members to be more satisfied with participatory leadership and that there was a positive correlation between group cohesiveness and participatory leadership, the overall results were mixed and mostly inconclusive. Stoghill concluded that while satisfaction and cohesiveness are probably associated with participative leadership, group productivity does not vary consistently with the different styles of leadership.

Stoghill's summary gives rise to the following sorts of thoughts about the leadership behaviors of teachers. Authoritarian teachers often do accomplish a great deal with their students, particularly when they are able to communicate a sense of openness and accessibility. But even though the highly respected authoritarian teacher exerts successful influence, and may even lead students effectively through the maze of academic learning, we should also be aware of other outcomes. It is likely that the actions of such teachers also encourage feelings of dependency, competition, and some powerlessness among the students and, at times, lead to the students feeling alienated from the subject matter.

Results of the studies that Stoghill reviewed, along with others reviewed by Weick (1978), and Schmuck and Runkel (1982), when interpreted in terms of power and status, suggest several negative outcomes. A leader who strongly emphasizes superior power and status may undermine group cohesion, frustrate group members' personal goals, induce discontent—even hostility—toward both other members and the leader, create pressures toward conformity, increase dependency, and lower an internalized commitment to work. On the other hand, a leader who does not actively use status and power to help the members of a group build their own problem-solving and decision-making capabilities and to develop their power over one another may find the members unwilling to work and feeling disorganized and dissatisfied.

Students, too, can often exert influence for unproductive ends. For example, Polansky, Lippitt, and Redl (1950) studied problem campers' influence attempts—those kinds of peer group influences about which teachers have nightmares. Even though the powerful youths in this study had severe emotional problems, their behaviors were not unlike those which might occur in average classrooms. Students with high emergent influence initiated lewd songs, threw food in the lunchroom, and generally disobeyed rules of the camp. Other less powerful students tended to imitate and follow them. The counselors were powerless to stop the misbehaviors. In many classrooms, teachers have experienced students seizing power and leading the class, however momentarily, in such games as, "Drop your pencil every five minutes," "Sharpen your pencil—everyone—at 3:00 P.M.," or, perhaps, "Everybody cough at 2:15 P.M."

With the possibility of such disruptions occurring in any classroom, it is important for the teacher to diagnose the power structure in the peer group and to work in concert with it rather than trying to run counter to it. Early in the school year teachers should look for cues that will help them predict which students will emerge as informal leaders. Generally, safe predictions can be made by following certain guidelines. Students who will emerge as classroom leaders usually possess fairly high self-esteem, are secure, intelligent, articulate (perhaps even verbose), flexible, low in anxiety, and often possess a high tolerance for ambiguity. Quite often they will also be risk-takers. Their followers, on the other hand, will tend to be characterized more by self-doubt, insecurity, lack of insight, quietness, rigidity, anxiety, and a low tolerance for ambiguity. Such personal characteristics of the followers undergird their propensity to be rather easily persuaded by others.

Goal-Directed Influence

Goal-directed influence occurs when the dynamics of interpersonal influence that we have just been discussing lead toward some valued outcomes. As such, goal-directed influence is synonymous with what Bass (1960) has called "effective leadership" and what Burns (1978) has labeled "political leadership." In relation to teachers, effective leadership would be measured by how successful the teacher's influencing behaviors are for achieving the overarching classroom goals of academic learning and positive personal development. In relation to students, effective leadership could be evaluated by how successful the student's influencing behaviors are for helping peers to achieve academically and to feel good about themselves as classroom members.

Many teachers can exert their imposed influence successfully but do not necessarily wield goal-directed influence effectively at the same time. One particular teacher, for example, had taught fourth grade for many years. Her teaching methods were highly structured and she acted in very controlling ways with the students. She was dictatorial, used a traditional curriculum, and ran a very well-ordered class in which the students did what they were told. She was highly respected by parents, teachers, students, and by us. She encouraged her students to do good work and she had successful teaching experiences with students who were unable to work well with other teachers. She was, in many ways, a successful teacher, and by observing only the immediate classroom processes, we would consider her as having goal-directed influence as well. After all, the students were learning and they felt good about it. For what more could we ask?

The major problem with that kind of influence was what happened to her students as they passed on to the fifth grade. They had learned subject matter, but they were unable to take initiative to learn some-

thing on their own. They had learned from the books that were studied in the fourth grade but were unable to search out new vistas of learning independently. They had learned to work quietly alone in their seats and to speak respectfully to adults, but they had not learned how to work effectively in small groups. They had worked hard through competition, but they had not learned how to cooperate. Even though they had respect for the rights of others, they did not know how to express their feelings to others and were afraid to state openly their frustrations and anxieties to the teacher.

We observed similar classroom dynamics in our observations of Belgium and Chinese schools. Teacher authority there was exerted sympathetically and with tact, but students were given little leeway for acting cooperatively or creatively. Current concern with the weaknesses of that sort of teacher leadership is so high in Belgium that there is considerable support in the Ministry of Education for experiments in more individualization, student choice, and cooperative learning. It is being realized more and more in Belgium that effective leadership in the classroom entails more than the students' rote mastery of academic subject matter. The same ideas and concerns do not seem to have reached many Chinese educators yet.

Goal-directed influence in the classroom should include concerns about both academic achievement and the development of autonomous, self-initiating students. Furthermore, a focus on both task and social-emotional group functions within the classroom group would be helpful for realizing goal-directed influence. If the teacher's leadership is shared so that many members of the peer group are performing both task and social-emotional functions, then goal-directed leadership will be more likely to be realized. It seems especially important that leadership in the classroom is shared by many members to achieve a favorable social climate. Our research has shown that *classroom groups with diffuse power structures—where most students have some degree of power over some other student—have more students who have high-esteem and are working up to their intelligence levels. Classrooms in which only a few students hold influence have more students who evaluate themselves negatively and are not working up to their intellectual potential.*

Our action research in schools indicates that, although classroom power structures are tenacious and difficult to change, they can be changed, and a greater dispersion of leadership throughout the peer group can be achieved. More sharing of goal-directed leadership can be encouraged through the teacher's working on the total group's orientations to influence. The teacher should also deliberately encourage and reward attempts at leadership of the less powerful students. Teachers can keep the group open for decision making and for the expressions of feelings. Teachers can give rewards for students' goal-oriented acts, even though at times the students' leadership may be ill-conceived and poorly executed.

Flexible Leadership

Since goal-directed influence requires an accurate diagnosis of changing social relationships within a group, as well as the ability to facilitate appropriate member behaviors, inevitably it must be flexible to be effective. In some kinds of group settings, direct leadership acts and close supervision will be appropriate. In other groups the

more effective leader will stand back and do very little. We will discuss briefly two classes of group situations which have been researched and which commonly occur in classrooms: situations which entail working alone or interdependently, and situations in which goals are either clear or unclear.

In research on industrial work groups, Dubin (1965) contrasted production that could be carried out by a single worker with production that required the interdependent actions of several workers. The individuated kind of work, termed "unit production," is illustrated by the cabinet-maker. The interdependent sort of work, "continuous production," is found on the typical assembly line. Dubin discovered that less direct supervision was effective in unit production, while more direct supervision was effective for continuous production. An analogy from Dubin's findings to learning activities fits the classroom. The effectiveness of direct supervision by the teacher will be low when students are working alone, but the stimulation of a very active and confrontative teacher leadership will be more effective when learning activities are being carried out in small groups of students.

In another series of empirical studies, Shaw and Blum (1966) found direct leadership to be highly effective when group goals and tasks were well understood and agreed upon. Conversely, they found that when the goals and tasks of a group were unclear, a more indirect style of leadership was superior. In the classroom, when most of the members are ready to "get going" and are clear about goals and tasks, direct leadership will be accepted, even wanted, to keep everyone on track. With the direction of action being clear to all, the stimulation of a direct leader will be encouraging and facilitative. On the other hand, in confusing learning situations with ambiguous goals and directions, students will be helped more by being able to ask questions and to enter into two-way communication with their teachers. Thus, a discussion style of leadership which entails a number of questions and answers is appropriate when students are not sure about where they are going and what they are doing.

Fiedler (1971) referred to that sort of leadership as "the contingency model." The effectiveness of particular leadership behaviors is contingent on both the nature of the group and the nature of the task. For the teacher, that means several kinds of influence are necessary every day with different topics and different students, and that from week to week and month to month, teachers should assess the effectiveness of their current leadership styles. Since no single leadership style will work with all students and with all academic tasks, teachers must adopt an expectation of flexibility and changeability.

Leadership for Effective Teaching

Saphier (1982) outlined four distinct phases of research on teaching which paralleled the research on leadership.

1. *Trait research* which emphasized the characteristics of individual teachers; characteristics such as intelligence, clarity of communication, imagination or perseverance were thought to be characteristic of teachers who taught effectively. The findings of that research paralleled the findings on trait theories in leadership—there was no evidence that personality characteristics were related to good teaching.

2. *Observation studies,* rich in description and detail, provided real life examples of teaching behaviors. Brophy and Good (1974, 1982), for example, showed the variety and complexity of the act of teaching and life in the classroom.

3. *Teaching research,* as well as *leadership studies* in other organizational contexts, focused on the dynamic transaction between leaders and followers. Teaching behavior was related to specific student outcomes; thus the situational characteristics of the leaders and followers were emphasized.

4. Finally, the *contemporary focus on teaching effectiveness* has distinguished between different styles of teaching, effective teaching in a particular style depending on the nature of the students and the lessons to be learned. Joyce and Weil (1980), for instance, distinguished between four different "families" of teaching; *social, behavioral, personal,* and *information processing.* In their words, the purpose of proposing alternative ways to teach is "to suggest there are many kinds of 'good' teaching and that the concept 'good,' when applied to teaching, is better stated 'good for what' and 'good for whom.' "

We do, in fact, know quite a bit about effective teaching. An effective teacher is also an effective leader; an effective teacher establishes academic goals and has the ability to motivate students to accomplish those goals. James McGregor Burns (1978) in his Pulitzer Prize winning book, *Leadership,* distinguished between a transactional leader and a transformational leader. *Good teachers are transformational leaders.* According to Burns, transactional leaders develop an implicit norm of reciprocity with their fellows. The leaders will give out rewards, information, and help in exchange for student conformity. Transformational leaders, on the other hand, inspire their followers to pursue values that both they and their leader believe in; such values capture the imaginations of leader and followers alike and they work closely together because they want to pursue these values together. The drama teacher who can inspire the students to work together for an aesthetic value, and the social studies teacher who can inspire the students to pursue a social project together are examples of transformational leaders.

Practical Issues for Classroom Leadership: Control and Responsibility

Sharing power with students represents one of the most serious and difficult instructional issues for teachers. Teachers who are sincerely interested in improving some of the unhealthy interpersonal dynamics within their classrooms are often reluctant to give up their legitimate authority for fear that "if I let the kids decide, they'll run wild. I'll lose all control." Those concerned teachers incorrectly assume that sharing influence with students is the same as abdicating their authority and their legitimate responsibilities. But shared leadership definitely does *not* call for the abdication of teacher power and responsibility within the classroom. Rather, it extends influence to students so that they can learn how to control their own behaviors and how to enter into collaborative decision making with one another.

Our views have been echoed by Ms. Lois Bergin, a fourth-grade teacher who used ideas presented in the initial edition of this book to share leadership with her students. Ms. Bergin wrote:

> The first big step to change came when the children and I together laid out our problems and began to attack them. . . . I learned to share power with the children to an extent I had never thought possible.

In her correspondence with us, Ms. Bergin went on to explain how she employed several action ideas for climate improvement described at the end of this chapter. Through these practices, she offered students greater opportunity to initiate their own ideas and to have more say into how they would carry out some of their academic assignments. Gradually, Ms. Bergin gave up some of her prerogatives, providing students with more and more personal control over their own learning goals and procedures. She put it well:

> A class that was once so uncontrolled that we could accomplish little has come through several developmental stages. A class once seated individually for best teacher control is now divided into groups of four who work together. The children use self-control when they are capable of it; when they aren't, I am their control.

Individual Control and Responsibility

Teachers who try to hold on to power and responsibility for student learning and behavior may well have orderly, quiet, and even pleasant classrooms—provided the students as a group are *not* "uncontrollable." In contrast, classrooms with teachers who share leadership with their students will often not be so neat and orderly—the problems that do arise will quickly come into the open, and the routines of group life will be analyzed frequently through discussions about immediate interpersonal concerns. Since the teachers of the second type will be allowing their students to learn about self-control and individual responsibility, they must expect that students will experience some difficulty in learning to control their own behavior, just as the students sometimes have trouble understanding a mathematical concept. What students do learn about their abilities to control their own behavior and to be responsible for themselves can also have direct implications for their academic performance. *Self-control and self-responsibility are not only concerns related to classroom discipline, but are also integrally tied to the behaviors required for pursuing academic objectives.*

Dweck and Rapucci (1973), in an empirical investigation of "learned helplessness" in fifth-graders, found that children who gave up quickly on academic tasks also took less personal responsibility for their behavior compared with those students who completed most tasks. The former students had learned to be "helpless;" they relied on forces outside themselves to guide how they behaved in the classroom rather than on their own initiative. Using the ideas of attribution theory, Dweck (1975) showed that helpless children, even after a series of successes, continued to predict that they would fail on similar tasks in the future.

In another study, Deci (1971) found that when a tangible external reward such as money was used, the subjects being studied gave up their intrinsic motivation for pursuing the activity. In contrast, Deci found that when verbal reinforcements were used as the external rewards, the subject's intrinsic motivation seemed to increase.

Since tokens similar to money or other tangible external rewards are often advocated for increasing the student's motivation to achieve or to take leadership, it is important to keep in mind the research which contrasts extrinsic and intrinsic motivational patterns. (See Bates, 1979, for interpretations of Deci's findings.)

Concrete rewards, such as money or candy, may add to the helpless orientation of students as studied by Dweck and Rapucci or to the pawn-like orientation as suggested by the work of DeCharms. DeCharms (1972) argued that students learn to act as pawns (helpless) or to act as origins (self-initiators) because of how they are taught by their teachers. The terms "robot" and "pilot" were used to describe similar power differentials by Ford and Urban (1965). Teachers who receive special practice in facilitating more origin-like student behavior can, with training, establish classrooms where more students can be classified as origins. Teachers who do not receive the training have fewer origins in the classroom. The trained teachers learn how to help students set their own goals, pursue those goals in their own ways, and take personal responsibility for their classroom actions. DeCharms found, moreover, that while the students were acting in a more origin-like manner, they were improving in their academic achievement as well.

Koenigs, Fiedler, and DeCharms (1977) also investigated whether the belief systems of teachers were associated with students' feelings of personal causation—that of being origin-like—and the students' patterns of academic achievement. Teachers were scored in four different categories on the complexity of their beliefs about causation of student behavior. Teachers characterized by what the researchers called "system 1 beliefs," for instance, had a simple cognitive structure. They categorized student behaviors as either good or bad and had definite opinions, whereas teachers characterized by "system 4 beliefs" did not make any judgments about how things "should" be. They sought information from a variety of sources and had flexible opinions about student behaviors, viewing most as multidetermined. The results were clear: teachers whose belief systems were open, complex, and interpersonally sensitive were more apt to accept and encourage influence from their students than teachers characterized by more closed and judgmental beliefs. Although the researchers attempted to relate teacher belief systems first to teacher behavior, then to classroom climate and, ultimately, to academic achievement, no relationship could be found between teacher beliefs and student achievement. Koenigs, Fiedler, and DeCharms state, "Clearly, this longest leap in the conceptual chain leaves room for many other variables to intervene."

Although significant relationships were not found between teacher belief systems and student academic achievement, the study above takes on particular interest. It has laid out a conceptual scheme for understanding the complexities of teacher influence upon classroom life, one that is mediated by the context of classroom interaction patterns. The authors state that "the chain of events is not made up of discrete links, but constitutes a stream that, when understood, is a meaningful and consistent whole." The interrelatedness of teacher beliefs and behaviors to power and influence can make a difference in classroom climate and, perhaps over time, in academic achievement.

It seems clear that teachers who wish to teach their students self-control, responsibility, and origin-like behavior must come to grips with how power and leadership are executed in the classroom. High teacher control typically does not facilitate self-initiative among students. Teachers cannot retain absolute power over academic goals and procedures and, at the same time, teach students to be self-controlling and responsible for their school related behaviors.

Group Control and Responsibility

Behavioral control and responsibility in classrooms are cultural as well as individual issues. In some classes the kinds of expectations that are shared in the peer group about what behavior is appropriate may be in opposition to the goals of the teacher and may hinder academic learning. Such a classroom group may be described by some adults as "uncontrollable," but it may be viewed by many students, in contrast, as having a regular and predictable interpersonal pattern. A vivid illustration was described by Ms. Bergin:

> The group of children I met in September are beyond anything I could ever have imagined. They are too many; but more than that, they have too many problems. Some have withdrawn tendencies, but most are very aggressive, keeping the classroom in almost constant turmoil with their disruptive behavior.
>
> They are hostile, noisy, explosive, and excitable. They seem unable to listen or to follow directions. They fight, kick, bicker, shout, stick pins and pencil points into each other. Their habit of tattling must be the worst on record. There

are cliques, loners, outcasts, liars, extortionists. They seem to hate each other, themselves, and me. They're full of headaches, toothaches, and stomach aches. Many are underfed, underclothed, and underloved. There are not nearly enough corners in the room to accommodate all the problem children, nor enough children who make good buffers to separate the rest.

Our room looks like a disaster area: more than half the desks have big shirttails of messy papers hanging out; pencils and crayons cannot be found because they are rolling down the aisles; the children cannot hit the waste can. It is rather like living in the city dump.

Ms. Bergin began by changing the expectations of the peer group by collaborating with the students in "laying out the problems" and then by attacking them one by one. She also faced the risk—and the joy—of sharing power. She had to give up some of her own plans because she decided to negotiate with the students so that some of their ideas would be used also. Perhaps, most importantly in relation to the work on belief systems by Koenigs, Fiedler, and DeCharms, she changed some of her expectations for what was "proper" to do within a classroom. She later wrote:

I think I am actually "putting up" with more, but am more comfortable and relaxed than I was last year when I had a group of children that was as trouble-free as any I'd ever worked with.

Ms. Bergin's example is illustrative of a point about "mutual control" made by Argyris and Schon (1974). They wrote, "Unilateral control is distinguished from *mutual control* in that collaboration occurs when *both* persons consent to act in mu-

tually advantageous ways." Mutual control, however, is extremely difficult to achieve in many classrooms. Like Ms. Bergin, all teachers face a number of difficult decisions every day about how much they will share leadership with their students. Because of the legitimate power vested in their authority, teachers cannot move too rapidly toward mutual control.

Many students will not understand how to act as *origins*. Teachers should carefully strive for mutual control in the classroom. Even though the peer group can wield significant influence in delaying a culture of mutual control, the teacher's choices about the sharing of leadership will usually have more significant implications for how the dynamics of the classroom group will be played out in the long run.

Student Responsibilities for Other Students: Peer Tutoring

In the Spring of 1989, the one-room schoolhouse at Ash Valley, Oregon, had just ten students, ranging in age from 5 to 13. Each student had a special job to do, be it locking up, emptying the pencil sharpener, or putting the chairs up. Not only did Ash Valley students answer the telephone or get the milk out at breaktime, but when students in class needed help, it was just as likely as not that another student would assist them. Often the students worked in older-younger pairs. Their teacher thought that such peer tutoring helped "the confidence of some students and reinforced their skills." Ash Valley students were learning to take on leadership, particularly in relation to academic learning.

One central reason for trying to increase student leadership in classrooms is, of course, related to academic achievement. While within our pluralistic society many people have different ideas about the purpose of schooling, subject matter learning is usually a universally agreed upon goal. Indeed, schools exist in order to teach students the basic skills of reading, writing, and computation so that they might later be able to compete for jobs. Whether or not students should learn to "adjust," develop "citizenship skills," or develop "social skills" is not always agreed on by the community. *Peer tutoring is one mechanism through which students are not only given responsibility for their own learning, but also for the learning of others as well.*

The idea of using students as tutors for other students has a long history. Certainly, for example, peer tutoring occurred in the one-room schoolhouse of early America, but its origins go back even further than that. Historians as early as the first century A.D. recorded the phenomenon of younger children learning scholarly lessons from older children. And from those early days on, it has been noted that the tutor and the tutee can benefit. In the seventeenth century, John Comenius, a Czech educator, discussed the benefits of peer tutoring in this way:

> The saying, 'He who teaches others, teaches himself,' is very true, not only because constant repetition impresses a fact indelibly on the mind, but because the process of teaching in itself gives a deeper insight into the subject taught (Crushschon 1977).

The research on peer tutoring has emphasized the benefits of teaching itself as an important vehicle for learning. (See Nelson, 1978, for descriptions of peer tutoring in inner-city America, and Rogacion, 1980, for uses of peer tutoring in rural Philippines.) The impetus for this view has come from the measurable benefits to the tutors resulting from their participation in helping. The academic benefits of peer tutoring were personally experienced by Patricia Schmuck when working with a group of teen-aged boys with severe reading disabilities. Their reading skills, as well as their understanding of personal problems, were greatly enhanced through tutoring younger students in reading. For instance, one uncooperative student, whom most teachers found to be a very difficult behavior problem, entered the program as a tutor and experienced a great deal of trouble relating to his student. In the clinic session devoted to helping the tutors solve some of their problems with students, he revealed an important insight into the younger boy. "I don't like him; he's a pain to work with." After a long pause, the tutor went on to reflect, "I guess I don't like him mostly because he's a lot like me."

Lippitt and Lohman (1965) experimented with a program of cross-age tutoring in which sixth graders tutored fourth graders. The formal steps of the program include: (1) several teachers getting together to establish agreements for cross-class tutoring; (2) teachers explaining the purposes of the project to the sixth and fourth graders; (3) teachers working with their own classes to build student attitudes in support of helping others and of receiving help; (4) some formal training for the tutors; (5) "at-the-elbow" help for tutors by teachers during the first few tutoring sessions; and (6) discussions within the sixth and the fourth-grade classrooms about how the tutoring is going.

Formal programs of peer tutoring can have many strengths. First, peer tutoring can be effective in increasing the learner's academic skills because of the long-term, one-to-one attention that the tutee receives—attention and support that is rare in relationships involving overtaxed teachers and masses of students. Second, it can offer a responsive system to the needs of a culturally diverse student body. Crushschon (1977) reports on several tutorial programs designed for minority youth—in particular, black students. She asserts that tutoring programs with their emphasis on interpersonal helping are consonant with the black heritage of our country. She argues that within black families, sibling roles and responsibilities tend to be clearly defined and understood, and older brothers and sisters are expected to share in the supervision, care, and training of their younger siblings. Peer tutoring, thus, may be one innovative procedure for capitalizing on cultural strengths in the school setting.

Peer tutoring can also serve as an excellent mechanism for students to have a hands-on experience of learning about functional leadership. The trust and care in providing a learning program for a younger student provides an invaluable experience, and most older students do not assume such a responsibility lightly. Since most student tutors are serious about their responsibilities, the relationships with their tutees typically last over an extended time period, and, consequently, the tutors receive a first-hand experience with the sequential stages of group development that were discussed in chapter 3. Perhaps more important, the tutors have a chance to experience empathy. Students who have just learned to control their misbehavior, or who have just learned to break the mystical reading code, may be in a better position to help the undisciplined student or the reluctant learner become motivated for self-improvement. For helpful reports on peer tutoring, see Allen (1976); Bloom (1978); Gardner, Kohler, and Riessman (1971); and Lippitt, Eisman, and Lippitt (1969). For a review of the research which is constructively critical, see Devin-Sheehan, Feldman, and Allen (1976) who point to several methodological weaknesses in research designs and data collection methods of several of the peer tutoring studies.

In a meta-analysis, Cohen, Kulik, and Kulik (1982) drew very optimistic conclusions about the value of peer tutoring. Their overview of findings from 65 evaluations of school tutoring showed that these programs have favorable effects on the academic performance and attitudes of those who receive tutoring. Tutored students outperformed control students on examinations, and they also developed favorable attitudes toward the subject matter covered in the tutorial programs. The authors' analysis also showed that tutoring has favorable effects on students who serve as tutors. Like the students they helped, the tutors gained a better understanding of and developed more favorable attitudes toward the subject matter in which they tutored.

Peer tutoring continues to be of interest to educators. Teachers, counselors and administrators alike are rediscovering that students teaching other students can be a fruitful avenue for harnessing student leadership in the school. Educational researchers also continue to give energy to determining the strengths and limitations of peer tutoring.

Implications for Teachers

The following statements summarize the key implications of this chapter's contents for teachers.

All human beings want to feel some influence and personal control toward important others.

Leadership entails not only interpersonal influence, but also the property of interaction between two or more persons within a group.

Because of their legitimate position of authority, teachers hold the most potential power in the classroom for executing leadership.

Functional leadership entails interpersonal influence in relation to group tasks and social-emotional concerns.

Students' attempts to gain classroom leadership are a function of their personal motives for power, their expectation for success, and the external incentives they perceive.

Students frequently attempt leadership in classrooms with favorable social climates.

Influence attempts in the classroom can facilitate or hinder academic learning. Goal-directed influence of either teacher or students—by definition—facilitates learning and personal growth.

A teacher's leadership will have significant influence on the climate of the classroom.

The influence structure of a classroom group can be changed. Teachers should take the initiative in working toward a dispersed influence structure.

Students will feel influential and learn to be self-controlling and responsible for their own behavior when they are helped by the teacher to share classroom leadership.

Action Ideas for Improving Climate

The following plans for altering leadership in the classroom so that climate might be enhanced were developed by public school teachers as part of several action research projects.

Role Playing Three Leadership Styles (Democratic, Authoritarian, and Laissez-Faire)

Role playing is a specialized technique that has been used in a variety of professions and settings (see especially Chesler and Fox 1966, and Shaftel and Shaftel, 1967), for applications to education. It helps to make new concepts and processes real for students by engaging them in make-believe approximations to the actual world of classroom group processes. We apply role playing here to the issue of leadership, but it could also be applied to most of the contents of this book.

The goal of this classroom activity is to help students recognize different styles of leadership and their effects. It should lead the students to become more aware of influence processes and to help them to talk about leadership in classroom discussions. *This action idea attempts to replicate the essential procedures of the classic Lewin, Lippitt, and White experiment of 1939, discussed previously in this chapter.*

The teacher arranges the seats in the class so that students are sitting face-to-face

---

INSTRUMENT 5.1

Reaction to Leadership Exercise

Check One: Discussion 1 ___, 2 ___, 3 ___,
Check One: Leader ___ Follower ___
For each question, please circle the number that best summarizes your feelings.

1. Who led in the interaction?
   9 Superior led completely.
   8
   7 Superior led somewhat more than the subordinate.
   6
   5 Leadership was shared; each led about equally.
   4
   3 Subordinate led somewhat more than the superior.
   2
   1 Subordinate led completely.

2. How much satisfaction did you derive from the discussion?
   9 Completely satisfied
   8
   7 Moderately satisfied
   6
   5 Neutral: neither satisfied nor dissatisfied
   4
   3 Moderately dissatisfied
   2
   1 Completely dissatisfied

---

in pairs. Six pairs are clustered in close proximity. Half the students are designated as leaders and half are called followers. The followers must have available another room where they can go while the teacher is coaching the leaders about their roles. Usually an aide, a counselor, or another assistant helps the teachers with the exercise by taking the followers to another place. Before the followers leave, they are told that they will be interacting with three different leaders on three different decision-making tasks and that they will be asked to react after each interaction to a questionnaire about what happened in the interaction. In other words, the work groups are to be pairs with one leader and one follower who will interact to reach a decision. After the decision, both parties will evaluate what happened on the "Reaction to Leadership Exercise" (Instrument 5.1).

Along with three of the reaction forms (one for each interaction), the followers and the leaders are given one each of three interaction forms (see Instruments 5.2, 5.3, and 5.4).

Next, the followers are asked to leave the room while the leaders are coached and to start work on the Interaction 1 form. When they are asked to return to the leaders, the followers will go to one leader to try to reach an agreement on a single rank-order with which both parties can agree.

INSTRUMENT 5.1 (Continued)
Reaction to Leadership Exercise

3. How much responsibility do you feel for the ranking you made as a pair?
   9 Feel complete responsibility
   8
   7 Feel some responsibility
   6
   5 Neutral
   4
   3 Feel very little responsibility
   2
   1 Feel no responsibility

4. How much hostility did you feel toward your partner?
   9 Felt completely hostile
   8
   7 Felt somewhat hostile
   6
   5 Neutral
   4
   3 Felt somewhat friendly
   2
   1 Felt completely friendly

5. Rate the quality of the ranking you made as a pair.
   9 Best possible ranking
   8
   7 Moderately good
   6
   5 Average
   4
   3 Moderately poor
   2
   1 Worst possible ranking

After the followers leave, the leaders are told briefly about the Lewin, Lippitt, and White experiment. This will be a replication of the leadership styles used in that experiment. In Interaction 1, the leader tries to be democratic. Interaction 11 is autocratic, while Interaction 111 is laissez-faire.

After each interaction, the followers leave the room again to fill out the reaction forms and to prepare the next interaction form. The leaders are also expected to complete the reaction forms and the interaction rankings. Hand-outs for the three leadership styles are as follows:

Instructions for Leader 1.

This interaction is a *joint* undertaking. Develop an acceptable basis for working together before you start into the rankings. For example, you and your subordinate might set the goal of agreeing on the items

---

INSTRUMENT 5.2
Interaction I

Rank the following eight traits in the order of their importance for being a competent parent. Place a number I by the most important trait, a number 2 by the second most important trait, and so on down to number 8, which will be the least important trait.

Rank	Trait	Rank	Trait
_____	Tact	_____	Compassion
_____	Honesty	_____	Energy
_____	Ambition	_____	Intelligence
_____	Courage	_____	Sense of Humor

INSTRUMENT 5.3
Interaction II

Rank the following eight items in order of importance for being a competent principal. Place a number 1 by the most important, a number 2 by the second most important item, and so on down to number 8, which will be the least important item.

Rank	Item

Rank	Item
_____	Has good understanding of the structure of the organization
_____	Able to give clear-cut, understandable instructions
_____	Keeps all parties who are concerned with a decision fully informed on progress and actions taken
_____	Willing to change own viewpoint when it proves to be wrong
_____	Able to make decisions based on facts rather than personal feelings, intuition, hunches, etc.
_____	Able to make good decisions under time and other pressures
_____	Able to delegate effectively
_____	Able to resist making a decision before all the facts are in

---

INSTRUMENT 5.4

Interaction III

Rank the following eight items in order of importance for being a competent teacher. Place a number 1 by the most important item, a number 2 by the second most important item, and so on down to number 8, which will be the least important item.

Rank   *Item*

_____   Communicates effectively

_____   Treats each student as an individual with unique abilities, interests, etc.

_____   Improves himself/herself by continuing formal education, reading current journals, attending workshops, training programs, etc.

_____   Relates well with colleagues, superiors, and subordinates

_____   Does research in his or her specialized field

_____   Takes an active part in community affairs concerned with education

_____   Able to effectively handle the "administrative" aspect of teaching

_____   Willing to try new teaching techniques and methods

---

that go at the extremes of the scale first and then resolving differences in the intermediate categories. Be sure every item gets a reasonable amount of consideration. Give your subordinate a full chance to participate. Even though you are the leader, you have high respect for the quality of your subordinate's thinking and ability; your goal, therefore, is to weigh his or her opinions and your opinions equally. Discourage the use of chance, like coin tossing, in any doubtful cases.

Keep in mind that after you finish, you will be asked to evaluate the efficiency of your subordinate in helping your pair develop the most adequate list. At the same time, your subordinate will be asked to evaluate *your* efficiency in acting according to the instructions. You are both responsible for getting a good list by working together in the manner described.

Remember, it is your responsibility to use the authority of your leadership to ensure that you and your subordinate come up with a ranking of the list that represents your *collaborative* thinking and that matches in quality the best ranking of the list. In the final analysis it is a joint effort.

Instructions for Leader 2.

In this interaction *you* are responsible for the activities and procedures followed by your pair. Assume that you have more knowledge, background, and skills than your subordinate. Take whatever responsibility into your own hands you consider necessary to get the job done. Your goal is to weigh your opinions much more heavily than your partner. You tell your subordinate the procedure you wish him or her to follow in working for you. As the supervisor in this situation, you have a better grasp of things and it is perfectly proper for you to bring him or her around to your point of view. In the final analysis *you* are responsible for the list. The criticism is all yours if your list is not good. Discourage the use of chance, like coin tossing, in any doubtful cases.

Keep in mind that after you finish, you will be asked to evaluate the efficiency of your subordinate in helping *you* develop the most adequate list. At the same time, your subordinate will be asked to evaluate your efficiency in acting according to these instructions.

Remember, you are responsible to use the authority of your leadership to ensure coming up with the best ranking of the list. In the final analysis it is a situation of *authority-obedience*.

Instructions for Leader 3.

In this interaction your goal is to *avoid active participation* in the content of the discussion insofar as possible. You are, however, to see that the work is done efficiently. If discussion gets off target, bring your subordinate back to the task. Avoid as much as you can giving your opinions, beyond expressing agreement when you feel it. You don't really care what order is produced, as long as your pair can establish an order or priority for the items. Your goal is

to weigh your follower's opinions much more heavily than your own. Discourage the use of chance, like coin tossing, in any doubtful cases.

Keep in mind that after you finish, you will be asked to evaluate the efficiency of your subordinate in helping your pair develop the most adequate list. At the same time, your subordinate will be asked to evaluate *your* efficiency in acting according to these instructions.

After each interaction, the teacher coaches the leaders about their next style and sums up the responses on the reactions forms. Each time a follower returns to the leaders for the next interaction, the follower goes to a new leader. At the end of the third interaction, the teacher reports the results of the reaction forms and raises several questions for class discussion. (1) What are the favorable and unfavorable aspects of each style? (2) Under what circumstances in the class is it good for the teacher to be democratic, autocratic, or laissez-faire? (3) What about the pupils in the class—when should they use one leadership style rather than another?

Encouraging Students With Interpersonal Influence to Pursue Constructive Goals: A Steering Committee

The goal of this practice was to improve the climate for learning in a classroom by helping students with high influence in the peer group to use it constructively. The teacher diagnosed members of the peer group, particularly the high-power students, as holding a preponderance of anti-learning, anti-school attitudes. The hindering influence of these students was causing a continual conflict between the teacher and a large part of the classroom peer group.

The teacher used objective sociometric questionnaires to measure the peer-group influence structure, (e.g., see Instrument 5.5 on page 142). Next, a six-member steering committee was appointed, consisting of the most popular and influential students in the class. The teacher worked with the committee every day for one week during lunch, training the members to understand and to use the task and social-emotional functions of group activity. After one week of training in leadership functions, the steering committee met twice each week to discuss problems, goals, and possible rules for classroom behavior and work. The teacher participated as a member in the discussions.

After about one month of these discussions, the steering committee presented plans to the class through a panel report. The plans were then discussed by the entire class. Following this, the steering committee was reconstituted and thereafter continuously changed its membership every two weeks—by election of the entire class—until all class members had served. The class decided to change only three steering committee members every two weeks so there would be a continuous overlap of membership.

The steering committee became more autonomous and self-regulating as the year went on. One member at each meeting was designated as an "observer" to make comments toward the end of the session on how the committee members had worked together. The teacher also gave the steering committee additional powers as the year progressed. The members were asked to discuss, to draw up plans, and to make decisions concerning the curriculum and instructional procedures in the class. After about three months of operation, the teacher asked the students to evaluate what they were doing. They developed brief questionnaires that they administered to their peers. Following the evaluation, still other changes were made in the operation of the steering committee. For example, the committee remained intact for three weeks instead of two because of the time needed before each newly constituted group could work well together.

This procedure is excellent for developing leadership skills and for dispersing student power and responsibility within the classroom. In this particular class, and in several others that tried the steering committee, there were significant changes in the negative and cynical orientations of the students. Several of these classes moved from interpersonally drab and hostile environments to exciting, curious, active, and warm environments. However, even though this procedure can be powerful for a classroom group's development, it is also very difficult to execute successfully.

The teacher who wishes to implement a classroom steering committee must relinquish power honestly and with patience. The teacher must clearly designate the powers given to students. For instance, if members of the steering committee want to decide about grading procedures, and the teacher wishes to maintain this prerogative, a discussion about grading should be ruled out of order. The teacher should *not* allow the committee to discuss a topic in hopes that its members will eventually agree with the teacher's position. Such hidden manipulation often backfires and leads to distrust between teacher and students. We believe that

---

INSTRUMENT 5.5
The Students in This Class

Date _____

Your Number _____

It is a job of teachers to find ways to make school life more interesting and worthwhile for all the students in the class. This form is your chance to give the teacher confidential information that will help the teacher to help each student. There are no right or wrong answers. The way you see things is what counts.

1. Which three persons in this class (excluding the teacher) are most often able to get other students to do things? Using your class list, write the number of each of the students you select.

    Student's Number

    The three who are most often able to get others to do things are

    _____
    _____
    _____

2. Which three persons in the class do the girls most often do things for?

    Student's Number

    They are

    _____
    _____
    _____

3. Which three persons in the class do the boys most often do things for?

    Student's Number

    They are

    _____
    _____
    _____

4. Which three persons in the class (not mentioned in the first three questions above) have strong potential for being leaders in the class?

    Student's Number

    They are

    _____
    _____
    _____

---

the teacher should limit the boundaries of decision making at the beginning of the year and broaden them gradually as students learn more skills and more trust is developed. The major theme of the steering committee should be to provide the opportunity for students to determine their fate in the classroom. Just making it a rubber stamp for a teacher's authority would be a mistake.

Diagnosing Influence Patterns in Class

The goal of this practice was to use an action research model in order to help students discuss the interpersonal influences in the class and to encourage them to make constructive changes. The teacher thought that the class had only a few informal leaders, and that by bringing this fact out in the open, the teacher might be able to facilitate a wider influence structure in the peer group.

The teacher started by passing out a class list to make sure that everyone knew everyone else's name. Next to each name was a number. The names were in alphabetical order. Next the teacher handed out a brief questionnaire (see Instrument 5.5).

The teacher's first step after collecting the data was to tally the number of times each student in the class was mentioned on each question. He did this by drawing four columns on a copy of the class roster and by marking the number of times a student was chosen in an answer next to that student's name on the roster. It was easy for the teacher to see which students were chosen often and which ones were neglected or seldom chosen. The data showed that five boys were chosen over and over again on questions 1 and 3, that most of the fourteen girls in the class were chosen by someone on question 2, and that about seventy-five percent of the students (twenty-two in all) were mentioned at least twice on question 4.

Next, the teacher formed a committee of six students to discuss the data with him. He chose three boys who were viewed as having potential for leadership. The teacher showed the tallies to the students and then asked them what they thought. At first the boys acted defensively by kidding around and by joking about some of the weaker boys in the class, but after an hour, the committee was agreed that a more dispersed leadership structure among the boys would make the class better and that everyone in the class should be given a chance for leadership.

The teacher and the committee in the form of a panel discussion brought their conclusions before the whole class the following week. After fifteen minutes of whole-class discussion, six small discussion groups were formed (each with half boys and half girls) to come up with ideas about how to increase leadership opportunities for every member of the class. The committee members acted as leaders in the groups. After thirty minutes, the groups brought their ideas back to the whole class.

Several ideas, such as rotating class officer roles, mixing up students more in the project groups, and listening more carefully to what others said were brought up by more than one small group. The teacher asked each small group to nominate someone to continue to work with him on implementing the ideas. Each small group chose someone other than their leader for the next steps.

Training Students in Goal-Directed Leadership

The goal of this practice was to improve the quality of group work in the classroom by dispersing leadership throughout the peer group. The two teachers involved—one an elementary teacher, the other a secondary teacher—were concerned that only a very few students were executing task and social-emotional functions. The elementary teacher developed the observation form in Instrument 5.6 for use with his students. The secondary teacher made use of the task and social-emotional group functions summarized in Instrument 5.7.

The training commenced in each classroom with the teacher leading a discussion about each point on the observation sheets. Then the teacher asked for six volunteers to form a discussion group, with the rest of the class as audience. The group was given an actual classroom problem to discuss, one that was relevant to the group processes of their classroom; for example, "Why do so few people participate in class discussion?" or, "Why don't more people in our class try to help one another to learn?" These discussion groups were given a limited time period to talk (usually about ten minutes in the elementary classrooms and twenty minutes in the secondary classrooms).

While the group discussions were taking place, the rest of the class used their observation sheets, marking down the initials of students whenever they performed one of the leadership functions. Next, the class discussed its observations and attempted to find uses of the observation forms in other class situations. One variation on the use of the sheets, suggested by a secondary student, was the idea that prior to a group discussion all student participants try to designate what functions they would especially wish to perform during the subsequent discussion. Then later, observers could see if they had been able to achieve their objectives. After using the sheets daily for several weeks, the teachers used them about twice each month in conjunction with regular class sessions.

Some precautions should be taken, especially with elementary students. In the beginning phases, the teacher may have to stop after each function is performed to ask the observers, "What happened there?" "What did you check?" Guidance such as that will be needed often but can gradually be reduced as the class becomes more comfortable with the observations.

Discipline Made Easy Through Teaching Responsibility

Donald Bates, principal of an elementary school in Pocatello, Idaho, helped develop what is nicknamed the "Master Plan" to teach students to become responsible for their own behavior. A how-to-do-it book, *Discipline Made Easy Through TR* (teaching responsibility), and a parent version, *How To Be a Parent in Three Easy Steps,* contain the procedures for teaching students personal responsibility. Those procedures support the following formula: (1) Set students up for success, (2) Catch them getting better, and (3) Use positive correction procedures to correct mistakes. Details can be received by ordering the booklets from Master Plan, 1340 West Quinn Road, Pocatello, Idaho.

Giving Students an Opportunity to Teach Their Own Lesson Plans

The goals of this action idea were to establish more power for students in implementing the curriculum and to help them in developing leadership skills through formally leading the class. The teacher involved in this innovation diagnosed the class as having low involvement in academic work. The teacher also hoped to find some

---

INSTRUMENT 5.6
Observation Sheet for Goal-Directed Leadership (Elementary)

Task Jobs   Jot Down Initials of Students

	Time 1	Time 2	Time 3	Time 4
Giving Ideas:				
Getting Ideas:				
Using Someone's Idea:				

People Jobs   Jot Down Initials of Students

	Time 1	Time 2	Time 3	Time 4
Being Nice:				
Saying How You Feel:				
Letting Others Talk:				

---

time to work with a small group who needed special attention and, therefore, wanted the rest of the class to be led by someone else.

The teacher started the practice by dividing the class into subgroups of six or seven students each. Each subgroup was told that it would work together for one hour daily to study designated topics. The concepts to be learned were listed on the chalkboard. Each subgroup was told that every student would be expected to be the leader of a group for one week of the term. The teacher described the responsibilities of the leader and asked each subgroup to select its first leader.

The initial leaders were asked to draw up lesson plans for one week. A lesson plan format was presented by the teacher. The teacher met with the leaders during lunch one day and went over their plans. Some leadership skills were discussed, and each leader was able to meet individually with

INSTRUMENT 5.7
Observation Sheet for Goal-Directed Leadership (Secondary)

Task Functions	Time 1	2	3	4	5
1. Initiating: Proposing tasks or goals; defining a group problem; suggesting a procedure for solving a problem; suggesting other ideas for consideration.					
2. Information or opinion-seeking: Requesting facts about the problem; seeking relevant information; asking for suggestions and ideas.					
3. Information or opinion-giving: Offering facts; providing relevant information; stating a belief; giving suggestions or ideas.					
4. Clarifying or elaborating: Interpreting or reflecting ideas or suggestions; clearing up confusion; indicating alternatives and issues before the group; giving examples.					
5. Summarizing: Pulling related ideas together; restating suggestions after the group has discussed them.					
6. Consensus testing: Sending up "trial balloons" to see if group is nearing a conclusion; checking with group to see how much agreement has been reached.					

INSTRUMENT 5.7 (Continued)
Observation Sheet for Goal-Directed Leadership (Secondary)

Social-Emotional Functions	Time 1	2	3	4	5
7. Encouraging: Being friendly, warm, and reponsive to others; accepting others and their contributions; listening; showing regard for others by giving them an opportunity or recognition.					
8. Expressing group feelings: Sensing feeling, mood, relationships within the group; sharing own feelings with other members.					
9. Harmonizing: Attempting to reconcile disagreements; reducing tension through "pouring oil on troubled waters"; getting people to explore their differences.					
10. Compromising: Offering to compromise own position, ideas, or status; admitting error; disciplining self to help maintain the group.					
11. Gatekeeping: Seeing that others have a chance to speak; keeping the discussion a group discussion rather than a 1-, 2-, or 3-way conversation.					
12. Setting standards: Expressing standards that will help group to achieve; applying standards in evaluating group functioning and production.					

the teacher if there was a need for additional help. The leaders were given total responsibility for both teaching and evaluating for one entire week. Their week's efforts were completed after they had supplied the teacher with written reports on the progress of their group.

Training Students as Group Conveners

Using a convener to lead small group discussions and rotating that role throughout the class are common procedures for providing dispersed leadership among the students. Conveners have legitimate authority to conduct the meeting. They are to facilitate discussion by following an agenda, calling on others for contributions, asking brief questions, and summarizing group progress from time to time. They should move the group efficiently through its tasks. Naturally, students will need some training and help to be effective conveners.

A senior high teacher used the following guide to help prepare student conveners for project groups:

Before the meeting, review the agenda by listing topics and issues to be discussed and making sure that a recorder (or secretary) is assigned to document proceedings and decisions during the meeting.

During the meeting, get started promptly and then: (1) lead the group to establish priorities among items on the agenda and to specify the time to be spent on each item; (2) keep the group at the task; (3) keep the group to its time commitments for each agenda item; (4) stay attuned to feelings of confusion and try to clarify them; (5) at the end of each agenda item (a) check

to be sure that everyone who wanted to has had a chance to contribute to the discussion, (b) check whether anyone is unclear about the topic, and (c) summarize or ask someone else to summarize, being certain that the recorder has written out the summary; (6) check whenever it seems appropriate on the involvement of group members and the decisions that are being made; and (7) conduct or ask someone else to conduct an evaluative discussion about the meeting during the last ten minutes or so.

After the meeting, meet with the recorder to check the clarity and completeness of the record and turn in to the teacher any reports or minutes that should be duplicated.

Dispersing Leadership Through Group Poetry

During our study of democratic participation in small-town schools we observed a creative method both for dispersing leadership and for motivating students to write poems. A local poet had volunteered to teach for 50 minutes a day in an alternative high school. She had 12 students sit in a circle, each with a pad of paper and a pencil. She asked each student to write a line of poetry near the top of a piece of paper and to hand the paper to the person on the right. In turn, each student added a line to each evolving poem. Once each poem had 12 contributions and was returned around the circle to the originator, the teacher asked each student to read the whole poem out loud. The activity helped the students to feel a part of the process and to begin to recognize how much fun there can be in writing poetry cooperatively.

Understanding Decision Making in the Class

A simple procedure for involving students in classroom decision making has been used by several teachers with whom we have worked. It takes less than thirty minutes, but it can help set up a constructive climate for shared decision making. The first step entails the entire class's brainstorming about decisions that must be made for the class to run smoothly. The teacher takes the lead by dreaming up several issues, but quickly moves to having students give their own ideas. The teacher records all ideas on the chalkboard. Next, the issues are categorized according to who should make the decisions. Typical categories are the teacher alone, the individual students, the whole class, or a leadership group in the class. After the issues are coded according to the four categories, the teacher reproduces the list of decisions on paper and passes it out for understanding and discussion. The teacher and a leadership group, such as the steering committee described above, monitor the class for the next month to see that decisions are being made and that follow-through on the decisions is occurring.

Exercise in Consensus Decision Making

The following exercise allows students to practice and consider the process of consensual decision making. Several teachers have used it early in the year to get their classes ready for cooperative decision making. The exercise is called "Lost on the Moon."

The class is divided into groups of five or six. Imagining themselves to be members of a space crew who have crash-landed on the moon some 200 miles from where the mother ship waits, students are given sheets of paper listing fifteen critical items left intact after the landing and are asked to rank them according to their importance in helping the crew reach the rendezvous point. Each student is given a sheet with the instructions at the outset (see Instrument 5.8).

Next, each student is given a sheet of "Instructions for Consensus." After reading this, students are told to reach a consensual decision of the best ranking of the fifteen items.

Instructions for Consensus

Consensus is a decision process for using all of the information and good ideas in a group. Consensus is difficult but not impossible. Use this exercise to see how well your group can do in achieving consensus. Try to avoid arguing just for the sake of argument. Present your point of view logically and listen to others' reactions also. Consider all points of view as potentially useful. Differences of opinion are natural and expected. Indeed, differences in experience and information can help the group find a better solution. Be sure to encourage all members to speak, and test to see if everyone agrees with a decision before moving on.

Allow groups approximately forty-five minutes to reach consensus about their ranking of the items and then ask them to tabulate the results. In each group, let one person act as secretary. As each member of the group calls out his or her private ranking of the fifteen items, the secretary records those on the scoring sheet as shown in Instrument 5.9. When each student's ranking has been recorded, the secretary sums the ranking for each of the items and ranks the sums, thus arriving at an average ranking

---

INSTRUMENT 5.8
Lost on the Moon

Instructions: You are a member of a space crew originally scheduled to meet with a mother ship on the *lighted surface* of the moon. Because of mechanical difficulties, however, your ship has been forced to land at a spot 200 miles from the mother ship. During the rough landing much of the equipment aboard was damaged, and, since survival depends on reaching the mother ship, only the most critical items must be chosen for the 200-mile trip. Your task is to rank the items below according to their importance for enabling your crew to reach the mother ship. Place the number 1 by the most important item, the number 2 by the second most important, and so on through number 15, the least important.

_____ Box of matches

_____ Food concentrate

_____ Fifty feet of nylon rope

_____ Parachute silk

_____ Solar-powered portable heating unit

_____ Two .45 calibre pistols

_____ One case dehydrated milk

_____ Two 100-lb tanks of oxygen

_____ Stellar map of moon's constellation

_____ Self-inflating life raft

_____ Magnetic compass

_____ Five gallons of water

_____ Signal flares

_____ First aid kit containing injection needles

_____ Solar-powered FM receiver-transmitter

---

for the group. (This could represent the ranking that might have been obtained had the group merely voted and not held a discussion.) The secretary also records the ranking that the group has reached by consensus.

The exercise works well when the groups sit in separate circles to minimize mutual distraction. When the secretaries of each group have completed their work, the teacher announces the correct answer to the exercise according to NASA. The secre-

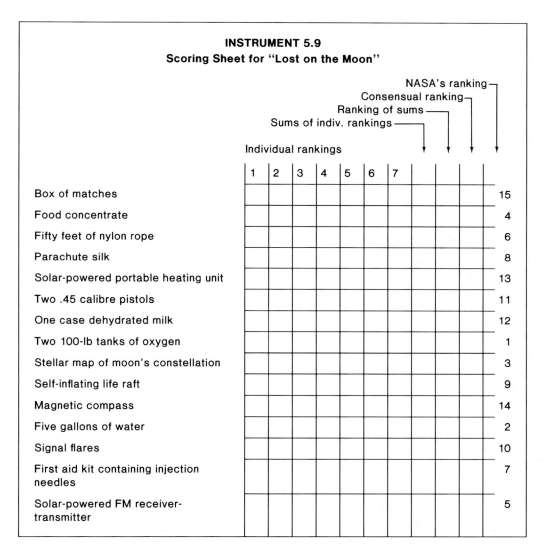

INSTRUMENT 5.9
Scoring Sheet for "Lost on the Moon"

	Individual rankings							Sums of indiv. rankings	Ranking of sums	Consensual ranking	NASA's ranking
	1	2	3	4	5	6	7				
Box of matches											15
Food concentrate											4
Fifty feet of nylon rope											6
Parachute silk											8
Solar-powered portable heating unit											13
Two .45 calibre pistols											11
One case dehydrated milk											12
Two 100-lb tanks of oxygen											1
Stellar map of moon's constellation											3
Self-inflating life raft											9
Magnetic compass											14
Five gallons of water											2
Signal flares											10
First aid kit containing injection needles											7
Solar-powered FM receiver-transmitter											5

taries also record this ranking on their sheets. Each group then computes three scores by summing the arithmetic discrepancies between the correct ranking and the ranking obtained through consensus, the average ranking of the group before discussion, and the individual ranking that came closest to the NASA ranking. Each group sees whether its "best" individual, its average produced before discussion, or its consensual product is superior.

After the students have inspected and informally discussed the charts for a few minutes, each group should discuss three questions: (1) What were my reactions to the exercise? How did I feel? What was I thinking? (2) How similar were our behaviors here to our usual behaviors in the class? How different? What are the implications of this exercise for the way our class operates? (3) How well did we use our group resources? What prevented us from using them better? How can the obstacles to better use of resources be avoided in this class? Later, the secretaries summarize the highlights of those discussions to the whole class.

Consensus Decision Making with Task and Social-Emotional Functions

An interesting variation on the exercise in consensus decision making is to assign several students the job of observing group behaviors during discussion with the task and social-emotional categories (see Instrument 5.7). Then, after the discussion is over, the student observers give feedback to group members on which of the twelve functions they performed and which of them were not performed.

The teacher who observes male students typically carrying out task functions and female students typically carrying out social-emotional functions might choose to run a consensus exercise with all male and all female discussion groups. Under such circumstances, some of the male students will usually perform social-emotional functions and some of the female students will perform task functions. Also, running the consensus exercise in sex-segregated groups often gives rise to total class discussion about sex stereotypes in leadership.

Classroom Government for Preschoolers

This historic project proved that even preschoolers can take the lead in formally organizing classroom life. In a unique two-year experiment in classroom self-government, Turner (1957)—reviewing her experiences as a teacher in the twenties—

showed how children ranging in age from four to six-and-a-half years old could be trained to take leadership in forming their own rules and regulations. During the first year, the teacher provided channels of communication for the entire class. When students found themselves in trouble and needing assistance, the teacher would summon a meeting of all the children in the group and, acting as chairperson, would call upon the individuals who raised their hands to say what they thought about the matter.

When the class sentiment had been revealed, rules or regulations were generalized in a summary by the teacher and voted upon by the entire class. These rulings were then hung on the wall as an article of a classroom constitution. Soon a classroom constitution began to take shape. During the second year, the children were able to conduct classroom meetings themselves under a chairperson chosen from among their group. Problem-solving sessions were held whenever a student felt an injustice had been done to someone. A constitution complete with amendments was published in the short but interesting report by the teacher, Marion Turner.

Even though Turner's experience was 30 years ago, it echos the sentiments of educators such as John Dewey 50 years ago and of contemporary educators such as the 27 distinguished Americans who issued the Thanksgiving Day Statement (see *Developing Character,* 1984). As a people and as individuals, we will continually struggle with good governance because each generation must face how it will govern itself anew. Preschool is a very good place to start. For examples of student governments in middle schools, junior highs, and senior high schools, see the action ideas in chapter 10.

Implementing Small Group Teaching

During the past decade a large amount of field research has been carried out in Israel on the topics of small group teaching and cooperative learning in the classroom. Sharan and Hertz-Lazarowitz (1981) summarized these efforts and have presented a practical handbook on how to do it. They worked directly with classroom teachers and hundreds of pupils to come up with these procedures.

In planning and carrying out a group project, students progress through a series of six consecutive stages: (1) the topic of study is selected and the students are grouped into teams of six to do research on the topic; (2) the topic is divided into subtopics and individuals or pairs of individuals within research groups select subtopics for study (decisions are made about what to study, how to study, and the purpose of the study); (3) the investigation is carried out first by individuals and pairs and later the research group integrates everyone's contributions into a single outline; (4) a final report is presented to the whole class (often the reports include activities and total class discussion); (6) finally, an evaluation is made of the final reports and of the work used by the research groups to construct the reports. The teacher can administer achievement tests and give an evaluation, but it is also important for cooperative evaluation involving students and the teacher to occur. This evaluation can include peer reactions and lead to revisions in the group procedures that will be used in subsequent research groups within the class.

Friendship and Class Cohesiveness

6

Human beings need close friends to feel secure and comfortable; they strive to be loved, or at least to be personally related to others. Without affiliation, feelings of loneliness, worthlessness, and anxiety arise preventing the maximum use of their potential. Friendship represents a very important interpersonal dynamic for the mental health of individuals. Groups, also, are replete with interpersonal feelings that influence members' performances on tasks. Soldiers perform more poorly in their combat units when interpersonal relations are unsupportive. Industrial work groups perform more successfully when workers "on the line" relate favorably to one another. And, participants' suggestions in many different kinds of problem-solving groups are accepted or rejected partly on the basis of their degree of popularity with other group members.

Cohesiveness deals with the feelings that class members hold toward the entire classroom group. A measure of cohesiveness can be taken by summing all of the individuals' feelings about the group.

Thus, friendship occurs between individuals; it is concerned with an individual's relationship with another individual. Cohesiveness, on the other hand, is a characteristic of a group. It differs from friendship in its emphasis on the individual's relation to the group as a whole rather than on the individual's relationships with other individuals, subgroups, or the teacher. Members of cohesive groups are typically more loyal to the group than are members of noncohesive groups and are more concerned with the feelings of the other group members.

Despite the importance of individual friendship patterns and group cohesiveness, some teachers still maintain that they are employed primarily to teach content and that they should not be concerned about students' liking for each other or for the closeness of the class. We think such a view is shortsighted and naive. It oversimplifies the social-psychological realities of the classroom and ignores the psychodynamics that are integrally involved in most learning processes. Teaching and learning entail an interpersonal process, and when that process is under way, it is complicated and affected both by the many relations among the students and by relations between the students and the teacher. The teacher's style and the curriculum, the students' feelings about themselves and their academic abilities, and their feelings for the group are all major influences on the teaching-learning process.

Objectives of this Chapter

In this chapter, we discuss the interpersonal variables that are associated with friendship and the group variables related to cohesiveness. We hope that teachers will see why it is important that students feel liked and accepted and how friendship can influence academic performance. There are many theories about why people like each other or why they don't. There are also theories about why some groups are highly cohesive and others are not. We review some of those theories in this chapter. Finally, we describe the ideas of the circular process model and suggest many practical action ideas for teachers. It is important to all of us to be liked and to value the primary groups to which we belong. Teachers can help create classroom climates where each student feels valued and where the classroom group can foster academic excellence.

The Concepts of Friendship and Cohesiveness

Friendship and cohesiveness are part of the dynamics of all classroom groups. Classrooms have a hidden world that at times too painfully reflects attraction and hostility among peers influencing the self-concepts and academic performances of the individual students. Classroom groups organized in such a manner that students feel liked and respected are more likely to have youngsters acting in ways that warrant the liking and respect of others. Conversely, when classroom social life is filled with anxiety, hostility, and self-doubt, the students will behave in maladaptive and unproductive ways, thus perpetuating a negative climate. At the "bottom line" we know that students with some support from friendly peers use their intellectual potential more completely than do their fellow students who are rejected by the group.

Cohesiveness is a characteristic of a group and contrasts, therefore, with feelings of inclusion or attitudes about involvement that are psychological in nature. A cohesive classroom group is made up of students who are actively involved with one another. Some typical psychological responses of students in a cohesive classroom are, "I really feel good when I'm in that class;" "I'm involved and a part of the action;" and "I know that I can contribute in this group." When responses like these reflect the attitudes of many students, the class is highly cohesive.

Although friendship and cohesiveness are discrete processes, there is a relationship between them. For instance, classrooms with high cohesiveness are more conducive climates in which to make friends. Students who care about their class and feel highly involved are more likely to communicate often with others, to be more open in expressing their own feelings, and to attempt influence more often within the peer group. A successful effort to raise the esteem levels of students represents one strategy which teachers might employ for increasing peer group cohesiveness—one that might also have the beneficial effect of increasing the dispersion of influence, the emergence of supportive norms, and communicative clarity.

On the other hand, cohesiveness is not only related to student behaviors that are favorably valued by adults; cohesiveness may also support concerted and spirited anti-adult behavior, as in delinquent gangs or defiant classroom subgroups. Subtle indicators of low amounts of cohesiveness might be frequent daydreaming in the classroom, fragmented subgroups that cannot wait to leave the class to interact, and low amounts of clear communication among the students. We would also expect to find a number of students who feel isolated and lonely in the class with low cohesiveness.

Indications of tardiness, absenteeism, or classroom vandalism can often be misleading regarding cohesiveness, since these indicators depend for their meaning not only on a group's cohesiveness but also upon the norms of the group or even upon prominent norms that are potent outside the group. For instance, students who share suspicions about the credibility of teachers hold common expectations that academic life is not very useful and, in general, hold negative feelings toward school. These students may reveal their cohesiveness in high rates of tardiness, absenteeism, and vandalism. In other situations such indicators may reflect low cohesiveness.

Cohesiveness is more than a mere summing up of interpersonal friendships within the classroom. Muldoon (1955) and R. Schmuck (1966) showed empirically that cohesiveness in classroom groups was related to the friendship structure. *Classrooms with more dispersed friendship structures were more cohesive.* Moreover, classroom groups in which the members could clearly point to their popular and unpopular peers had less cohesiveness and did not work well as a total group. When there was a more diffuse attraction structure, however, there was also a classroom group with clear goals and an appreciation for individual diversity.

Cohesion is also based on several psychological aspects of attraction, such as feelings of membership, identification with other group members, and good feelings about participation, working simultaneously. Cohesive classrooms may tolerate flare-ups and heated arguments, but they are *not* characterized by sustained friction and hostility among members. The emotional investment and deep involvement of students in the group support rapid solution to interpersonal problems by joint collaboration to reduce tensions.

Personal and Social Variables Related to Liking

Do you like me? Who is your best friend? Those are common questions asked openly or silently by people of all ages. Whether you are liked or not liked, whether you like another person or not are the topics of interpersonal attraction and friendship. One must like another person before friendship can occur (see Segal, 1979, for details). Peer relations and friendship choices have captured the attention of many psychologists,

social psychologists, and sociologists because social relations are critical in understanding human behavior. Glidewell et al. (1966), Bersheid and Walster (1969), Rubin (1973), and Tajfel (1982) provide excellent reviews of the literature. Rubin (1980) gives a non-academic review of children's friendship, Asher and Gottman (1981) provide a detailed accounting of the development of children's friendships, and Epstein and Karweit (1983) look at the social context of schooling in friendship choices.

We summarize that *"liked" students—more than unpopular students—will be physically attractive, well-coordinated at motor skills, outgoing, socially effective, intellectually competent, and mentally healthy.*

Looking at the attributes of the person who is liked or unliked has been the kind of research typically undertaken. The typical study presents correlations between certain personal attributes and a student's "liking" status in the classroom. From such findings we are unable to draw causal inferences, except when an obviously static antecedent condition—such as the physical attributes of a student—is studied. Nonetheless, much of the research can be valuable in helping to sketch a picture of the kinds of students who are most likely to be attractive and those who will most likely be the unfortunate recipients of hostility.

In addition to the personal variables, we will also review some of the social variables at work in liking. Liking another person can depend upon other situational factors such as the classroom structure or the ways in which teachers behave; thus we will discuss the attributes of groups that influence liking.

Personal Variables Related to Liking

Research on the characteristics of liked and disliked students indicates that the former are often physically attractive, have well-coordinated motor skills, are outgoing and socially effective, are intellectually competent, and are mentally healthy. Some differences between students of different social classes have also been noted. For example, lower-class boys in schools in predominately lower-class neighborhoods gain acceptance by taking risks and by being physically aggressive. Students are often rejected if they are limited in their physical ability, if they have difficulties in relating socially to others, if they have intellectual limitations, if they lack a sense of humor, and if they have mental health difficulties. In many classrooms, the social behaviors of lower-class students lead to their being rejected because their overt aggression or passive dependency run counter to middle-class values.

These findings about interpersonal popularity within the classroom peer group can be understood in light of a theory developed by Lippitt et al. (1952) and elaborated by Gold (1958) and Tajfel (1982). The theory states that all students possess human properties which are causally critical to ways they are perceived by others and to how they behave. Physical attributes, personality characteristics, and intelligence are examples of these personal properties. These properties, in turn, become converted into resources when they are valued by members of the group. Since different students and classroom groups will value different human characteristics, a property of a student which is a resource in one social context may not be a resource in another.

So, for example, while the properties of physical size and fighting skills may be im-portant resources in some classes, others may undervalue those attributes so much that students manifesting them may have difficulty in becoming accepted and gaining friends. Similarly, as the same classroom group faces various social situations or developmental stages, different properties of class members may be valued by the group. Thus, a student who talks a great deal may be highly desirable when the teacher is asking the whole class questions, but that same student may be viewed as overbearing during informal gatherings of the students. In the following sections we will discuss the personal attributes of those who are liked and disliked.

Physical Attributes

Physical appearance, although often considered to be a superficial psychological variable, can be an important initial factor in making friends, choosing dating partners, and in selecting marital partners. Gold (1958) discovered that physical attributes were considered to be valued resources by elementary students. Terms denoting attractive physical appearance such as "pretty," "good looking," "dresses well," "looks nice," as well as terms denoting skillful use of the body such as "participates in sports well," "is coordinated," and "can do things well," were offered by students as highly valued resources and as reasons for liking other students. In heterosexual relationships physical attributes also play an important part. Walster et al. (1966) showed that a college male's liking or not liking his date and his wanting or not wanting to date her again were largely determined by her physical attractiveness, as judged by disinterested observers. Clore (1975) pointed out that even though some elements of the youth culture and the women's movement have forcefully rejected physical beauty as a primary value, this protest has not changed the commercial value of cosmetics and clothes—it has only changed them to more "natural" appearances.

Touhey (1979) used an instrument called a "Macho Scale" to measure the degree of male and female traditional sex role adherence. To test whether the endorsement of physical attractiveness is related to adherence to sex role stereotypes, he asked subjects to rate their liking for a person of the other sex. They were given pictures as well as biographical information. High scorers on the macho test were more affected by the physical attractiveness of the person, and low scorers on the macho test were more influenced by the biographical information. Touhey suggests some reason for these differences: "High scorers judge the opposite sex largely in terms of socially desirable role performance, while low scorers evaluate potential dates in terms of capacities for personal involvement and emotional intimacy" (p. 288).

Conversely, it also appears that persons with obvious physical handicaps, as well as those with peculiar psychomotor disabilities, often are not chosen as friends by students. Indeed, students with such disabilities are frequently ignored and not chosen as participants in group activities. Moreover, even very minor physical drawbacks such as a lack of coordination in playing ball, in jumping rope, or in running very fast may lead to peer group rejection. Such prejudices toward the disabled and those with limited physical abilities seem to arise because of the high value placed on youthfulness, physical prowess, and beauty in American society. Students simply copy the norms of the adult society, making attempts at "mainstreaming" special education students within regular classrooms a difficult challenge for educators.

Social Behavior

Although physical attributes can have a significant impact on liking patterns, the social behaviors of students, once they become acquainted with one another, appear to be much more important. Social behaviors refer to interpersonal acts carried out in relation to one or more others.

Lippitt and Gold (1959) in their extensive research on the social behavior of liked and disliked students found that students who were rated as attractive by their peers exhibited interpersonal behavior that was enhancing, supportive, and helpful to others, rather than threatening and hostile. Rejected students expressed more negative affect toward others—both verbally and physically—and often behaved in either actively aggressive or passively hostile ways. Their highly attractive counterparts were friendly, empathic, and outgoing.

Lippitt and Gold went on to present data about differences between the sexes in relation to social behaviors that were associated with friendship. Aggressive hostility, physical abuse, and overt defiance were associated with boys who were disliked by their peers. For girls, passive dependency and social immaturity were associated with rejection. Both overt aggression on the part of boys and passive dependency on the part of girls made others in the class feel uncomfortable and insecure.

The findings of Lippitt and Gold appear to be most applicable to classrooms with predominantly middle-class students. Aggression, physical fighting, and high amounts of dependency run counter to middle-class values and expectations. Lower-class settings sometimes can be quite different. Pope (1953) showed, for example, that in predominantly low socioeconomic settings, the students who were often held in highest esteem by their peers were the ones who were defiant, belligerent, and nonconforming. Pope pointed out that such defiant students were not necessarily liked, but they were respected. In the same vein, students who regularly conformed to classroom rules and to teacher demands were often rejected by peers.

The prevailing social class structure of the school makes a difference in the kinds of social behavior that will be liked or disliked by the students. Pope found that boys in lower-class schools valued physical strength, group loyalty, physical prowess, and cool friendliness; whereas, Lippitt and Gold found that middle-class boys valued physical coordination, strenuous activity, and fair competition in games. Boys in both social classes valued friendliness, but its expression was much more physical and subtle in the lower class than in the middle class. These striking differences between the social classes did not exist for the girls. In both social classes girls valued social skills and cooperation, the exception being that middle-class girls placed greater value on cheerful behavior and skill in group activities.

In schools with mixed populations of middle and lower-class students, the norms of the middle-class typically prevail. The social behaviors of middle-class students are usually more appropriate for the demands of the school and, therefore, the middle-class students tend to receive rewards and to achieve success more easily than do the lower-class students. In one study, Cook (1945) showed that the middle-class students in a school with almost equal distribution of middle and lower-class students received more nominations from their peers along such dimensions as best-dressed, best-liked, more fun, and real leaders.

Even after an intensive intervention for change that sought to increase social interaction among students and to democratize classrooms, Cook's findings showed that a social class stratification of friendships still prevailed. Students of higher social class levels were being chosen more often for a variety of attractive attributes than students of lower-class backgrounds. Unfortunately, awareness of social class differences gains importance as the student gets older. High school students generally are well aware of such differences, and their preferences for relating to others are influenced by these perceptions and comparisons. We address some of these findings in chapter 7 by describing how group norms work to shape the behaviors of secondary school students.

In another program of research on popularity in the peer group, Lawrence W. Sherman (see Sherman and Burgess, 1985; and Sherman, 1985) has been studying the social behavior of popular and unpopular elementary and junior high students. In a study of six junior high classes, for example, in which developmentally handicapped students had been mainstreamed, Sherman and Burgess (1985) demonstrated that the handicapped students were not more rejected than their normal peers. Rather, their results showed that rejection in mainstreamed classrooms is more a function of being viewed by peers as unassertive, passive, and socially incompetent. Handicapped students who were positively assertive and active in the peer group were highly accepted by their peers. The researchers concluded that peer rejection is more a function of perceived behavioral attributes than the label "developmentally handicapped." For more evidence for the social deficit hypothesis of children's low sociometric status, see Renshaw and Asher (1982).

As part of the same program of research, Sherman (1985) showed that students who are viewed as having a good sense of humor were more accepted by peers than were students viewed as relatively humorless. Apparently humor facilitates social behavior and social acceptance. Conversely, the absence of humor or the capacity to laugh and share funny stories may provoke social distance in children which, in turn, can lead to social rejection.

Intelligence

Scores on intelligence tests have been found to correlate positively with acceptance in the classroom (see Gronlund and Anderson, 1957, and Richards, 1967). While these correlations tend to be small, the associations between intelligence and liking in the classroom are particularly high at the extreme ends of the intelligence range. Mentally retarded students in normal classrooms, for example, are often the most rejected by their peers (see Jordon 1960, 1961). Torrance (1963), studying highly intelligent students, found that social acceptance was high for intelligent students who were also conformists, but that acceptance was not nearly so high for bright students who were, at the same time, creative. The highly intelligent, creative students were viewed as being odd and different; they received low acceptance ratings by both their peers and teachers.

The studies by Jordon, Torrance, and Sherman suggest that the critical antecedent factor for acceptance is not so much intelligence as it is a cluster of social behaviors that are concomitant with high intelligence. In the case of mentally retarded students, it is likely that they often behave in socially inappropriate ways. They may lack, for example, a sense of timing. They are often clumsy and poorly coordinated. They might not share in the humor of the group. In addition, they might not keep up with the jargon of the peer group, especially when it changes rapidly from month to month. In a similar vein, highly creative students may often behave in divergent and unexpected ways. Nonconformity, especially when it is unexpected, can be uncomfortable and threatening to others.

Little relationship between achievement and liking appears to hold in the early primary grades, but that relationship does become significant in the fifth grade and continues to get stronger as students move into high school (Buswell 1951). In Richard's research, he has shown that fifth and sixth-grade students who are rejected by their peers do not achieve at a level that would be concordant with their intelligence (Schmuck, 1963). A large discrepancy exists between the intelligence and performance levels, especially of those upper elementary students and junior high youngsters who are rejected. Rejected students, particularly during early adolescence, experience alienation from the learning environment, develop reduced self-esteem as students, and are unable to concentrate for long periods of time on intellectual tasks.

Acceptance by peers, on the other hand, can increase students' self-esteem and facilitate their working up to potential. The statistical association between liking and using intellectual potential is correlational, and its causal direction is therefore unknown. We believe that several directions of causation are clearly possible and, indeed, that multiple dynamics linking friendship and achievement are occurring every day in our schools. Students who enter a classroom group as underachievers may manifest fear and confusion in relation to peers and thereby find themselves being rejected. Other students may reduce their likability by initially doing unkind things to others. Subsequently, they are unable to perform well on their studies because of the anxiety they feel in being rejected.

Mental Health

Acceptance by peers is also related to the overall psychological well-being of individual students. Numerous studies that have made use of teachers' ratings, personality inventories, and student nomination questionnaires to assess mental health of students have shown significant correlations between being rejected by peers, on the one hand, and high anxiety, maladjustment, primitive defense mechanisms, hostility, and personal instability on the other. The association between liking in the peer group and mental health appears to be monotonic. That is, the greater the severity of psychological disturbance, the more likely that such students will be rejected. Students whose thoughts stray and who frequently are inattentive—not to speak of those who periodically lose contact with reality and hallucinate in the classroom—respond inappropriately because they are listening to their inner selves instead of attending to others and tuning in on external social situations. Autistic students need special teaching but, unfortunately, they generally need more help than even the most accomplished teacher can provide.

Many students who might be categorized as "mental health problems" are not extreme enough to require special teaching

or counselling. While their behaviors may often be inappropriate and their ability to concentrate is too frequently spasmodic, such students can be helped in a regular classroom as long as the climate is interpersonally supportive and psychologically nonthreatening. Unfortunately, the label "emotionally disturbed" is too often used as a rationalization by teachers who are frustrated in their efforts at disciplining particular students. Some teachers justify ineffective teaching behaviors by pointing out that many of their students are mixed-up and disturbed. Such disturbances are typically viewed by such teachers as developing out of inadequate family experiences, rather than as resulting from an unsupportive and uncomfortable classroom climate.

As a result of an inservice workshop that Richard designed and implemented (Schmuck 1968), the teachers who participated began to cope effectively with the behaviors of students whom they had previously labeled as "disturbed." They came to refer to those students as energetic, active, or lively. These new, more constructive psychological concepts that were developed by the teachers enabled them to view many of the deviant behaviors of the students, at least initially, as divergent, creative, and, perhaps, as uniquely individual. Moreover, some of these student behaviors did indeed become more constructive when the teachers responded to them as arising out of restlessness, anxiety, and energy, rather than interpreting behaviors as being "crazy" or weird in nature.

Sex and Race

Young boys and girls seem to differ in their social experiences; one fairly consistent research finding is the fact that girls tend to interact in small groups, particularly dyads, while boys tend to interact with larger groups. Eder and Hallinan (1978) studied the exclusiveness of children's friendships and found, as expected, that girls tend to be more exclusive in their friendships than boys. That is, two girls playing together tended more often to exclude a third person as compared to two boys playing together. There appear also to be some sex-related differences in friendship patterns. The feelings of boys appear to be influenced more by having low influence or power in the peer group. Girls, in contrast, are affected more emotionally by having low attraction status (Van Egmond 1960). Girls without friends feel isolated, insecure, and anxious about their own worth. In attempting to specify variables affecting the academic performance of boys and girls, Schmuck and Van Egmond (1965) found that girls were significantly influenced by their position in the peer group, their satisfaction with the teacher, and by the level of perceived parental support for school. Boys, on the other hand, were influenced only by the peer group and teacher and not so significantly by their parents.

Karweit and Hansell (1983) reviewed four dimensions along which sex differences have been reported: (1) strong sex segregation in peer friendships from nursery school through early adolescence; (2) the pattern of small friendship groups for girls and larger ones for boys, (3) the different functions of friendship for girls (intimacy, loyalty, and commitment) and boys (achievement, leadership, and competitive advantage), and, finally, (4) sex as a basis for friendship selection.

While it is difficult to explain why such sex differences appear so consistently in the literature, some studies show such patterns differ because of the social structure of the school or classroom. For example, Hallinan (1976) showed that classrooms structured to provide a great deal of student interaction showed little differences in exclusivity of boys and girls. Her study indicates the importance of socialization differences between boys and girls and in the future we may expect to see some changes in the literature about sex-related differences. One study illustrates that point. There are differences in the choices of games preferred by girls and boys today compared to thirty years ago. Girls and boys choose similar games today, whereas thirty years ago there were much more noticeable differences in their choices (Sutton-Smith and Rosenberg 1971). There is no doubt, however, that sex is a personal attribute affecting friendship patterns because of the social meanings connected to being male and female.

Tajfel (1982) argues that sex is a fundamental status factor in virtually every society and particularly in American classrooms. Being male or female places each student into a social category. By interacting more with peers in one's own category than outside of it, a social identity as a male or female is formed. To reinforce the group identity, comparisons are frequently made between the groups and differences are accentuated. Finally, as group members engage in social comparison, there arises an interest in protecting and preserving the distinctiveness of each group. In an empirical study by Sherman (1984), regardless of whether elementary students were participating in a cross-age class or an age-homogeneous class, cross-sex social distance ratings were significantly greater than same-sex ratings. In other words, there was a definite tendency for girls to choose girls and for boys to choose boys, regardless of age differences. At the same time, there was an indication from the statistical analysis that girls were much more cohesive and had a stronger preference for in-group interaction than boys. Moreover, girls were more rejecting of boys than boys were of girls.

Another personal attribute with social meaning is race. Janet Ward Schofield (1978) has followed the patterns of peer relations in an integrated, interracial school. Her studies are particularly exciting because she tests the assumptions of contact theory developed by Gordon Allport in his 1954 book, *The Nature of Prejudice*. Allport set the criteria vital for promoting positive interracial attitudes and behavior; they are equal status within the contact situation, shared goals, cooperative dependence in reaching those goals, and the support of the authorities, law, or custom. Schofield's series of studies in an integrated, middle-class school tested Allport's assumptions. In one article Schofield and Sagar (1977, p. 130) stated that the school "comes perhaps as close as we can realistically expect, at this point in our society's history, to meeting the Allport criteria." And data suggested that integrated, interracial schooling did indeed foster increased voluntary associations between blacks and whites. The data also indicated these associations varied, depending upon the structure of the situation. The seventh graders, who were mixed in most of their classes, had a high rate of interaction, whereas the eighth graders were less integrated because they were streamed into different classes based on previous achievement. The eighth graders showed less voluntary association. Schofield and Sagar also pointed out that sex served as an even more powerful attribute than race; girls interacted more with girls and boys with boys.

And boys had more mixing across racial lines than girls, primarily through contact during team sports.

Other research on prejudice and racism, reviewed by Jones (1985), suggests that providing students with personal information about every other student in the class reduces the tendency to judge a peer in terms of race. That research also suggests that teachers ought to create a sense of "we-ness" within the class as a way of reducing interracial boundaries. One means of accomplishing that is to bring students of different races together for mutual problem solving. Either the minority student is given a position of strategic centrality (such as being appointed convener) or each of the students is given information without which the entire group cannot solve the problem. According to Jones, each of the successful strategies demonstrates Gordon Allport's claim that equal status and intergroup contact, sanctioned by teachers and administrators, will reduce intergroup hostility.

Social Variables Related to Liking

Of course personal variables, such as physical appearance and physical proximity, represent the starting points of the forming friendship. Students who appear attractive to one another, as well as those who initially sit close to one another, commence interaction. Then, as long as there are no significant threats made to either of the students' psychological needs for status and security, communication between the students will be encouraged to continue. The discovery of shared and common attitudes, values, and interests can deepen the relationship, increase the time of interaction, and encourage informal meetings outside the classroom. Favorable reactions from the other can enhance a student's self-worth, leading the recipient to react supportively in the style of a favorable, interpersonal, circular process. The presence of complementarity in terms of interlocking personality needs buttresses the relationship and helps to maintain it.

Friendships are nurtured in social settings; some social settings facilitate the bonds that form between people and other settings discourage them. How the class is structured and how teachers behave toward students are important aspects in the formation of friendships.

Classroom Social Structure

At the group level, classroom friendship patterns have been described in terms of peer group sociometric structure (see Schmuck 1963, 1966, for two empirical studies). Two types of sociometric structures were described: (1) *centrally structured groups,* characterized by a narrow focus of interpersonal acceptance and rejection; and (2) *diffusely structured groups,* characterized by a wide range of supportive and nonsupportive choices, with little or no focus on interpersonal acceptance and rejection. In centrally structured groups, a large number of students agreed in selecting a small cluster of their classmates as students they liked or toward whom they felt friendly. Diffusely structured groups, on the other hand, were *not* typified by small clusters of highly accepted and highly rejected students. These groups reflected a more equal distribution of liking choices, with the absence of distinct subgroups whose members received a large proportion of preferences. Furthermore, there were very few, if any, entirely neglected students.

Research by Marshall (1978) showed that in centrally structured groups there was a less supportive emotional climate and more criticism of the less competent students than in the diffusely structured classrooms. In the centrally structured classrooms, there was a tendency for the academic superiority of a small group of students to prevail.

Richard Schmuck's research indicated that students were more accurate in estimating their friendship status in centrally structured groups than in diffusely structured groups, and, in particular, the low-status children were more aware of their low status. The greater accuracy of perception in the centrally structured class was interpreted in terms of the clarity of status positions. The theoretical bases for that interpretation originated with Gestalt perceptual theory on the one hand (Kohler, 1947, and Lewin, 1948) and group dynamics theory on the other (Cartwright and Zander, 1969).

The assumption from Gestalt theory about sociometric structures was the idea that at least one significant determinant of perceptual veridically lies in the structure of the distal stimulus object, i.e., its "good form," clarity, symmetry, and distinctiveness. Centrally structured peer groups represented clearer and more distinct social stimuli for individual students. Almost every student knew who was liked and who was disliked. From group dynamics, studies on communication nets and group structure (Leavitt, 1951) indicated that task leadership was recognized more quickly and easily in centrally structured groups. Social-emotional status would also be expected to be more easily recognized in groups with centrally structured liking patterns. Thus, in centrally structured classes there was an absence of generalized emotional support that might otherwise obscure a student's low status.

Hallinan (1976) carried out a related study to test whether friendship patterns differed as a function of the pedagogical strategies of the teacher or the school. In relation to the former, Hallinan made use of the concepts of the centrally and diffusely structured friendship patterns. In relation to the latter, she compared traditionally organized classrooms to open schools.

The *traditional arrangements* were defined as self-contained classrooms in which students of the same chronological age were grouped, often homogeneously for purposes of pedagogy or efficiency. In contrast, the *open arrangements* were characterized by classes with considerable variation in the ages of the students, the transitory nature of seating arrangements, and the complexity and variety of ad hoc subgroupings for purposes of instruction. Moreover, many of the open classrooms had resource centers where students might go for informal discussions as well as study carrels where they could isolate themselves to work alone or perhaps with one other person.

Hallinan found that the open classes did, indeed, allow for much more peer group interaction than did the traditional arrangements. Moreover, *a less hierarchical distribution of friendship choices, with fewer social isolates and fewer sociometric stars, was found in the open classrooms as compared to the traditional ones.* In other words, centrally structured friendship patterns were more likely to be formed in the traditional classrooms than in the open school arrangements, and diffuse friendship patterns arose more frequently in open schools than in the traditional ones.

In another analysis, Hallinan (1979) uncovered some unexpected results. Students in the traditional classrooms, with limited social interaction, named more best friends than students in open classrooms with a lot of peer interaction. In an article prepared by Hallinan and Felmlee (1979) this seeming paradox was resolved. Children in classrooms where there is a lot of peer interaction may be more realistic about their friendships, because they have had more of an opportunity to test them out than they would in classrooms where there is little peer interaction. A student can name potential friends, but once the relationship has been found wanting, he or she might no longer list that person as a friend. Thus the inverse relationship between more classroom interaction and fewer best friends is not so surprising.

In a longitudinal study of 4,163 students in four different grades, Epstein (1983) showed how the *physical condition* (the architecture and room arrangements), the *instructional condition* (the degree to which students were grouped and regrouped), and the *psychological condition* (the degree of encouragement of tolerance and acceptance of others), influenced friendship patterns in "high participatory" and "low participatory" classrooms and schools. In the high participatory schools there were fewer social isolates; almost everyone had the opportunity to find a friend. Furthermore, there was not a hierarchy of choices, there were no "stars" chosen over and over again as in the low participatory schools. Students had more diverse friendships, often choosing students of a different sex or race. Finally, self reliance was an important criterion in friendship. As Epstein notes, teachers and administrators have a great deal of influence in providing an educational environment which supports the basic motive for affiliation. The way classrooms and schools are organized directly influences the way friendships are organized and formed in schools.

Teacher Behavior

Naturally, teachers' attitudes toward their students can also be fraught with affect. Teachers tend to prefer those students who are attractive to peers, who exhibit supportive feelings toward other people, and who adjust to the school's demands for academic work and discipline. On the other hand, teachers tend to dislike students who create disturbances and who keep other students from attending to schoolwork.

In general, girls tend to have more compatible relationships with their teachers than boys. Boys more often than girls are disliked by teachers. Teachers have been found to give more negative feedback especially to boys with low status in the peer group liking structure. Lippitt and Gold (1959), for example, showed that teachers often paid closer attention to the social behavior than the academic performance of low-peer-status boys and that those same boys received more overt rebuke and criticism than other students. At the same time, teachers appeared to grant low-peer-status girls support and affection. Those findings were accompanied by the facts that low-status boys were aggressive and disruptive, while low-status girls tended to be more dependent, passive, and affectionate.

Flanders and Havumaki (1960) carried out a field experiment to show how teachers' behaviors can influence the friendship patterns in a classroom group. They asked teachers to respond support-

ively and consistently to selected students and not to others. For a week, teachers interacted with and praised only students seated in odd-numbered seats, while in comparison groups, all students were encouraged to speak and the teachers' praise was directed to the whole class. Students in the odd-numbered seats, in the former classroom situation, later received more peer-group sociometric choices than students in the even-numbered seats. In the comparison classrooms, the difference between sociometric choices of students in the odd and even-numbered seats was insignificant. The peer choices were spread around more evenly, indicating greater general acceptance.

Chaires (1966) attempted to improve the acceptance of low sociometric status students in special classes for the educable mentally retarded. By means of a sociometric scale, she identified the four lowest status children in each of sixteen special classes. Those classes included eight at the intermediate and eight at the junior high level. In half the classes, two of the four lowest status children were chosen randomly to take part in an experimental program, and the other two were identified as being within-class controls. The experimental subjects, along with two of their popular classmates, were then removed from the classroom twice weekly for fifteen-minute sessions in which they practiced a skit to be presented to the class at the conclusion of the program. The experimental program lasted for five weeks. The eight classes not involved in the treatment provided an outside control group. As a result of this intervention, the low-status children improved significantly in sociometric status, in comparison to both the within and the outside class control groups.

Lilly (1971) attempted a replication of Chaire's research, applying a tighter research design in an effort at improving the social acceptance of low sociometric status, low achieving students in regular classrooms. A five-week treatment was used in which low-status students were taken out of class to work with popular peers making a movie to present to the class. Some interesting variations in the treatment were designed to specify the variables involved in the improvement process, including amounts of interaction with high-status peers. High involvement with popular peers in making the movie and in presenting it to the class produced significant gains in social acceptance; however the gains did not endure over a six-week, follow-up period.

For modifications in classroom sociometric structures to be maintained, there must be a continually sustained strategy employed, in contrast to short-term interventions. Retish (1973), for example, showed that if the planned and systematic reinforcement behaviors of teachers toward rejected students were sustained over several months, then significant net gains of the targeted students did result and did seem to continue over time. Still few research efforts can continue on long enough to test sufficiently whether current interventions make a difference. There is a need for longitudinal research on the relationship between teacher behaviors and peer sociometric structures.

In relation to how day-to-day classroom events might relate to sociometric structures, some research by Richard indicated that teachers of more diffusely structured classrooms, compared with other teachers, attended to and talked with a larger variety of students per hour

(Schmuck 1966). Teachers with centrally structured peer groups tended to call on fewer students for participation and seemed especially to neglect the slower, less-involved students. Teachers with the most supportive peer groups tended to reward students with specific statements for helpful behaviors and to control behavioral disturbances with general, group-oriented statements. Teachers with less supportive friendship patterns in their classrooms tended to reward individuals less often and to reprimand particular individuals more often for breaking classroom rules.

Stensaasen (1970), in a lengthy study of classroom interpersonal relations, showed how teacher approval and disapproval is linked to student status in the classroom. Students who are perceived as approved by the teacher have high status and students perceived as disapproved have low social status.

Hallinan and Tuma (1978) point out that the way teachers group students, even though the reasons for grouping are for pedagogical considerations, profoundly influences children's affective relationships. In a study of 32 fourth, fifth, and sixth grade classrooms, Hallinan and Sorensen (1985) found that when teachers used ability groups frequently, students with similar abilities were more likly to become friends. Conversely, the students in ability groups were less likely to make friends with students of differing abilities. Thus, the research demonstrated that *tracking does affect friendship formation.* Bogen (1954) demonstrated that teachers who are aware of the sociometric patterns in the peer group typically have greater rapport with their students. Teachers influence peer relations in the classroom by the way they structure the learning environment, by their attitudes toward students, attitudes that are communicated in covert and overt ways, and by certain specific behaviors such as praising or criticizing.

Satisfaction with the teacher is an important facilitator of a student's academic performance. Students are attracted to teachers who provide them with a boost of status in the peer group and who grant them security. Teachers who reward frequently and who do not rebuke or demean students in the eyes of their peers are attractive. Students who are satisfied with their teachers usually feel good about school, learning, and themselves. The continual rejection of an overtly aggressive student by both his or her classroom peers and the teacher feeds the negative cycle of low self-esteem, unfriendly approaches to others, and poor performance in academic work.

Some Bases of Attraction and Friendship

Everyone gains self-esteem, at least in part, by being *competent, influential,* and *attractive.* The last of these is especially important to the developing child and adolescent. Indeed, interpersonal attraction and hostility are primary forms of social behavior among elementary and secondary school youngsters. Students' personal assessments play a significant part in how attractive they are to their peers. But the psychodynamics of attraction and friendship are, of course, considerably more complex. Four salient and relevant theories from social psychology can shed light on how classroom friendships come into being and how they are perpetuated.

Cognitive Validation Theory

Pepitone (1964), a major proponent of cognitive validation theory, argues that persons have a drive for veridicality. That is, we each strive to perceive the external world as it really exists. According to Pepitone, each of us wishes to read the external world correctly and to behave in appropriate social ways because such reality-oriented and functional behavior will facilitate effective survival. Bizarre, inappropriate, autistic behaviors are maladaptive because they satisfy only internal needs without connection to the external social world. Over time, such maladaptive behavior will become destructive in relation to social effectiveness. Consequently, we strive to adjust to the world around us by trying to tune in on reality. Pepitone states:

> The validation motive is the need for an individual to maintain a cognitive structure which correctly maps physical and social reality concerning the value of himself and others along some dimension. Generally implied by this formulation is that whenever an estimate of his own worth deviates from estimates of objective valuation in a given respect, the individual will tend to change his cognitive structure so that such valuations are more in line with reality (p. 50).

Thus, persons seek to know and to check and recheck their attitudes by mapping them against what is outside. If stimuli from the social world communicate to them that they are worthy and have value, then they will be attracted to that part of reality. If, on the other hand, interpersonal events prove to persons that they are worthless and without value, then they will feel hostile toward that part of social reality. Attraction and hostility toward others, in particular, are built up especially out of the messages about self that a person perceives as being sent by others.

Pepitone carried out a series of experiments to test aspects of this theory and to seek information about the bases of interpersonal attraction and hostility. His general hypothesis stated that interpersonal attraction grows out of others' rewarding expressions that serve to enhance *status* and *security*. In simple terms, Pepitone argued that persons are attracted to those who assign them a position of high status or who help them to feel secure. Persons tend to feel hostile toward those who demean them in the eyes of others or of themselves.

Pepitone designed interrelated laboratory experiments to test the functions played by the variables of status and security in relation to interpersonal attraction. In one experiment, subjects were interviewed by an actor performing as a braggart who made invidious comparisons between the subjects and himself in order to demean the subjects. For example, while looking at his own stylish sport coat and slacks, the interviewer would snidely ask, "Do you always come to appointments dressed as you are now?" Under conditions like that, most of the subjects would feel angry and act in uncooperative and hostile ways toward the interviewer.

Next Pepitone was interested in studying conditions under which boastfulness would or would not arouse hostility. In a second experiment, researchers presented a taped recording of a highly technical discussion on the subject of industrial development in Liberia. One of the participants on the tape sounded extremely omniscient. He acted as though he knew all about the problems and would present solutions for each of the problems in highly technical, flowery language. This omniscient participant in the taped discussion was introduced differently to each of three experimental groups: first, as a student (low status); next as an official of the State Department (high status); and finally as a world-renowned technical expert (super status). Subjects showed most hostility toward the participant when they thought that he was a student and the least hostility when they thought that he was a world-renowned technical expert.

Pepitone argued from this theory of cognitive validation that interpersonal attraction entails checking perceptions against reality. When a person's expressed presentation of self agrees with our view of that person's professional status, we tend to agree with those valuations of high self-worth and to be attracted to the person. If, however, there is some discrepancy between the person's presentation of self and that person's status, such as a student acting as though he or she is omniscient, that person's statements are not consistent with reality and we tend to feel hostile toward his or her mannerisms.

In another of Pepitone's experiments on self-evaluation, subjects were made to believe that they had violated a commonly shared societal norm. As members of a fictitious College Disciplinary Committee, they were induced by stooges to deal harshly with a misbehaving student. Later, they were informed that the student was under intensive psychiatric care and that they had overdone their condemnations and had therefore dealt inappropriately with him. In the end, the subjects essentially had two choices, either to deny that they had violated a societal norm (thus maintaining self-esteem) or to re-evaluate and devalue their reactions (thus diminishing their self-esteem). Pepitone found that most subjects would use all the information available and take all available opportunities to maintain their self-esteem.

The subjects, indeed, did look to authorities, did project blame on others, did rationalize their own behavior, and did defend what they had done as the "only way." Wherever legitimate "outs" were available, such as a letter from the misbehaving student's psychiatrist saying that the student "had not been putting forth effort to improve," subjects tended to defend the correctness of their behavior, thereby keeping evaluations of themselves high. But when all avenues for rationalization were finally closed off, the subjects did tend to re-evaluate themselves and did begin to express dissatisfaction with their own behavior. Thus reality pressures could be made strong enough so that the subjects were compelled to view their actions as inappropriate.

Those experiments supported Pepitone's general hypothesis that we strive to assess ourselves and others in comparison to our understandings of social reality. Moreover, the studies indicated that two social-psychological facets of the real world, *status* and *security,* are integrally related to attraction and hostility in interpersonal relations. And these findings have direct implications for the classroom. Students react to one another according to their expectations of the other's behaviors. They tend to evaluate themselves, in part, according to the enhancement or reduction of their own status in the eyes of their peers, as well as in terms of the security they feel in knowing that they responded appropriately to social reality. *Students will tend to feel friendly toward those peers who enhance their needs for status and security and to feel unfriendly toward peers who behave in ways that are threatening to their desires for status and security.*

Balance Theory

Balance theory states that when behavioral systems are out of balance, forces arise to restore the balance such as in the case of the students in Pepitone's Disciplinary Committee. Imbalance occurs between two people when they are attracted to each other, but hold opposite attitudes about something important to both. Price (1961) showed, for example, that when two people like each other very much but hold different attitudes about others, they feel uneasy and strive to reduce the discrepancy.

Research on balance theory (see Zajonc, 1960, for theoretical background) has focused either on twosomes or on one person's thoughts concerning his or her relationship with another. However, we believe that balance theory can also contribute to an understanding of classroom liking relationships.

Balance theory differs from cognitive validation theory in its emphasis on internal consistency within the individual's psyche. Whereas validation theory leads to an analysis of the social stimuli emanating from the environment, balance theory focuses more on the need to organize thoughts, beliefs, attitudes, and behavior in a psychologically consistent manner. Such striving for consistency frequently constitutes aspects of the psychodynamics of stereotyping and prejudice. Allport (1954) presents the following examples of balance from his studies of prejudice:

MISTER X: The trouble with Jews is that they only take care of their own group.

MISTER Y: But the record of the Community Chest shows that they give more generously than non-Jews.

MISTER X: That shows that they are always trying to buy favor and intrude in Christian affairs. They think of nothing but money; that is why there are so many Jewish bankers.

MISTER Y: But a recent study shows that the percent of Jews in banking is proportionally much smaller than the percent of non-Jews.

MISTER X: That's just it. They don't go in for respectable business. They would rather run night clubs.

The psychological press for balance also manifests itself again and again in perverse social logic about American blacks and is related to the self-fulfilling prophecy discussed in chapter 4. Before World War II, for example, blacks were typically denied admission to labor unions because, it was argued, "they lacked a necessary appreciation of unionism." This supposed "fact" was clearly evident to powerful whites because blacks were continually acting as strikebreakers. But, in reality, the self-fulfilling prophecy was at work. Blacks became so-called "scabs" because they were denied union membership and, consequently, the only alternative way of making a living was to work. Their taking jobs had little if anything to do with a "low sense of unionism."

Balance theory argues that some persons tend to dislike those whose values and attitudes are quite different from their own, and may even express hostility toward people who confront or upset their well-organized images of the world. The original supposition that "blacks lack a sense of unionism" can evoke behaviors of denying union membership which, in turn, can lead

blacks who try to work to be viewed negatively as strikebreakers. Balance theory also argues, of course, that persons tend to like those people who agree with them and to like especially those who hold similar attitudes and values. Indeed, as blacks and whites worked together to pursue common goals within unions they did form a number of interracial friendships. Balance theory emphasizes the need to achieve psychological consistency among people's cognitions and attitudes, as well as a social balance between their views of reality and the views of those with whom they interact.

Newcomb (1961) did extensive field research to test aspects of balance theory. Twice he offered free rent for a semester to seventeen college students who agreed to be observed or interviewed once each week. His overall findings substantiated balance theory; that is, those students who, before meeting one another agreed on a variety of attitudes, were attracted to one another after they had lived together for a time. Furthermore, such attraction became stronger as students learned of more similarities that they shared.

In a parallel sense, elementary and secondary students in classrooms continuously check one another's beliefs and attitudes. Liking takes place between those who share similar attitudes and values. Of course, children's friendships undergo more changes than adult friendships. Students change grades, teachers, schools and after-school activities with unusual frequency. Hallinan and Tuma (1978) report that mutual friendships of elementary students last an average of 90 days and high school students have a pattern of changing friendships (Epstein, 1983). The development of a close friendship increases the probability that the friends will find more and more ways in which they are similar. Once this process gets going it tends to reinforce itself as in the manner of the circular interpersonal process.

Self-Esteem Theory

In contrast to balance theory, which emphasizes the importance of internal consistency within the human psyche, proponents of self-esteem theory argue that enhancing self-esteem is a more powerful motivator in more circumstances than achieving cognitive balance. A key hypothesis in self-esteem theory is the concept that people are attracted to those who give them favorable feedback and not attracted to those who demean them, regardless of whether or not the feedback is consistent with the recipients' views of themselves. A contrasting hypothesis coming from cognitive balance theory would lead us to predict that persons with low self-esteem would react favorably to negative evaluations—since such feedback would be consistent with their own self-image.

Jones (1973), a proponent of self-esteem theory, has argued that balance theory does not often hold up under conditions of favorable and unfavorable feedback. He wrote that the unhappy self-derogator seems to glow when praised and glare when censured, even more than his self-confident counterpart. Jones poetically states the importance of self-esteem for understanding the attraction process by rewriting one of the paradoxical psychological "knots" presented by Laing (1970). Whereas Laing wrote: "I am good—you love me—therefore you are good"; "I am bad—you love me—therefore you are bad," Jones rewrites the second part, "I am bad—you love me—therefore you are truly beau-

tiful." And Jones's own research, along with an experiment by Krauss and Critchfield (1975), tends to substantiate that point.

Although Jones may be correct where the particular topic of love is concerned, both the balance and the self-esteem theories are useful for understanding attraction and friendship in the classroom. Depending upon the social-psychological circumstances, one theory or the other may take precedence in explaining interpersonal attraction. Favorable feedback usually takes place within an interpersonal context that has a history as well as a cluster of contemporaneous, impinging forces. Jones discusses, for example, two psychological climate conditions in which the desire to enhance self-worth may be temporarily suspended in favor of either cognitive validation or cognitive balance. The first condition occurs when the consequences of favorable evaluation are perceived by the individual as being unrealistic. The favorable feedback is viewed as being dysfunctional or undesirable for the recipient over the long term. The second condition takes place when the motivation behind the favorable feedback is distrusted by the recipient.

Let us first discuss the former condition as it might occur within the classroom. Most classrooms are replete with feedback in the form of interpersonal evaluation—either friendly pats on the back or negative putdowns. In particular, students are frequently formally evaluated on their schoolwork by teachers, and even more frequently, informally evaluated about their interpersonal behaviors by their peers. For students who very much want to become competent in an academic subject, in a psychomotor skill, or in their personal interactions, feedback from others will be essential to keeping them on a correct "learning track." Unrealistically favorable feedback will not be helpful in overcoming tough obstacles during the learning process, since it might be misleading and dysfunctional.

As Nyberg (1971) has indicated, learning is both "tender and tough." Only through straightforward, honest feedback that is *right-on* and *authentic* will a student be able to learn new competencies, and be guided in new, more functional behaviors. Students who begin to notice that some kinds of favorable feedback from particular people are not helpful to them in achieving their own goals will not be attracted to the giver of that kind of feedback. In this circumstance, the desire for self-worth is delayed for future gratification, and tough feedback is valued as being instrumental to the achievement of higher levels of self-esteem.

The second condition discussed by Jones concerns the motivational basis of the approving feedback. Students wish to think of themselves as having some control over their own fate (see Coleman et al., 1966, and DeCharms, 1976, 1977, for empirical support). When students believe that their own behavior has prompted approving feedback, they may view themselves as being the cause of the favorable response and probably will become attracted to the giver. However, if the teacher indiscriminately praises everyone in class, any particular student who receives such praise will not necessarily feel personally responsible for having behaved in ways that warranted the supportive feedback. After all—the student may think—our teacher makes those nice comments to everyone.

This psychological process can be explained by balance theory. The student is attracted to the giver of both favorable feedback and unfavorable feedback when the student views the cause of either type of feedback as coming from his or her own behavior. The psychological balance is rewarding because either kind of feedback fits the reality of the student. In other words, authenticity may be more attractive than perceived dishonesty.

While cognitive balance may function in this way when the authenticity of the feedback is problematic, self-esteem theory better explains our reactions to others when the feedback comes from people with high prestige. According to Krauss and Critchfield (1975), when prestigious people give favorable feedback, they take on lower potency for the recipient of the feedback than when they issue criticism and negative feedback. Thus, even though the recipient of the negative feedback may not believe that the criticism is warranted when it comes from a prestigious source, the recipient's self-esteem is reduced and his or her friendly feelings toward the source of the feedback are reduced and may even be transformed into hostility and rejection.

The cognitive validation, balance, and self-esteem theories of attraction and friendship formation can be useful for understanding the effects of different sociometric group structures. Validation theory would argue that students will strive to assess themselves in the eyes of their peers by trying to discover their status position in the classroom "liking" structure. If the sociometric structure is organized so that only a few students are clearly the most attractive to others, then it should be relatively easy and straightforward for a student to determine his or her place in the peer group. The perceptions of students in centrally structured classes are in close agreement with the actual, obvious structure.

With a striving for psychological balance at work, a sense of rejection by others can lead to negative opinions about self-worth which, in turn, can lead to a perception of the classroom as a threatening environment. And, according to the self-esteem theorists, rejection by others can usually lead to frustrations in enhancing self-worth and dislike for those who are negative. Even though the need for validation is just as strong for students in diffusely structured classes, the status patterning is unclear, and a more generalized pattern of emotional support is more apparent. Students receive about the same number of positive choices as their peers; more students view themselves as highly liked or at least as secure. In diffusely structured classrooms, the students' self-perceptions of high status and general emotional support from the peer group encourage the high self-esteem and low anxiety that help the students perform well in their academic studies. The classroom is not a threat and students feel a sense of security and status.

Need Complementarity Theory

This theory states that persons become attractive to one another when their contrasting psychological needs are gratifying in an interlocking, complementary manner. Need complementarity theory focuses upon the exchange of dovetailing personality needs through interpersonal transactions. Thus it differs in emphasis from the other three theories which place greater emphasis on either the social forces outside relationships or the internal, cognitive, and affective dynamics of the interacting individuals.

In an empirical study of the need complementarity theory, Winch et al. (1955)

discovered that marital partners often chose each other in part to satisfy complementary needs, e.g., assertive persons tended to marry receptive persons, and dominant individuals seek more submissive ones. Schutz (1958) made use of this sort of formulation in his theory of interpersonal relations, arguing that persons relate to one another primarily in terms of inclusion, control, and affection needs. Attraction occurs between two persons when they each satisfy the other's needs in these areas, e.g., a person with a strong need to express control will be attracted to one who wants to be controlled.

Need complementarity may also be the basis for some of the friendships that form in classrooms. Students who want to be very affectionate will like peers who need to receive a lot of affection. Students who want very much to be included in games and activities will like peers who strongly wish to include them. Students who are dependent and anxious about their status in the group may like peers who show them what to do and who exert a good deal of leadership.

The Relationship Between Friendship and Cohesiveness

Attraction processes relate to cohesion with more complexity than a mere summing up of interpersonal friendships in the class. An individual's attitudes about a group are related both to how attractive other members are *to* the individual and to how accepting the others are *of* the individual. The psychodynamics of attraction and acceptance of a group are integrally associated with the self-esteem levels of the participants. And the relationships among attraction, acceptance, and self-esteem are circular in nature. Thus, students who are attracted to a class and who feel accepted by the members of

FIGURE 6.1   Johari Model of Awareness in Interpersonal Relations

	Known to Self	Not Known to Self
Known to Others	1. Open Area of Sharing and Openness	2. Blind Area of Blindness
Not Known to Others	3. Hidden Area of Avoided Information	4. Unknown Area of Unconscious Activity

Reproduced by permission of J. Luft, *Of Human Interaction*. Palo Alto, Calif.: National Press Books, 1969.

that class will experience enhanced self-esteem. Conversely, students who enter a class with high levels of self-esteem will behave in ways which lead to their being accepted and will tend to perceive the environment of the classroom—both physical and psychological—as attractive.

Trust and openness are also related to the psychodynamics of attraction, acceptance, and self-esteem. Students develop trust and openness with others in the group depending upon the emotional closeness or distance they feel toward one another. In emotionally distant interactions, students know little about one another and view one another as objects that can either fulfill or frustrate their wishes and expectations. In emotionally close interactions, students recognize their interdependence with others, realizing that the other person's behavior simultaneously influences and is influenced by their own behavior.

In a useful conceptual model on the topic of psychological openness, Luft (1969) has described interpersonal relationships in a helpful way for understanding some of the psychodynamics of cohesiveness. The four quadrants presented in Figure 6.1 are the basic ingredients of his graphic model. This so-called *Johari Awareness Model*—named by combining the first names of its authors, Joe Luft and Harry Inghram—can also be used by the teacher as an instructional device for helping a class to look at itself as a group. The basis for division into the four quadrants is the awareness of behavior, feelings, and motivation on the part of the individuals in the group. An act is assigned to one of the four quadrants based on "who" knows about that act. Thus, quadrant 1 refers to behavior, feelings, and motivation known both to oneself and to others. Acts in quadrant 2 are known to others, but not to the self. Those in quadrant 3 are known to oneself, but not to others. And acts in quadrant 4 are known neither to the self nor to others.

Luft argues that productive working relationships with others as well as the cohesiveness of a group can be facilitated by increasing the area of quadrant 1 in relation to the other three quadrants. The theory states that as group members interact openly in order to reduce blind spots and to reveal hidden areas of personal concern, they become emotionally closer. Moreover, as communication increases among students, more openness and spontaneity will also arise among them. They will reveal more of what is on their minds, and they will be less afraid of giving feedback and talking frankly to one another. Increasing the area of quadrant 1 is one way of describing what happens psychologically as a classroom group becomes more cohesive. We believe that classes become more cohesive and stronger as groups when the students share more of what so often is hidden from public discussion.

Effects on Academic Performance

A student's perceived sociometric position within the classroom peer group has definite implications for the accomplishment of that student's academic work (Schmuck 1963, 1966, Glick, 1970, and Lahaderme and Jackson, 1970). Students who are accurate when estimating their position in the friendship structure, and who are negatively placed within that structure, tend to use their academic abilities at a lower level and have less favorable attitudes toward self and school than students who are accurate and favorably placed in the friendship structure. Moreover, students in diffusely structured classrooms quite often think of themselves as being liked by at least a few peers, use their abilities more highly, and have more favorable attitudes toward self and school. This occurs even though, objectively speaking, they often hold low status in terms of the classroom pecking order of

choices. Finally, research has indicated that students who have very few friends outside the classroom group are more influenced by their liking status in the classroom group than are students who have more non-class friends. Thus, the detrimental impact on academic performance of a student's holding low status in a centrally structured peer group is even greater when that student has no close friends outside the class.

Those findings were essentially corroborated in an important study by Lewis and St. John (1974) which dealt with the achievement of black students within classrooms with a majority of whites. In an effort to study the dynamics of racially integrated classrooms, Lewis and St. John set out to test the concept garnered from the 1954 U.S. Supreme Court decision that integrated school experiences would facilitate the achievement of black students. They collected extensive data from 154 black sixth-graders in twenty-two majority white classrooms in Boston. Their results showed that a rise in the achievement of blacks depended on two factors: (1) norms stressing achievement in the classrooms; and (2) acceptance of black students into the classroom peer group. This second factor was shown to be especially important. The mere presence of academically achieving white students was not sufficient to raise achievement levels of black students. The performance of blacks was strongly influenced by their being accepted as friends by white students.

It is also important to note once again that some research evidence indicates that girls are affected more by an absence of friends than boys. According to a review by Hoffman (1972), affective relationships are paramount for females, and much of their achievement behavior is motivated by a desire to please others. Thus, in school situations where excellence in academic performance might threaten affiliation, Hoffman argues that girls may well sacrifice performance to maintain friendships. Apparently the anxiety a girl experiences over loss of friends is stronger than the anxiety felt by failure to master some aspects of the academic environment.

One clue as to how the needs for affiliation and achievement might be integrated and formed into an enhancing relationship comes from a study by Lucker et al. (1965). This action research compared the academic performance of fifth and sixth-graders, including both girls and boys as well as Anglos and minorities, working in small, interdependent learning groups in traditional, teacher-focused classrooms. The interdependent learning groups' style of working together was based on what Deutsch (1949) has labeled "promotive interdependence." The model stressed the use of small, interdependent learning groups in which students taught one another the material to be covered. A covariance analysis indicated that while the Anglos performed equally well in both interdependent and traditional classes, the minorities performed significantly better in interdependent classes than in traditional classes. Unfortunately the researchers did not compare the performances of boys and girls.

In any case, for many students, being attractive to peers can be a very important variable within the matrix of forces facilitating or inhibiting achievement. Students who receive unfavorable and negative feedback from their peers are put in a threatening environment for many hours each day. A lack of peer acceptance undermines a student's self-confidence and hinders his or her motivation to persist in the face of tough academic obstacles. The feelings of interpersonal support and helpfulness along with actual interdependence with others can enhance a student's achievement efforts and subsequent academic performance.

Effects on Group Production

Members of cohesive groups invest energy in their interpersonal relationships, tune in on the expectations of others, and gradually make many of the others' expectations their own. In this way, group norms become crystallized and members feel interpersonal pressure to conform. Such interpersonal stress need not lead to dehumanizing pressures toward conformity that reduce the individual's autonomy and creativity. On the contrary, when the norms support individual differences and autonomy, the interpersonal pressures to abide by them will free students to seek their own unique ways to gratify themselves.

Indeed, research in industrial organizations has demonstrated that cohesiveness is correlated with the productivity of a group, provided the norms are supportive of production. Cohesive groups are more goal-directed than noncohesive groups, and as long as the shared goals of the individuals are in line with productivity, cohesiveness is a facilitating factor. One way of describing the relationship between cohesiveness and norms, delineated by Seashore (1954) and generally replicated by Stodgill (1972), is illustrated in Figure 6.2.

Seashore found that the performance of highly cohesive individual work groups, in comparison to those having low cohesiveness, was either very low or very high. He argued that the U-shaped curve shown in Figure 6.2 was indicative of the role played by norms in relation to cohesiveness.

FIGURE 6.2   Relationship between Cohesiveness and Performance

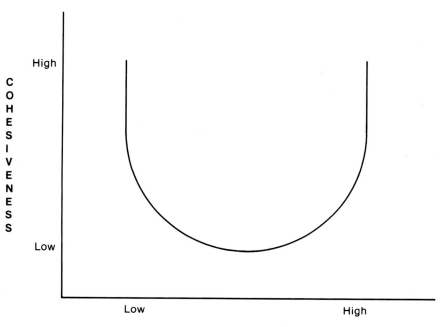

Work groups whose norms opposed high output performed poorly, especially when the groups were cohesive. In such groups, cohesiveness diminished productivity. Similarly, research by Stodgill indicated that industrial groups had highest productivity when they were cohesive and when members possessed "high drive," that is, when the members were motivated and enthusiastic about the group and its intended purposes or products.

It is clear that similar group processes could prevail in the classroom. Students who share negative attitudes about academic learning and who make up a cohesive peer group probably would achieve at low levels. Conversely, student groups with supportive norms for learning would attain high achievement, especially as such groups increased in their cohesiveness. In other words, *high cohesion typically means that students will be more susceptible to interpersonal influence than usual, the direction of influence being regulated by the group's norms.*

Kafer (1976) illustrates the relationship between productivity, norms, and cohesiveness in elementary classrooms. He studied the capacity of students to influence the work levels of others. He found that students who are in highly cohesive, small friendship groups abided by the work norms of the groups and were very resistant to change. When the norms of these friendship groups were task oriented, the student was more productive; if the work norms were antiproduction, the student followed likewise. Students from groups with low cohesiveness were more amenable to their teacher's influence on their attitudes toward work.

Reynolds (1977) demonstrated how a buddy system could improve the attendance of students in a junior high. To commence the program, thirty students with moderate attendance problems were selected by school counselors. These students were asked to choose a buddy—"someone who lived close to them or someone who had a telephone to call them." If the buddy were willing to take part, the pair would check in with a counselor each morning to record their attendance. Before beginning the program, the counselors held a party with refreshments; during this party the pairs were told that for improved attendance they would receive awards of record albums, picnics, or pizza parties. After six weeks, Reynolds reported significant gains in attendance and that many of the pairs had become friends.

Types of Classroom Cohesiveness

Students are attracted to classrooms for a variety of reasons. Some students like the challenge of certain kinds of schoolwork. Some like to be near particular students. Some simply like to be rewarded for extra efforts. And some students believe that they will gain prestige when they are perceived by others to be part of a particular class. Just as youngsters feel differently about their classes, classroom groups can also be described as being cohesive for various reasons. Back (1951) carried out an experiment in which he investigated various "pulls" that groups have for individuals. In his research, the subjects worked cooperatively in pairs on a task. The pairs were formed to be cohesive or not, and the cohesive pairs were arranged in one of three ways: (1) attraction to the group because of a liking for the other member of the pair; (2) attraction to the group because of mutually held high interest in the task; and (3) attraction to the group because of its prestige for the members. Even though the three types of cohesiveness were different, the groups that were cohesive in one way or another worked more effectively on the tasks than the noncohesive groups.

These three sources of cohesiveness are visible in school settings. Attraction to other students is often the primary source of cohesiveness for extracurricular clubs, for informal gatherings at lunch, and for parties. Common interest in an activity or task is often the basis of cohesiveness in the school's drama group or on the basketball team. Prestige is often a powerful source of cohesiveness for members of the football team, the cheerleader's rally squad, and some special, advanced classes. Indeed, any group in the school can possess one or more of these bases of cohesiveness, and each gains higher amounts of overall cohesiveness as it incorporates one or more of them. For instance, the student council will work in a more concerted fashion if it performs activities enjoyable to the members, or if it has some prestige within the school, or if the members feel friendly toward one another. Groups with fewer bases of cohesiveness, of course, will work less coherently. Unfortunately, classroom groups often lack cohesiveness, especially when compared to other student groups, because common interest in the tasks, prestige, and friendship are missing.

The sources of attraction in any particular group obviously will differ for the individual students who make up the group. For example, when in 1990 we interviewed a cluster of junior high students who were very enthusiastic about their class in local government, we heard a variety of answers to the question, "What do you like most about this government class?" Some of the answers were: "I get to study with my two best friends;" "It's interesting to find out how this town operates;" "I'm going to have a chance to be a mayor for the day;" "I'm getting a chance to know more people in the class;" "I'm thinking about politics for a career;" and, "The work is fun to do." While each of these answers revealed a different interest on the part of an individual and several different sources of cohesiveness, together they added up to a highly cohesive class.

As the cohesiveness of a classroom group increases, the more students feel they are satisfying their interests, values, and motives. Such satisfactions, both according to Back's research and to our observations of students, center on the activities, prestige, and friendships that a class offers its members. Psychologically speaking, students' feelings about themselves as students become more or less favorable, depending upon how much their achievement, power, and affiliation motives are satisfied. Thus, executing a task productively and efficiently can reward students' achievement strivings, while being part of a group that many others respect can satisfy power needs. And associating closely with friends on a regular basis can satisfy the motive for affiliation. In contrast, if students continually fail at learning tasks, they often will also experience unpleasant interpersonal relations with peers. Also, students' feelings about the class will be negative and their involvement will tend to be low.

The teacher's classroom influence extends only to providing a *setting* for students to fulfill their achievement, power, and affiliation motives. The teacher's influence cannot *assure* that such satisfactions will be met. Students will generally attempt to satisfy their personal interests and motives when they view themselves as valuable in the eyes of their peers and as contributing members of the group. Teachers facilitate the emergence of such feelings by being clear themselves about learning goals and by helping students to choose ways of arriving at the goals. It is in the area of increasing the flexibility of arriving at learning goals that open, two-way communication is so important in the classroom. If channels of communication are closed, and feelings or concerns are hidden, little chance for establishing multiple avenues for satisfying individual interests is possible. When many people participate actively and openly so that the air can be cleared and interpersonal problems can be publicly discussed, more chances arise for the students to find ways of satisfying their own interests and motives.

For some individual students, however, cohesiveness can have negative consequences. Students who are attracted to the class and wish to belong, and who, at the same time, view themselves as being rejected by some of their peers, will experience negative feelings about themselves and their schoolwork. Such negative emotional states often arise when a student's initial attraction and involvement are based primarily on interest in the task or the prestige of the group. Subsequent interpersonal rejection, after becoming involved, can be psychologically painful. Empirical relationships linking sociometric status, self-esteem, and academic achievement are especially strong in highly cohesive classroom groups. *Students who are accepted members of cohesive classrooms with a dispersed friendship structure experience high self-esteem and typically are working up to their intellectual potential.*

The Circular Interpersonal Process: The Case of the Rejected Student

In chapter 4 we explained the circular interpersonal process, a useful way to describe the friendship patterns in a classroom that are based on enhancing or resisting the exchange of personal resources. Students who view themselves as competent in physical skills or in their academic abilities may attempt to actualize their resources by offering to help someone with less skill (transmit some of their resources) or by using their physical prowess to force someone to do what they want him or her to do (convert resources into personal power). In the former case, they will probably become attractive; in the latter case they will probably become disliked. Students in need of help with their schoolwork may initiate an effort to use the resources they perceive a classmate as having by asking for help. The resource of being liked can be understood in terms of the actualization efforts initiated by the possessors of the resource to express friendly feelings toward others or to exert influence over those who are attractive to them.

Interpersonal relationships that entail the exchange of resources become stable and predictable in many classrooms and can be conceptualized by using the model of the circular interpersonal process. Moreover, the circular process is helpful for understanding how friendships remain stable over time. It includes attitudes toward the self and others, how these get expressed behaviorally, and the perceptions and reactions of the others in the interaction.

As we noted in chapter 4, expectations form a fundamental part of the circular interpersonal process. Even when a rejected student makes a valiant effort to change his or her own style of relating to others, it will be difficult for others in the peer group to notice the behavioral changes because they believe so strongly that he or she will behave negatively and with hostility sooner or later (for supporting research, see Northway, 1968). Often the rejected student's expectations influence his or her perceptions so that the incoming information received is biased. Thus, a student in a negative cycle might try to act friendly, by perhaps tapping a fellow student softly on the back or by nonverbally agreeing with another, but because the others' expectations are so strong, the negative student may be viewed as "hitting" or as "acting smart" or trying to perpetuate an argument. Negative cycles of interpersonal relations become emotionally vicious when behaviors intended to be benign are seen as negative and, therefore, as confirming the original expectations.

In a program of classroom research in Australia, Kafer (1981 and 1982) demonstrated that rejected students experienced problems both in perceiving others and in reacting to them. In a study of person perception, Kafer showed that rejected and isolated students made more errors in recognizing the emotional expressions of others than did normal children. And in another study, Kafer demonstrated that the interpersonal strategies of unpopular children backfire much more frequently than the interpersonal strategies of popular children. Unpopular children, more frequently than popular children, became noisy, obstinate, boastful, and rebellious to their teachers and peers. While children with moderate popularity often hesitated in initiating interactions, the most unpopular students continued to make inept attempts to be accepted by their peers.

Students who are rejected by or isolated from their peers typically have had the sympathy of their teachers. While the reality of rejected students has always been with us, the concept of "rejected student" took classic form with Moreno (1934) and with the idea of sociometric testing. Indeed, there is a long-standing debate about whether instruments such as sociometric tests should be used because they point out an unpleasant reality (see Stensaasen, 1967, for details).

And the current task of moving physically or mentally handicapped students into regular public schools raises the issue of rejection to a different level. Handicaps such as blindness, deafness, confinement to a wheelchair, speech impediments, and emotional disturbances are often upsetting to other students (Woodward 1980) and people who have handicaps are often rejected. One student, who walked laboriously dragging one foot, a useless arm crooked in front of her, admitted to problems. There are three kinds of kids, she said. "There are the curious ones who ask questions, the friendly ones who are too shy to ask questions, and

the rude, mean ones who tease me, push me into lockers and throw my books on the floor" (Woodward 1980).

Although the research already described (Lilly, Chaires, and Retish) is not overly optimistic about teachers changing the sociometric status of rejected students, we are hopeful that sensitive and dedicated teachers can use the knowledge gained from this book to improve the status of rejected students.

Implications for Teachers

The following points summarize some of the most important implications of the contents of this chapter for teachers.

All human beings strive to be attractive to someone else. Although the degree of affiliative motivation will differ from person to person, all people will look for some friendship in most groups.

Friendship relationships within the classroom cannot be separated from teaching and learning; they are integral to instructional transactions between teachers and students, and among students.

Cohesiveness is an attribute of a group, not of individuals. It entails shared feelings of loyalty, membership, closeness, and trust.

A classroom group is cohesive when most of its members, including the teachers, are strongly attracted to the group as a group, and when most group members are highly accepted by the others.

Attraction to a classroom group occurs for individuals when their self-esteem in relation to membership is raised. This takes place when their desires for achievement, power, and affiliation are satisfied through interactions with other group members.

Students who view themselves as being disliked or ignored by their peers often have difficulty in performing up to their academic potential. They experience anxiety and reduced self-esteem, both of which interfere with their academic performance.

The instructional behaviors of teachers can have a significant impact on the peer group friendship patterns that develop in the classroom.

In highly cohesive classrooms, students' involvement in learning may be high or low, depending upon the particular norms of the group. Productivity in learning will tend to be high in classes where there is high cohesiveness and where the norms support academic involvement.

Action Ideas for Improving Climate

Some of the practices used by teachers or consultants are discussed below.

Diagnosing Classroom Sociometric Structure

Kafer (1979) found that while teachers were accurate in assessing the measured sociometric status of children, they were quite inaccurate in assessing the class social structure. The following sociometric instrument with directions for coding and analysis can be used in a variety of ways illustrated below.

Preparing the Class

Instrument 6.1 is useful for gathering data relevant to classroom liking patterns. Beforehand, the teacher should duplicate an alphabetical list of the class members with a number in front of each name; these numbers should be those assigned to students for identification of the forms. Each student should receive a copy to refer to and record classmates' numbers rather than names.

Students may require the teacher's support in one special area. Everyone forms positive and negative feelings about his or her associates. Negative feelings may be harder for students to accept than positive feelings, for society often frowns on their expression, and most children have been rebuked for too free an expression of their dislike of someone. At the same time, the expression of negative or critical feelings is often necessary for constructive change and development. Those students who fear to express their negative feelings about others even when this expression might be helpful, or who have not even permitted themselves to accept the fact that they have such feelings, may need reassurance about the naturalness of these feelings. Some help may be needed, too, in the expression of positive feelings. For example, the student who is shy or withdrawn may find it difficult to name anyone whom he or she likes, or a boy who is attracted to a girl may hesitate to admit it for fear of being razzed by his male peers. Treating the task in an objective, routine manner is a real help to students who have difficulty in recognizing and expressing the way they feel. The teacher might help students by reading the top paragraph of the questionnaire to the class, making sure that everyone understands the confidential nature of the responses.

Modifications in the tools are necessary at early grade levels. To measure patterns of classroom liking, one teacher of very young children used small school photos of each student and five plastic freezer boxes with simple faces drawn on them illustrating five degrees of feeling as indicated in Instrument 6.2.

Each child, working privately, sorted the photos and put them into the appropriate boxes according to the way he or she

---

INSTRUMENT 6.1

How I Feel about Others in My Class

Everybody has different feelings about everybody else. We like some people a lot, some a little bit, and some not at all. Sometimes we think it is not proper or polite to dislike other people, but when we are really honest about it, we know that everyone has some negative feelings about some of the people he or she knows. There are some people who like you a lot and some who don't like you at all. If the teacher knows the way you really feel about other members of your class, he or she can often plan things better.

There are no right or wrong answers. (Use the class list to answer the following questions.)

1. Which three persons in this class do you feel most friendly toward? Using your class list with names and numbers, write the three numbers in the blanks.

The three I like most are: Student's Number

                                                             _____

                                                             _____

                                                             _____

2. Which three persons in this class do you feel least friendly toward?

The three I like least are: Student's Number

                                                             _____

                                                             _____

                                                             _____

Instrument 6.2

**How I Feel about Others in My Class
(for Young Children)**

| Very Nice | Nice | So-So | Not So Nice | Not Nice at All |

felt about each person. They were questioned about the reasons for their feelings toward classmates whose pictures were put in the extreme boxes. The teacher who used this method reported that selected sixth graders had been taught to do an effective and confidential job of testing the younger children individually and recording their responses. The sixth graders also analyzed the data by constructing matrices and targets of the type described below.

Analyzing the Data

After the data are collected, they can be tabulated in various ways, depending on the problems to be solved. A basic kind of tabulation that gives the most information for the least effort is a matrix with as many rows and columns as there are students in the class. As shown in Figure 6.3, prepared for a class of sixteen students on the liking dimension, positive choices are indicated by 1 and negative choices, or rejections, by -1. Each row across contains the choices made by the student whose number appears at the left; the columns contain the positive or negative choices received by the student whose number appears at the top of the column. By adding the total number of positive and negative entries in each column, the choice pattern is evident at a glance.

Inspection of this matrix shows a classroom that is narrowly focused, with a few very popular students, several who are quite unpopular, and others who have few, if any, friends. Student 11 is clearly the star of the class, with twelve positive and no negative choices. Students 2, 5, and 9 are also highly liked, although one student dislikes 5 and another dislikes 9.

On the negative side, students 13 and 14 are widely disliked, with ten and eight negative choices respectively. Students 6, 10, and 12 may be thought of as isolates, for they are mentioned by no one, either positively or negatively.

In many cases the choices are mutual. For example, student 1 chose students 2 and 5, and students 2 and 5 similarly chose student 1. Numerous mutual negative choices are also apparent, as between 3 and 13, 4 and 14, and 9 and 15. In these cases the students have made their feelings toward each other clear enough to be recognized and reciprocated. But in some cases opposite feel-

FIGURE 6.3 Matrix for Sociometric Analysis

	1	2	3	4	5	6	7	8	9	10	11	12	13	14	15	16
1		1			1		−1				1			−1		−1
2	1				1		−1		1				−1			−1
3	1				1			−1			1		−1		−1	
4		1			1		−1		1				−1			−1
5	1			1				−1			1		−1		−1	−1
6		1		1			−1				1		−1		−1	−1
7		1							1		1		−1	−1	−1	−1
8				1			1		1				−1	−1		−1
9		1		1			−1				1		−1		−1	
10		1			1		−1				1		−1	−1		
11		1			1			−1	1				−1		−1	
12	1							−1	1		1		−1			−1
13			−1	1	1						1			−1		−1
14				−1	1			−1			1		−1			1
15	1			−1	1				−1		1		−1			
16			−1		−1				1		1		−1		1	
Total +	5	7	0	5	9	0	1	0	7	0	12	0	0	0	1	1
Total −	0	0	2	2	1	0	6	5	1	0	0	0	10	8	4	9

ings are expressed. For example, student 7 names 2 as liked, whereas 2 names 7 as not liked. Findings such as these challenge the teacher to try to change perceptions and feelings.

A separate matrix of this kind might be prepared for each dimension—such as a liking, influence, or cooperation—that the teacher wants.

To summarize the data from a matrix and point them up more graphically, the target method is useful. To construct a target, draw four concentric circles, as shown in Figure 6.4.

In the center of circle A, the bull's-eye, place the numbers of the students who receive more positive choices than would occur if the choices were evenly distributed among all the students. If each student is asked to choose three others he or she likes, an even distribution would give each student three votes. In this case students who receive four

FIGURE 6.4   Sociometric Target

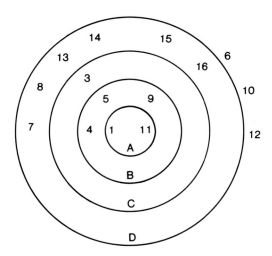

or more positive choices and no negative choices are placed in the bull's-eye.

In ring D place the numbers of those students who receive four or more negative choices or rejections and either one or zero positive choices. In ring B place the numbers of those who are more liked than disliked, even though they are not highly chosen. In ring C place the numbers of those who are more disliked than liked. Place the numbers of the neglected students outside the whole target. In Figure 6.4 the data shown on the matrix from Figure 6.3 have been recorded on the target.

Another organization of sociometric data is a series of class maps, or sociograms. A simple procedure is to arrange the class in circular fashion on a large sheet of paper, each student represented by a number. Then lines are drawn between circles to represent choices; a solid line indicates a positive choice, a broken line a negative choice. An arrowhead points toward the person chosen. Where there is a

mutual choice, there is an arrowhead at each end of the line. Lines of different colors can be used to include more information or to clarify a sociogram.

The sociogram shown in Figure 6.5 represents a class of fifteen students who were asked to name the person or persons they would most like to sit next to in school and the person or persons they would least like to sit next to. In this case there was no attempt to make the students give a specified number of choices. Numbers 1 through 8 in the diagram represent girls; 9 through 15 represent boys.

In this class there is a rather clear split between boys and girls, with only one girl, 5, who makes a positive choice of a boy, 15, and no boys who make positive choices of girls. Among the girls, 3 is the most popular, with five positive choices, three of which are mutual. Moreover, this girl has no negative choices. According to the questionnaires on which the sociogram was based, there is no student who would dislike

FIGURE 6.5   Simple Sociogram

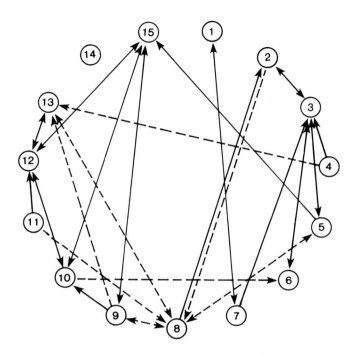

sitting next to her and none whom she rejects. In sharp contrast to this is 8, who is rejected by three boys and two girls. She herself rejects three of these students, and the one student whom she does choose positively, 2, rejects her. This appears to be a girl who is in trouble because of her interpersonal relations and who needs help. Another person who might be in need of help is 14, who made no choices himself and was chosen by no one. Students 4 and 11 were also unchosen by any of their peers. The pattern of choices for student 13 suggests that he has one good friend, 12, but that he is otherwise rather disliked.

Instead of preparing a matrix, a target, or a sociogram, a teacher might find it easier merely to make tallies on the alphabetical

name list of the class, recording after each name the number of positive and negative choices a person receives on each of the dimensions being studied. This would not, of course, illustrate how and to whom individual students interrelate.

Using the Data

Data analyzed on a matrix, in a sociogram, or in some other way are useful in answering a number of questions.

Which students need special help in improving their interpersonal relations because they are rejected or ignored by their peers? By looking at the sociogram or data sheet, the teacher can spot those students with a high number of negative choices and those with no choices. Those are the students who may need special assistance, either from the teacher or from some other source.

Which students are overchosen and which are underchosen? Since students are asked on these tools to make three positive and three negative choices, each student would receive from two to four choices of both kinds if the choices were nearly evenly distributed. How many students receive one or no choices? How many receive a large number of choices? The target method described is useful for such an analysis.

Which high-influence students are liked by their peers? Working from the matrix or from a tabulation, the teacher can list the names, in order of the most liked. These are the leaders in the eyes of the class.

Going further in this direction, are these influential, well-liked students seen as good students and cooperative with the teacher, or are some of the most influential students in the class seen as being against schoolwork? The comparison of a list showing ratings for cooperation with the lists already made will give this information.

How might students be grouped so that certain ones can have a good influence on their peers? The "whom I want to be like" questions may show which good students might be the most constructive models for some of the poorer and less motivated students.

Picture Method for Measuring Friendship Structure

A sixth grade teacher we observed last year in a small town, elementary school used Instrument 6.3 to measure her students' perceptions of friendship in her class and to find out where each individual student placed herself or himself in the classroom friendship structure.

Diagnosing Acceptance of Outgroup Members

The lion's share of studies on sociometric choices in the classroom use the traditional peer nomination method. In that method, each student is asked to list a few (usually 3 to 5) classmates who are friends or best friends. By so measuring, the teacher does get a good idea of the classroom sociometric structure, but the peer nomination method does restrict (by design) the number of others a student can choose. When no out-group members (those of a different sex or race) are included among the top choices, a teacher could erroneously conclude that out-group members are not accepted. Schofield and Whitley (1982) recommend using a "roster-and-rating" method to study the acceptance of out-group members.

In the roster-and-rating method, each student is given a list of all of his or her classmates and indicates on a 4, 5, or 7-point scale the degree to which he or she would like (for example) to work or play with each classmate. It is important to keep in mind that while the peer nomination method is best for diagnosing friendships and friendship structure (central vs. diffuse), the roster-and-rating method is better for assessing interpersonal acceptance, a less close, affective relationship. Schofield and Whitley point out that "since interracial acceptance (or we might add intersex acceptance) rather than close friendship is one of the basic goals of school desegregation," roster-and-rating methods are more appropriate than peer nomination methods.

INSTRUMENT 6.3

The Classroom Group (A Method for Measuring Friendship Structure)

If you were to think about this class as a group, which one of these drawings would most nearly resemble your class?

Pretend that each circle stands for a person in this class. Circles that are close together stand for people who are friends. (Check the one most like your class.)

Place an "X" within the circle that stands for your position in the group.

a. _____

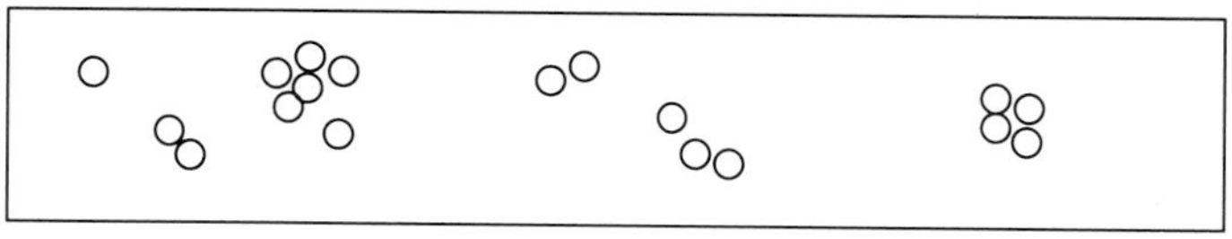

b. _____

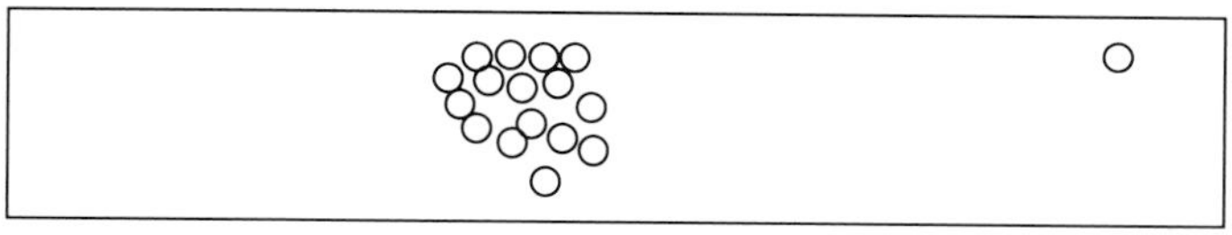

c. _____

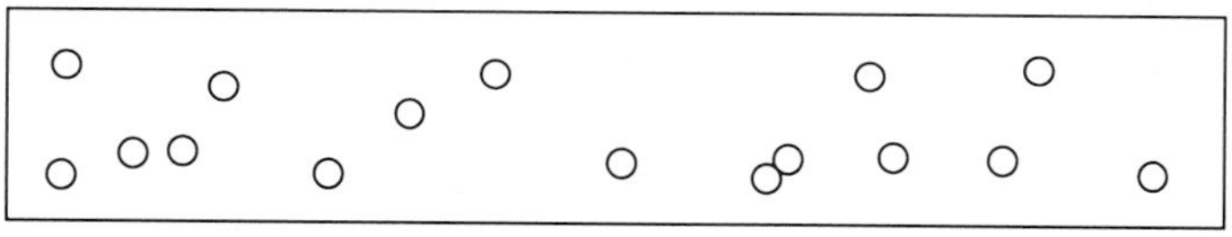

d. _____

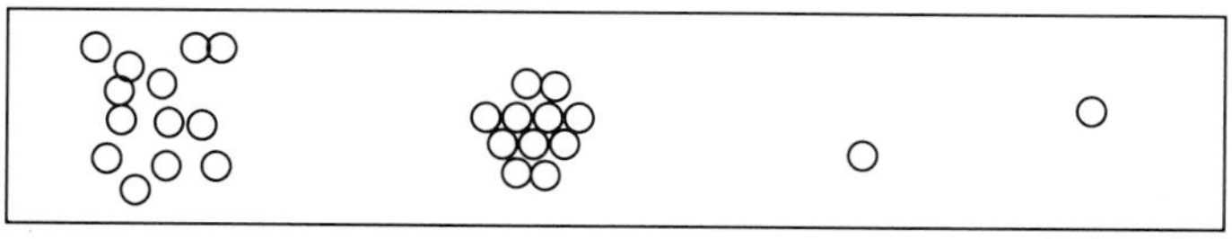

Other-please draw

e. _____

The method is as follows: "Everybody has different feelings about working and playing with everybody else. Rate each person in your class, first on how much you'd like to work with them on a class project and second on how much you'd like to play with them in games outside the classroom."

After collecting these data, the teacher uses a matrix such as in Figure 6.6 to implement the roster-and-rating method.

1.   Working on a class project

Rating

Class Roster	A Great Deal	High	Medium	Low	Not at all
1.					
2.					
3.					
4.					
.					
.					
.					
N					

2.   Playing in games outside the class

Rating

Class Roster	A Great Deal	High	Medium	Low	Not at all
1.					
2.					
3.					
4.					
.					
.					
.					
N					

Becoming Friendly by Becoming Better Acquainted

Several elementary and secondary teachers have used the following procedure for helping students to become better acquainted. Each student is given a large index card (8 1/2″ × 6″) and each student working alone is instructed to do the following: First, in the very center of the card, print your first name or the nickname you want others to use in this class. In the upper left-hand corner of the card, print at the top the city and state in which you were born, and right under this print the name of the place that you most like to visit, such as a vacation place or the place where your

FIGURE 6.6   Matrix for Roster and Rating Analysis

Student nos.	1	2	3	4	.	.	.	.	.	N
1										
2										
3										
4										
.										
.										
.										
N										

grandparents live. Next, in the upper right-hand corner of the card, print two of your favorite leisure-time activities. Now, in the lower left-hand corner of the card, print two of your favorite TV programs. Next, in the lower right-hand corner, print something fun that you did last summer, and next to it, print something fun that you hope to do next summer. After you are finished, walk around the room and pair off with other students so that you can read each others' cards. Tell each other about yourselves. Try to get to meet everyone in the class!

After the preceding process, the teacher holds a discussion with the whole class to see where the similarities and differences are in the group. The teacher stresses how important it is for a good class to have lots of both personal similarities and differences.

Improving the Acceptance of Rejected Students

The goal of this practice was to improve the peer group environment for rejected students by training the class in empathy and by taking the role of another person. The teacher started by administering a sociometric questionnaire (see Instrument 6.1) to see which students had high and which had low friendship status in the group.

After analyzing the data that were collected, the teacher began by working first with a group of low-status students, next with a group of high-status students, and finally finished the design by working with the whole class. She used a chair to stand for a fictitious person. The chair was placed in front of the group and given human characteristics. Low-status students were asked to sit in the chair and to express behaviors that they thought would "turn other people off." The high-status students were asked to sit in the chair and to express understanding, acceptance, and inclusion of others. Both groups discussed the behaviors and the feelings related to them and then talked about their relevance to the classroom. After these discussions had gone on in separate groups for about one month, the entire class met to enact classroom situations of acceptance and exclusion through role playing.

In the evaluation of the practice, the teacher said that considerable amounts of interpersonal strain had been reduced among many of the students, and that several of the low-status students now had a few friends.

Using An Art Project to Measure Friendships

A sixth-grade teacher employed an art activity as a vehicle for measuring the friendship structure in her class. All students were urged to think creatively about the following art project. They were to use "bubble letters" in printing the names of everyone in the class in an artistic arrangement on an 8 1/2 by 11-inch sheet of paper. After all of the students had prepared their own posters, the teacher read these instructions: (1) Find the names of people you wish were your friends—color them *red*. (2) Find the names of people you know very little about—color them *green*. (3) Find the names of your friends—color them *blue*. (4) Find your own name—color it *yellow*. (5) If you cannot fit some names into the above categories, leave them *blank*.

Then the teacher collected the posters and designed some action steps for improving relationships within the peer group.

Making A Book About Friends

In our travels during 1989 to small town schools, we met a second-grade teacher who was spending one hour a week with her class to have the students create their own class book about friends. The initial activity, carried out in groups of four, was for the students to come up with their own sayings about friendships. For example, two small groups came up with, "Friends are there when you need them," and, "You can be yourself with your friends." Next, each small group drew a picture to depict their saying. Then all sayings and pictures were put in a class book. Next, the students were formed into new groups of four to discuss the characteristics of their friends. They came up with such things as: "We have fun together," "We watch TV together," "We do sports together," and, "We play together." All of these characteristics of friends were also printed in the class book. Still, later in the year, pairs of students got together to write a story about friends. Again, after the stories were finished, they were printed in the class book.

Diagnosing Classroom Cohesiveness

Perceptive teachers can easily make note of classroom behaviors that indicate the cohesiveness of a class. They can, for example, count the number of times plural pronouns in contrast to singular pronouns are used during classroom discussion. Classroom groups in which "we" and "us" are frequently heard are usually more cohesive than ones in which "I" and "me" are more often expressed. Members of cohesive groups see themselves not so much as individuals set apart from the other students, but rather, as being part of the class. Teachers, also, might watch for students to offer and accept help from one another. Generally, cohesive groups are characterized by more cooperative relations among themselves and more competitive relations with outsiders.

Another indication of a class's cohesiveness is its internal flexibility in accommodating individual differences. Students in a cohesive class take pride in the group, even in the physical appearance of the room, and can work easily with a variety of their peers. Work groups can be changed easily. Members take one another's place when a substitute is needed. And students want to fill in where they can be helpful. Another indication occurs when students participate with other class members in out-of-classroom activities. Examples include playing together at recess, having lunch together, walking home together, and studying together. Helpful, friendly, and cooperative relationships with classmates both inside and outside the classroom are indications of cohesiveness. At the same time, competitive circumstances outside the classroom will find members of the cohesive group upholding and supporting one another.

Teachers will also find it useful occasionally to gather data about cohesiveness with questionnaires. The questions should not be elaborate; often simple and straightforward items will suffice. For example, a number of questions could be answered by students using the following multiple-choice answers: (a) All of the students; (b) All but a few; (c) More than half; (d) About half; (e) Less than half; (f) Only a few; and (g) None. Sample questions might be: (1) How many students in this class would you say you know pretty well? (2) How many students in this class do you think you could easily work with in a small group? (3) How many students in this class do you think feel friendly toward one another? (4) How many students in this class would you say you like quite a lot?

Negative answers to questions such as these, or the absence of very many indicators of cohesion, are not necessarily reasons to be alarmed. In some respects the search for high classroom cohesiveness can be carried too far. However, there is enough research evidence available now to argue that the achievement of at least a minimal level of classroom cohesiveness can enhance student academic performance, and that, therefore, a teacher's attempt to establish peer group cohesiveness is worth the building of new and better teaching strategies.

Public Discussion of Cohesiveness

A junior high teacher wished that his students would discuss their feelings of involvement in, or alienation from, the class as a means to more interpersonal openness in the group. He structured the initial discussion in relation to the Johari Awareness Model by first taking several minutes to present the four quadrants and then asking each student to think about the question, "How do I really feel about this class?" As an example, he began filling out a blank Johari model on the blackboard, as portrayed in Figure 6.7. The teacher next asked the students to fill out quadrants 1 and 3 by themselves. After giving them about five minutes to work on each quadrant, he organized the students into groups of four. All members of any one small group filled out quadrant 2 in reference to each of the other participants in their same group. Quadrant 4 was skipped altogether.

The purpose of the exercise was to reveal many private feelings that might have been hidden and to discuss those feelings so that they would be understood by others. Since a cohesive group may be achieved, at least in part, by building trust and openness, it was important for this kind of sharing to occur. The exercise worked well in that most of the students became actively involved. It also served to launch the class on once-a-week debriefings about the group, discussions that were very fruitful in building cohesiveness. It should be kept in mind, however, that some cohesion and attraction must already exist in a classroom group before public sharing will be carried

FIGURE 6.7   How I Really Feel about This Class

1	2
I don't like to read out loud. I like to have class discussions. I think this class is "cool."	You act mean when you get a low score. You say "ah" a lot when you talk out loud in class.
3	4
I am afraid of making mistakes. I like to work with Joe.	

out in a forthright fashion. The next two activities can be helpful in producing a beginning level of cohesion.

Involving Students in Evaluating Their Curriculum

A secondary English teacher thought that her students felt close to one another, but that their interpersonal involvement did not extend to supporting one another in learning English. She thought that they were poorly motivated for academic work, even though they were already fairly cohesive, so she sought to modify the group's norms so that the members would band together in the study of English. As a way of changing group norms, she hoped to involve them in curriculum building more than she had in the past.

She decided to begin by asking all students to report their feelings about classwork that had already been accomplished. She developed a format for student evaluation of past classroom activities which en-

tailed the following steps: (1) She discussed the reasons why the evaluation of past events was important for building a more interesting English course. (2) She presented an evaluation sheet for the week's studies. (3) She had the students fill out the sheets and prepared a summary of the data for a discussion the next day. (4) She revised the curriculum based upon these evaluations. (5) An evaluation sheet was filled out every week. (6) Feedback was given every Monday, and revisions in the curriculum for that week were presented.

After carrying out several months of evaluations and incorporating the results into weekly lesson plans, the teacher was convinced that students' ideas were useful and sensible. The students liked the procedure and, most importantly, from the teacher's point of view, the close interpersonal relationships that energized many actions of the peer group were now being more fully used in supporting the learning of English. Although this activity added more routines for the teacher to be concerned about, the increased motivation and learning of the students reduced her frustrations and worries.

Discussions on the Commonality of Problems

A fourth-grade teacher wanted to demonstrate to his students that many of them shared very similar interpersonal and emotional concerns. He wanted his classroom to be a setting where students would feel free to discuss problems, and, perhaps, to receive help from other students. He also hoped to increase feelings of interpersonal support and closeness in the peer group. He began by using an "unfinished story" about a fictitious boy who wanted to learn to speak French but who didn't want to admit it to his friends. The teacher asked his students to brainstorm for some possible endings to the story. Later, the teacher asked all the students to write out real or fictitious problem situations for the class to consider. Discussions on these were held by the whole class or by various subgroups. The teacher noted a definite increase in sharing and communicating among the students—a development which had an especially enhancing impact on the increased involvement of the *least* active students.

Discussions on Affirmative Action

An eleventh-grade social studies teacher wanted her students to grapple with their own information and values about affirmative action. She believed that open debates about affirmative action could be one way of reducing prejudice, racism, sexism, and ageism among adolescents.

She told the class that affirmative action is a policy taken by an organization such as a governmental office, a business such as McDonalds, or a high school to hire or to promote people in groups that in the past have suffered discrimination (e.g., blacks, women, and senior citizens) ahead of people in the previously advantaged or preferred groups. In other words, affirmative action argues that to right the wrong of history, we should take action based on individuals' membership in groups. But, then, isn't affirmative action exactly what prejudice is defined to be: a judgment of an individual based on group characteristics?

How can we embrace a policy that would commit the same mistake it was intended to correct? If we don't pursue affirmative action, how do we correct the negative situation for outgroup members? How do we personally resolve this dilemma? What is your position? Present your arguments. Now, reverse your position and argue the other side.

After students had time to work alone and in pairs on the questions above, the teacher randomly selected 2 teams of students to debate each other. The other students described what they heard and how they felt about the debate after it was over.

A Film on Prejudice

A film, "The Eye of the Storm" (1968), portraying a classroom experiment on prejudice conducted by a sixth grade class in Nebraska, can be useful for facilitating a class discussion on prejudice. The teacher was aware that her students, who were growing up in an entirely white town, would have very little real idea of how black people might feel as the target of prejudice. She divided the class into brown-eyed and blue-eyed students and conferred superior status on those with blue-eyes. The film reveals how the teacher implemented the experiment and what the results were within the peer group in real, behavioral terms. The film ends with a class discussion about how it felt to have brown or blue eyes (ABC Films, Communications Park Video, P.O. Box 1000, Mt. Kisco, NY 10549 or Koral Media, 22 Riverside Drive, Wayne, NJ 07470).

The Jigsaw Puzzle Method

Aronson and his colleagues (1975, 1978) have developed a classroom technique that has been tried in several schools and that has proven to be a useful way of increasing interpersonal acceptance and friendships, particularly among students of different racial and ethnic groups. Students working in six-person teams are each given one paragraph to study from a multiparagraph lesson and are asked to teach their peers the content of their particular paragraph. For example, if the lesson is about the Life of Martin Luther King, each of the six students would be given one of six paragraphs pertaining to Dr. King.

One paragraph might relate to his ancestry, the next to his development as a youngster, the next to his college years, etc. Each student would be given one and only one paragraph to study. The student's job, then, is to prepare to teach the contents of the paragraph to the other members of the learning group. To enhance pressure toward cooperation within teams, the students are given a quiz on the life of Dr. King later on. Since the only way that each student can learn all about him is to listen carefully as others are teaching, there typically develops a highly cooperative relationship among the peers rather than one in which each student is pitted competitively against the other. Aronson et al. found, moreover, that if a few students in the study group are having difficulty in articulating their paragraphs, instead of putting them down, the others gradually learn that interpersonal ridicule is dysfunctional. Indeed, the participating students learn to become probing interviewers, asking their teaching peers the sorts of questions needed to learn the material.

In our travels to small town schools in 1989, we observed an excellent use of the jigsaw puzzle method in a ninth grade English class. After going through *Romeo and Juliet* once with the whole class, the teacher divided the students into five groups. Each group was responsible for becoming expert on one of the acts of the play. Then each expert group taught the rest of the students about the fine points of a particular act. The teacher felt very good about how motivated the students became in teaching the other students. He thought, too, that these students learned a lot more about *Romeo and Juliet* than did other students he had taught in more traditional ways.

The Five Square Puzzle

The jigsaw technique is not unlike a group exercise called the "five-square puzzle"— one that has been used successfully with both elementary and secondary students to create increased interpersonal attraction and helpfulness within the peer group (see Schmuck and Runkel, 1988, for details). In groups of five, the students are given exactly enough puzzle parts to construct five complete squares. At the outset, no individual can complete a square with the pieces he or she is given. The rules create a reason for interdependence and cooperation. Only giving pieces to others is allowed. There can be no taking, no motioning or beckoning, no grabbing, and absolutely no talking. The group's task is not completed until there is a completed square in front of every group member. After the group task is completed, the ensuing discussion should focus on problems of coordinated effort and on the implications of the exercise for relations among the students of the class.

Strength-Building Exercise

The goal of this practice was to build the self-esteem of individual students by the group's sharing favorable characteristics of everyone in the class. The teacher first led a discussion on the large variety of personal traits of people, moved next to the traits that are valuable, and then on to the importance to the classroom of knowing who is good at what things and of having people who are good in different things. Students were then given a large sheet of newsprint paper and asked to put their names at the top and to list in large letters what they considered to be their most important strengths as persons.

Every student was encouraged to have at least three important items on his or her list. These sheets were hung up around the room, and the students were asked to add strengths to other students' lists, strengths that they had perceived in the past. Each student was encouraged to add something to the other sheets, or, at least, to point out agreement with what others had written previously. Later, the teacher mimeographed sheets about all the students' resources and discussed ways of using the strengths in the class. In most classrooms where this practice has been employed, the results have been an increase in interpersonal closeness and friendship among some of the students.

Building Academic Work Groups to Change Classroom Friendship Patterns

The main goal of this practice was to change a centrally structured friendship pattern into a diffusely structured pattern. The teacher organized small work groups to work on social studies projects. The groups were formed to include a heterogeneous mix of high, medium, and low-status students. The groups were altered every month so that almost every student had a chance to work with every other student during the year. The teacher felt that this simple procedure increased the friendship status of most of the students who initially were not viewed as very attractive to their peers.

Norms

7

Norms influence patterns of interpersonal interaction by helping individuals to understand what is expected of them and what they should expect from others. Group life is usually orderly and predictable because of norms that take the form of shared expectations and attitudes about thoughts, feelings, and actions. Without such social-psychological guideposts for individuals, group processes could be confusing, unpredictable and, at times, chaotic. Moreover, norms can help a group to clarify what is distinctive about itself and central to its identity.

In the classroom, norms are shared expectations or attitudes about appropriate school-related procedures and behaviors. Students tend to behave predictably most of the time because of their adherence to norms. Norms serve, therefore, as strong stabilizers of behavior because the members of the classroom group monitor one another's behaviors. The strength of group norms in the classroom arises out of four kinds of forces: (1) forces within the individual to reduce conflict felt when personal actions are different from those held by others; (2) forces induced by others who wish to influence the person's behavior; (3) forces induced by the activity structures such as reading circles, one-way presentations, and seatwork through which students interact with the teacher and with one another; and (4) forces induced by the group to maintain its own distinctiveness and identity.

Objectives of this Chapter

In this chapter we aim to help students understand the relevance and importance of norms for classroom life. Since norms are often difficult to diagnose, we define them in detail so that their measurement will be more straight-forward, both for classroom teachers and their students. The chapter summarizes up-to-date theory and research on norms, particularly as they relate to classroom situations. It proceeds to point out several implications for action, particularly actions that teachers might take but also the potential actions of students who wish to change classroom norms. We end the chapter by proposing various teaching strategies that have been successfully used by teachers to establish constructive norms for learning.

Norms in the Classroom

Important norms in classrooms are those which exercise influence over the student's involvement in academic work and those which influence the quality of interpersonal relations between the members. Because there are so many individual differences in the classroom, it is important for norms to be flexible and changeable. A supportive classroom climate has a broad range of tolerable behavior and considerable latitude for idiosyncrasies and individual differences.

Unfortunately, the norms of many classrooms are not characterized by flexibility and a wide range of tolerable behavior. Traditional classrooms, for example, in which the students sit in assigned seats, organized in neat rows, and where the teacher organizes and directs most of the learning activities are frequently characterized by a narrow range of individualistic norms. Each student is on his or her own to carry out assignments alone and without the help of, or even without interaction with, other students. Often such classes are also characterized by norms of competitiveness:

students pitting themselves against one another in trying to obtain the support, favor, and good will of the teacher. In those competitive settings, the urge to work together or even to act in a friendly way toward one another may get very little support from the teacher. As a result, there is a low amount of congruence between the formal and informal life of the peer group in such classes.

Too many classrooms that we have observed over the past 25 years, and even into the 1990's, have group norms that are not conducive to learning. For example, we have observed norms in support of students talking at the same time and not feeling obliged to listen, students interrupting one another in disrespectful ways, students using sarcasm, ridicule, or put-downs to express insulting disapproval of other students, and students pushing and shoving one another during periods of academic learning. Perhaps even more unconstructive have been norms that support teacher and students paying *no explicit attention* to whether their ways of working together are helpful for learning. Moreover, in such classes a norm sometimes exists with the concept that problems are a sign of weakness and that classroom life is supposed to have no problems. Any problems that surface are the responsibility of the teacher to solve. Students do not view themselves as being responsible for making the classroom environment more supportive and constructive for learning.

Even though there are still many classrooms that lack constructive norms, there is also a trend, particularly in the 1990s, that runs counter to the individuated and competitive norms of traditional classrooms. More and more, contemporary teachers are stressing interpersonal helpfulness and group cooperation. Students are expected to work on projects cooperatively, to study together, to drill each other, to form tutoring relationships, and to move quickly and efficiently from one "ad hoc group" to another.

Ideally, classrooms should have room for a variety of norms which would support different sorts of students doing different tasks at different times. For some activities, and especially when interpersonal trust and support are low or when friendships require some buoying up, cooperative projects could be emphasized. At other times, using special activities such as writing compositions or reading for book reports, students could be expected to work alone and silently at their own desks. For still other activities, such as athletic games or intergroup projects, competition could be appropriately emphasized. The most ideal mix of norms must be tailored for a particular teacher with a particular cluster of students in relation to the subject matter of class focus.

Arranging a supportive climate for learning can also be viewed as facilitating the development of group norms that permit a lively intellectual life within the classroom. Thus, interactions between students are open and direct, with agreements or disagreements stated clearly about what is being studied; conflicts are considered natural and seen as cues that it is time to enter into more discussion and cooperative problem solving. These norms permit the public expression of a student's ideas. They also offer feedback to the student about the adequacy of these ideas, offer friendly relationships that permit the student to look at any cognitive inadequacies, and offer support for risk-taking in order to learn new ideas and to express them to others.

The Theory of Norms

Any conceptualization of norms emphasizes *interpersonal sharing;* thus, norms occur in groups and are not psychological processes alone. The proper psychological counterpart of a norm is an attitude—a predisposition to think, feel, and act in particular ways. An example of an attitude is a student's feeling of friendship toward a peer. The student thinks nice thoughts about the peer and acts toward the peer in friendly and supportive ways.

Norms, on the other hand, are individuals' attitudes that are *shared in a group.* Thus, an example of a norm is a class that acts friendly toward a new student and class members who expect one another to act friendly toward the newcomer. The interpersonal and intrapersonal dynamics of expectations that were presented in chapter 4 undergird norms. In this chapter we move beyond individual expectations to investigate *shared* expectations held by group members, and how these expectations function in the classroom. These shared expectations are part and parcel of norms. When a norm is present, most group participants know that their class attitude is also held by others, and that the others expect them to have that attitude and to behave accordingly.

Sociologists and anthropologists have been more interested in norms than have psychologists. There have been several significant high-points of that history. Sumner (1906) popularized the concept of *folkways* to depict the power of the normative culture of a society or community. Later, the Lynds (1937) and Warner and Lunt (1941) described the social classes of American communities as having very different norms, thereby attempting to explain the differences in behaviors between middle and lower-class persons. Still later, Whyte's (1943) classic study of delinquent gangs offered poignant illustrations of group norms in action, while Cohen (1955) spelled out a theory of norms to explain the delinquent activities of urban gangs. Whyte and Cohen demonstrated that delinquent gangs hold high standards for themselves and exert a great amount of influence on their members to abide by norms. Still later, Angell (1958) described current crises in our large cities as a condition of unclear and unshared moral norms.

Goffman (1959) demonstrated in a host of everyday situations, including schools, that group members very naturally exchange information about norms, thereby sharing expectations, usually implicitly, about how they are to behave toward one another. Goffman likened interaction in schools and other organizations to being on stage, initially without a script, but learning what the play is all about after interacting for a time with the other actors. People are very, very gradually socialized into the norms of a group. Hargreaves (1967) demonstrated the impact of peer group norms for school achievement in England, and Wax (1971) described the problems of Indian education as emanating largely from the strength of peer group norms emphasizing low initiative and achievement. The importance of norms has also been applied to corporate cultures by Deal and Kennedy (1982), Schein (1985), and Kanter (1989). And, although school cultures have not been discussed much in the literature, except by Sarason (1982) and Goodlad (1984), some school administrators have been influenced to analyze their schools' climates by using the ideas from writers on corporate cultures.

Sociologists and anthropologists have also been interested in connecting the absence of clear norms with individuals' feelings of alienation. Faunce (1968) proposed, for example, that "normlessness" is a predisposing condition to alienation. By normlessness, Faunce referred to the circumstance of an individual who recognizes very few effective rules or standards for guiding personal behavior. In effect, the predictable social system and its behavioral regularities have broken down. Normlessness refers, therefore, to the emotional condition of the individual for whom there are few guidelines and few expectations shared with others. Alienation, on the other hand, represents a sense of social isolation and estrangement from the group. Normlessness, while rare in classroom and schools, does affect some subgroups of students, particularly those most "at-risk." Alienation from the ambiguous and inconsistent norms of many classrooms is quite widespread in our public schools.

Norms in schools typically develop gradually and informally as students learn what behaviors are necessary for their class to function effectively. Most classroom norms develop: (a) as the result of explicit statements by the teacher; (b) as the result of critical events in the class's history; (c) as a result of what the teacher emphasized during the first week of school; or (d) as the result of routines and behaviors learned by the students in other classes.

Norms can be categorized as either *static* or *dynamic,* depending upon the amount of active interpersonal influence, and as either *formal* or *informal,* depending upon how codified, public, or traditional they are. Static norms make up the basic, unconscious culture of groups. Group members tend to abide by them without much interpersonal pressure being actively exerted. For example, a shared expectation that all students will have their own textbooks for a class is a formal, static norm in many schools. The traditional principle of "one student—one book" is regularly written, or at least assumed, within the policy handbook of the school district or even in some state laws. And, until it is questioned by several students, teachers, or by members of a community or a legislature in a public arena, it will remain static.

Norms of greater interest to the teacher are dynamic and informal. In some classrooms, for instance, a norm exists specifying that students should *not* help one another with schoolwork, especially when tests are being taken. If fellow students and the teacher take action to keep one another from sharing and discussing an assignment, they are actively supporting the norm through their interpersonal influence. A contrasting norm may exist in other classrooms—that of helping one another on schoolwork and viewing it as a valuable activity. Such a norm probably would not be sustained without the active support of a large part of the class, since the norm of surrounding classrooms, in many instances, would not support it.

Figure 7.1 delineates these distinctions in more detail by offering some typical examples. A norm could, at any time during its development, be placed in any of these four categories. Generally speaking, norms develop first as dynamic and informal and next become either static and informal or dynamic and formal. Static and formal norms usually have existed for a long time and are a fundamental part of the assumed classroom group processes. Classrooms in which even the most straightforward and traditional norms are dynamic are typically in trouble because so much time and energy must be spent in just maintaining order.

FIGURE 7.1   Examples of Classroom Norms

	Formal	Informal
Static	Rules followed with little prompting: 1. No cheating 2. Asking permission to leave the room 3. Addressing teacher when seeking permission to change something in the room	Procedures and routines: 1. How students enter the room 2. Who talks to whom for how long 3. Saying, "Good morning," "Thank you," etc., to the teacher
Dynamic	Rules in need of at least occasional enforcement: 1. No talking during story time or individual study time 2. Turning work in on time 3. Using correct grammar in talking and writing	Interpersonal actions which involve active monitoring: 1. Addressing teacher in a nasty fashion 2. Wearing hair in an extremely different state than other students 3. Acting abusively toward others

Schools and classrooms are replete with a multitude of examples of all four types of norms that influence the behaviors of teachers and students. But while norms are pervasive in educational settings, only a few systematic studies have been done on the ways in which they function in classrooms. Many of the ideas in this chapter are taken from social-psychological theory and research on industrial settings. On the other hand, most of the examples we present are from actual classrooms where we have worked or observed, particularly during the 1980s and 1990s.

The Nature of Norms

Norms are group agreements, usually implicit, which help to guide the psychological and behavioral processes of the group members. They influence *perception*—how members view their physical and social worlds; *cognition*—how they think about things, other people, and themselves; *evaluation*—how they feel about things, other people, and themselves; and *behavior*—how the members overtly act. In the real world of any particular group, it is difficult to separate perceptual, cognitive, evaluative, and behavioral processes. Nevertheless, we will keep them separate here to provide a clear conceptualization of the complexities of norms in action.

Perceptual Norms

During perception, the person derives meaning from sensory experiences. Sometimes perception acts as a straightforward process in a group when persons agree on what they see. But at other times, individual group members differ widely on the meaning they attribute to a set of sensory experiences. Furthermore, groups can have a decided effect on how individuals perceive a particular sensory experience. A first-grader's perceptions of his or her teacher may be quite favorable. The child views the teacher as a beautiful, supportive, and gentle person. However, if the youngster's peers were to speak about the teacher in critical ways, describing the teacher as cruel, judgmental, and aggressive, the student might begin to look for different behaviors from the teacher. The student could begin to look for cues of negative attributes and most likely would perceive behaviors that would confirm the group members' comments. Through an interpersonal influence process, perceptual norms are formed and students are affected psychologically.

Sherif (1935) conducted a classical experiment on the dynamics of perceptual norms in which he used the "autokinetic phenomenon"—a stationary pinpoint of light that appears to the human eye to be actually moving when viewed in a totally darkened room. Subjects were asked to estimate the light's movement for 100 separate trials at two-second exposures. Initially, one-half of the subjects worked alone and declared their estimates of movement to the experimenter, thereby establishing personal standards of perceptual judgment. During this initial phase of the experiment, subjects generally settled on a range of movement between two and ten inches. Next, subjects worked in groups with two to four members in which one-half had already established a perceptual standard, while the other half had not had an experience with the autokinetic phenomenon.

The subjects were then asked to declare their individual estimates publicly. In this small group situation, all the subjects of a particular group developed group agreement, even though such agreement was not stressed by the experimenter. If the group norm centered on eight to ten inches of movement, those who previously saw the light moving three or four inches changed in the direction of the group, and vice versa. Variation between groups was greater than the variation between individuals within the same group, even though individuals of the same groups initially held very divergent perceptual standards.

To complete a sequence of research, Sherif asked the subjects once more to make individual judgments of the light's movement. Most of them—even with no apparent pressure to conform—persisted in estimating the amount of movement that had been established by their small groups. The ambiguity of the sensory data, along with the public sharing of estimates within the small group, lead to the development of a perceptual norm. Once established, this norm continued to be influential, even when subjects were alone, because for most subjects it had become an internalized attitude, guiding their perceptions in an ambiguous, confusing circumstance.

The classroom with its many sensory experiences has all kinds of ambiguous and unclear events. Teachers, for example, are especially important figures for the development of perceptual norms because they possess significant potential power. But they, in fact, represent an unknown factor—especially as the school year begins. What will the teacher be like? Will the teacher be tough? Can the teacher be trusted to be kind? Can the teacher be believed, or will he or she have a change of mind and be confusing? How will the teacher behave toward us?

Students begin unconsciously to establish perceptual norms on the meanings of the teacher's actions. Frequently, students bring negative attitudes toward active and open participation in class discussions from their previous classroom experiences. Those attitudes quickly become shared and solidify into perceptual norms, particularly if the teacher dominates and cuts off students as they begin to speak. Ambiguity and confusion may arise when a new teacher states a desire to hear what is really on students' minds. Is it for real? Can the students trust the teacher not to punish them for being outspoken? How direct can they afford to be?

In our observations, perceptual norms of suspicion for the teacher's actions can be so strong and severe in some classroom peer groups that participation will remain low, even as that teacher states the desire for participation to be much higher. Norms for low participation are tenacious because students fear that the teacher does not really mean what is said. Moreover, students fear that fellow peers will not be supportive in collaboratively testing the teacher's earnestness. The persistence of norms of suspicion for authority can be broken only by the teacher's continuing to reiterate a genuine interest in openness. In addition, he or she must behave congruently with student requests over a considerable period of time. Students may gradually be willing to take risks to test the teacher, and the norm may eventually give way if they are successful. Of course, if the situation becomes unclear again, students will rely more on strong, powerful peer group members than on the teacher to help them clarify their perceptions.

Cognitive Norms

Cognitive norms, which entail sharing thought processes such as reasoning, remembering, analyzing, and anticipating, may or may not correspond to a physical reality. Those that do not correspond can have just as real effects as those that do. The power of cognitive norms arises when classmates believe that others in the class should think as they do, and when each student comes to think that his or her classmates actually do hold similar beliefs. Some examples may be that books are to be studied or carried carefully and not thrown around; that other students should be respected, not ridiculed; and that teachers are to be thought of as helpers instead of as controllers. The development of such shared understanding which gives critical support for academic learning can generally be divided into two subcategories: (1) *cognitive norms as classroom goals;* and (2) *cognitive norms which deal with the processes of classroom learning.*

Intellectual and emotional development of students occurs more effectively when formal educational goals and a number of the cognitive norms of the informal peer group are consonant. Conflicts between the two lie at the core of many current tensions in schools. For example, schools in which the formal goals focus on preparation for the long-term objectives of jobs may be in conflict with informal peer group goals reflecting immediate relevance and satisfaction. Classes in which the formal goals emphasize freeing students to make more choices may be in conflict with informal peer group expectations that adults are supposed to make educational decisions. Schools which stress public displays of school spirit through football games and concerts may be in conflict with students' expectations that educational activities should focus on solving social ills.

Perhaps the most serious contemporary conflict between the informal norms of the peer group and formal school goals concerns the students' role in decision making. Modern technology, more and more, allows for the individualization of instruction. Class schedules and individual programs can be computerized to render numerous creative permutations, and curriculum materials can be made more diversified and individualized. Students themselves can be used to tutor and learn from one another. But cognitive norms in the peer group to support such a modern design are often absent. Defining the norms for supporting independent study time—for either students or teachers—is difficult. Questions arise: Should a group of students work separately from an adult? If so, what rules should be established? Old expectations do not work. Only by engaging in effective discussion and arriving publicly at group agreements can appropriate norms be established.

Cognitive classroom learning can be divided into two groups: the norms that deal with the content of classroom learning; and those that address the processes used during teaching and learning. *"Content learning"* refers to subject matter, curriculum packages, and texts that are deemed valuable for classroom study. *"Process of learning"* refers to the procedures teachers and students use to learn that content. Students appear to pursue learning content most energetically if they are involved, along with the teacher, in establishing cognitive norms that deal with the processes of learning. Focusing upon teaching and learning itself is one good way of helping students understand how to learn, as well as how to take responsibility for their own learning. Unfortunately, many teachers assign too many laborious tasks requiring recitation of facts and focusing on the conclusions of a content field rather than on the inquiry methods of that field.

From that kind of teaching, students learn about the subject rather than really immersing themselves in the dynamics of the subject. For example, they learn about social studies as though the problems of society were removed from life, or they parrot back mathematics, in contrast to experiencing its basic idea of order. One third-grade teacher we observed summed up a year of modifying cognitive norms about learning in this way, "I worked with the students on ways in which to learn until the Christmas vacation. During the winter, we learned a lot of things and, starting in the spring, I tried to prepare them for continuing to learn on their own, even if another teacher might stand in the way." It is likely that this teacher's efforts would have been futile unless the norms of the class were actually modified, and unless a substantial part of the group moved on together into the fourth grade. Nevertheless, attempts to establish cognitive norms that support inquiry and discussion about how the learning is taking place can increase students' abilities to learn independently and can, with the support of the next teacher, carry over.

Evaluative Norms

Evaluative norms entail high amounts of favorable or unfavorable feeling. To be cruel to another student may be very bad in one class or highly respected and socially reinforced by members of the peer group in another. In large segments of our contemporary youth culture, to wear loose clothes is "in"; interest in rock and roll is fading; lots of TV viewing is expected; powerful authorities are often "bad"—especially government officials; and smoking pot can be either very good or very bad depending upon the subgroup. Evaluative norms are typically dynamic, and should not be confused with cognitive norms which become static and elicit little intense feeling. That the students rush out-of-doors in a scramble at recess may not be preferred by the teacher, but it is expected and, after a time, taken for granted. It represents a cognitive norm. There are few active attempts to embarrass those who rush out. In contrast, evaluative norms are at work when a student swears at the teacher or uses the teacher's first name, and criticism results, either from the teacher, or from looks of disgust or criticism from peers.

Especially for evaluative norms, teachers should attempt to develop group agreement within the peer group that supports individual diversity and uniqueness. Students should strive for that agreement, not only because such norms are valuable in themselves, but also because the learning of academic subject matter by individuals tends to progress with less anxiety when students feel supported by their peers. Overly strict evaluations about hair style, dress, appearance, and behavior by the teacher or by peers can lead to alienation and feelings of low self-respect in some students.

As in the case of cognitive norms, it is important that evaluative norms be shared and discussed throughout the school year so that students can understand and share in the definitions of good taste. Should students chew gum in class? Should they talk and share during a work assignment?

Should they interrupt the teacher to ask questions? Should students decide how certain lessons will be taught? Should students help one another with academic assignments? These and other concerns can be discussed by the entire class or by specially formed subgroups. The teacher should vigorously confront evaluative norms held by the classroom peer group, norms that tend to restrict and isolate others in an academic or social-emotional manner from participating effectively in the group.

Behavioral Norms

Individual behavior is influenced by perceptions, cognitions, and evaluations as well as by the circumstances of the situation. As Lewin argued, *behavior is a function of both the psychodynamics of the person as well as how a person perceives the social environment.* Behavioral norms operate, on the one hand, to guide a person's actions through a complex psychological process involving perceptual, cognitive, and evaluative norms simultaneously; or, on the other hand, through cues and pressures to conform, received from important others in the social environment. The latter type of social process, termed *external conformity,* does not entail the sharing of internalized processes of other norms but, rather, has to do with an individual behaviorally subscribing to other persons' behaviors when those others are present.

The norm of reciprocity, first defined by Gouldner (1960) as constituting an integral part of most cultures, is an example of one made up of perceptual, cognitive, and evaluative norms all working simultaneously. For a norm of reciprocity to take hold, there are two sets of understandings that must be held and shared by group members: (1) that members should help those who have helped them; and (2) that members should not injure (or ridicule) those who have helped them. The key to generating a norm of reciprocity within the classroom lies in the teacher's finding avenues for increasing the amounts of positive social reinforcement that are initiated from one student to another.

Several observational studies of elementary classrooms have indicated a positive and significant correlation between the emission of supportive reinforcement and the receipt of supportive behaviors. In one study, Charlesworth and Hartup (1967) showed that the amount of reinforcement emitted by a student toward other students was positively associated with the amount of reinforcement that the particular student received from peers. Charlesworth and Hartup noted, furthermore, that often the consequence of dispensing social reinforcement was the continuation of the recipient's activity at the time of reinforcement. Moreover, approximately one-half of the peer reinforcement observed was in immediate response to positive overtures by another person, indicating that the dynamics of the norm of reciprocity worked in the fashion of a supportive, circular interpersonal process.

Another empirical study by Hartup, Glazer, and Charlesworth (1967) indicated that there was a highly significant positive relationship between the frequency of a student's emitting social reinforcement to peers and that student's friendship status within the peer group. Corroborating results were reported in an earlier study by Marshall and McCandless (1957). They showed that the degree of a nursery school child's participation in friendly social interactions was related to the child's socio-metric status in the peer group, as well as to the teacher's judgment of the child's social acceptance by peers.

The teacher can go a long way toward encouraging the development of a reciprocity norm in the classroom. By introducing activities, such as the "jigsaw puzzle model" and the "five-square puzzle" (see chapter 6), he or she can prompt students to be interdependent and cooperative. And by issuing a large number of reinforcing statements, especially when the students are helping one another to learn assignments, the teacher can develop and enhance that behavior. We will describe some concrete activities toward the end of the chapter.

In studying behavioral conformity to the pressures of others, it's important to remember that *perceptual, cognitive, and evaluative norms do not always combine to constitute behavioral norms*. Asch (1952), for example, conducted a field experiment to explore the effects of group pressure on behavioral conformity. The study highlighted differences between behavioral norms, on the one hand, and perceptual or cognitive norms on the other. Fifty groups, each consisting of eight male college students, were asked to match the length of a line presented on a chalkboard, with one of three other lines, and to declare their judgments on twelve different trials. All of the members of each group, except the single subject, had been instructed by the experimenter to give a wrong answer. The subject confronted a social environment in which his senses were in contradiction to the reports of all the other group members.

One-third of Asch's subjects, labeled as yielders, conformed to the group's wrong answers approximately half of the time. According to interviews immediately following the choice situations, very few of the yielders reported having distorted their perceptions; almost all gave in in order not to stand out and be different. They could not understand the apparent contradiction between their perceptions and what the others were saying, but were unwilling to be unique and risk rejection in front of the others.

Asch's experiment may shed some light on the dynamics of behavioral conformity in schools. Often students have not internalized peer group norms to the extent that their perceptions, cognitions, or feelings have truly been modified. They conform to the expectations of their peers so that they won't appear to be different and risk being rejected. The norms of the peer group become the student's personal standards, but only superficially. Once students move outside the presence of peers, their behavior is no longer influenced by them.

Similarly, teachers are aware that many students who appear to have internalized a lofty regard for intellectual values are merely conforming while in the teacher's presence. Their work is done on time, but they do just enough to get by. Their classroom behavior is seldom objectionable, and their apparent attitude toward school is passive acceptance. They have not internalized values of involvement, academic interest, and curiosity, nor do they deviate from the typical demands of the school. Even some defiant students conform in ways that do not run deeply into their cognitions and feelings. They might deviate from adult expectations by going along with hostile peers while not feeling deeply counterdependent or aggressive toward the authorities. Their behaviors are guided by a desire for acceptance by deviant peer group members, but are so-guided without the internalized feelings of hostility and destructiveness.

Some teachers find it useful to differentiate between perceptual, cognitive, and evaluative norms on the one hand, and behavioral norms on the other, since the latter are easier to modify. Behavioral norms can be modified through open, public communication with members of the class. The teacher can encourage the class to discuss circumstances in which superficial allegiance to behavioral pressures has kept them from being effective. *Since sharedness is the essence of normativeness, the teacher who wishes to modify behavioral norms must hold discussions with the entire class.* A classroom group can share the students' views of various classroom objects and behaviors and the meanings they have attached to them if the class hopes to establish helpful, influential, perceptual norms. It might share "where it is going" (content goals) and "how it plans to get there" (learning processes) if it hopes to establish influential cognitive norms. And it might share the deepest feelings that members have about one another's behaviors in order to shape agreements about new evaluative norms. The most significant thing to be done about behavioral norms is to work toward establishing a norm of reciprocity supported by a dispersed friendship structure within the peer group.

Sometimes students' behaviors are influenced by misreadings of shared attitudes in the peer group. A special condition, called *"pluralistic ignorance,"* takes place when incorrect estimates of others' expectations influence a student's behavior. Pluralistic ignorance occurs without a "true norm" existing. In such instances, students are influenced by what they *believe* others are thinking, even though their conceptions of the others' orientations are erroneous. Especially during the preadolescent years, the fear of being rejected by one's peers is so strong that misperceived expectations are not tested. "I wouldn't dare wear my hair that way; others wouldn't like it;" "I couldn't possibly go with that person; what would others say?"; "I can't carry this book around," and so forth. In this way, adolescents conform to perceptions of fictitious norms. Conditions of pluralistic ignorance can be diminished both through data feedback strategies—during which individuals state how they actually think and feel about a matter—or through structured classroom discussions about the norms of the group.

Open sharing of norms allows all students to become more realistic about their peers' reactions to various behaviors. For sharedness to take place, three conditions must be present within the classroom group: (1) students recognize what others expect of them to perceive, think, feel, or do; (2) students accept others' expectations for themselves, abide by them, and, in some instances, exert pressures upon violators; and (3) students recognize that other students share in their acceptance of the expectations.

Frequently students perceive a more restricted range of legitimate behavior than their teachers will tolerate and accommodate. Open sharing allows for widening the range of alternatives for perceptions, cognitions, feelings, and behaviors. Also, public sharing of norms produces greater social support for the agreement eventually decided upon. Changes in methods of working in the group are brought about most effectively when students are involved in planning the changes. Imposed alterations often cause resistance and the development of counterproductive norms that may impede the class's group processes.

Interpersonal support for a new norm is usually increased when group members are actively involved. Open sharing and discussion about classroom norms can also increase feelings of group solidarity as well as the sense of responsibility for pulling together. Students are more attracted to classes where they can voice their beliefs and attitudes and share in influencing the group's direction. Also, when students have trust in and feel close to their classmates, they tend to apply group norms more to themselves. Sharing those norms that are real and desirable contributes to higher involvement in the classroom group and often to more satisfaction with school.

Individual Reactions to Group Norms

Relationships between group norms and individual attitudes entail bilateral, reciprocal influences and cannot be understood without considering both. Group norms have brought influence over individual attitudes when the individuals willfully accept the norms. But some individuals are so constituted cognitively and affectively that they are influenced very little by interpersonal pressures, regardless of the strengths of group norms. Let us consider, first, some general reasons why group norms influence the psyches of individuals.

Groups help to define social reality for their members. Many of the individual differences that occur in society can be accounted for by the different group memberships and social roles of individuals. For instance, a militant teachers' union defines political and educational issues and develops solutions and action recommendations that are quite different from an association of school administrators—especially when the latter is locally based. There are considerable variations between the two organizations in the information discussed, the attitudes expressed, and the actions considered. Social reality takes on different priorities and meanings for the members of each group. Likewise, different student peer groups communicate various meanings and priorities to their members. Within any classroom group, there are subgroups and cliques of students that define reality in different ways.

Moreover, individuals rely on group norms to guide them, especially when they are unsure about the meanings of a complex social reality. Existential uncertainties encourage a search for an understanding of the social world as others see it. During this psychological search, individuals are aware that their immediate social surroundings are commonly shared with the members of their group, and they therefore expect the others to be experiencing the same reality. For students, especially, there is a definite pull toward the peer group to make the complex academic and social worlds of the school more understandable. For example, students perceive the teacher or a textbook and, at the same time, realize that their peers' perceptions are also converging on the same teacher or same text. It is reasonable, then, for the co-participating students to expect their peers to be helpful in clearing up ambiguous events. Or at least it appears legitimate for students to share doubts, concerns, and hypotheses about the unclear environment.

Students may feel insecure when their response opposes a group norm. Experimentally this was shown by Hoffman (1975) in a study of the relationship between anxiety and disagreements with group norms. He had students state opinions about a set of social attitudes, and then, six weeks later, all students were asked again for their attitudes on the same items—that second time after hearing the experimenter present false

group norms. Hoffman, measuring anxiety with galvanic skin responses, found that the subjects' skin responses were measured lowest when their opinions were in agreement with the norms established both times. As the subjects changed their opinions, however, from the first to the second time toward the bogus norms, there was a moderate degree of skin response. But those subjects whose opinions both times were quite different from the group norms exhibited the highest amount of galvanic skin response, indicating the highest amount of anxiety.

Many students, struggling with the fear of being rejected by their peers, tend to go along with their peers' perceptions of the group norms in order not to be rejected. Students internalize the norms of the peer group as their own attitudes when they become more and more involved in and rewarded by the group. Students who hold high influence status among their peers usually exhibit most allegiance to group norms and hold attitudes very similar to the norms. Peer groups also have goals toward which they are moving, and highly involved students become committed to these more than do alienated students. Indeed, students who are actively working toward peer group goals, and who are committed to them, may willfully allow themselves to be imposed upon and will expend a large amount of energy to help the group.

Group norms, when in the dynamic state, can take the form of intense, interpersonal pressures on members to conform. An experiment by Schachter (1951) demonstrated how group pressures can be brought to bear in ways that make it difficult to resist. Schachter asked groups to make a judgment about handling a juvenile delinquent named Johnny Rocco who was awaiting sentencing for a minor crime.

Group members were each asked to choose a scale position on an attitude inventory, ranging from love and kindness at one end to extreme and harsh discipline at the other. Three prompted subjects (stooges) were a part of each group. The stooge playing the *model role* took the typical position of most members of the group. The stooge called a *slider* first took the extreme punishment position, but eventually moved toward the softer, majority position of group members. And the stooge playing the *deviate* differed the most from group members, maintaining throughout that there should be extremely harsh discipline for Johnny Rocco.

Schachter's results indicated that the *deviate* was rejected in groups with a high degree of cohesiveness and interest in the activity. The *sliders* received the most communication during the discussions, especially during the time that they were making the gradual move from the deviate to the *modal* position. The person playing the modal role received no more special attention from others than any other group member. The strongest interpersonal pressures and most hostile criticisms were leveled at the *deviates*. In many classrooms similar phenomena occur weekly. Students who dare to adopt different attitudes from the predominant norms of the group may risk peer group pressure to conform, followed by eventual rejection if they fail to do so.

Group pressures need not always be restrictive and inhibiting of individuals, however. Groups can support and liberate their members so that all members can react as they personally think and feel. Milgram (1965), for example, experimented with the freeing effects of a group by having group members support a person's resolution of a value conflict in favor of that person's own values.

Milgram's classic research focused on the effects of group support and pressure and was carried out by a design with a sequence of three experimental conditions. In all of them, the subjects were asked to teach a confederate of the experimenter a list of paired associations, by administering electric shock whenever the learner made a mistake. The subject was also told to increase the voltage intensity of the shock after each error. The subject was in front of a pseudo voltameter which described the degrees of shock as slight, moderate, strong, very strong, intense, extremely intense, and dangerous-severe. Actually, the learner did not really receive shock. Clearly, the experimental situation set up a conflict for the subject between the experimenter's demands to increase the shock and the pseudo cries, discomfort, and vehement protests of the confederate, acting as a learner.

In the first experimental situations, the subjects acted alone with only the experimenter and the experimenter's confederate, the learner, being present. Of the forty subjects, only fourteen withdrew before the completion of "dangerous" shocks. The majority of subjects continued to administer shocks at the supposedly highest voltage points. In the next two experiments, two additional confederates joined the subject. One read the list of words, the second informed the learner if he or she were correct, and the subject administered the shock. In the second experiment, even though the experimenter pleaded, prodded, and cajoled, the two confederates refused to continue after a "very strong" shock level was reached. Ninety percent of the subjects also defied the experimenter by refusing to continue.

Just the opposite condition was set up in the third experiment. The confederates continued to obey up to the "maximum shock," and only 27.5 percent of the subjects refused to continue, compared with about 35 percent refusers in the first experiment. Other data indicated that subjects removed from the interpersonal pressure of the experimenter would not continue to shock to maximum levels. Thus, interpersonal support by peers strongly influenced whether or not a subject continued to shock the learner. This experiment indicated how group pressure can help or hinder an individual from resolving his or her own value conflicts.

It may be noteworthy to point out that these experiments on obedience and interpersonal pressures demonstrate the strength of normative phenomena in two other ways. First, the content of the experiments themselves reveal how powerful the norms of our society can be for acting in the legitimate name of science. The experimenter in each of those studies dressed in a white coat and acted very objectively, formally, and without emotion, as he firmly directed the subject to administer shock. Indeed, Milgram's studies can be interpreted as demonstrating the extent to which people have come to trust and believe in the scientist. The white coat and scientific demeanor have become very important legitimating symbols.

Second, the national attention given to these experiments triggered a response of challenge to the prevailing norms of science, at least to science as it is practiced in the psychological profession. During the past 25 years, as experimental social psychology has rapidly increased in prominence, concern about the ethics in carrying out research with human subjects has also rapidly increased. The manipulative techniques used by Milgram and his associates to study obedience in the laboratory have been criticized as examples of scientific procedures that may, in fact, have harmful or disturbing consequences for the subjects. In virtually all universities in the 1990s, psychologists are obliged to have their research designs and procedures approved by committees for the protection of human subjects.

Research carried out in natural settings has shown that group norms are influential in the following circumstances: (1) when the group is a highly cohesive unit; (2) when the norm is highly relevant or intense; (3) when the group is crystallized so that individuals know where the group is going and share their opinions; (4) when the group is a source of gratification for the individual; and (5) when the situation facing the group is ambiguous to the members. At the same time, research has also shown that the personality attributes which people bring to a group also determine how much they will conform.

Crutchfield (1955), in an empirical study of the personality characteristics of conformists, found them to be less able to make decisions, more anxious, and less spontaneous when compared with persons he called independents. Furthermore, his research indicated that the conformists had pronounced feelings of inadequacy, low self-confidence, and unrealistic pictures of themselves. The independents, conversely, had high ego strength, favorable self-esteem, and realistic images of themselves. Conformists were more conventional and moralistic; independents showed greater tolerance for differences and ambiguities in their world views. Conformists also tended to be more dependent and passive in their interpersonal relationships as compared to the independents.

FIGURE 7.2   Behavioral Dimensions of Times Participating

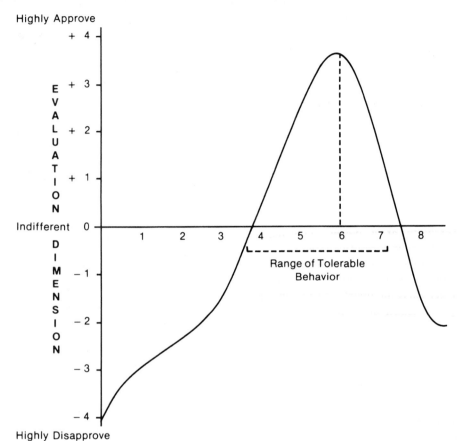

Adapted from J. Jackson, "Structural Characteristics of Norms." In *The Dynamics of Instructional Groups*. Chicago: National Society for the Study of Education, 59th Yearbook, part 2, 1960.

Structural Characteristics of Norms

Jackson (1960) developed a systematic framework for analyzing the structural characteristics of norms that can be useful for educators. His theory describes a norm as specifying the amount of particular behaviors which are expected of a person through the use of two dimensions, behavioral and evaluative. The behavioral category includes perceptual, cognitive, and behavioral norms as we have already described them. Jackson's model specifies that for any behavior executed within a group, the amount of approval or disapproval felt by the group's members may fall anywhere along the evaluative dimension from highly favorable, through neutral, to very unfavorable. Figure 7.2 depicts a norm for oral participation where low amounts of participation (three or fewer) are disapproved and where high amounts (eight or more) are also disapproved. For this group, emotional support is given for moderate amounts of participation. The curve in Figure 7.2 describes the behaviors that have "oughtness" attributed to them. It shows the amount of supportive or unsupportive *return* that members will *potentially* receive if their participation during a discussion is at different rates.

Jackson's model serves as a guide for plotting out classroom norms. Some of the many facts that have to become known before the model can actually be used to describe classroom norms follow.

1. Intensity of a Norm—The teacher might ask about normative intensity. What behaviors really make a difference in how class members feel? What behaviors actually get class members "turned on" positively or negatively? With students in nursery school and kindergarten, for example, behaviors concerned with sharing toys could constitute an intense norm. During the upper-elementary years, norms about how students work together on classroom projects could be intense. During high school, strong norms tend to govern dress, dating, and classroom participation.

2. Range of Tolerable Behavior—The range of tolerable behavior, shown in Figure 7.2, depicts those rates of participation that are approved by the group. Relevant questions about a group's degree of tolerance are: Is the range narrow or broad? Is it low or high on the behavioral dimension? Classroom life could be threatening and insecure if only very narrow ranges were allowed for many behaviors. Moreover, if the narrow ranges are close to the negative end of the behavior dimensions, restrictions are placed on individual students to withhold many behaviors. For example, the likelihood

would be quite great of breaking a norm which specified that no class member may speak out without the teacher's permission, for such a norm would constitute a restricted, unrelaxed learning environment. The focus of attention would be on the teacher; students would not be free to help one another; the peer group would have little opportunity to become cohesive; and a great deal of the teacher's time would be spent in maintaining order and enforcing rules.

Jackson showed that when a group has norms characterized by very narrow ranges of tolerable behavior, the likelihood of breaking a norm is very high and, consequently, the probability of being punished is high. He pointed out that the range of tolerable behavior can be placed on a continuum from very narrow to very broad. In a class where the normative ranges are broad, there is a climate of encouragement and flexibility rather than one of restraint and rigidity. When the range is narrow, it is likely that norms will be broken because the environment is threatening and restrictive.

3. Crystallization of a Norm—Jackson uses crystallization to refer to the extent of agreement among group members about what is approved or disapproved behavior. The curve in Figure 7.2 was plotted by taking the average curves for all members of a class in which there was high agreement among the members and, consequently, high crystallization. In other classes or with other norms, subgroups of students may differ widely in their approval or disapproval. A low amount of similarity across the subgroups of a total class represents low crystallization of the norm.

High crystallization among the members of a group concerning the appropriateness of important behaviors is a basic ingredient for an effective group and should be worked on through group discussions. It is important to keep in mind, however, that high crystallization does not mean that all class members think and act alike. It means simply that all class members agree on a norm's intensity and on a particular range of tolerable behavior. Discussions aimed at bringing about high crystallization should focus on making the ranges of tolerable behavior as wide as is feasible.

4.   *Ambiguity of a Norm*—Jackson uses ambiguity to refer to a special case of low crystallization where there is high agreement within two or more subgroups of the total class, but where those subgroups are definitely in disagreement. Classroom groups often exhibit ambiguity either at the beginning of the school year or when high conflicts occur within the class between two highly influential members of subgroups. Sometimes normative ambiguity occurs between two easily recognized subgroups—for example, of male and female students—with each subgroup expecting the teacher to behave differently.

In some high schools, normative ambiguity for an entire student body occurs between subgroups of students in different curricula tracks. College-bound students often hold a norm for high involvement in school programs (curriculum, student council, and football). General, business, or vocational students, on the other hand, are sometimes apathetic about the school's educational goals and embrace norms that are opposed to active school participation. Such normative differences are maintained easily because the several subgroups seldom intermingle and communicate with one another. The ambiguity of a norm is the

presence of two opposing norms which are intense and highly crystallized in themselves.

5.   *Integration of Norms*—Integration of norms deals with how an entire cluster of norms in a group relate to one another. Inconsistency among norms can lead to confusion and frustration: e.g., a classroom in which a norm for independent study exists but where the students also expect the teacher to monitor their behavior from moment to moment. Teachers should look at the consistency of their rules and at how inconsistent norms might keep a supportive and effective climate from developing. For example, a teacher who is set on establishing a norm of peer group helpfulness about learning may also have to consider student involvement in setting classroom goals. Weekly class discussions and periodic data feedback on students' perceptions about normative consistency within the class may be necessary. That is especially true when the teacher is trying to introduce some innovative classroom procedures.

6.   *Correspondence   of   Norms*—Correspondence refers to the depth of student attitudes about the norm of the group. A teacher can attempt to diagnose normative correspondence by administering two parallel questionnaires to the students of a class. One of the questionnaires would investigate the norms of the group, while the second would measure the individual students' attitudes toward the same issues.

For example, the issue might be, "It is good to take part as much as possible in classroom work." Each student would be asked to report first on "how many of my classmates feel a certain way about this

FIGURE 7.3   Norm Incongruence

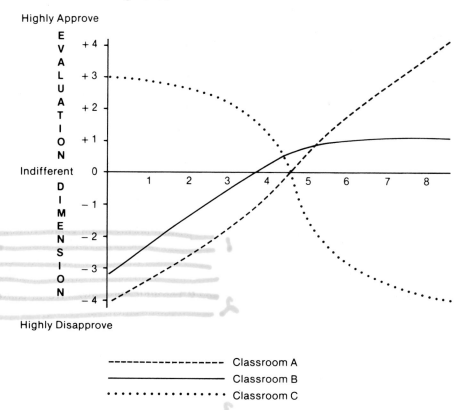

Highly Approve

EVALUATION DIMENSION

Indifferent

Highly Disapprove

----------- Classroom A
——————— Classroom B
· · · · · · · · · · Classroom C

Adapted from J. Jackson, "Structural Characteristics of Norms." In *The Dynamics of Instructional Groups.* Chicago: National Society for the Study of Education, 59th Yearbook, part 2, 1960.

issue" (almost all; many; about half; some; only a few). Next, each student would report on "how I feel about this issue" (agree almost always; agree more than disagree; half-and-half; disagree more than agree; and disagree almost always). A teacher might also have students estimate how the instructor feels about a variety of issues, thereby attempting to learn about the correspondence between peer group norms and the teacher's philosophy and instructional strategies.

7. Congruence of Norms—Normative congruence refers to agreements of norms

across the several classes to which one student may belong. Students have to deal with confusion and inconsistencies when expectations are radically different from one classroom to another. One norm that frequently differs from class to class is the amount of time students should actively spend participating in classroom discussions. An example of norm incongruence in one school is illustrated schematically in Figure 7.3.

Notice that a high amount of congruence does exist between classroom A and B, but in classroom C, the norms do not support high student participation. Students moving from classroom A or B to classroom C will be likely to experience confusion and will have to change their frames of reference, at least temporarily. Incongruences across classes are the bases of many interpersonal tensions in senior high schools, but this phenomenon is seldom addressed directly by school staffs.

To make use of Jackson's structural model and some of his theoretical concepts about norms, the teacher should follow these steps: (1) Choose one perceptual, cognitive, or behavioral dimension of high interest to the class that has a definite evaluative aspect. For example, students' following directions, students' levels of oral participation, students' helpfulness toward one another, students' independence, students' behavioral manifestations of interest in the class or their productivity. (2) Plot a curve to show feelings of approval or disapproval of class members (an average) as you see it. Ask the students to draw a curve to make a composite of their reactions and yours. With regard to student productivity, for example, ask where students "draw the line" for "how little" or "how much" work should be produced? (3) Check the range of tolerable behavior to see how broad or narrow it is. (4) If the curve turns out to be flat, check to see if it means that the norm has low intensity (is unimportant), or that there is low crystallization, or that there is normative ambiguity with two or more subgroups holding quite different norms. (5) To get additional data on crystallization, as well as to obtain information about normative correspondence, use parallel questionnaires—one to measure student perceptions of group norms, a second to measure student attitudes. (6) Share the findings with the class to see if this is the sort of norm that the students wish to hold. The teacher should also tell the students how he or she feels about the norm.

Affecting Classroom Norms

The norms of a class play a large role in determining whether the students will work together effectively. Teachers should strive to establish norms that dovetail with their own leadership and teaching styles. To accomplish that, teachers should remember a few guidelines.

First, the most important time for affecting classroom norms is during the first two weeks of school. It is much more effective to establish formal norms at the beginning of a relationship than to change them later. Second, teachers should be tuned in to group norms that the students are bringing from their last year's class(es). Teacher should hold discussions early with other teachers and with the class about rules from the last year which were perceived by the students to be helpful or unhelpful for their own learning. Third, very early in the semester teachers should draw students' attention explicitly to potential problem areas, e.g., respecting other people's property and feelings, acting in a safe manner in relation to others, turning work in on time, and legitimate ways of helping one another with school work. Fourth, norms will truly change only after all students understand and are motivated to go along with the new norms. *Participation* is the way to achieve that condition. Teachers should hold class discussions during which they help students to put the new norms into their own words. Moreover, teachers should seek ways of getting the students to state publicly that they agree with the new norms.

We like to distinguish between *implicit norms* and *explicit group agreements*. The former are not articulated and are not written out. The latter are discussed and are written out. Indeed, this is the bridge that teachers should help their students walk across—from implicit norms to explicit group agreements. In some elementary classes we have observed, the teachers and students have printed their explicit group agreements on poster boards and have displayed them prominently in their rooms. Senior high teachers prefer to put their classes' explicit group agreements on ditto sheets so that each student has one for his or her notebook.

Instructional Goal Structures

Instructional goals can be viewed as special kinds of classroom norms. Indeed, they can be defined as shared expectations about the proper ways for achieving knowledge or mastering skills within the classroom. As such, they can be treated as highly important classroom norms that should be understood by all members of the class. They should also receive a focus as key normative issues for teachers who are self-consciously striving to help their students make explicit group agreements to guide teaching and learning processes.

During the 1980s and 90s, considerable research and theory development have been carried out on instructional goal structures, particularly on cooperative goal structures. Now well into its second decade, the "International Association for the Study of Cooperation in Education" has spawned three books (Sharan, S., et al. eds. 1980; Slavin, R., et al. eds. 1985; and Sharan, S.,

ed. 1990) each of which is replete with theory and research on cooperative goal structures.

Comprehensive treatments of that important topic were prepared by Johnson and Johnson (1987 and 1989). These authors present definitions and extended discussions of the three fundamental instructional goals, originally described by Deutsch (1949), as *cooperative, competitive,* and *individualistic.* Johnson and Johnson summarize a considerable body of both laboratory and field research—especially on the first two types of goal structures—and they offer a number of ideas for the appropriate uses of the three different goal structures. Finally, these authors describe a large number of action ideas and instructional strategies that teachers might employ to make any of the three goal structures a reality within their classrooms.

When students work together within the framework of a *cooperative goal structure,* each student seeks an outcome that will be beneficial to all other group members. The respective goals of the different individual members are linked together interdependently so that there is a positive association among all members' goal attainments. A clear example of a cooperative goal structure occurs for a basketball team: the primary goal is to win the game, and if one player excels in helping the team win, every other member of the team also benefits. Indeed, interdependence can be so high that one player's failure to cooperate can undermine the team's achievement.

In a *competitive goal structure,* in contrast, a student seeks not only to succeed but also to cause other participants to fail. Thus a competitive social situation is one where the goals of the individual participants are related in such a manner that there is a negative correlation between their goal attainments. Within the framework of pure competition, an individual student can obtain his or her goal if, and only if, the others with whom the person is competing cannot obtain their goals. An example occurs when two basketball teams play a game against each other or when two high jumpers put on a duel for first place.

An *individualistic goal structure* is one in which the goals of individuals are independent of one another. Thus, whether or not an individual accomplishes a goal has very little, if any, bearing upon the accomplishments of others. Individualistic classroom situations lead the students to seek outcomes that are best for themselves, without regard to the goal attainment of others.

While most of the theory and research reviewed by Johnson and Johnson argues that cooperative goal structures are superior to the other two instructional goals for desirable educational outcomes, there are many classroom situations in which one of the goal structures may be preferred to the other two. So, for example, competition is probably superior to cooperative or individualistic goals when an academic task calls for a simple drill activity or when a quantity of work output is desirable. (This often occurs on mechanical or skill-oriented tasks that require little help from other people.) However, when the instructional tasks entail some kind of problem solving or complex thought process, the research indicates that a cooperative goal structure results in higher achievement than does a competitive goal structure. And, of course, when the instructional tasks call for students to work interdependently, cooperative structures are necessary and competitive behaviors will be interfering and destructive to the group's

problem-solving efforts. In extensive empirical research, Slavin and Karweit (1985) demonstrated how cooperative and individualistic goal structures can be combined to foster math instruction.

In a meta-analysis of 121 empirical studies on instructional goal structures, Johnson et. al. (1981) compared the relative effects of cooperative, competitive, and individualistic goal structures on achievement. In all, the studies produced 286 findings which were content analyzed using three meta-analysis procedures. The results indicated that cooperation was considerably more effective than were competitive and individualistic efforts in promoting student achievement. Cooperation with intergroup competition was also superior to interpersonal competition and individualistic efforts in promoting competitive and individualistic efforts in affecting achievement. In another extensive review of studies carried out in secondary schools during the 1980s, Newmann and Thompson (1987) showed that cooperative goal structures can be quite successful in helping high school students raise their achievement scores. The authors of both reviews conclude, *"Educators may wish to increase considerably the use of cooperative learning procedures in order to promote higher student achievement."*

While this analysis does not give much support to individualistic goal structures, we should point out that programmed instruction can be effective once students have a clear understanding of what they are to learn and possess sufficient intrinsic motivation to learn the material on their own. Moreover, it seems likely that particular kinds of creativity such as writing a poem, painting a picture, or carving a piece of wood could be more successfully and effectively accomplished within individualistic goal structures. However, the processes of creativity can also be stimulated through cooperative discussions with others. On the latter point, Barbieri (1978) and Smith (1987) have devised useful techniques to foster cooperation on writing assignments and have shown how to combine individualistic and cooperative goal structures in English in order to enhance the learning of writing skills. An important idea, then, to keep in mind is the concept that individualistic goal structures can be productive when planned for within the context of the other two types of goal structures.

The same sort of a principle—sequencing and designing the flow of goal structures—applies to competitive relationships within the classroom. As Johnson and Johnson point out, when competition is executed during "low-anxiety-producing, relatively unimportant activities," it can take on excitement, release energy, lift the spirits, and energize the participants to work more productively within a cooperative goal structure. Thus games, athletic events, or other kinds of recreational activities can be invigorating and psychologically healthy. As Clifford (1971) has shown, however, clearly specified competitive goals encourage superior results compared to relatively ambiguous competitive goals that usually lead to inferior results.

In summary, the teacher is advised to make use of all three of the instructional goal structures, but to try to do so within an overarching cooperative goal structure. Indeed, herein lies one sort of vocabulary for explaining a fundamental theme of this book. In general, classroom life, and in particular, academic learning, will tend to go better when the norms of the peer group support cooperation, helpfulness, supportiveness, and interpersonal empathy. However, there will be appropriate contexts, involving both tasks and people, that call for either individualistic or competitive goal structures. It is therefore of the utmost importance that the teacher and the peer group understand and agree on the appropriate perceptual, cognitive, and behavioral norms of the three goal structures.

Since competitive behaviors can be expected to dominate in schools, both because of historical tradition in American education and because of the social milieu of many American communities, teachers will have to educate all students in the skills of engaging in cooperative action. Unfortunately, trust, openness of communication, mutual attraction, and problem-solving effectiveness in groups can be destroyed very easily by the competitive teacher or student who takes advantage of others. Thus, the group skills offered in this book should be viewed as a curriculum for helping to establish effective cooperative goal structures in classrooms.

Peer Group Norms and Academic Performance

The peer group constitutes perhaps *the* most important normative force on students' school performance (for corroborating data, see Goodman, 1969). One particularly dramatic example of the strength and impact of peer group norms on school achievement was illustrated vividly by David Hargreaves (1967) in his study of "streaming" in an English secondary school for boys. Hargreaves researched the psychological and behavioral characteristics associated with the individual members of several different types of peer group cultures. The extreme differences he unearthed among the several peer group clusters were obviously heightened by the traditional British custom of streaming students according to their scores on examinations. Nevertheless, Hargreaves' research is very instructive in demonstrating how powerful associations with particular peers can be in relation to academic achievement. Even though it is the case that American, Canadian, and Australian schools typically do not make quite such blatant distinctions based upon a student's level of achievement, Hargreaves's results show how deeply the norms of a peer group can affect the behavior of individual students. Moreover, the norms of these student peer groups in England are also present to some degree in schools of most cultures, and have, we believe, similar effects to those noted by Hargreaves.

Hargreaves focused his analysis on the interpersonal interaction patterns within the peer groups of the fourth (or last) year boys. These students represented the "final products" of schooling and had spent the longest time being initiated into the values of both their peer group and the school. The fourth-year class, similar to all the others, had been divided into five streams when the pupils entered school. Hargreaves studied only four of those streams, excluding the fifth, which was composed mostly of retarded or minimally educable students. His study showed that each stream had its unique set of norms that persisted, even when the composition of the streams changed when boys were shifted among them.

The highest stream, labeled A, held norms that were consonant with the school's formal goals. These boys valued academic achievement, looked down upon "mucking around" in class, discouraged fighting, thought that teachers should be obeyed, and believed that plagiarism and cheating were strictly against the student code and should be strongly punished.

Boys of the B stream had quite a different culture. For one thing, they were characterized by less corresponding norms, i.e., less agreement among the boys between their privately held personal attitudes and the group norms that guided behavior. Stream B also exhibited several norms that were incongruent with academic goals and the rules and procedures of the faculty. The following quote from a high-status student within stream B highlights the differences between streams A and B.

> We like boys who don't mess about. We don't like boys who answer a lot of questions. If you answer all the questions, the lesson goes all the quicker, doesn't it? I mean, say you have two periods and you start having all these questions; right then it would take a period to do, and then you have another period and then you'd have to do some new work. If they start asking questions and we don't answer them, they have to start explaining it all to us and it takes two periods. So we don't have to use the pen (p. 27).

Stream C was actually composed of three subgroups. It was similar to B in that most of the members strongly devalued academic work. But whereas in B "fun" was valued more than work, and "messing around" was encouraged for its own sake, the high-status members of the cliques in stream C apparently were primarily interested in behaving contrary to school values and defying the school administration. In other words, the C group was negatively oriented toward the authorities of the school, while the B group was more fun-loving and devilish. One subgroup in C, however, continued to hold norms very different from the rest of that group. For example, this deviant C subgroup valued work, obeyed teacher demands, dressed well, and attended school regularly.

The D stream had an even more diffuse leadership than the other streams, but like most members of stream C, the members of D shared expectations of defying the school's authorities and generally challenging faculty demands. In fact, one criterion for status seemed to be doing poor academic work. Tardiness and truancy were encouraged; physical pressures were applied to the low-status boys who went along with the teachers; threats were issued to fellow members of stream D who weren't going along with the group; and delinquent acts of all sorts were frequent and valued by members of the high-status clique of stream D.

Members of the four streams entered into very little interaction across streams, except when students were switched from one stream to another by the faculty, or when there was some mixing while participating on the school's rugby team. Most of the participants in the school—both students and staff—maintained stereotypic conceptions of members in the different student subgroups. For example, the A's were viewed as snobbish, while the D's were seen as delinquent. Hargreaves also showed that the students' identifications with their own group were very strong. For example, at times, the boys in streams C and D reinforced the importance of their norms by decreasing their test-taking performance on purpose so that they would not be moved up to a higher stream. They deliberately kept their academic achievements mediocre to

poor, apparently to buttress the security of their peer associations. Hargreaves concluded that:

> The streams exert a powerful influence on the extent and form of interaction between age-mates in the same neighborhood school. Boys tend to interact with and choose friends from boys in the same stream and only rarely from streams more than one removed from their own. As the predominate norms of each form become differentiated and the various barriers to communication between streams are erected, negative stereotypes develop. These serve to reinforce the normative differentiation and inhibit further cross-stream interaction, and thus the incentive value of the "promotion" system is undermined for the low stream boys (p. 82).

There seems little doubt that peers can have a significant impact on the academic life of individual students. A national survey, for example, by Coleman et al. (1966) showed convincingly that variations in students' attitudes and achievement were accounted for not so much by the teachers, but more by the educational and economic levels of other students in the school. Students not only have an impact on one another because of their classroom interactions. But, as Hargreaves has shown, their relationships outside classes and throughout the daily life of the school organization also influence how individual students relate to the school.

Another study, also carried out in England on twelve secondary schools in London, showed even more clearly than the Hargreaves' study that organizational norms present in a school can affect student motivation and learning. Rutter and his colleagues (1979) carried out a three-year longitudinal study in twelve typical, big-city, comprehensive high schools. The authors' primary concern was to investigate differences between schools in terms of various measures of pupil behavior and attainment and to determine in what ways the interactions in the school might influence these pupil outcomes. Although we shall present a more thorough summary of that research in chapter 10, it is relevant to mention here that the schools did differ in their norms and that these differences were correlated with different student outcomes. Some of the more important findings follow: (1) Pupils achieved more in schools where staff members shared expectations to plan the courses of study cooperatively. In such schools, the group planning provided opportunities for teachers to encourage and support one another. (2) Pupils achieved more and had fewer behavior problems in schools where the disciplinary rules for the pupils were set by the teachers as a group—in contrast to letting individual teachers work out the rules of discipline for themselves. Again, the more successful schools had staff norms in support of team work and cooperation. (3) Pupils achieved more in schools where staff norms supported being open and direct with one another. In the less successful schools, faculty members expected one another to be autonomous, private, and aloof.

Other research during the 1980s showed that ability grouping, one of the most common of practices in American elementary schools, can depress achievement of students assigned to the low groups (see Peterson, P., Wilkinson, L. C., and Hallinan, M., eds., 1984; and Slavin, 1988). The research indicated that students in low ability groups were more likely to be inattentive compared with classmates in high groups and that the difference lay in the group environment rather than in individual ability. Whereas students in the high groups helped peers to focus on reading, students in the low groups frequently distracted one another. The teachers unwittingly fostered inattention of the low students by also behaving in ways to further distract the students and to send negative ripple effects throughout the low groups. To summarize, the researchers concluded that *ability grouping has very few benefits, if any, for low-ability students, and the culprit seems to be group norms that support poor performance, norms that are very strong in the low-ability groups.* Unfortunately, many teachers make the mistake of adopting expectations for such groups that are too low and of under emphasizing competent performance when teaching the low ability groups.

Norms and the Evaluation of Performance

Evaluation of performance is an integral aspect of both formal and informal classroom life. Academic evaluation is typically represented by a formal static norm. Teacher and students share the expectations that evaluation will occur often and that it will be issued by adult professionals and received by students in the form of a grade, a star, a missed recess, a pat on the back, making a team, or staying after school. We believe that the evaluation of academic performance should take the form more of a dynamic classroom norm. Thus, students and teacher would be questioning the evaluative procedures as a normal part of their daily interaction.

Evaluation could be organized so that it would take place equally across hierarchic levels in the classroom. For example, students could be involved in evaluating both their own academic performance and the instructional behaviors of their teachers, while the teachers could be evaluating both student performances and their own. This democratic departure from the traditional hierarchic arrangement would put teacher and students into a normative relationship of *mutual accountability*. Furthermore, evaluation could be used not only to assess individual performance within the classroom, but also to enable students and their teacher to assess where they are as a group and to formulate improved group processes collaboratively.

Summative and Formative Evaluation

Two ways of doing performance evaluation have become prominent and are worth considering when discussing classroom norms. They have been labeled by Bloom et al. (1971) as *summative* and *formative* evaluation. Summative evaluation is the typical, formal, static norm found in most traditional classrooms. It is the assessment of what finally has been accomplished, usually in student achievement. For instance, a student's grade ostensibly reflects the level of mastery that a student has reached in a subject. Summative evaluations are helpful primarily to policy makers and decision makers, e.g., should the student be encouraged to move on to a more advanced level in the school? They are helpful to the teachers and parents who act as decision makers in the students' academic careers.

Formative evaluations, on the other hand, aim to present information about the next steps which should be taken to move closer to a particular goal. The astute teacher continually sizes up the social situation of the class as well as the needs of each student to ascertain the next move. Informally, most teachers make use of formative data as they perform their daily functions. The teacher develops a sense of whether students are involved, bored, or excited about a particular assignment.

A formal example of formative evaluation is a diagnostic performance test used with young students in particular skill areas such as reading. Test results give the teacher information about how to proceed in developing reading skills. Its purpose is not to evaluate summatively (such as in giving a grade) but to pinpoint the skills—as well as lacks—the youngster has developed and to indicate the appropriate kind of future instruction. Formative evaluation provides objective information to pinpoint problems and to suggest alternative paths of action for solving the problems.

Multiple Accountability in the Classroom

Classrooms with norms which support students evaluating students, and students and the teacher evaluating one another, can make use of both summative and formative evaluations in new, more equalitarian and collaborative ways. As such, traditionally elitist procedures of evaluation can become more constructive aids to improving everyone's performance.

For students, evaluations by peers can be much more powerful than evaluations received only from the teacher. We already know this to be true from observing both the constructive and the destructive power of informal peer relationships. Why not use the power and energy of peer group relationships constructively? Students can help one another in ways that teachers cannot.

For example, often a student can hold the attention of a friendly peer for much longer than the teacher. A student can also successfully paraphrase concepts to another student when a teacher's logic and phraseology do not seem to communicate. Students can often recognize the difficulty that another student is having because they have experienced the same difficulty just a short time before. In helping students learn to write well, peer feedback and peer criticism can be strong facilitators. Our experiences in working with peer tutoring and in researching cross-age tutoring have proven to us that the tutors themselves often learn just as much, if not more, than their tutees.

Student evaluations of teachers also represent a very powerful tool for improving teacher performance. In fact, our experiences, along with some systematic research, have shown that student feedback can be more influential on teachers than feedback from the principal or from parents. In a field study, Gage, Runkel, and Chatterjee (1963) asked fifth-grade students to fill out one questionnaire telling the extent to which they saw their teachers performing certain visible actions and another questionnaire telling the degree to which they would *like* teachers to perform those actions. Summaries of the responses were given to the teachers. Later ratings by the students showed a relative trend of changed action on the part of teachers who were given this feedback on the wishes of the students, compared to teachers who were not given feedback. In another study, Tuckman

and Oliver (1968) found that the instructional behaviors of teachers in the classroom were changed more often as a result of student appraisals and feedback than by the appraisals and feedback of colleagues or supervisors. A similar phenomenon has been documented by Margaret Nelson (1972) in a study of short-term change among substitute teachers. Nelson supplied the substitutes with systematic formative evaluations from their students about the substitute teachers' classroom behavior and showed that the feedback triggered significant behavioral changes in a very short time.

In conclusion, norms are powerful guides to classroom behavior. Most important are the norms that govern academic performance and the use of evaluation of school achievement. When members of a classroom are guided by the shared expectation that all persons—students and teacher alike—should be developing better ways of learning and developing both as individuals and as a group, they will work collaboratively on generating formal procedures to evaluate one another in helpful, growth-enhancing ways.

Implications for Teachers

The following summary statements capture the most salient implications of this chapter for teachers.

Norms are *shared expectations* for how the participants of a classroom should perceive, think, feel, and behave.

Norms influence the perceptions, cognitions, evaluations, and behaviors of the individual members of the class.

While individual students and teachers will react differently to the pressure of classroom norms, all will be affected by them.

Classroom norms can be pinpointed and measured. Moreover, there are some useful conceptualizations that can be applied to the analysis of classroom norms and which can guide planned change attempts.

Student peer group norms frequently will be in opposition to the goals of the professionals of the school. Such opposition can be counter-productive to individual student growth and development.

Cooperative peer group norms enhance student self-concept and academic learning more than norms in support of competition or of individualistic ways of learning.

Teachers will be most successful where they can flexibly use cooperation, competition (particularly intergroup competition), and individualized structures for learning within an overall cooperative classroom climate.

Action Ideas for Improving Climate

The following descriptions of classroom practices were employed by teachers in their attempts to develop more supportive norms to enhance academic learning in their classrooms.

Clarification of Classroom Norms

The main goal of this activity was to help a sixth-grade class openly discuss norms that were operating in the peer group. The teacher wanted the students to regulate their own behavior, and this was a first step toward encouraging them to take more responsibility for making up the rules of the class and for reaching group agreements about how the class should be run. The teacher presented the idea of a norm to the class by saying that it was a shared feeling in the group about the ways a student ought to behave or the things a person ought to do as a class member. She explained further that norms can be formal or informal.

The teacher next asked each student to write examples of formal and informal norms on a piece of paper. The students were given about ten minutes to write down their own ideas. The students were then asked to share their ideas in small groups of five and to make up a group chart which represented the consensus items for that particular group.

The various items of the five-person groups were recorded on a large sheet of paper for the entire class. The following are examples of formal norms: (1) Don't shout or talk loudly in the classroom. (2) Act in friendly ways toward the teacher, especially inside the school building. (3) Get to school on time in the morning. (4) Don't sit in someone else's seat until the teacher says we should. (5) Be careful not to mark up the textbooks.

In contrast, some of the informal norms were: (1) Don't be a tattle-tale—that is, don't tattle to authorities such as teachers, principals, and parents. (2) When you are new to the class, don't boast or tell others what to do. (3) Don't let the teacher or other students know your deepest feelings. (4) Don't ask a student to go steady with you or to be friends with someone who is not like you or your group. (5) Unless all your friends really like certain things about your teacher, you should not try to be like her.

As a continuing activity, the teacher and the students looked at the lists of formal and informal norms each week, made additions and deletions, and had discussions in order to make plans for changing some of the less helpful norms. Most changes occurred in the informal norms. Some of them were modified slightly and transformed into formal norms, while others were dropped for lack of continuing support by a majority of the class.

Classroom norms can be changed through the concerted, collaborative efforts of teacher and students. Members of learning groups can gain control over themselves and their own culture through data collections about themselves and group discussion methods. School staffs that have cooperative norms in support of joint course planning, setting disciplinary rules together, and open communication will be more successful with their students' learning than staffs with more competitive or individualistic norms.

Using Questionnaires to Explore Norms

A fifth-grade teacher also sought to get his students to discuss classroom norms openly, particularly norms having to do with helpfulness and emotional support. He believed that his students would have difficulty understanding the concept of a norm. He also believed that the class norms called for a lower amount of helpfulness and support than was beneficial for learning. The teacher decided to use Instruments 7.1 and 7.2.

The teacher collected the students' responses and found that although all but two students indicated more personal agreement than disagreement with the four statements on Instrument 7.2, more than half the students thought that their peers would disagree with statements 1, 3, and 4 on Instrument 7.1. Thus, there was a condition that sociologists call "pluralistic ignorance" in the class. Individually, the students thought that helpfulness and support were valuable, but collectively they believed that their peers in the class would not go along with high amounts of helpfulness and emotional support. And the teacher noted that most student behaviors were more closely following the collective response instead of individuals' attitudes. Many classroom behaviors were unhelpful, even antagonistic and emotionally unsupportive. The teacher presented the data to the students, asking them to think of reasons for the discrepancies between the two questionnaires. Then he explained how he stood on each item (in high support of helpfulness and support) and asked the students to brainstorm ways in which helpfulness and support could become realities in the class.

Considering The Feelings of Others

An eighth-grade language arts teacher whose class was 35% Native-American believed that in order for his students to work together collaboratively in project teams, they would have to understand one another more and to think more empathically about one another. He decided to ask his students to do a sentence completion inventory and to share their answers with other members of their project teams. Some of the incomplete sentence stems were: (1) Studying is

---

INSTRUMENT 7.1
How This Class Thinks

Classes are different from one another in how students think about the class—about what's right and wrong behavior in the class. How do you believe your classmates think about the following things? Put a check in one of the boxes under "How many think this way?" for each of the statements below:

How Many Think This Way?

	Almost All	Many	About Half	Some	Only a Few
1. It is good to help other pupils with their schoolwork, except during tests.					
2. It is good to ask the teacher for help when you need it.					
3. It is good to give encouragement to one another when you are working on schoolwork.					
4. It is good to say nice things to one another.					

. . . (2) I learn best when . . . (3) Homework is . . . (4) Learning out of books is . . . (5) I can't learn when. . . . After sharing their answers with one another, the students were asked to brainstorm ways in which they could work and learn together—methods that would be helpful and interesting to all of the team's members. Finally, the teacher asked the students to review the brainstormed lists and to make group agreements about those ideas they definitely wished their teams to follow.

After the students made group agreements about how they would work on teams, the teacher gave the teams academic tasks such as analyzing a story together, writing a team poem about multicultural differences, and paraphrasing some Native-American poetry. When we saw the teacher in the late spring of 1990, he told us, "There really is a strong need for us to develop the social skills of students along with their academic skills. I believe now that cooperative learning in teams can give us academic gains, improved ethnic relations, and better social skills for a wide range of students. If we teachers become committed to teamwork, schools will be much better places."

INSTRUMENT 7.2
How I Think about These Things

Put a check in the box that tells how you think about each of the statements below.

How I Think

	I agree almost always.	I agree more than disagree.	Half and half	I disagree more than agree.	I disagree almost always.
1. It is good to help other pupils with their schoolwork, except during tests.					
2. It is good to ask the teacher for help when I need it.					
3. It is good to give encouragement to one another when we are working on schoolwork.					
4. It is good to say nice things to one another.					

Shifting Among Three Cultures

A senior high school social studies teacher successfully taught her students to change normative cultures in the classroom at will. After a brief presentation on norms, with examples from other cultures, the teacher said that there would be three cultures in this class that would each help to facilitate learning about social studies. She explained the cultures as follows: (1) *A Personal Culture* is one in which we present our own thoughts, feelings, and values about a topic. An important norm is respect and appreciation of differences, and an important verbal reaction is "I think . . .," or "I feel . . .," or "I value. . . ." (2) *An Academic Culture* is one in which we study the ideas, research, and practices of experts. Here we must learn to move out of ourselves to listen and to read carefully the complex ideas of others. Important norms are curiosity, hard study, and trying to commit information to memory. (3) *An Application Culture* is one in which we find out about problems in our community or school and seek to use information we have about ourselves and have learned from the experts to find solutions to those problems. Important norms are collaborative problem solving, trial and error, and evaluation of effects. The teacher found that class members learned the three cultures well enough to go from one to the other easily and cooperatively.

In Atlanta, Georgia, senior high school students are required to take a course called, "Duties to the Community." That course entails 75 hours of unpaid volunteer service in community agencies under the supervision of school staff. The program aims to increase students' awareness of their civic responsibilities. Along with the hours of service, the students must write an essay or keep a journal throughout the experience which gets turned in to the Language Arts Department. Atlanta has developed an excellent means of realizing the *application culture* in its secondary schools.

Planning A Time Sequence For Academic Work

A high school English teacher became concerned with the large number of incompleted assignments in one eleventh-grade class and felt that his students' quality of work was very poor. He brought the matter up with his students and discovered that papers and homework assignments in other subjects were falling due at about the same times as the ones in his class. The students were unable to cope adequately with these time pressures. So the class, with the help of the teacher, decided to plan jointly at the beginning of each unit to space the assignments in a convenient manner for everyone.

At the outset of each new study unit, the teacher held a planning session with the students. The scope of work was discussed, and dates were established for papers and exams. The students became involved in the decision making for curriculum sequencing, and the teacher decided to prepare the final examination on the basis of student questions. The class was divided into three groups, each being responsible for one section (grammar, literature, or vocabulary). The test turned out to be difficult and

long, but offered an excellent learning experience for the students and teacher. Those planning sessions helped the class to establish a norm of high productivity and of high participation in English.

Regular Review of Classroom Norms

A sixth-grade teacher used the action idea entitled "Clarification of Classroom Norms" and added to it a regular, monthly review so that new, formal norms would be continually created and clarified. The teacher called her monthly meeting, "a debriefing session." She explained that debriefing is a popular activity used by many groups, for example, a football team watching movies of its performance, an army unit discussing a recent battle, or teachers talking together about how the school year is going. She said that she wanted the class to debrief for two hours at the end of each month, particularly on the subject of classroom norms. The teacher divided the total class into four-person groups at the start of each debriefing so that each student would have a chance to speak. The students were to list the norms they liked and wanted to keep and the norms that needed changing. Each small group shared its ideas with the total class while the teacher printed the ideas on newsprint. The teacher asked all class members to brainstorm new behaviors they'd like to try during the succeeding month and then asked for some explicit group agreements about the top three or four new behaviors to try.

Forming A Classroom Student Council

The teacher of an upper-elementary class felt that her students lacked a sense of being deeply involved in classroom affairs. She wanted the students to think that their contributions were worthwhile, that they could be responsible ultimately for the effective functioning of the classroom. She decided to establish a rotating student council that would be concerned primarily with establishing and enforcing classroom rules. The council, composed of six students, made recommendations to the class, and each class member, including the teacher, had a single vote. Punishment for infractions of the rules were also recommended by the council and voted on by the class. In the beginning, the rules were very strict and the punishments were harsh. The teacher voiced her concern about the narrow ranges of tolerable behavior of the council's norms, but did not interfere with the harsh decisions of the students. Even though at times it appeared as though a student kangaroo court might be forming, rotations of the council members helped the students to become more realistic, empathic, and tolerant in initiating ideas and enforcing rules. The teacher was pleased to see the youngsters begin to internalize many of the council's rules as their own attitudes and to feel more responsibility for establishing supportive interpersonal relationships within the class.

Cooperative Investigations

In Israel, Sharan and Hertz-Lazarowitz (for details, see Sharan, ed., 1990A) have successfully changed classroom norms toward increased cooperation by having students work together on academic tasks. The tasks are typically short and focus on a particular topic, such as a famous person's life, a social problem, a short historical period, a book, or a play. All activities performed by group members take place as part of a collective effort. Each activity requires group deci-

sion, and thus constant coordination among participants is required during performance in order to carry out the task.

In planning and carrying out cooperative investigations, students progress through a series of six consecutive stages. Stage 1 consists of specifying the task and organizing students into investigation teams. Typically, the teacher presents a general area of study, encouraging the students to suggest specific topics for study. After discussion, the students select topics and join investigation teams. Stage 2 includes planning the learning task. Here the teams determine what to study, how to study, and the purpose of the study. Stage 3 consists of carrying out the investigation. Stage 4 comprises the preparation of a final report. Stage 5 is a presentation of the report to the rest of the class, and Stage 6 is a cooperative evaluation of each of the investigations by all students and the teacher.

In a field experiment in Israel, Sharan and Shacher (1988) compared students who used the above six stages in social studies and geography with students taught by the traditional, whole-class-recitation method. They found not only that there was much more cooperative give-and-take between students of different ethnic groups in the cooperative investigations, but also that the achievement levels of the students who worked cooperatively were higher than the achievement levels of students taught in the traditional manner.

Sharan and Shacher (see Sharan, 1990B) showed also that Middle-Eastern students, a minority group in Israel, gained even more than the predominant Western students from the cooperative investigations. There is also evidence from California, Oregon, and Texas classrooms that

Hispanic students can make significant achievement gains when they are taught to cooperate and to help one another in academic learning. Sharan does a superb job of summarizing the theory that undergirds these findings in his 1990 book entitled *Cooperative Learning: Theory and Research.*

Developing Norms of Interest and Relevance

A high school social studies teacher wanted to encourage his students to use community resources in their studies of social problems. He hoped to establish expectations that such an activity would be interesting and relevant. The whole class was engaged in a unit of careers and decided to find out what careers were available in the community. They planned the general sequence of their research as a total class, but broke up into small groups to tackle specific methodological aspects such as questionnaires, interviewing, compilation of data, writing up the study and discussing ways of using the information to make choices and act on recommendations. The experience provided opportunity for taking both initiative and responsibility in planning a research design. The students were highly motivated and involved at every step, and they developed the shared expectation that to participate actively in this class was a valuable experience.

Student Team Learning

Slavin (1983) has developed and successfully tested several innovative strategies for using the norms of cooperation and competition to facilitate academic learning. One strategy is entitled "Teams-Games-Tournament," in which students are assigned to learning teams of four or five members. After the teacher presents a lesson, he or she hands out worksheets to each team. The team members work together, trying to make certain that each teammate knows the material, because the team will not be able to win (intergroup competition) if some students are not prepared. At the end of the week, students from each team compete with one another on simple learning games to add points to their team scores.

In another strategy developed by Slavin and others, labeled Team-Assisted Individualization (TAI), students work in small heterogeneous learning teams on individualized, math materials. Students check one another's work and manage the mechanics of the curriculum, freeing teachers to provide tutoring to individuals and small groups. Because TAI fosters constructive student interaction, students find the curriculum fun rather than boring. Research indicates that most students like to be able to progress at a rapid rate through the individualized materials and to receive the support of their peers for doing so.

The TAI packet includes a diagnostic placement test, a method for assigning students to 4 or 5 member learning teams, individualized curriculum materials, a method of team study and peer feedback, a method for getting team scores, and an overview of a cycle of individualized, small group, and whole-class instructional activities. For further information about TAI or "Teams-Games-Tournament," write to: Student Team Learning, The Johns Hopkins University, 3505 N. Charles Street, Baltimore, MD 21218.

Judicious Discipline

Gathercoal (1989, 1990) has helped many teachers and school staffs use what he has termed, *judicious discipline.* The philosophy behind it is the concept that classroom group processes will go better if teachers and administrators teach students about their individual rights as citizens of the United States. Students are taught that they may do what they want in the school, unless what they do interferes with the rights of others. Students are taught that their constitutionally protected freedoms must be kept within sensible bounds, and that in some instances, the needs and interests of the majority carry greater weight than those of individuals. In legal terms, the interests of the majority are *compelling state interests.*

According to Gathercoal, students should be taught that in reaching some equilibrium between individual rights and compelling state interests, the school (as a state institution) has the legal right to establish rules in four areas: (1) avoiding property loss and damage; (2) serving legitimate educational purposes; (3) fostering health and safety; and (4) avoiding serious disruption of the educational process. Gathercoal encourages teachers to work collaboratively with their students to come up with classroom group agreements in each of these four categories. For example, in one Oregon fourth-grade class, the students agreed on these rules: (1) Respect other people's property; (2) We are in class to listen and learn; (3) Conduct yourself in a safe manner and be healthy; and (4) Do not disrupt the class.

Gathercoal argues that judicious discipline should not rely on authoritarian decision making or on punishment. Rather, it should focus on helping students learn "correct behavior" through discussion, participation, and collaborative decision making. For more detail about how to implement *Judicious Discipline,* see the 1990 second edition of the Gathercoal book by that title, available from Caddo Gap Press, 317 S. Division St. Suite 2, Ann Arbor, Michigan 48104.

Activity Structures

Berliner (1983) showed how classrooms might be described through the activity structures teachers use. For example, activity structures such as reading circles, mediated presentations, two-way presentations, and seatwork call for different functions and norms to guide the behavior of students in the structure. Many classroom teachers use a variety of activity structures in their classes, but don't take time to establish group agreements with the students on how behavioral norms should differ from structure to structure. Berliner recommends that teachers set aside time to establish "rules of behavior" for each prominent activity structure they will use. For example, in reading circles students don't have to raise their hands to ask a question, whereas when doing seatwork they should raise their hands if they want help. Or, all mediated presentations will be followed by small discussion groups during which students discuss what they learned from the presentations. During two-way presentations, the teacher will try to paraphrase each student's remark before responding to it. Teachers might develop lists of rules under each activity structure early in the year and have the class review them once a month.

Developing Norms of Helpfulness

A high school English teacher, looking for ways to improve the ability of her students to write clearly, decided to form students into helping pairs to give feedback on writing. The instructional sequence was first for the teacher to present a list of guidelines for good writing, second for the students to write a brief essay on their own, third for the helping pairs to meet and for their members to read and criticize each other's essay, fourth for each student to rewrite his or her essay, fifth for each helping pair to meet with another pair and for all four to go over one another's essays, sixth for each student again to rewrite his or her essay, and, finally, seventh for the students to turn in their essays to the teacher.

The teacher reported back to the whole class that the papers were much improved compared to how they read before the helping pairs and asked the students to continue on with helping pairs for writing. She also asked each student to find a new pair-mate. After the new pairs were established, the teacher lead a discussion with the whole class on how to give helpful feedback about another person's writing. After that discussion, the class went through another complete cycle as described above. The teacher and most students felt good about how the new norms of helpfulness were facilitating improved writing and decided to continue the practice throughout the term.

Communication

8

Communication is uniquely human; it is verbal and nonverbal dialogue between people. Through communication, people both participate in groups and develop as individuals. Indeed, it is primarily via communication with parents, siblings, teachers, and peers that youngsters come to know themselves as people.

Many different actions, from the principal speaking to every class over the loud speaker to a small group of students engaged in oral reading, might be categorized as communication. However, this chapter will emphasize the face-to-face verbal and nonverbal interactions that occur in the classroom between teachers and students and among students.

Classroom participants communicate many different kinds of information to one another. They talk about the content of the curriculum, the methods they use to learn, and sometimes about the group processes of the class. Frequently, very personal messages with idiosyncratic actions are exchanged, messages that carry special meanings for that particular class.

Objectives of this Chapter

In this chapter, we strive to help readers develop analytic schemes for understanding and mapping communication in the classroom. The process of classroom communication entails a synthesis of expectations, leadership, friendship, cohesiveness, and norms. We conceptualize communication first by using George H. Mead's "symbolic interactionism," and second according to its circularity in reciprocal, interpersonal relations. We illustrate these concepts in communicating about sex roles and status in the classroom. This chapter reviews concepts and research on miscommunication, the multiple levels at which people communicate, and typical communication patterns in the classroom. It proceeds to suggest several communication skills that can raise the level of communicative effectiveness in classrooms, points to how teacher communication can facilitate or inhibit student learning, offers useful procedures for developing effective classroom discussions, and gives suggestions for reducing communication gaps among classroom participants. We end the chapter by proposing classroom strategies that teachers have used successfully to develop effective communication.

Communication as Symbolic Interaction

Although animals emit sounds and make gestures, such as a hen's clucking to her chicks or a wolf's cuddling her cubs, they do not communicate or interact symbolically. Humans share in the attitudes and feelings of others by giving and receiving symbolic messages. An outstanding difference between animal noises and human communication is the human ability to be able to project oneself into the role of another person. It is distinctively human to recognize psychological states of others through the messages they communicate, whether the messages are nonverbal or verbal. For a teacher to look into a student's eyes, to know that there is hurt inside the student, and to respond with an affectionate hug can nonverbally communicate a strong message of concern, compassion, and caring. To say, "I feel bad," or "I care about you," in such a way that the student will know how the teacher feels can constitute a tender moment of human empathy and compassion.

An infant's initial gurgling and cooing contain sounds of all potential languages. By hearing specific sound patterns repeatedly, the infant eventually expresses some of the myriad of potential sounds and starts to eliminate others. Preschoolers incorporate some sounds into their personal repertoires, begin to understand that particular sounds have referents, and start to develop understandings about themselves and others by imitating others' verbal exchanges or by rehearsing conversations within their thoughts. Beginning at about three years of age, children's discussions with peers become exchanges, play and language become interactional, and peers respond to one another realistically rather than autistically. Both as preschoolers and students within classrooms, youngsters' sharing of feelings with others and the development of their self-concepts occur simultaneously and interdependently.

Members of classroom groups can come to understand one another by communicating verbally, even though the individuals come from different social backgrounds and have different personalities. Language, the primary medium for exchanging messages, is composed of symbols associated with referents, e.g., the sound "chair" calls up an image of an object to sit on, with a back, seat, and legs. Of course, there are various concepts inherent in "chairness," ranging from an artistic creation to a hewn log. And, thus, additional words must be used to communicate the differences. At the same time, most persons will know what another is talking about when the word "chair" is used.

Symbols are constituted of more, however, than shared meanings with specifiable referents. They also take on special connotative definitions that are not necessarily widely shared. Often differences in understanding occur in classrooms because of changes in inflection, mannerisms, or intonations. The teacher who says to a student, "Well, you certainly did a good job on that," could either be intending sarcasm or be making a favorable evaluation. The student who says, "I'm uptight with arithmetic," could mean to indicate either anxiety about arithmetic, or high interest and involvement in it, depending upon the cultural contexts and the manner of speech.

Nonverbal communication, also, is understood differently in different cultural contexts. Byers and Byers (1972), for example, described the culturally different meanings of direct eye contact between people. American children, for example, are often expected to look directly at an instructing or chastising adult to show that they are "paying attention." Yet, in contrast, Puerto Rican children are expected to show respect toward adults by looking down. Indeed, direct eye-to-eye contact is viewed as disrespectful, challenging, or arrogant. This cultural difference can be a source of conflict when children of the two cultures come together. Many Puerto Rican children in mainland schools may be chastised for disrespect by behaving in the very ways that signaled respect in their own culture.

Discussing nonverbal interaction, Hall (1971) describes the different orientations to personal space that people may learn from their culture. (Personal space is the preferred distance for each individual when interacting with other people.) There are differences, of course, between individuals and there are also significant cultural differences. Latin Americans, for example, generally prefer less personal space in interactions than do North Americans.

Observations in the natural world, along with experimental laboratory studies (see Evans and Howard, 1973) have demonstrated that adults of both sexes tend to approach females more closely than males and to seat themselves closer to females. Those studies also reveal that the nonverbal behavior between men and women in our society reflects status differences. Whereas men display dominant nonverbal behaviors such as directly approaching a woman and touching, women's behaviors are submissive. They avert their eyes, move away from a man, or step aside when they are in the same path. These differences between interacting men and women also have been observed in other cultures. An interesting question, nowadays, is whether such nonverbal interactions involving males and females will gradually change as women take on higher status roles in the work force.

Language Communication and Sex Roles

Some anthropologists, such as Benjamin Whorf, maintain that language provides people in a culture with a conceptual map to their own phenomenological world. The psyche takes on meaning through the importation of language. Patterns of verbal interaction are associated with "what it means" to be a male or a female in our society. The use of language in social interaction, as well as the nuances of expression and gesture, identify and stereotype males and females.

Research has emphasized the detrimental effects of sex bias in everyday language and usage (e.g., see Thorne and Henley, 1975, and Thorne, Kramarae, and Henley, 1983). To assist teachers in identifying language that is sex biased, we offer

four rules of thumb. Does the language *label* by sex? Are male or female *markers* necessary? Is one sex *omitted*? Are males and females treated in *nonparallel* ways? (see Kalvelage, J., and Schmuck, P., 1981).

Sex-labeling is prescribing an occupational role to a man or a woman. "Policeman" and "housewife" are examples of sex-labels. Research by Lord (1976) explored the effects of sex-labeling of occupational roles on young children's images of males and females. One group of youngsters studied occupational roles with no sex labels (i.e., firefighters, law enforcement officers, and mail carriers). Another group of children were given the conventional names of fireman, policeman, and mailman. When asked to draw a picture of a "firefighter" or a "mail carrier" the children using the nonsexist experimental materials were more likely to draw pictures of males and females in non-sex-stereotyped roles. The youngsters who studied sexist materials on occupations drew male figures more often. Thus, the language used to describe occupations can influence girls to grow up aspiring to be nurses or teachers and boys to grow up aspiring to be doctors or superintendents.

Sex-marking is a form of normative compliance in the language. Although the word "nurse" carries no sex label, the norm frequently exists that a nurse is female. Thus the word "nurse," when referring to a man, is marked with the adjective "male." The addition of the suffix, "ess" to non-sex-labeled words, such as steward, author, or poet, is also an example of sex-marking. Marking can be used also to identify people of color; Shirley Chisholm is described as a "black, female congressman." Mark Hatfield is described as the Senator from Oregon; he is not described as a "white, male senator."

Omission occurs when one sex, usually female, is excluded from the language. The use of the word "man" is perhaps the most obvious and debated example. Does the word "man" include the female part of the species? Here are some examples of the ambiguity of the word "man." Erich Fromm, the noted psychoanalyst, described man's vital interests as "life, food, and access to females. . . ." Clearly, in this instance, "man" means male. "The Ascent of Man" was an acclaimed television program depicting the evolution of culture. Presumably, in this instance, the word "man" includes the female of the species. Finally, here is an example where the word "man" clearly means *only* female: "Man, being a mammal, breast-feeds his young" (Miller and Swift 1977).

In an exercise developed by Wells (1976) to raise consciousness about language and sexism, the audience is asked to listen to a historical reading on "Woman, Which Includes Man, of Course." It traces the history of Neanderthal Woman to the current state of womankind, "which includes man, of course." Each historical episode emphasizes the women in history and not the men. It is a revealing exercise for both women and men—some men report feelings of "rejection and failure" after completing the exercise.

Curriculum materials, tests, and the public media use language that tends to ignore females. Several content analyses by WOWI (Women on Words and Images 1972) and Britton (1973) on the numbers of male versus female referents in popular reading materials have been completed. They indicate a male referent (either a human, an animal, or a male-linked role) approximately 90 percent of the time compared to 10 percent representation of females.

Nonparallel form is our fourth example of sex bias in the language. Usually nonparallel form diminishes the status of a person such as the use of "boy" to refer to an adult black male. Yet it is common to hear about the "girls" and "men" at the office, even though the females and males are probably the same age. The use of the term "girl" frequently diminishes the status of females. The use of Mrs. and Miss compared to Mr. is perhaps the most common example of nonparallel form. Women's marital status is indicated by their title. "Mr." carries no such information. Therefore, many women choose to use the title "Ms." which is parallel to "Mr." in that it conveys no information about marital position. The explicit messages of sex stereotyping in our language are only beginning to emerge, both for students and for educators. The teacher who wishes students to work up to their potential will be wise to pay attention to the subtle—and not so subtle—nuances of the manner in which our language differentially treats boys and girls.

Communication and Status in the Classroom

Cohen (1986) has examined the effect of status relationships among students on their classroom communication, involvement, and learning. In particular, she has studied how status distinctions emanating from sex roles, ethnicity, and socio-economic position affect student participation. Over and over, her data have demonstrated that low status, whatever its basis, is associated with low peer-group participation, and that even in small, cooperative learning groups, those with low status learn less. In the style of a negative circular process, reduced learning serves to reinforce low status in the classroom.

Cohen exhorts teachers to become aware of status differences among their students, particularly as they attempt to communicate together within small learning groups. A common problem, she argues, will be domination by a few students and a lack of participation by others. She encourages teachers to create ways to raise the participation levels of low status students.

Cohen suggests, for example, what she calls "expectation training" during which low status students are given the role of "expert" within a cooperative learning team, or during which the teacher communicates the value of a wide range of talents and how every student in every learning team has certain unique talents (for more examples, see chapter 4). Cohen goes on to discuss how teachers should strive to transform implicit norms so that "whoever wants to participate does so at whatever level they choose," or so that there are explicit group agreements that "everyone participates and everyone helps." Cohen also emphasizes group discussion techniques such as rotating group conveners, recorders, or facilitators to insure equal participation. (For more examples, see chapter 7.)

Cohen encourages teachers to watch carefully for signs of status differences and to construct training exercises or other interventions that are integrated into the regular curriculum. The six communication skills and the ten group discussion techniques discussed later in this chapter are the sorts of classroom interventions that can go a long way toward helping teachers deal constructively with the important issue raised by Cohen—classroom status.

Communication as a Reciprocal Process

Verbal and nonverbal messages constitute the core ingredients of communication. Verbal communication is important to many aspects of life. How one communicates and how much one communicates are related to the motives of achievement, power, and affiliation. As an empirical study, Ahlbrand and Hudgins (1970) investigated the relationship between the amount of verbal participation of boys and girls in grades four through nine and their scholarship, leadership, and popularity. High verbal participators were viewed by their classmates as top scholars, leaders, and popular students. Whether the high verbal participation caused the favorable ratings or whether their high status caused them to be verbally active is unclear. It is clear, however, that Cohen (1986) has made a convincing argument that a relationship exists between the status achieved with peers and participation.

Although words are a principal vehicle of communication, the meaning of verbal messages is not based upon words alone. Verbal communication entails interpersonal relationships. How one reciprocates in the interaction depends upon how the receiver interprets the words that are sent when they are augmented by such nonverbal cues as bodily gestures, intonations, situational factors, and previous relationships with the communicator. Sometimes verbal or nonverbal messages do not clarify the relationship between people; rather, they tend to confuse it.

For example, some youngsters are exposed to contradictory verbal and nonverbal messages. Their parents say, "I love you," but communicate bodily messages of hostility and anger toward the youngster. If the child responds to the messages of hostility, the response may be, "Why do you do that to someone who cares so much for you?" On the other hand, if the child responds to the verbal message of love, the response may be, "Don't hang on to me so much." The child's interpersonal interactions with such a parent are continuously confusing, and soon the child is unable to respond appropriately to others' communications. The child's self-concept becomes as confused as the interpersonal environments, and the child begins to send unclear, confusing messages to others.

Messages with multiple meanings are frequently communicated. In fact, received messages are discrepant from the intentions of the sender in many settings, especially messages involving children. Such miscommunication is often observed in a family with a new baby. An older sibling, learning the appropriate behavior toward a new infant, might say, "You're a nice baby," and then match the loving remarks with a hug resembling the hold of a sumo wrestler. The baby may get hurt physically while being loved with words. Similar confusions occur daily in classrooms. The teacher gives an assignment and smiles. Some students read the message as pleasant and supportive while others see it as a show of power and authority. Only continuous checking with students on what messages they actually receive will keep communication channels open and clear in the classroom.

Communication flows from the needs, motives, and desires of individuals toward others. It entails the sending of messages about personal intentions, whether these intentions are desires for control, in-

formation, love, or anger. Effective communication exists between two persons when the receiver interprets the sender's message in the same way the sender intended it. The message in this way does not belong to the sender alone.

Communicative messages entail encoding, transmitting, receiving, and decoding, and, as such, they involve relationships between sender and receiver. The bridging of gaps between separate individuals entails specifying the congruence among intentions, behaviors, and interpretations. That reciprocal communicative process is depicted graphically in Figure 8.1. In effective communication, the messages of the sender (person A) reflect the person's intentions, and the interpretations by the receiver (person B) match the intentions of the sender.

Miscommunication

Miscommunications are gaps between the intended message and the received message. They frequently occur because messages sent do not accurately reflect intentions. For example, Bill, a student, feels embarrassed, guilty, and inferior when called upon to recite. He does not know what to answer. He responds with defensive wisecracking which the teacher interprets as defiance and low interest in the subject matter. Bill's true feelings, which are actually intentions to please, are masked by his verbal joking and nonchalant behavior. The teacher misreads Bill's inner state, becomes angry, and scolds him. Bill unhappily returns to his seat, feeling rejected.

Part of the answer to why messages do not reflect intentions is the fact that certain behaviors are more difficult than others for

FIGURE 8.1   Reciprocal Communication Process

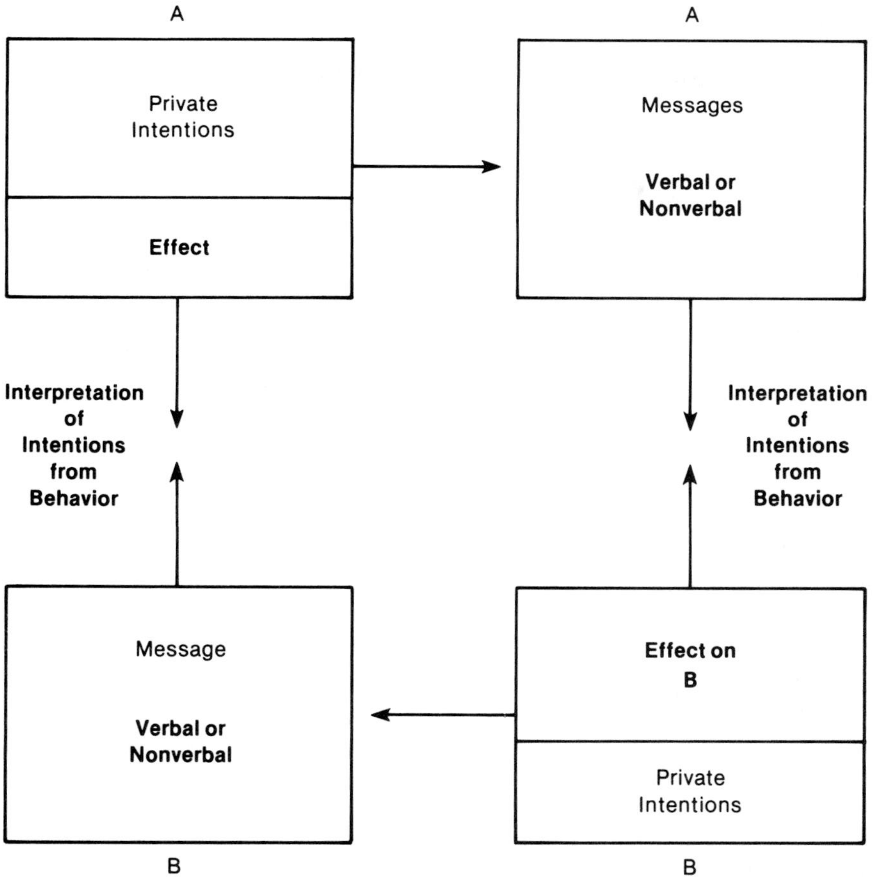

persons to perform. Some words, phrases, or mannerisms are not a part of some people's behavioral repertoires. In the previous example, the student lacked skill in transforming the feelings of embarrassment, guilt, and inferiority into appropriate verbal behaviors. Another instance of a discrepancy between intent and action occurs as people try to reveal affection for one another. Tongues become tied, bodies frozen,

and eyes no longer make contact when some people attempt to show their attraction for another.

Studies of teachers' influence on students frequently assume that all students make the same response to teachers' behavior as perceived by observers. A study by Takanishi and Spitzer (1980) showed that students' perceptions of teachers' behavior were different, depending on the age and sex of the students. In a number of the classes studied, Takanishi and Spitzer found miscommunication between teachers and students because the students' perceptions were quite different from those of the teachers.

Takanishi and Spitzer studied seven nongraded, multiaged teams of teachers and students in a laboratory elementary school. Students ranged in age from four to twelve years. The teachers told the students that an advantage to working together as a team was the situation that there would be more helpers for learning than in regular classes and that regular opportunities for working with teachers, peers, or other adults would occur.

Observers substantiated the teachers' views that their students, regardless of age or sex, were making use of the variety of resources in the teams. Students regularly worked with each teacher, with several peers of both sexes, and with a few adults other than teachers; however, perceptions about what was happening were often quite different between teachers and students and among the students.

Takanishi and Spitzer interviewed the students to obtain their perceptions of the classes. The results indicated significant variations among the students. The younger students, for example, did not perceive peers to be resources for learning. They thought that only the teachers were helpers and that time with peers was unrelated to learning. Sex differences were also pronounced. Girls, more frequently than boys, spoke about specific girls who were helpful to them as resources, but boys frequently indicated uncertainty about peers being resources for learning at all.

Perhaps such variations would not have been difficult for the classes had the teachers known more about the students' percep-tions, but no time was spent in class discussion about the helping relationship. Students were often confused about what they were to do when interacting with peers or when working with adults other than teachers. That study is an illustration of the multiple realities of classroom life and the need for two-way communication to increase the clarity of messages between teachers and students.

Discrepancies between intentions and messages also occur because of confusion between students' expressing themselves directly and students' trying to impress others so that the others notice these students' attractive attributes. To *express* is to allow the self to be known to others with authenticity. It is making the self transparent. To *impress* is to put on a mask and to perform in ways that will be attractive to others. Much classroom interaction arises from the desire to impress. In class, students may present images which convey curiosity and interest in the curriculum, primarily to impress the teacher. The teacher may attempt to present an impression of omniscience or of distant control. In either case, real selves are being concealed in order to maintain a stable and predictable social scene. It is as though all parties are taking part in a play. The classroom becomes the stage and class members perform as the actors. When class members, intentionally or unintentionally, attempt to impress, they set the stage for distrustful communication. All members become aware that others are playing the same game, but no one wants to change his or her act because each is a crucial player in the drama.

To impress is not unnatural nor is it always "phoney." It is, rather, a natural human state that allows people to cope more easily with a number of superficial social events. Unfortunately, superficiality and the concealment of self in teaching are detrimental to the development of autonomous students and effective classroom communication. Teachers who continuously attempt to create impressions are finally "discovered," thereby rapidly losing their students' trust. The "omniscient" teacher will make a mistake that some students will notice. The teacher may attempt to hide the error by defending, justifying, or even falsifying the point, just to maintain the impression of omniscience. But students will perceive the behaviors as defensive and soon will begin criticizing the teacher outside of the classroom. Eventually, the students will challenge what the teacher is doing, either covertly, by not following directions, or overtly, by acting out in class.

Gibb (1961) defines defensive communication as interpersonal behaviors that occur when individuals see the environment as threatening and therefore must protect themselves. Gibb presents some categories of climates which can be characterized as defensive or supportive. Defensive climates include those that have high degrees of evaluation, those that attempt to control others' behaviors, and those where there is competition to be superior. Supportive climates, on the other hand, permit more descriptions of behavior, empathy for others, and collaborative relationships. Defensive communication is intended to protect and guard against others and does not yield dialogue or reciprocal communication.

Effective communication occurs in classrooms where trust and empathy are present. Teachers who communicate their own complex humanity directly by discussing their feelings, and who listen to descriptions of students' feelings, have a good

chance of engaging students in effective dialogue. On the other hand, teachers who fashion false impressions encourage their students to play a game of impression-forming also and increase the probability that the curriculum will be a meaningless ritual.

The teacher's warmth, concern, and acceptance help to facilitate interpersonal trust, as long as these qualities are communicated in a genuine sense. To behave as consistently accepting, when the teacher is truly feeling annoyed or angry, presents a phoney facade which, over time, will reduce trust between students and teacher. In our teaching experiences, students tend to trust those teachers who are open and honest about their thoughts and feelings. Authenticity on the part of teachers is more important than a rigid consistency of warmth and acceptance which has the "ring" of dishonesty. Those teachers we know who are authentic have worked diligently to become more aware of their teaching values, beliefs, feelings, anxieties, and behaviors.

Levels of Communication

Communication is an intricate bevy of spoken and unspoken behaviors occurring at several levels of human interaction. Some parts of communicative acts are obvious and easily understood while others are covert and ambiguous. Using the analogy of a complex novel can help in understanding communication as a multileveled process. Hemingway's novels, for instance, can be read simply as stimulating and interesting stories with exciting details and action. The characters are real, facing authentic issues. Their lives are easy to grasp. Hemingway as the great storyteller and entertainer is communicating overtly, concretely, and descriptively. But those who read Hemingway's novels only at this level of communicative reality miss a good measure of his complexity. The stories portray depth, compassion, empathy, and sometimes offer an allegory which can be useful in arriving at a more complete understanding of human existence. Basic psychological themes underlie the concrete events, and the lives of the characters constitute a covert, emotional level of communication.

In *For Whom the Bell Tolls,* for example, Hemingway presents a captivating adventure story, full of intrigue and romance, set in the fury and destruction of the Spanish Civil War. Like most of Hemingway's novels, *For Whom the Bell Tolls* offers a thrilling story for Hollywood. But there is much more than a romantic adventure story in this novel. It also tells about two contrasting styles of leadership, thereby contributing an understanding about leadership to those of us interested in group processes. *For Whom The Bell Tolls* shows how military morale is affected by leadership style. Hemingway tells the story of Robert Jordan, an American professor of Spanish, who fought as a demolition expert with the Loyalists. Jordan decided that he could best help the Loyalist platoon to accomplish its mission of destroying a key bridge by being invited by the troops to become the group's leader. His story provides a view of leadership based on influence rather than authority. In contrast, Hemingway tells the story of a Fascist captain whose authority was tied to his gun and to the intimidation of his troops. He ignored his subordinates and, in the end, was left alone to carry out his own orders. Thus,

Hemingway teaches us that even during war, leadership based on knowledge and friendship is more powerful than leadership based on coercive authority.

Classroom communication can be just as complex as Hemingway's novels. Different levels of feelings, motives, thoughts, and intentions exist simultaneously. Some comments and behaviors are easy to understand, but others represent underlying messages in the lives of the teacher and students. Teachers are often aware that events must be occurring at home which are affecting the student's behaviors in school. Or perhaps, while a student is talking to a teacher, the student may also be addressing peers in that the student hopes that the conversation will be overheard by peers. Teachers may say something to the entire class, intending for only a few students to listen to it.

Paul Byers (1972), an anthropologist, and Happie Byers (1972) a practicing educator, have written about the implications of their studies of nonverbal communication for the classroom, and they point out the importance of the context by which communication occurs—the human relationship.

> When we examine a human relationship, such as a simple conversation between two people, we almost immediately discover that there are multiple modalities or channels operating in addition to language. We discover that the modalities, verbal and nonverbal, are learned as patterns of a culture (as language is learned) and that they are systematic (as language has grammar, for example). Furthermore, we discover that they all fit together; they are systematically interrelated (p. 6).

Increased awareness of different levels of communication should assist teachers in relating more effectively to the class. The teacher's talking about something that heretofore has been an unspoken subject, or even a subject about which the students have not been aware, increases the likelihood that communication will be clarified.

In an analysis of classroom communication, Hurt, Scott, and McCroskey (1978) discuss some feelings which will cause students to close up and to avoid communication: (a) a desire to be left alone because of preoccupations with other events, (b) a fear of disclosing thoughts because they might appear to be incompetent and stupid, (c) a dislike for school, (d) a perception that their best friends do not value communication with teachers, and (e) an apprehension about communicating because of previous unsatisfying experiences with the same teacher.

Aside from the first of these, all of the circumstances listed by Hurt, Scott, and McCroskey that retard effective dialogue in the classroom can be altered by the teacher. Since it is clear that the members of classroom groups have feelings, expectations, and thoughts that remain below the surface unless they are raised for discussion, the teacher must be alert for opportunities to bring things into the open. When hidden psychic processes and idiosyncratic perceptions are brought into the open for discussion, they can be worked on through group problem solving. A classroom group that delves into subsurface levels increases its freedom to improve itself.

Four relevant levels of classroom communication are spoken-unspoken messages, surface-hidden intentions, work-emotional activities, and task-maintenance functions.

Spoken-Unspoken Messages

It is difficult, if not impossible, to discuss nonverbal communication in words. Something is inevitably "lost in the translation." Unspoken messages are part and parcel of human communication. For communication to be clear in the classroom, the spoken and unspoken messages should be consonant. If they are in conflict, students will be confused and often will continue to communicate unclear messages in a circular fashion.

Surface-Hidden Intentions

Classrooms are made up of a variety of personal goals, some of which are in conflict. In competitive classes, for instance, a surface intention to do better than others exists. A preference for high performance may be communicated directly, while a wish to be better than competitors could be revealed in offhand, negative remarks about other students.

Work-Emotional Activities

Messages communicated in the classroom about the curriculum typically have emotional meanings. Feelings about classroom work influence ways in which the work is accomplished. Long periods of inaction in improving feelings about work can lead to apathy and resistance toward learning.

Task-Maintenance Functions

In chapter 5, we discussed how communication can be directed toward moving the class forward on its assignments (task), or toward keeping members of the class working together smoothly (maintenance).

Communication Patterns

Communicative acts in the classroom develop into routine and regular patterns that can become self-perpetuating. The teacher who dominates discussions tends to train students not to take the initiative. The student who is ignored in discussions for a week stops speaking the next week, and may be ignored for much of the rest of the year. Teachers and students can become victims of their own self-perpetuating routines unless they feel encouraged to raise them to an awareness level for discussion. Public recognition of communication patterns is the first step toward making constructive changes. Classroom communication patterns can be analyzed in the following three ways which we'll examine in some depth.

Verbal Communication

During the last 25 years, instruments to measure classroom verbal communication have grown by leaps and bounds. Whereas in 1967 Simon and Boyer catalogued 26 instruments, a 1986 newsletter entitled *Communication Quarterly* (produced by the Institute for Research on Teaching at Michigan State University) presented over 150 annotated references, many of which included an instrument to measure classroom verbal communication. At the 1990 national convention of the American Educational Research Association, over 200 quantitative and qualitative strategies were offered for measuring classroom communication. These many instruments capture both affective and cognitive aspects of classroom communication. The affective systems measure classroom emotional qualities by coding the teacher's reactions to feelings of students. Cognitive systems deal with different types of information giving, questioning, and offering. They emphasize how the formal classroom curriculum gets communicated. Contemporary instruments also measure time allocation, the integration of assessment and instruction, and teaching styles.

The single, most important pioneer researcher on the verbal communication of teachers during teaching was Ned Flanders. Starting in the 1950s with the small-group research of Bales, Thelen, and Withall, Flanders worked for 20 years on the development of procedures for classroom observation. His students and followers at the University of Minnesota, Temple University, the University of Michigan, and the Farwest Educational Laboratory have produced a large body of research literature (e.g., see Furst and Amidon, 1965; Amidon and Simon, 1965; or Simon, Samph, Soar, and Amidon, 1966, for important early papers).

One set of categories for analyzing classroom verbal communication, based on Flanders' system of Interaction Analysis (1960, 1970), warrants special consideration. It is the Verbal Interaction Category System (VICS) developed by Amidon and Hunter (1966). Amidon was a very close collaborator with Flanders as the latter's graduate assistant at Minnesota. VICS systematizes classroom verbal exchanges within an objective category system in order to describe verbal messages sent by teachers and students. By using the VICS, teachers can discover whether their verbal communications are consonant with their intentions. The VICS is a valuable tool for checking what teachers are actually communicating rather than what they think or want to be communicating. The VICS categories are as follows:

Teacher-Initiated Talk

1. gives information or opinions
2. gives directions
3. asks narrow questions
4. asks broad questions

Teacher Response

5. accepts
    (a) ideas
    (b) behaviors
    (c) feelings
6. rejects
    (a) ideas
    (b) behaviors
    (c) feelings

Student Response

7. responds to teacher
    (a) predictably
    (b) unpredictably
8. responds to another

Student-Initiated Talk

9. initiates talking to teacher
10. initiates talking to another student

Other

11. silence
12. confusion

After observations are collected, the data are compiled into a scoring matrix. Each square represents one characteristic; for example, "teacher rejection of student responses," or, "extended student-initiated talking to the teacher or other students." By glancing at the matrix, the teacher can readily perceive what patterns of communication exist in his or her classroom. Teachers should read Amidon and Hunter (1966) for an array of details, situations, and skills dealing with improving verbal communication in the classroom, Simon and Boyer (1967) for a variety of analyses of communication networks, and Good and Brophy (1973) for ideas on what to look for when observing communication in the classroom.

One-Way, Two-Way Communication

In our study of 80 schools and 119 teachers in small towns (for details about the research, see Schmuck and Schmuck, 1990), we observed in 80% of the classes we studied what Ned Flanders called the rule of two-thirds; i.e, two-thirds of classroom talk is teacher's talk, and two-thirds of that is unidirectional lecturing. In our extensive research, we modified Flanders' maxim to the rule of three-fourths. The classes were typically teacher-centered; we saw teachers standing up front lecturing to rows of students, with only occasional student talk as a response to teacher questions. In only ten of 119 classes did we see student-to-student talk that was planned by the teacher. Four times we saw students in pairs conferring together in response to the teacher's questions, and six times we saw students in small groups working together on a problem or a project. Our experiences were especially sobering, considering that we had deliberately asked principals to introduce us to teachers who were using learning groups or cooperative learning. Indeed, even in 1990, a considerable number of principals thought about ability grouping when we asked them if any teachers in their school used groups for learning.

FIGURE 8.2 Geometric Patterns Used in One-Way, Two-Way Communication Activity

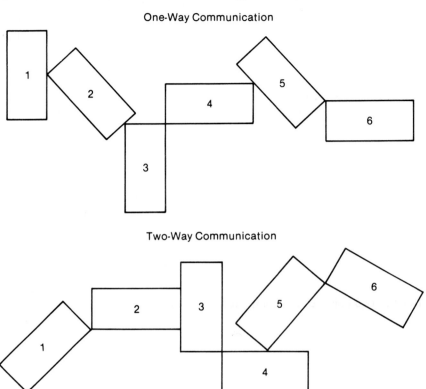

Research using the VICS or similar verbal communication system has also shown that verbal interaction occupies a great deal of class time and that the preponderance of interaction is teachers "talking to students." One-way communication from teacher to students is not, however, usually the most effective means for student learning. Many teachers wish to reduce the amount of talking they do by eliciting comments from students, but they are stymied as to how to do it. One way of increasing student talk is to change classroom norms that support more two-way communication (see Tesch, Lansky, and Lundgren 1972, for some research data). This is an exercise that can be used in the upper elementary grades, the middle school, the junior high, and the senior high. The class is divided into groups of approximately eight students each. One member of each group is chosen as coordinator and another is asked to be the sender of the communication. The remaining six members are asked to perform as receivers. The coordinator signals when to begin, keeps track of the amount of time spent during each phase of the activity, and makes observations of the receivers' nonverbal reactions.

To commence the activity, the coordinator gives two geometric patterns of rectangles to the sender without showing them to the receivers. The two patterns of rectangles, shown in Figure 8.2, are equal in complexity. One pattern is presented to the receivers in the fashion of one-way communication; the other is given by two-way communication. During both types of communications, the sender sits with his or her back to the receivers so that facial cues and hand movements do not influence the process. The receivers are asked to draw the patterns as accurately as possible. During one-way communication, they may ask no questions and must remain silent. In the two-way communication episode, receivers are encouraged to interrupt at any time to raise questions and to interact verbally with the sender.

After the two episodes are completed, the coordinator helps the receivers determine the number of correct placements in their drawings. A correct rectangle touches one or two other rectangles at the matching location on the sides of the other rectangles. It also should be oriented vertically, horizontally, or diagonally modeled on the sender's page. Scores in this exercise can range from 0 to 6 for each type of communication. A receiver looses one point each time two adjacent rectangles fail to touch at the correct place, making a total of five points possible. The sixth point is lost if the vertical, horizontal, and diagonal orientations of any of the rectangles are clearly wrong.

After the receivers score their own drawings, both the sender and the receivers are asked to answer the following questions. How much time did each type of communication take? Then, for each of the following questions, three alternative answers are possible, one-way, two-way, or no difference. With which communication were you most satisfied? With which communication were you more frustrated or tense? Which type would you prefer to use as a sender? Which type would you prefer to receive? The coordinator guides the ensuing discussion, using the following questions as guides. When is one-way communication efficient in our class, and how might we improve it? When is two-way communication necessary in our class, and what can we do to improve it? What are other implications of this activity for our class, and what keeps us from using two-way communication more often?

To complete this activity, the small group coordinators report to the entire class on the primary outcomes of their group. All class members then discuss what they learned from the activity, and make recommendations for improving classroom communication. To further enhance the exchange, perhaps a small committee of students could be constituted for continued work on improving clarity of communication in the classroom.

Both one-way and two-way communication can be useful for teaching and learning, provided they are employed appropriately. Although one-way communication places a student in a passive role, evidence indicates that lectures are valuable for students who are highly motivated and who are eager to learn specific information. Students are ready to hear one-way communication when they are listening for answers to questions they have already raised for themselves.

Two-way communication promotes more active inquiry and listening, and is especially valuable when the learning requires behavioral changes. For example, two-way communication is more valuable than one-way communication when students are asked to show insight into the real psychological problems of children or to manifest the ability to act appropriately with disturbed youngsters. Two-way communication consumes more time than does one-way communication in getting work done. However, the work is generally of higher quality and is accomplished with less confusion and negative feeling.

Nonverbal Messages

A large amount of effort during the past twenty-five years has gone into research on the influence of the nonverbal domain on interpersonal communication. Although much of this work has been done outside of educational settings, Smith (1979) in a review indicated that educational researchers are beginning to recognize the importance of nonverbal communication in teaching.

During the 1980s and 90s teachers have become much more aware of the classroom's silent language. It includes eye contact, nodding and gesturing, modulating tone, assuming a posture of attentiveness, and smiling. This silent language is particularly powerful when it is issued in different ways to different students. It is how teachers either reinforce or alter the status differences between boys and girls, among members of different racial or ethnic groups or members of different social classes.

Nonverbal messages usually entail expressing feelings by bodily changes, gestures, or various shades of facial coloring. A remarkable thing about classroom participants is the fact that while feelings are perhaps the greatest determinants of their actions, these feelings are very seldom communicated in words. In communicating emotions, too often language is used as a way of disguising real feelings rather than as a way of expressing them. Classroom communication would be enhanced more if a teacher caught in making mistakes would say, "I'm embarrassed," or "I feel uncomfortable because of what I just did," rather than attempting to justify the error by covering up nonverbally.

Nonverbal messages are inevitably ambiguous, and therefore the recipient is often unclear as to what the sender is feeling. Expressions of feelings can take the form of many bodily changes. Thus, a specific feeling, such as anger, can be expressed by great bodily motion or by a frozen stillness. Any single nonverbal expression also may arise from a variety of feelings. For example, a blush may indicate embarrassment, pleasure, or even hostility. Nor is a specific feeling always expressed in the same nonverbal way. A student's attraction to a teacher may manifest itself in many ways, from blushing while standing near the teacher to watching from a distance, bringing presents, or even doing work well. In perceiving nonverbal messages, the receiver must interpret the sender's actions and, as those actions increase in ambiguity, the chance for misinterpretation increases. The receiver's own emotional state is also very important in interpreting the sender's action. And so, for example, if the receiver feels guilty about previous actions, nonverbal messages of confusion might be received from the sender as accusations of negative judgments.

Nonverbal messages are continuously expressed among peers in the classroom. Nonverbal peer group communication is triggered especially rapidly when highly influential students are scolded by the teacher.

The response of a highly influential peer to a teacher's disciplinary action elicits a similar response in other observing students. If the disciplined student submits to teacher influence by remaining silent, others will also remain silent. Highly influential students may induce others to do as they do, even when they do not intend to influence others directly. Peers watch the nonverbal gestures of their highly influential peers to receive cues to guide their own classroom behaviors.

Teachers should be aware that certain non-verbal behaviors will generally facilitate supportive relationships in the classroom. Promptly recognizing and greeting students as they approach will help them feel accepted. Making eye contact when addressing a student could help that student to feel important. Moving one's eyes around the whole group can help students feel that the teacher is aware of what's going on in the class. And, of course, frequent smiling and pleasing facial expressions can communicate a positive tone to everyone.

Seating Arrangements

Ecological psychology deals, in part, with the physical arrangements of the classroom environment. Classroom communication flows through space and is influenced by physical phenomena, especially seating arrangements. A number of researchers have shed light on the effects seating arrangements have upon classroom communication.

Leavitt (1951) experimented with the effects of four physical structures on communication within five-person teams. The four structures placed different limitations on the teams. One pattern was formed as a circle. Each subject could communicate to persons on either side, but to no one else. This structure was equalitarian; each subject could communicate with only two others, and no single subject was in a position to dominate. A second structure took the form of a line. This was similar to the circle, except that the subjects on the ends could communicate only to one other person.

The two other patterns were more centrally structured in that they possessed focal points through which communication was to pass. One was shaped like a square, with four subjects at each corner, and the fifth subject in the center. This pattern was the most centralized structure, with most communication passing through the center person. The last was shaped like a Y, with two subjects at the upper points, one at the juncture, and two below the subject in a line. The four communication structures of Leavitt are depicted in Figure 8.3.

All four groups were given problems to solve in a manner requiring information exchange. The results showed the diverse effects of the physical structures. Groups 3 and 4 were more efficient than the first two groups, but the errors they made persisted longer, and their feelings of dissatisfaction with the exercise were much higher. The circle pattern, group 1, was inefficient in time, although few errors were made and the subjects felt more comfortable compared with all other groups. The line pattern, group 2, was also inefficient, but it offered more satisfaction than groups 3 and 4 reported.

Leavitt's research has implications for the classroom. Certain communication patterns give rise to feelings of being a peripheral or an unimportant member. This would be most obvious in classes where commu-

FIGURE 8.3   Leavitt's Four Communication Structures

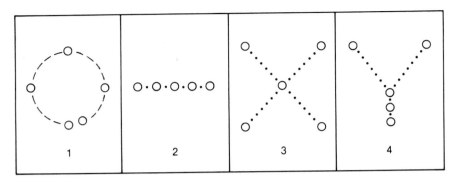

nication is focused on an elite peer group, or where it emanates primarily from the teacher in the directive style of one-way communication. Feelings of being peripheral to the group can lead to a reduction of communication with others, and possibly also start a negative circular process. It seems clear that when the class is organized so that the possibility exists for communication to flow equally—as in the circle—everyone will participate to some degree during an hour's time. In the circular structure, communication remains open and is dependent on participation of most members. *In classrooms where issues are discussed by most everyone and where different people become central to the discussion at different times, greater feelings of involvement, satisfaction, and a steadier flow of communication will occur.*

Sommer (1967) adapted Leavitt's ideas to carry out research directly on classrooms by studying the relationships between seating arrangements and classroom participation. The primary seating arrangements were *seminar style*—where the students and instructor sat around in an approximate circle—and *lecture style,* where the instructor faced the students who sat in rows. In the seminar-style arrangement, Sommer found that students directly facing the instructor participated more than students sitting off to the sides. In classrooms with straight rows, students in front participated more than students in the rear, and students in the center of each row participated more than the students at the sides.

Sommer argued that direct visual contact between persons increases the amounts of communication between them. Sommer's results had been corroborated in an earlier study by Steinzer (1950). The latter found that persons seated opposite each other interacted more than people who were seated side-by-side. The ability to see another is decreased when people are seated beside one another, and more talk occurs when participants are visible to one another. Thus, different arrangements for learning call for different nonverbal behaviors. For individual study, for example, eye contact should be minimized, whereas in small-group discussion, maximum eye contact would be best.

Seating patterns within a school cafeteria were used by Schofield and Sagar (1977) as an index of the degree of racial interaction in a newly desegregated middle school. The index of seating patterns was used as a measure of voluntary interracial contact. The researchers counted the number of instances of cross-race and cross-sex pairs seated next to each other as well as across the table. They argued that across-the-table seating, which allows eye contact, may elicit a higher degree of interracial interaction than side-by-side seating.

Interviews with students also confirmed the importance of sitting across from people with whom they ate lunch. The findings indicated that race is an extremely important criterion for voluntary association, but that sex was an even more important criterion than race. Interracial associations were higher for seventh-graders who had more instances of mixed classes than they were for eighth-graders who were tracked into a heavily white "accelerated group" and a heavily black "regular group." Interracial associations were also more frequent among boys than among girls. Schofield and Sagar suggest the greater incidence of male interaction may be due to the male sex-stereotyped role requiring boys to establish a position of dominance over both in-group and out-group members.

Research by Schofield and Sagar offers support for the contact theories of Pettigrew (1973) and Allport (1954), who argue that full integration by race or by sex will entail contact between equal status people, shared goals, cooperative interdependence, and the support of law and custom. When people voluntarily place themselves next to members of another race or sex, it is one indication of the degree of interpersonal communication that is possible among them. At the same time, we should keep in mind that proximity is no guarantee of favorable cross-race or cross-sex attitudes. We always

have the dilemma that some kinds of familiarity breed discontent. What does seem to work is involving blacks and whites or girls and boys together in cooperative learning and in working together toward an agreed-upon, superordinate goal. We will be saying more about that in chapter 9.

Communication Skills

The development of empathy—the ability to put oneself psychologically within another's thoughts and feelings—is essential to skillful communication. Empathy is important in the classroom because with increased compassion and caring for others, the self-esteem and general comfort of everyone can be enhanced.

There is a negative correlation between empathy and aggression. As empathy for others in the class increases, the number of aggressive acts decreases. To communicate with empathy takes skill and such communication skills can be practiced effectively as part of the regular classroom routines.

The skills presented below were first developed by Wallen (1969) and further explicated by Schmuck and Runkel (1985) to facilitate more effective communication and dialogue in the classroom and school. They are *techniques* and not ends in themselves. Indeed, while skillful communication is important, it alone cannot engender interpersonal warmth, openness, or intimacy. Although we believe the following skills can be very useful techniques for facilitating more effective communication, the growing feeling of alienation in our society will not be dispelled by teaching people techniques alone.

FIGURE 8.4 Six Communication Skills

	Receiving Skills	Sending Skills
Ideas	Paraphrasing Ideas	Making Clear Statements
Behavior	Describing Others' Behavior	Describing Own Behavior
Feelings	Checking Impressions	Describing Feelings

Moreover, although these skills may appear simple, they are difficult to execute—both effectively and humanistically—on a continuous basis. They are merely tools that can be used to foster communication. We have seen at least one instance where individuals adhered to these techniques so rigidly that the techniques became routines that denied dialogue between people. In consulting with a school faculty, we spent the first two sessions teaching them how to use the following skills in their staff meetings and other related work settings. When we returned, we were appalled by the methods they had used to incorporate the communication skills into their meetings. Rather than using these skills to enter into more authentic dialogue, the skills had been used strictly and had become wedges and bludgeons which fostered alienation, distrust, and frustration. The tools had become valued for their own sake, thus losing their main intent.

The communication skills described herein are tools to continue and to enhance dialogue between people. They are not meant to close off communication, but to extend it and capture the messages entailed in talk. Communication entails skill in both receiving and sending information about ideas, behavior, and feelings. Figure 8.4 summarizes six communication skills which are defined as follows:

Paraphrasing Ideas

Paraphrasing entails using one's own words to restate what another person has said. It focuses on receiving cognitive messages from others—it is an attempt to understand the ideas that have been communicated. Paraphrasing is a communication skill that implies caring for the other person's ideas. It also conveys a desire to respond with an accurate mirroring of that person's thoughts. Some lead-ins to paraphrasing are, "I understand you said. . . ." or, "Did I hear you say . . .?" The function of paraphrasing in the classroom is twofold: to check to see that the student understood the communication and to communicate to the student that he or she has been understood.

Describing Others' Behavior

The skill of behavior description entails noting in words the overt actions of another person. It is initiated by a receiver to call attention to particular behaviors and, like paraphrasing, it focuses on cognitive content. Behavior descriptions do not impugn motives by giving psychological meaning to the actions of the other, nor should they imply unalterable generalizations about the actions of the other. Looking beyond behavior for psychological interpretations is a common cause of miscommunication and interpersonal friction. Moreover, implying that the other's behaviors are unchangeable leaves little room for dialogue. Some differences between behavior description and impugning motives are expressed in the following examples.

Someone *describing* behavior would say, "Jim and Sarah have talked the most during this discussion," or, "That's the third time you interrupted," whereas, "Jim and Sarah are the only ones who are interested in the discussion," or, "You never listen to what I'm saying and never will!" represent *value* judgments, not behavior descriptions. The latter statements will tend to create defensiveness on the part of the receiver and to close off chances of continuing dialogue.

Checking Impressions

Impression checking entails a receiver's describing in a tentative fashion what he or she perceives to be another's affective state. It is similar to paraphrasing but requires tuning in on the feelings rather than the ideas or overt behaviors of the other. Impression checking must always be tentative. It attempts to open communication channels so that others will wish to describe their own feelings directly. When teachers carry out an impression check, they should avoid implying disapproval until some dialogue has occurred and the feelings of the student have been described directly. Some exemplary instances of impression checking are: "I gather from your loud and fast

speech pattern that you are angry with me right now. Are you?" And, "Your fidgeting movements and pacing up and down indicate to me that you're concerned about something today. Is that right?" Examples such as, "Why are you angry with me?" or, "Why aren't you doing what you're supposed to be doing?" are not impression checks because they imply knowledge about another's emotional state and sound like commands or threats.

Making Clear Statements

The most important sending skill is to tell others very clearly and succinctly about one's ideas. This usually means that the sender should try to use only three or four sentences in stating his or her idea. Longer, more strung-out paragraphs that are uneven and disconnected make it difficult for receivers to paraphrase. The test of clear statements is whether they can be successfully paraphrased by a receiver.

Describing Own Behavior

This skill of behavior description entails telling about one's own behaviors. It is initiated by a sender to illustrate or explain how the sender acted in a particular situation. The primary aim is to inform receivers about oneself, while a secondary aim is to communicate empathy for others.

Describing Feelings

The direct communication of one's own feelings—the sending of affective messages—is probably the least used communication skill. Unfortunately, its lack of use creates many possibilities for misunderstanding in the classroom. To express feelings directly places one in a vulnerable position with others because one is revealing an emotional state. Trust is an unknown quantity in many classrooms, and feelings tend to be expressed in indirect ways. Consequently, these feelings are often misunderstood. The following examples illustrate differences between *direct verbal descriptions and indirect expressions of feelings.*

Direct Description of Feeling	Indirect Expression of Feeling
"I feel embarrassed."	Blushing—saying nothing.
"I feel pleased."	Withdrawing—saying nothing.
"I feel annoyed."	"Why do you do such bad things?"
"I enjoy her sense of humor."	"She's a wonderful person."
"I like her ability."	
"I am impressed with her facility with language."	

The indirect expression of anger—both suppressing the anger or venting it through rage and fight—can be detrimental not only to one's mental health but also to one's physical well-being. In a twelve-year, longitudinal study carried out in Tecumseh, Michigan, by Harburg (1986), adults with high blood pressure who in the early 1970s scored high on suppressing anger were two times as likely to have died during the previous twelve years than those who said they would directly describe their anger or frustration. Other epidemeologists believe that it is important to recognize the connection between the communication of emotion and biological outcomes, such as elevated blood pressure. The direct description of emotion, when accompanied by a spirit of problem-solving promotes not only better interpersonal relations but also better health and possibly longer life.

Feedback

Feedback is a reciprocal process. It consists of one person sending information about the effects of another's behavior on himself or herself, and the other, in turn, accurately receiving that information. Typically, *feedback entails putting together in a single statement a feeling description and a behavior description,* for example, "I feel frustrated when you ask me to repeat the directions several times." This is direct feedback involving feelings (frustration) and behaviors (requesting directions several times). It is often difficult, however, to give feedback without impugning negative motives to the other, thereby creating a negative circular process. While letting off steam, or catharsis, may be the behavior that seems appropriate, many times such behavior can lead to defensiveness and anger on the part of the recipient, thereby closing off dialogue. Of course, constructive feedback is very difficult to give when one is very angry or frustrated. To be constructive, feedback should usually be given under planned and deliberate conditions in which the sender consciously makes an assessment of the recipient's readiness to hear the feedback.

One guide to constructive feedback is to use only the three sending skills illustrated in Figure 8.4 and to accentuate the feedback with "I" statements. For example, start with a feeling description, *I feel trapped and constrained,* continue with a description of self behavior, *when I try to communicate with too many people at once,* and complete the feedback with a clear statement, *so I need to talk with you about a schedule for our working together.* This statement was actually made by a high school student who was feeling overwhelmed by the time demands being put upon her by a younger student she was tutoring. The important point to note in the feedback is the attempt of the sender to talk only about herself. The form of the statement is: I (*direct description of feeling*), when I (*description of own behavior*), so I (*a clear statement of what is desired*). Dialogue between the two parties will be enhanced when the last desire is to talk about the problem.

In most of the literature on feedback, the emphasis has been put on the need for the sender to develop tact and skill in rendering constructive feedback. Porter (1974) points out that giving feedback, however helpfully intended and skillfully delivered, may be risky and could turn out to be destructive. Thus Porter focuses on the *receivership* of feedback. He suggests that individuals model being the recipients of feedback by soliciting information about the effects of their behaviors on others and using the skills of paraphrasing to confirm their understanding of the feedback they have received. We believe Porter's model may be effective in classroom situations, especially where teachers hold legitimate power over students.

Teachers should keep in mind that for feedback to be effective in enhancing dialogue with students, it should not be evaluative or judgmental. Feedback should bring out the teacher's personhood; the teacher, too, has feelings, and sometimes student behaviors affect those feelings. At the same time, teachers should be careful that their feedback not come across as requiring student change. The recipients should be free to accept or reject the information. Feedback will be most helpful when it is specific and concrete, when it is requested and not thrust upon a person, and when the sender checks to see if the feedback was received accurately.

A number of books dealing with communication skills have been written, many of which can be very useful to classroom teachers. Bandler and Grinder (1975) have prepared an analysis of communicative difficulties patterned after the creative work by Virginia Satir. Following the theoretical lead taken by Berne in his transactional analysis, Harris (1967) has produced a popular book for enhancing communicative clarity. Gemmet (1977) has compiled a practical handbook on interpersonal communication for teachers, while Gazda et al. (1977) have compiled a manual of techniques for educators. Also a useful text focusing on classroom communication was prepared by Hurt, Scott, and McCroskey (1978). Many of those concepts and techniques have been summarized by Schmuck and Runkel (1985), and by Garrett, Sadker, and Sadker (1986).

Developing Effective Group Discussions

Effective communication is necessary if interpersonal relations and group processes are to proceed smoothly. However, when a group discussion is conducted with more than just a handful of people, communication skills alone will not suffice to assure all members a chance to participate. In such situations, important information will be brought out quickly, and it may be difficult to arrive at decisions which will satisfy all or most of the members. Moreover, task-oriented classroom discussions having to do with history, math, or language arts cannot—nor should they—focus upon interpersonal communication alone.

Classroom groups do function at an emotional level, but they must also carry out the work of academic learning. Some teachers who have used the earlier editions of this book have pointed out that, for example, impression checking is not necessarily a useful skill when thirty students are involved in a discussion about the causes of the Civil War. We agree. Messages of an affective sort are not always appropriate and might serve to delay accomplishment of a task. The following discussion skills build on the communication skills. They are useful tools for keeping discussions flowing in an orderly fashion and for helping everyone keep on track during content discussions.

Orienting statements lay out the information, the goal, the objective, the problem, or the task to be accomplished. For instance, an orienting statement might be, "The task for the next half-hour is to determine how we will break up into groups to accomplish our fund-raising activity;" or,

"This hour we will brainstorm the possible consequences of the space walk." The orientation should provide an opportunity for everyone to be clear about the goals of the discussion.

Agenda setting is a more formal way of orienting the group to work on tasks in an orderly manner. All tasks that the group should take care of during a meeting are listed. Times and names are often written next to each task. The times show the number of minutes to give to the task while the names show the person who will take leadership on that task. Often high priority tasks are worked on first to ensure accomplishing them.

Summarizing statements are comparable to paraphrasing at the group level. "So far, we have identified three major economic consequences of the exploration of space; they are. . .," is an example of a summarizing statement. Summaries should be recorded on newsprint or the blackboard so everyone is clear about what has been accomplished.

Recording is a more formal way of keeping a written history of a meeting. The recorder writes down high points, major topics, and decisions. Later, notes can be circulated to group members to remind them of the results of the meeting.

Procedural statements reflect on the processes of the discussion. For instance, "This discussion has already taken twenty minutes; do we want to continue this, or should we move on to the next item?"

Taking a survey is an excellent technique for finding out where a group is on a given topic. It is merely a method to discover quickly if there is agreement or disagreement on a given topic. "Have we come to an agreement that our next field trip will be to the museum? Let's go around the group to see!" A survey can be undertaken by going from individual to individual so that all members have a chance to speak as to whether they agree with the decision. Or, one can survey via a show of hands. If all people are not in agreement, the discussion is continued. The point of a survey is to get *information* about where individuals stand on a given topic. It is not a time for evaluating or disagreeing about the merits of their thoughts.

Gatekeeping entails observing which group members are not saying much and attempting to bring them into the discussion. Frequently, people who wish to speak but can't seem to get in the flow of the group must be helped to contribute. Someone asking them for their ideas can be very helpful, both to the quiet individuals and to the group.

Encouraging is associated with gatekeeping in that it, too, facilitates the participation of typically quiet members. More than gatekeeping, however, encouraging calls for a more active support of the others to contribute, for example, "I would really like to hear your ideas about that because I know you've got some good ideas."

Process checks are statements that invite evaluations of *how* things are going. They are comparable to impression checks at the group level, i.e., "The discussion seems to be getting bogged down and we often are digressing from the main point." Or, "People really seem to care about this discussion and we are making good headway on the problem." Similar to an impression check, a process check is a tentative impression about the group processes and not an evaluation or judgment about the group's productivity.

Debriefing is like a process check, but occurs at the end of a discussion. "How did it go today?" "What did you like about our discussion?" "What didn't you like?" These are useful ending questions that can lead to improvements in subsequent discussions. Debriefing includes messages of both a cognitive and an affective sort. It also provides information about areas of group discussion which need to be improved upon. For example, perhaps only a few group members were really contributing while others were "hitch-hiking," or perhaps some of the former were talking too much and were not giving the latter group members much of a chance to speak. Some teachers have a short debriefing session at the end of each class period, or at the end of each day or week if they are in a self-contained classroom. *Debriefing is elaborated on below as one of the action ideas for improving classroom climate.*

Reducing the Communication Gap

Today teachers are given extra assistance in employing one-way communication. Computers, movies, audiotapes, television, and other technological developments have been created as effective ways of passing on information to students. Yet, even though technological advances have opened the way for teachers to put more of their time on two-way classroom communication, impersonality and lack of dialogue still characterize classes. Instead of using the advances for more humanized classroom relationships, teachers too often have incorporated the "machine orientation" into their interpersonal relationships with students. The mechanical orientation of one-way communication is perhaps safer and more comfortable. Teachers can remain aloof and uninvolved, thereby keeping themselves from being hurt by negative feedback from students.

True dialogue is not safe; it is unpredictable, and it makes the teacher vulnerable to negative criticism. Yet its absence creates communication gaps between teachers and students. A communication gap occurs when there is a lack of consonance between the behavioral actions of the teacher and the interpretations of those same actions by students. Communication gaps are pervasive in modern society; they are basic to generation gaps, racial gaps, gender gaps, and international gaps. They occur when language is used to conceal and veil, rather than to reveal and openly express. The phoniness of a teacher's concealment leads students to be alienated from school and to feel cynical about the shallow adult world. For some innovative ways of coping better with communication gaps in the classroom, see the ideas in Hurt, Scott, and McCroskey (1978) and the ideas of William Glasser (as summarized by Rothstein, 1990), along with the action ideas suggested below.

Implications for Teachers

The following summary statements characterize the key implications of this chapter for teachers.

Communication entails the human capacity to hear and to understand one another's inner thoughts and feelings. The process of classroom communication entails a synthesis of expectations, leadership, friendship, cohesiveness, and norms. The most important psychological process inherent in human communication is empathy.

Communicative acts are reciprocal. Like the circular interpersonal process, they entail the intentions and message of the sender and the interpretations of that message by the receiver.

Communication is both verbal (relying on language) and nonverbal (represented by bodily cues and voice sounds). As such, communicative acts exist at several levels at the same time and usually carry multiple cultural meanings as well as different personal meanings.

Regular and stable communicative patterns develop over time between people, within groups, and within organizations. Along with interpersonal expectations, leadership hierarchies, friendship constellations, and group norms, we can speak of such regularized communication as culture.

Environmental considerations, such as seating arrangements or physical positioning and proximity to the teacher, affect the patterns of communication.

Miscommunications are discrepancies between what the sender intends and what meanings the receiver picks up. Effective communication means the receiver correctly interprets what the sender intends to communicate.

Communication can be made more effective by using the communication skills of paraphrasing, behavior description, feeling description, impression checking, and feedback.

Teachers can model feedback skills by actively soliciting feedback about the impact of their own behaviors from students.

In soliciting feedback, teachers model openness, thereby making students more receptive to solicit feedback about themselves from the teacher and from their peers.

"I" statements should be used in giving feedback, i.e., I feel _____ , when I _____ , so I'd like us to talk about it, because I want some help.

Teachers should incorporate the communication skills into their instructional behavior and deliberately teach these skills to their students.

Communication skills are necessary, but not sufficient tools, to assure high participation and the learning of content in classroom group discussions.

Teachers should make use of orienting statements, summarizing statements, procedural statements, surveys, process checks, and debriefing to develop more effective discussions.

Action Ideas for Improving Climate

The classroom practices that follow were created by teachers in order to reduce communication gaps in their classrooms.

Data Feedback to Facilitate Openness

A sixth-grade teacher wanted to create conditions for more open and honest communication in the class. He decided to ask for feedback about himself in order to model openness and a willingness to receive feedback. He used a questionnaire which he administered once every three weeks (see Instrument 8.1).

INSTRUMENT 8.1
Our Teacher

Pretend that I (your teacher) could change the ways I relate to you in school. For each number, check the box that best tells how you would like me to act in this class.

	Much more	A little more	The same	A little less	Much less
1. Help with work					
2. Yell at us					
3. Smile and laugh					
4. Make us behave					
5. Trust us on our own					
6. Make sure work is done					
7. Ask us to decide					
8. Make us work hard					

He asked a few students to tally the data and to pick out at least two things on which change was desired by the students. Then the teacher led class discussion about those two things to get ideas on how to improve them. One week later the teacher asked the class how he was doing on making the changes that were discussed the week before. One week after that he asked the students to discuss changes that they might make in order to improve how the class was operating.

Using Students as Observers of Communication

A junior high social studies teacher decided to supplement her curriculum on "group relations" by having the students study their own classroom dynamics one day a week. During the first two weeks of the course she trained the students in the Verbal Interaction Category System (VICS) which was described earlier in this chapter. Then, on subsequent weeks (and for one day per week), two students each week served as observers of the class. They recorded behaviors using the VICS categories, tallied them on a matrix, and gave the data back to the class the following week. This process made the class much more aware of the need for more student-initiated talk to the teacher. For the next five classes, before the teacher would present any new topics or assignments, the students would divide up into three-person groups all around the class to brainstorm questions or points to raise from the previous day's class. That procedure led to much more student-initiated talk in subsequent classes and to an improved attitude on the part of most students toward social studies. Later, with that same class, the teacher introduced the idea of each student keeping a personal log to write down his or her personal reactions to the topics of the class. That practice gave still more ideas to the students about the relevance of social studies to their lives.

Developing Communication Skills as Part of the Curriculum

The teacher spent a few weeks early in the year introducing paraphrasing, behavior description, feeling description, and impression checking to sixth graders. Then he told the students that several times each week he wanted to check to see if the skills actually were being used. He introduced a plan of having three students fill out observation sheets during a regular lesson and for those students to give feedback to the class about their observations. Before any observations took place, every member of the class was handed an observation sheet, shown in Instrument 8.2, and the categories were discussed at a total class meeting. The observations took place during small group or total class discussions. After each discussion, the observers were asked to give feedback on what they saw. The teacher selected a few incidents for further discussion and, sometimes, class members were asked to practice some of the communication skills over again.

The One-Way, Two-Way Communication Exercise

A large number of teachers at all grade levels have made use of the One-Way, Two-Way Communication Exercise described earlier in this chapter. *It can be very useful, for example, to use the exercise during the*

INSTRUMENT 8.2
Observation Sheet for Communication Skills

Directions: During the observed time period write down the initials or first names of people who used the following communication skills.

Evidence of Listening

    1. Paraphrasing _____

    2. Checking out the feelings of another _____

Evidence of Making a Contribution

    1. Giving direct impression of feeling _____

    2. Describing another's behavior _____

    3. Contributing an idea or suggestion _____

Evidence of Feedback

    1. Telling how others affected you _____

    2. Receiving feedback by paraphrasing and impression checking _____

---

first week of class in order to accentuate the need for two-way communication for clarity and learning. Other teachers have used the exercise to highlight the different skills required to learn from lectures and discussions. Still others have developed variations, either simplifying or making more complex the figures that are to be communicated. Several teachers have followed the exercise with instruction and practice in the six communication skills summarized in Figure 8.4, presented previously in this chapter.

Some discussion questions that teachers have used are: (1) What problems do you have in following my lectures? (2) Are there any of the communication skills that I should be using more often? (3) Would it be OK for me to ask you to paraphrase my ideas once in awhile? (4) In what ways might we improve upon our small group discussions in class? and (5) Which of the communication skills should we all be using more often?

Fighting Fair

A middle school teacher uses the curriculum by Schmidt and Friedman (1986) called *Fighting Fair: Dr. Martin Luther King, Jr. For Kids.* Every Wednesday for two hours the class role-plays a vignette from the life of Martin Luther King. The themes of this curriculum emphasize communicating about problems and conflicts rather than succumbing to irrational anger or overt, physical fighting. The curriculum consists of 15 lessons spread over four months. It can be obtained from The Peace Foundation, Inc., Miami Beach, Florida 33119.

Shared Information About What It Means to be a Male or a Female In Our Society

In a junior high school class, a teacher used the following exercise to open communication about sex roles. Students were divided into same sex groups of three or four people and asked to answer four questions on large sheets of newsprint to be displayed to the whole class. The four questions were:

For Girls' Groups:

1. What is good about being a girl?

2. What is bad about being a girl?

3. What do boys like about girls?

4. What don't boys like about girls?

For Boys' Groups:

1. What is good about being a boy?

2. What is bad about being a boy?

3. What do girls like about boys?

4. What don't girls like about boys?

Each group was given a half-hour to answer the questions by listing all the ideas suggested. No attempt was made to come to agreement or consensus about the items listed. After the groups completed their assignment, the newsprint was hung up for everyone to see. The discussion focused on the differences in perceptions between the girls' and boys' groups.

These questions were raised by the teacher:

1. Do girls/boys like the same things about themselves that the other sex likes about them?

2. Are there differences between what girls/boys think the other sex likes and doesn't like about themselves?

Since the purpose of the exercise is to illustrate giving and receiving information, the skills of paraphrasing should be emphasized. It is not as important to come to an agreement or decide whether a statement is right or wrong as it is to understand what different people think. For younger students who do not have writing skills and who have a shorter attention span, the teacher may ask each question of the girls and of the boys in a total class session and write the responses on the board.

Using Time Tokens With Fourth Graders

The time token is a device for dealing with students who contribute too little or too much to classroom discussion. During a planned discussion about how to improve interpersonal relationships in the class, a fourth-grade teacher distributed four tokens (poker chips) to each student to be redeemed for a specific amount of discussion time which, in this instance, was gauged at about fifteen seconds. As a student used up the tokens, he or she could not say anything else in that discussion. The activity made each member's degree of participation obvious and salient. In this particular class, it helped a few "long-winded" students to make their contributions more concise. Gradually, it was noted that the students became much more conscious about bringing everyone into the discussions.

Matching Behaviors to Intentions

The major goal of this practice was to increase student awareness that any behavior may be expressive of several different intentions. The teachers who used this practice asked their students to enact, in the form of role playing, short vignettes as take-off points for discussion. At the elementary level, the teachers used the following situations: (1) you want the teacher to help you with your math; (2) you have finished your assignment before anyone else in the class is finished; (3) a classmate grabs a paper you have been working on; and (4) you wish to welcome a new student to the class. In the secondary classes, the teachers used these situations: (1) you want to introduce one of your friends to your teacher; (2) you borrowed a pen from a classmate and accidentally broke it; (3) you want to get to know another student in one of your classes; (4) someone asks you to go to a movie—you wish to go very much but cannot; and (5) you come to class late, but it is not your fault.

Several students were asked to role play how they might behave under each of these circumstances. After several enactments for one situation, the teacher raised some of the following questions for discussion: (1) What do you think were the intentions of each of the role players? (2) Which of the actions gave you that idea about the intentions? (3) What other actions might the actor have taken to communicate those same intentions and to communicate why he or she behaved this way? How else might the actor have expressed intentions? In some instances, other students were asked to enact how they would try to put their intentions into action. The exercise works best when the class is comfortable with role playing.

The Card Discovery Problem

Several sixth-grade teachers who have used the Jigsaw Puzzle method for learning (described in chapter 6) have found it useful to precede work in such groups with a communication exercise called the *Card Discovery Problem*. In groups of six, the students are given five cards each. On the cards are printed 12×12 matrices with 144 points, each of which is either on X or 0. *Only one card in the deck of thirty is unique.*

Detailed instructions about how to construct the deck of cards can be found on pages 272–275 in Schmuck and Runkel (1985).

The task for the group of six is to communicate orally about their cards without showing one another the cards. They are to talk about their cards until they discover the unique matrix. After the problem is either solved or not solved, the ensuing discussion should focus on problems of clear communication and coordinated effort, and on the implications of the exercise for working together on jigsaw tasks.

Closing the Communication Gap

A teacher wanted to set time aside each week for open communication about her class's group processes. Clearing the air was not always possible in the midst of daily activities, so she sought special time, with no limitations or boundaries on the content for discussion. She planned one hour per week for "gap closing." The agenda was prescribed as follows:

1. Class specifies individual and group concerns, likes and dislikes (try to use behavior descriptions and descriptions of own feelings).

2. Class chooses one or two of the concerns for concentrated work.

3. Class divides into small groups of four to work on concerns.

4. Each small group makes plans for solving concerns.

5. Small groups report back to total class.

6. Class evaluates the solutions and comes up with actions to be taken.

Initially, the students did not know what concerns were appropriate to discuss, and so the teacher made suggestions. For example, "Sometimes it's difficult to concentrate when the teacher is presenting a topic;" or, "I'm not very much interested in the way we're studying social problems." The students tried to test the teacher's limits by suggesting concerns such as doing away with grades, doing away with homework, and closing school early. The teacher had to be patient and persistent in her desire to find legitimate concerns for discussion. At first, even the most outrageous demands were explored as possible classroom concerns. But, as the students developed trust in the teacher, they began to discuss critical areas that were feasible for improvement. Before long, "gap-closing" discussions were held each day for short periods soon after the problems occurred. Although problems in communication arose throughout the school year, few of them lasted very long.

Circle Discussions

A first-grade teacher routinely uses circle discussions to raise students' awareness of feelings, to teach empathy, and to help stu-dents learn to use communication skills. She had been influenced by Glasser's *Schools Without Failure* (1969). While an aide tutors half the class in reading or math, the teacher takes the other half of the class behind a screen and asks the students to sit on a rug in the form of a circle. The teacher also sits on the floor in the circle with the group. Some of the topics she uses are the following:

For *awareness,* (1) think of something that makes me feel good, (2) think of three wishes, (3) a thought that keeps coming back to me is . . ., and (4) something about this class that I like very much is. . . .

For *mastery,* (1) think of something that I can do well, (2) think of something I want to learn to do better, (3) think of something I wish I could do, (4) think of a time I had to make a hard decision, and (5) remember a time when I was part of making a group work well.

For *social interaction,* (1) I did something that someone liked, (2) think of a time when someone did something that I didn't like, and (3) I made someone feel included when. . . .

The teacher tries to be a facilitator and a listener. She paraphrases and accepts, but does not probe or analyze. She gives the responsibility to the student to take part or to be a silent listener in the circle. She attempts to establish an atmosphere of acceptance and of affective support.

Another teacher uses circle discussions with his kindergarten class. He asks only 8 students at a time to become part of a circle. Some of the topics he uses to guide the discussions are the following: (1) Something at home that makes me feel good, (2) Something at school that makes me feel good, (3) A time someone made me feel good, (4) A time I made someone else feel good, (5) Something I can do now that I couldn't do when I was a baby, (6) A favorite game I like to play, (7) Something I can help someone else do, (8) Something I like to do with an adult friend, (9) Something I like to do with a friend my age, and (10) Something about school that I like.

Some tips to teachers who wish to try circle discussions are: listen and repeat feelings, accept feelings and don't hurry, make sure everyone gets a chance, model the value of listening (moments of silence can be good), use whispering sometimes (if it relaxes group members), restate the feeling behind a student's remark and overtly accept what was said (even if it was silly), and ask disrupters to help choose the next person to speak.

Additional ideas for facilitating circle discussions at all grade levels are available from Cooperation Unlimited, P.O. Box 68, Portage, Minnesota 49081. Ideas can also be found in Johnson, Johnson, and Holubec's *Circles of Learning: Cooperation in the Classroom,* published by Interaction Book Company, 7208 Cornelia Drive, Edina, Minnesota 55435 (June, 1986). In addition, suggestions are disseminated through a newsletter issued by The Cooperative Learning Center, 202 Pattee Hall, University of Minnesota, 150 Pillsbury Drive, S.E., Minneapolis, MN 55455.

Debriefing as a Regular Part of Classroom Life

Debriefings are class discussions about how the class performed together on a particular task or during a certain period of time. They are reflective, self-analytic discussions during which feedback can be exchanged. Sometimes debriefing is referred to as *group processing*. The main purpose of group processing is to discuss what group actions were helpful or unhelpful in getting the task done so that in the future, the group will learn from its mistakes of the past.

Many teachers now make debriefings a regular feature of their teaching, holding formal debriefing discussions at least once a week and frequently even once a day. Some teachers make a definite point of using the communication skills summarized in Figure 8.4, going so far as to train the students to use the skills during debriefing. Others treat debriefing more informally. Some use questions like the following: (1) Are we listening to one another? (2) Are we working well together? (3) How might we improve our working relationships? (4) Are we focusing on our school work? (5) What sorts of distractions are there in the class? (6) Are we respecting one another's contributions? (7) Are we helping one another to learn? and (8) How might we help one another with our school work? One teacher told us, "I saved time twice a week to debrief how the class was going. One of those times, routinely, was Friday afternoon. It became a useful time to set the stage for what we were planning to do on the next Monday."

Evaluation can be done by simply raising hands or by putting thumbs up or down to indicate positive or negative feelings. A simple rating scale can also be used. For example, on a scale of 1-to-5 with one being at the negative end and 5 being at the positive end, which number fits your perception of how we are doing? The class might also be encouraged to brainstorm ideas for improvement and then to pick a few that seem to be the most crucial for the immediate success of the class. The top 2 or 3 ideas could be written on a chart and posted as a reminder.

A study by Yager et. al (1986) confirmed the value of debriefing. Yager and his colleagues compared the impact on achievement of cooperative learning with debriefing, cooperative learning without debriefing, and individualistic learning without any special debriefing. The results showed that high, medium, and low-achieving students who worked in cooperative groups with debriefing scored higher in daily achievement, post instruction tests, and retention than their counterparts in the other two learning settings. Students in cooperative groups that did no debriefing did not achieve as well, but they did achieve better than the students who worked individually.

Conflict

9

Students in a high school social studies class are discussing the forthcoming political elections and what they understand to be the differences between views of Democrats and Republicans on welfare reform. One student says, "My mom said if that position is accepted, it will be the poorest people who suffer the most." Another student retorts, "But there already is too much government interference. People need to be more responsible for themselves." Voices and tempers rise. The argument gets hotter and the adversaries have stopped listening to one another. What should the teacher do?

In a kindergarten, some children are taking roles in the area of the playhouse, a favorite place to try on different clothes and to act grown-up. A boy and a girl both wish to wear the single pair of fancy silver shoes. They pull at the shoes, but neither can control both shoes at the same time. The boy attempts to resolve the struggle by suggesting that the two of them should take turns. He also suggests that he should go first. She wants to be first. An argument follows with yelling and crying. Should the teacher intervene? What should the teacher do?

A fifth-grade teacher designates students to work together in small groups on an English assignment. One student frowns and fidgets, finally approaching the teacher privately to say, "I don't want to work in that group. I don't want to be with Martha. She's stuck-up and always picks a fight with me. She pushes kids around on the playground." Should the teacher change the group assignment? How might the teacher handle this tension?

The local teachers' organization has voted in favor of a teachers' strike. Two teachers who have just begun to team-teach and are responsible for the same students have assumed opposite points of view about the strike. One of them plans to strike and to carry a picket sign in front of the school; the other plans to cross the picket line and to teach their joint class with a substitute teacher for whom the first teacher uses the label, *scab*. When the strike is terminated and an agreement is reached, what will happen between these two teachers? What might take place in their classroom?

These four vignettes offer examples of fairly commonplace events in the lives of students and teachers. We have witnessed all four during the past several years, some more than once. Conflict in schools is indeed pervasive, emanating from difficulties between students, between student and teachers, between teachers, and between teachers and administrators. One simply cannot avoid conflict when people come together in groups to work and to learn.

We take the view that conflict is part of human relations, an inevitable group dynamic, an integral part of everyday life in schools. In fact, we would go so far as to argue that without conflict, schools would not be vibrant, growth-inducing institutions. We give special attention to conflict upon the advice of teachers and professors who take the position—with which we agree—that conflict is at the same level of importance for classroom groups as expectations, leadership, friendship, norms, and communication. Conflict arises in classrooms whether one likes it or not, or whether one plans for it or not, and the best teachers are prepared to guide and direct the energy that adheres to conflict in constructive and educational ways.

Objectives of this Chapter

We commence this chapter with a working definition of conflict in order to organize our very diverse experiences with conflict. We go on to discuss the functions that conflict can play and elaborate on four frequent types of conflict: conflicts over *procedures, goals, concepts or opinions,* and *interpersonal relationships.* The last can be the most psychologically draining and the least manageable. We also indicate how the sources of conflict can emerge from intra-psychic, personality dynamics of individuals; how interactions between individuals can give rise to conflict; and how the social structure of the classroom group can work to maximize or minimize the emergence of conflict. We go on to discuss conflicts as power struggles between persons and subgroups, role conflicts, and differentiation of function in the classroom. A section on conflict resolution and a listing of current resources are new to this edition. Finally, as in the other chapters, after a summary of the implications of the contents of this chapter for teachers, we present concrete action ideas that teachers might use in their classrooms.

Definition of Conflict

For many people, the word *conflict* carries a negative, emotional loading. The connotation inferred gives rise to feelings of discomfort and to the defense of denial. "Oh no, there wasn't any conflict; they just had a difference of opinion." We eschew any predominantly negative meaning for conflict. Rather, we believe that conflict can be good, indifferent, or bad, and that it need

not have an emotional loading of any kind. Moreover, conflict can be positive, neutral, or negative in its consequences. The value or emotional sense that conflict will take on depends on how the circumstances are perceived and how they are treated by the participants. As an endemic property of classrooms, conflict is perhaps best construed as being amoral. Conflict simply exists.

Deutsch (1973), an expert on the social psychology of conflict, conceived of it in this way: *A conflict exists when incompatible activities occur—when one activity blocks, interferes with, injures, or in some way makes a second activity less likely or effective.* Two children who want to wear the same pair of shoes at the same time are in conflict. Either the Democrat or the Republican position on welfare wins; the other takes second place. The students who hold different beliefs are in conflict. The teachers who carry out diametrically opposite activities during a strike are in conflict, particularly when they face each other in front of the school at the picket line. We like Deutsch's above definition of conflict because it is straightforward and because it has been used widely by researchers. Although our focus is primarily on conflicts between individuals in classrooms, Deutsch's definition also applies to conflicts between groups, within organizations and communities, and between nation states.

Functions of Conflict

Since for many of us conflict is construed as evil and destructive, we can go to considerable lengths to avoid or cover up even the appearance of conflict. Think of how embarrassing it is, for instance, when a stranger enters the room in the midst of an argument between you and your spouse, or when the principal enters your classroom just when you and a student are having a heated exchange. We remember one first-grade teacher who was taking an inservice course on teaching social science concepts that Pat Schmuck was teaching. The lesson for the day, drawn from Lippitt, Fox, and Shaible (1969), was about "feeling angry." The teacher decided not to use that lesson in her class, because as she argued, her first-graders did not have angry feelings. Moreover, she pointed out, "I don't allow angry feelings in my classroom." What she meant, of course, was that she tried to keep her students from making overt expressions of anger. She might also have been saying that she did not recognize anger, even when it was expressed by her students. That teacher went to great lengths to avoid conflicts in her class. "Either silver shoes for everyone or no silver shoes at all."

It is true that conflict often does create tension, anxiety, and unpleasantness. But like anger, these feelings in themselves are not always bad. They can supply the punch and push needed for growth and development. We believe that conflict in the classroom can provide a creative tension that serves to inspire problem solving and to motivate enhanced individual or group performance. We believe that the effort it takes people to resolve some conflicts constitutes a needed step toward personal learning and the process of change. Indeed, we can make an even stronger statement about the function of conflict in the classroom.

We should not expect young people to be able to work constructively with conflict without their having the opportunities for learning to do so, any more than we can expect them to learn how to read without coaching and practice. In many ways, the students' futures are being plotted and planned right now. As they play out the drama of their current life in the classroom, they are, at the same time, rehearsing the drama of their future. Thus, the teacher should seize opportunities to help students learn how to handle conflict. The fight over a pair of silver shoes or the disagreement about who goes first will be rehearsed again and again later in life. At the moment of the heat of the battle, as well as during subsequent discussions, the teacher can help both the individuals and the class as a group understand alternative ways of coping with conflict.

Even while advocating the learning potential in conflict-laden events, it is important to point out that not all conflicts should be faced head on. Some conflicts are best left alone and sometimes the avoidance of a public discussion about the conflict is a favored strategy. Perhaps the conflicting parties aren't really very serious or perhaps they will resolve the difference quickly without intervention. Perhaps emotions are running too high and rational discussion isn't possible. Perhaps the conflict is over a very trivial matter of low importance to both parties. It is, of course, a mark of wise people that they know which battles to enter and which ones to avoid. And it is the wise teacher who will use only particular conflicts for purposes of instruction, while down-playing public demonstrations of others. The key is whether the conflict has strong potential for constructive consequences.

Let us, for example, look at two potential scenarios on the conflict over the teachers' strike. This conflict is over differences in values. One teacher believes that the strike is a vehicle for improving the profession of teaching, and the other teacher believes, just as firmly, that a strike constitutes unprofessional behavior. Their difference, when taken from this point of view, is irreconcilable. According to Deutsch, "A conflict has destructive consequences if its participants are dissatisfied with the outcomes and feel they have lost as a result of the conflict" (1973, p. 17). As long as the teachers believe they must persuade each other to agree on the strike issue, the outcomes are not promising. More than likely, stereotyping and increased social distance will arise between the one labeled "scab" and the other labeled "unprofessional." It seems wise to leave this value difference alone.

On the other hand, they both are teachers, responsible for teaching the same students. They already have had some experience and they have made tentative commitments to team teaching. When the strike is resolved, they will presumably return to teaching together. Deutsch defines a conflict that has productive consequences as one where "the participants are satisfied with the outcomes and feel that they have gained as a result of the conflict" (1973, p. 17). In this teaching situation, the conflicting parties must initially resolve that it is O.K., indeed—perhaps it is even a strength—to agree to disagree about the strike. But the strike is over and classroom instruction is what really counts. In agreeing to disagree, the teachers can lay the groundwork for collaboration in the classroom. They can both benefit, moreover, by sharing more information with each other about their different strengths and interests in teaching. When the strike issue can be seen as having opened the door to a fuller

use of their resources in team-teaching, then it is worthwhile to agree to disagree about it.

Perhaps the most important function of conflict is to raise the possibility of a more mature and complete relationship between the warring parties once the focus of the initial conflict can be worked through. It means that the parties must agree to disagree about some points, but it also carries with it the potential of opening up new avenues of relating. Could the boy and girl perhaps brainstorm together about the characters they would be or the roles they would play if they were wearing the silver shoes? Could the Democrat and the Republican carry out some interviews together with poor people? Could the teacher invite the two students who dislike one another to think together about a class party? Perhaps. Perhaps not! But, it is important to keep in mind that quarrels will be inevitable in the classroom and that they can lead either to increased bitterness or to increased intimacy, depending on how they are handled.

Types of Conflict

As we have seen, conflicts differ with regard to their focal issues and the context in which they occur. Not wishing to participate in the same learning group with a disliked peer represents a more complex issue than arguing over who will wear silver shoes first. And the ideological conflict over a teachers' strike occurs across more contexts than the classroom argument over welfare reform.

Conflicts in school take at least three basic forms for teachers: (1) prescribed conflict, featured by intentional competition based on standard rules, as in an athletic contest, a game, or a debate, (2) emergent conflict, featured by unplanned battling over incompatible interests, as in arguments over silver shoes or welfare issues, and (3) destructive conflict, featured by intentional efforts to dissolve working relationships, something that could happen if the two teachers in conflict about the strike refuse to resume their team teaching after the strike. Prescribed conflict is really no problem because, if set up right, it can be satisfying even to the losers, but destructive conflict should be avoided. The teacher's dealing effectively with emergent conflict will frequently ward off destructive conflict. When, however, emergent conflict is viewed as another kind of prescribed conflict, it will frequently escalate into serious cleavage and eventually into destructive conflict. We shall review four types of emergent conflict here, all of which frequently arise in the classroom.

Procedural Conflict

This is characterized by *disagreement over a course of action* that should be taken to reach a goal. Here we are referring to conflict over "instrumental means"—what we should do to reach our objective. Procedural conflict is common and perhaps one of the easiest types of conflict to resolve. Let us look at a few examples.

A teacher wants all students to prepare a library research paper on the topic of the city government. His goal is for the students to learn about city government; the means to that end is the paper. One student prefers not to prepare a library research paper, but rather wants her term project to be a series of interviews with city government officials. If the teacher cares more for the goal of learning about city government than the preparation of a research paper, the decision probably will be to go along with the student. However, if the procedure of preparing a library research paper is also a kind of subgoal, the teacher and the student will be in conflict. Perhaps, the procedural conflict can be mitigated by the student's agreeing to use the library to prepare for the interview and to write out a summary of the interview.

In a third-grade classroom, the students line up each day at the door before being dismissed for recess. One day, they are more fidgety and noisy than usual. The teacher's patience is tried; he requires the whole group to return to their seats because of the unruly behavior. The students resent the intrusion into their recess time; some of them think that the teacher is unfair for punishing all when only a few of the students are moving around and making noise. Now students and teacher alike are angry. From the teacher's point of view, the rule is clear. If the students don't behave themselves when lining up for recess, they won't have the privilege of getting a full recess. The students aren't all that clear in their minds about this rule. In this example, the teacher and the students have a procedural conflict because the rule is a means to an end. Perhaps the teacher could reduce the conflict, at least in the future, by discussing the reasons for the rule with the students. If they realize the goal that the teacher wishes the class to pursue, perhaps they will go along with the rule more fully.

In the main, procedural conflicts arise in classrooms because group norms—particularly the formal norms that are often called rules—are unclear or poorly defined. There are not, in essence, clear, *shared agreements* about how the class is to proceed. Procedural conflict occurs when the classroom rules are determined and announced by the teacher without classroom discussion and clarification. Many of these conflicts can be circumvented when the class has regular discussions about classroom rules and regulations. In the chapter on leadership we showed that shared leadership in the classroom is quite feasible and that it can go a long way toward building student involvement and interest in the class. Moreover, in the chapter on norms, we showed that student groups that decide with the teacher on classroom rules are more likely to follow the rules, in contrast to classes where only the teacher decides. Notwithstanding these facts, procedural conflicts will arise, even when there is shared leadership and student involvement in making rules. They can provide the impetus for class discussions and group decision making. The effective teacher will use instances of procedural conflict as signals that new discussions are required for clarifying classroom norms.

Goal Conflict

This type of conflict is characterized by *disagreement over values* or end states. Here we are referring to conflict over "terminal ends" or targets. Goal conflict can be more difficult to resolve than procedural conflict. Clarifying discussions alone usually won't be enough. Let us consider a few examples.

A teacher is concerned about a student's lack of academic progress and prepares a plan for how the student should proceed to improve in school work. The teacher brings the plan to a special meeting with the student. Part of the teacher's plan calls for the student to spend less time watching television and less time social-izing with friends. The reduced time with television doesn't faze the student but less time with friends is an anathema. The student is deeply concerned with peer acceptance and would like to spend even more time with friends. There is here a basic disagreement over goals between the teacher and the student. For the teacher, academic performance is the ultimate goal; for the student, a day without friends is meaningless.

It will be very difficult for this teacher and student to discuss directly their goal differences. Very likely, the teacher will focus the discussion on the school work, its quality and quantity. The teacher will probably offer ideas about study procedures and about scheduling study time. The student may or may not go along with the teacher's suggestions. But the real conflict goes unspoken. If the student could only articulate the high interest in being with friends, or if the teacher were sensitive enough to perceive it, perhaps a study plan could be constructed that would include some kinds of collaborative work with peers. Teachers who don't recognize goal conflicts with students will have difficulty reaching their students.

Frequently we have observed classes in which there are goal conflicts between the teacher and virtually the entire classroom group. The teacher's goal is the ideal that students perform well on tests, but the students support one another in not studying and in not valuing the tests highly. The students' goal is to attract attention and to inspire laughter, but the teacher's goal is to achieve classroom control and disciplined student behavior. The list of examples is long. As we indicated in the chapter on norms, the normative structure of the classroom peer group can, in fact, work in opposition to the teacher's goals. In such cases, the teacher will have to find ways of working with the class to bring about an understanding and acceptance of the teacher's goals.

It is important to note that a focus on procedures won't serve to resolve goal conflicts. Some teachers try to "tighten the screws" on their discipline procedures or assign more academic work in the face of poor test performance by students, but typically procedural shifts won't resolve differences of goals. Only by taking the goal conflict head on, and by negotiating to find ends upon which the teacher and the students can agree, will it work out. What serves the teacher best is to give to the students several times early in the year a list of course objectives—concretely and behaviorally stated—with ample time for discussion and opportunities for revision.

Conceptual Conflict

This type of conflict is characterized by *disagreement over ideas, information, theories, or opinions.* Here we are referring to conflict over the "way the world is viewed." Conceptual conflict occurs when two parties conceive of similar phenomena in very different ways; they have different cognitive maps of the same actual phenomena.

Consider, for example, the very different conceptual frameworks of organizations such as the Ku Klux Klan and the National Association for the Advancement of Colored People. While these are extremely different world views, the school is often confronted with situations in which widely divergent views should be presented and studied. An important function of social studies classes, for instance, is to offer conceptual conflict as food for thought and discussion. The two students in our earlier examples who debated welfare reform were embroiled in conceptual conflict. We believe that well-organized discussions that are focused on such conceptual conflicts should be encouraged in schools.

Johnson and Johnson (1984) argue that controversies and arguments over concepts can be excellent sources of motivation for learning as well as opportunities for higher levels of cognitive reasoning and critical thinking. They outline the process in this way. The student starts by organizing all the available information and comes to certain personal conclusions. That might have to do with the Democratic and Republican views in the case of social welfare, the differing opinions on race in the situation of the KKK and the NAACP, or the diverse views about the history of humanity in a conflict between the creationists and the evolutionists. All of these offer strong confrontational issues for discussion. It is primarily the conclusions of previous learning and understanding that the student brings to a debate. During the debate itself, new information is brought out—at least new from the student's viewpoint—and the student is pushed to self-analysis and to a consideration of alternative conceptualizations. Some of the student's previously held conclusions do not hold up. Personal ideas are confronted and a state of internal conflict or disequilibrium arises. Some psychologists call this a *state of cognitive dissonance.*

Cognitive dissonance arouses an active inner search for new understandings and new conclusions. The student learns to consider two very different conceptual schemes simultaneously and is energized to develop his or her own unique version of the issue. This kind of academic, conceptual conflict is precisely the sort that Socrates was striving for in his teaching and that Plato memorialized in the *Dialogues*. It is very important for the learner that the conceptual conflict take on the form of a self-confrontation. How can I resolve these two divergent conceptualizations for myself? This is the type of conflict that teachers can use best for instructional purposes.

The S-T-P Model

Let us step back for a moment from our discussion of the types of conflict to offer another model that will help us develop a better understanding of procedural, goal, and conceptual conflict. In the S-T-P model, S (situation) refers to the features of a current circumstance or condition, T (target) to a desired state toward which we are striving, and P (proposals) to action plans aimed at bringing about the desired state. The S is commonly associated with facts, opinions, explanations, perceptions, and feelings; the T with goals, aims, ends, values, purposes, and objectives; and the P with plans, strategies, procedures, and implementation. This S-T-P model can be used to describe the above three types of conflict.

Conceptual conflict (type S) entails argument about the realities of a situation—either debate over easily discoverable facts or over facts more difficult to gather. Goal conflict (type T) encompasses arguments over values, goals, or objectives ranging from highly specific phenomena, such as students' behavior or achievement, to more abstract events, such as debates over different educational philosophies. Procedural conflict (type P) entails arguments over the best way of moving from a present condition to a valued future condition.

A teacher will find it useful to keep this model in mind. Considerable movement can be made toward the resolution of a conflict just by being able to categorize it as an S, or T, or P type. In S conflict, we look together for additional information. We recognize that there are different ways of viewing the world. With T conflict, we decide to agree and disagree at the same time or we negotiate a third goal that is desired by both of us. In P conflict, we try to assess the different effects of our procedures. We come to some agreements about the procedures we will follow until we have an opportunity to discuss them again.

Interpersonal Conflict

This type of conflict is characterized by *incongruity over personal styles and needs;* it is perhaps the most difficult type of conflict to handle. It often entails great amounts of psychic energy and can grow out of all proportion, even with low social contact between the conflicting parties. Interpersonal conflicts can occur, of course, between students, as in the example above, between student and teacher, and between adults. They frequently occur between people who are not fully aware of the conflict styles or needs that they have.

Holmes and Miller (1976) have made a useful distinction between realistic conflict and what they refer to as "autistic conflict." Conflicts over procedures, goals, or concepts they categorize as realistic because an objective referent can be demonstrated to be the nub of the conflict. Person A and person B are in disagreement over referent X where X is symbolic of a procedure, goal, or concept. In contrast, conflicts over interpersonal style or need they refer to as autistic because such conflicts "have no basis in the objective set of rewards and costs associated with a situation." Holmes and Miller view autistic conflict as being "rooted in the personal, internal states of the participants." Indeed, in such conflicts, the hostility and emotional tenor in the relationship are out of line with the obvious rational or objective issues at stake.

The social psychologist, Ted Newcomb (1950), referred to what transpires between adversaries embroiled in interpersonal conflict as "autistic hostility." As conflict grows in the relationship, less interaction occurs between the parties, and less and less objective information about the other party is available. When sharing of selves breaks down, the parties conjure up in their own minds the evils inherent in the others. The hostility felt is autistic and in the style of a negative circular process; it feeds upon itself.

Think of what might have happened in the relationship between teachers who were in conflict over the strike. In the S-T-P model, they differed in their view of the S (conceptual conflict), one T (goal conflict), and several P's (procedural conflict). Those are rational bases for conflict; they can be handled by discussion, negotiation, and agreements to disagree. Yet, if they had not been able to settle their differences by agreeing to disagree, their conflict could have escalated into autistic hostility and such an acrimonious relationship that they would not have been able to teach together.

Interpersonal conflicts are best handled in one of two ways. If the conflicting parties do not have to be interdependent and if they can quite easily go their separate ways, leave the conflict alone. Chalk it up to two people with different personality styles. But, if you are in a circumstance where the parties must work together, like students together in the classroom or a teacher and student, then seek assistance from a third party who can be objective and neutral. Teachers and students can successfully serve as third party mediators, roles that are outlined in a following section. Mediators bring the adversaries together for discussion and problem solving. They seek ways in which collaborative work might mitigate the conflict. The poet, William Blake, offered good advice:

> I was angry with my friend,
> I told my wrath, my wrath did end
> I was angry with my foe,
> I told it not, my wrath did grow.

The Social Psychology of Conflict

An important insight of social psychology is the concept that social situations influence individual behavior and that individual variations will occur, even in the most pressing of situations. Social psychology, in other words, is the interface between sociology and psychology. In the same classroom, under the same teacher and within the same general peer culture, individual students behave very differently from one another. People also react differently to the same behavior of another; thus in one class, a student's behavior might drive the teacher up the wall, whereas that same behavior could go unnoticed or even be viewed as positive energy by other teachers. And, of course, each person adapts his or her behavior, depending on the situation; in one class a student can be helpful and friendly, while in another class, the same student may be withdrawn and unfriendly.

Conflict, its cause and its nature, is similarly influenced by a variety of personal and situational factors. In this section, we turn to three contexts from which to view conflict—personal, interpersonal, and situational. We discuss how conflict arises, depending upon: (1) the intensity of self-interest in the issue, (2) the nature of the interpersonal relationship between the conflicting parties, and (3) how the nature of the classroom situation enhances or minimizes the conflict. We will see that the frequency, strength, and endurance of the conflict varies according to these contextual factors.

Self-Interest

Conflicts arise when an activity one person wishes to pursue is interfered with by another. In other words, conflicts occur when self-interest is thwarted. A student who wants to sit quietly to daydream is in conflict with the scolding teacher who demands work. The youngster who wants to play with a toy that another youngster is currently using is in conflict. The student who wants to spend an evening watching television is in conflict with the teacher who demands that a take-home exam should be completed before the next morning.

Resolution of such conflicts will depend on the strength of the conflicting parties' self-interest in the issue at hand. According to Holmes and Miller (1976, p. 8), "The more personal identity or investment one attaches to the attainment of a goal, the more likely that one will engage in conflict." Thus the student who has arranged to watch a favorite television program with a close friend will feel in stronger conflict with the teacher's assigned take-home exam than will a student who casually planned to

watch television because that would be better than working on the exam. Of course, the student who wishes to maintain a self-concept of an effective student will give up the television viewing faster than one who doesn't care much about being a good student.

Self-interest will, of course, vary for the same individual from situation to situation, and from one individual to another in the same situation. As an aid to conflict resolution, it would be useful to understand the depth of a person's interest in the issue. One mechanism we have employed to deal with this kind of conflict is to ask the conflicting parties for a description of how strongly they each feel about the issue. A useful guide in raising the query is a ten-point scale where a number 1 indicates very low strength and a number 10 indicates very high strength. If everything else is equal, the person with the stronger level of self-interest attains the immediate goal, providing that the "winner" is willing to give up something of importance to the "loser." So, for example, the student may be allowed to watch the television program if he or she prepares a written review of it *and* agrees to complete the take-home final in a few days.

It is important for the teacher to try to develop a classroom norm that supports the concepts of (1) being public and articulate about self-interests, (2) trying to satisfy individual self-interests whenever feasible, and (3) being willing to give up something in order to satisfy self-interests. On this last point, the teacher should attempt to communicate the idea that "there is no free lunch. If you're going to get something, you're also going to have to give up something." Both personal and academic growth should be facilitated by that way of working with conflicts of self-interest.

Interpersonal Relationships

Conflicts sometimes arise when participating parties have inaccurate perceptions of each other. Indeed, this is perhaps the most frequent kind of conflict between teachers and students. For example, a teacher believes that most of the lower-class students in her inner-city class are not motivated to learn. She sees them as being preoccupied with games and fighting in their relationships with her and with their peers. "If only they liked intellectual things," she thinks. "If only they wanted to go to college." The teacher prepares a fairly tight schedule of study with high amounts of accountability to prevent the students from goofing-off. "Keep them on task"; that's what she learned at the university. The tight schedule leads students to believe that they are not trusted and respected. They resent the teacher's sense of superiority toward them. Who does she think she is? They complain that the teacher is stuck-up, too strict, disrespectful, and insensitive. The teacher complains that the students are irresponsible and lazy, and she refuses to let up. Distrust, suspicion, and hostile feelings escalate. The teacher, who believes she is operating in the students' best interest, is guided by stereotypes and only partially correct versions of reality.

Deutsch (1973) describes part of what is taking place here in this way:

> "Given the fact that the ability to put oneself in the other's shoes is notoriously underemployed and underdeveloped in most people . . . it is not surprising that there is a bias toward perceiving one's own behavior as being more benevolent and more legitimate than the others' behavior toward oneself."

Only through effective use of the communication skills described in chapter 8 is it possible to break through the negative emotion of interpersonal conflict.

Today a common source of misperceptions and stereotypes has come about as part of the mainstreaming of handicapped students into regular classrooms. In many schools, mainstreaming has meant that students with rather obvious physical handicaps have been placed into classes in which the students have had little previous face-to-face experience with handicapped persons. There is, of course, a great deal to be said for providing students with and without handicaps the opportunity to interact in the same classroom. How else will empathy and understanding develop? Unfortunately, it isn't that straightforward.

Many teachers have found that mainstreaming is frequently accompanied by interpersonal tension, by misperceptions, prejudice, and outright rejection. In particular, the teacher is challenged to reduce the all-too-frequent student misperception that physically handicapped students are inferior intellectually. They face the "elephant-man" syndrome over and over again, whereby a physical deficiency is interpreted as including a mental aberration. Even though there are no simple answers, opportunities for getting acquainted, for talking to one another, for working collaboratively together, and for airing publicly feelings about the class ultimately are the best techniques for reducing interpersonal stereotypes. Throughout this book, but particularly in chapter 6, we have offered activities used by teachers to break into the vicious cycle of interpersonal rejection. There is, in general, no better method than to have a handicapped and a nonhandicapped youngster working together on an academic task that interests and pleases them both.

Conflict Resolution

Certainly the poignant and dramatic international events of the 1990s—the collapse of the Berlin Wall, the prison release of Nelson Mandela in South Africa, the challenge to peace in the Middle East, the movement for national independence among some Eastern Bloc countries, and the diminishing tensions of the cold war between the United States and Soviet Union—offer opportunities for successful conflict resolution.

Yet in our own country, conflict and violence is an increasing social problem. "Violence is as American as Cherry Pie," H. Rap Brown said during the 1960s in the often violent struggle for civil rights. Today violence on our streets and in classrooms is a widespread national concern.

Although Mary Parker Follett wrote about conflict resolution for business managers as early as 1924 in her book, *Creative Experience,* it has been only in the last few decades that conflict resolution, negotiation, mediation or dispute resolution has found its way into many realms of social interaction. As conflict has emerged as a major social issue, so has the role of conflict resolution. Disputes about child custody, neighborhood problems, rental agreements, and building permits are increasingly being mediated. The movement to use mediation was motivated by concern with a "litigation explosion" where interpersonal issues created a backlog in the judicial proceedings (Folberg and Taylor, 1984). Best selling books such as Roger Fisher and William Ury's 1981, *Getting to Yes: Negotiating Agreements Without Giving In,* attest to the popularity of strategies to solve conflicts.

Conflict Resolution in the Schools

In 1972, Pricilla Prutzman (see 1988), under the auspices of the Quakers, set about teaching non-violence to children in New York City schools. By the late 1970s many educators were discussing problems of peace education as well as the roots of violence in their own classrooms. The Educators for Social Responsibility was formed in the early 80s and curricula began being developed for teaching conflict resolution to children. The formation of the National Association for Mediation in Education (NAME), formed in 1984, is testimony to the growing proliferation of school-based conflict resolution programs which have grown to over 100 (Lam, 1989).

Special Training in Conflict Resolution

Curricula are available for special training in conflict resolution for children. Workshop models, special classes, or activities to incorporate in the classroom are available from several sources. The following materials and organizations provide resources for school programs:

National Association for Mediation in Education (NAME). 139 Whitmore St., Amherst, MA 01003. (413–545–2462).

Cheatham, Annie, 1988. *Directory of School Mediation and Conflict Resolution Programs.* From NAME, 1939 Whitmore St., Educators for Social Responsibility. 23 Garden St. Cambridge, MA 02138.

Kreidler, William. *Creative Conflict Resolution: More Than 200 Activities for Keeping Peace in the Classroom, K-6.* 1984, Glenview, Ill: Scott Foresman.

Prutzman, Pricilla, Lee Stern, M. Leonard Burger, Gretchen Bodenhammer, 1988. *The Friendly Classroom for a Small Planet.* New Society Publishers. Box 528, Santa Crux, CA. 95061.

Children's Creative Response to Conflict, Box 271, Nyack, NY, 10960.

Roderick (1988) reports that all students in Chicago's 67 high schools now have a course in dispute resolution as part of the social studies curriculum, and in the New York City Community School District thousands of students participate in the Model Peace Education Program. In the Northwest a special program developed under the Oregon Law-Related Education Project (Coddington, 1985) has been implemented in several school districts. Emerson (1990) studied four elementary schools where children were trained to be peer conflict managers on the playground. Emerson found that:

1. Students can participate in running their schools and intervening in minor discipline cases before they get out of hand.

2. Training of peer conflict managers is essential; training should involve role-playing, communication skills, and specific guides for conflict manager behavior. Peer conflict managers must employ problem-solving skills and not "police like" behavior.

3. Students must have designated duty times to act as peer conflict mangers. That is, on the playground they are more effective when *on-duty* than while playing.

4. All participants in the school (faculty, students, and parents) must be clear about the purposes and practices of conflict managers.

5. Training and problem-solving must be on-going for the peer conflict managers.

Setting a Classroom Environment for Conflict Resolution

Special training for conflict resolution is of growing interest to many educators. Yet, we must remember that students learn effective or ineffective ways to deal with conflict within their own classroom as they cope with their own inevitable emergent conflicts. The silver shoes and the debate about welfare are potentially instructive activities for learning about conflict and its resolution. In this section we will review how norms and instructional goal structures influence the ability to resolve conflict in the classroom.

As we have noted in chapter 7, norms offer the most potent situational variable in the classroom. Perhaps the most important norms on conflict have to do with cooperation and competition. Under cooperative norms, students perceive that they will attain their self-interest only if other students also achieve theirs. It is the spirit of teamwork wherein it is in students' self-interest to behave cooperatively with others. In contrast, under competitive norms, students perceive that they will attain their self-interest only at the expense of others. It is the spirit of win-lose; one party achieves a goal only if others do not.

Deutsch (1973) provided an illuminating example in an experiment on cooperation and competition with college sophomores. He used student grades to develop two different normative structures. The class was divided into small groups to study and solve different problems. Some of the problems entailed exercises in logic and they had a correct answer. Other problems were much less clear; they entailed a human-relations issue that had no single correct answer. Half the groups were put into a competition. They were told that their individual grades would be determined by how well they did compared to members of their group. The best contributor was to receive an "A," the next best a "B," and so on. The other groups were graded cooperatively; that is, every person in the group would get the same grade, based on the group's performance. Under the condition of cooperation, all members of the best groups would receive the highest grades. The results were striking in showing the power of the different normative situations. Individuals in the cooperative groups, in contrast to the competitive groups, showed more (1) effective member communication, (2) friendly and helpful behavior, (3) coordination of effort, (4) division of labor, (5) orderliness, and (6) task orientation. The most obvious finding was the fact that conflict was enhanced in the competitive situations and minimized or erased in the cooperative situations.

Another important study is also worth mentioning here because of its focus on the social situation and conflict. The Robbers' Cave experiment (Sherif et al., 1961), discussed more fully in the section on "Action Ideas for Improving Climate," was conducted at a special summer camp for boys aged 11 and 12. The experimenters divided the study into three different experimental stages. First, they formed two separate groups of boys, the Rattlers and the Eagles, and developed each group into a highly cohesive unit. The boys ate together and slept together in each of their separate groups. There was a minimum of contact between the Rattlers and the Eagles. In the second stage the experiments arranged for contact between the two groups of boys; most formal contact was in athletic competition. Great feelings of animosity arose between the two groups. In situations that were not competitively based, such as in the dining hall, fights erupted and conflict escalated. Finally, the third stage of the experiment was to reduce the conflict so the members of the two groups would work together harmoniously. Many things failed. Finally a situation emerged that reduced the conflict and created a cooperative situation. Both the Rattlers and the Eagles were riding to a swimming hole in a truck; the truck broke down and all the boys were obliged to work together to get the truck, with all their gear, to the swimming hole. Getting the truck to the swimming hole became a *superordinate goal;* both groups had to work together to accomplish one common end.

Their previous strategy of win-lose behavior would not work in this instance. Another similar challenge to work together on a superordinate goal occurred when an emergency arose in the dining hall and both groups had to work together to bring enough food to the cook for dinner. The common goal of relieving hunger brought the Rattlers and the Eagles together into cooperation.

We have seen a similar event in the relationships between students as our own children have engaged in competitive athletics at the elementary, junior high, and high school level. At the elementary level, they competed against students at other schools. Here there were important school rivalries which sometimes led to unfavorable comments and dislike for students—especially the highly skilled players—playing on the other teams. Then students from several elementary schools combined as a single student body at the junior high level, and the disliked players from the competitive elementary schools of the past became favored teammates and good friends. The story repeated itself again as our children moved from the junior high school to the senior high school.

Despite the techniques for assessing self-interest, for clearing up misperception and miscommunication, as well as for arranging the situation to decrease the likelihood of conflict arising, many conflicts cannot be resolved constructively. People cannot always assess their motives accurately. Sometimes their skills in communication are so ineffective that they cannot convey their intentions, and often the degree of interpersonal animosity is so great that the conflicting parties cannot interact in a constructive manner. Some situations are of a win-lose character, and constructive conflict resolution is just not possible. All the same, the teacher can make inroads into working constructively with conflict by using the concepts and procedures described above.

Along with these ideas from social-psychological theory and research, it is relevant to keep in mind the practices that teachers have used for years. Providing a cooling-off period, for example, makes sense in many conflict situations. Holmes points out that "the more interruptions in the course of the interaction, the less likely that autistic conflict will escalate. Interruptions or breaks provide an opportunity for hostilities and tempers to subside." In some cases, teachers should stop the public demonstration of conflict when rational problem solving cannot take place. We do not believe, however, that such conflict situations should be allowed to fester; they should be brought into the open for discussion and attempted resolution.

Another useful practice is to change the situation from a public to a private setting. Public settings too often bring courtroom drama where players are directing their behaviors toward a jury of peers rather than toward the resolution of the conflict itself. A fight on the playground or in the locker room can often be resolved better in a school office or in a quiet room without the aid of others cheering on the sidelines.

And, in some cases, conflict can be resolved between individuals or groups when the teacher or administrator throws the opposing parties together and forces them to work things out. "Come and see me when you have come to a satisfactory resolution of differences," has been a workable and standard procedure for many years.

Teachers should not expect every conflict to end in a constructive manner. The fact is that conflict is an inevitable consequence of human relations, and it cannot always result in beneficial outcomes. But teachers can use the actual drama of human events to provide opportunities for students to try new behavioral skills and to expand their levels of awareness and behavior to include appropriate conflict resolution techniques, depending on the situation. While there will always be conflict, there are more or less constructive ways of coping with that conflict.

Implications for Teachers

The following points summarize some of the most important implications of the contents of this chapter for teachers:

Conflict is natural and inevitable in human relations. In schools it occurs most prominently between individuals and between groups.

Conflict is either good, neutral, or bad; it can have positive or negative consequences.

Conflict in classrooms offers the opportunity for individual and group growth.

Conflict exists when one activity blocks, prevents, interferes, injures, or in some way makes another activity less likely or ineffective.

Conflicts occur over incompatible procedures, goals, concepts, or interpersonal relationships.

Conflict resolution can—and should be—taught to children of all ages.

The S-T-P model can help to categorize incompatible procedures (P-conflict), goals (T-conflict), and concepts (S-conflict) for rational problem solving.

Interpersonal conflicts can be handled effectively by assessing self-interests, clearing up misperceptions and stereotypes, and developing a cooperative normative structure within the social situation.

Conflicts are resolved constructively when both parties get something that they want.

Action Ideas for Improving Climate

The practices that follow have been tried successfully by classroom teachers in order to understand and deal with conflict.

Overview Strategy for Secondary Grades

Successful tactics for resolving emergent conflicts, whatever their type or source, are organized into three steps: (1) distinguish between *miscommunication and conflict,* (2) assess the *seriousness of the conflict,* and (3) respond appropriately to the *source of the conflict.*

Miscommunications are not conflicts; they are gaps between intended messages and received messages. They occur when messages sent do not directly reflect intentions, or when messages sent are inaccurately understood. Miscommunications can be reduced by improved articulation and listening. Use the skills of paraphrasing and summarizing to enhance listening. When miscommunication might escalate into conflict, seek face-to-face meetings with the parties involved. If clarifying the communication accentuates differences between the parties, assume there is conflict and proceed to assess it.

Assess the source of the conflict, and respond accordingly. With power struggles, talk separately with the conflicting parties about your perception of their conflict. Often just bringing an unconscious power struggle into the open with conversation can reduce its intensity and disruption. If, however, the struggle does not subside, recommend that a third party with authority be introduced to help resolve the conflict. That neutral party could be a teacher aide or a committee of trusted students. Once the conflict has surfaced and you have made a tentative assessment of its source, look for ways to engage the conflicting parties in cooperative work toward common ends.

When role conflict is the source, and the above tactics don't work or seem inappropriate, ask each party to write three lists addressed to every other party in the conflict as follows:

To help me carry out my role, I'd like you to do the following more or better _____ ; To help me. . . , I'd like you to do the following less often _____ ; and . . . , I'd like you to continue doing the following as you are now _____ . Give the responses to the parties, encouraging each to question others for clarification, but not to argue about the information. After the messages are understood, ask the parties to choose issues to negotiate, with each participant prepared to offer some temporary behavior change. The role negotiation takes the form of an exchange: If I do _____ ,

you will do _____ . After the parties are satisfied that each will receive a return for what they are to give, record the agreement, and move to another issue. Agree on a date and time and a negotiator to check whether the actions occur.

If differentiation of function is the source of conflict, and the above tactics don't work, ask each party to write descriptions, both favorable and unfavorable, of itself and of the other party. The parties convene next to share their images with one another. Then separate the parties once more, and ask each to recall instances when its behavior supported the impressions of the other party. In other words, each party confesses that it did, at one time or another, behave in ways that might have exacerbated the conflict. Finally, reconvene the parties to share the confessions and to specify the underlying issues that are pulling them apart. Although this procedure is unlikely to resolve all existing differences, it can set the stage for collaborative problem solving.

The S-T-P Model

A high school social studies teacher used the S-T-P model to teach his students about different sorts of conflict. He explained situations (S), targets (T), and proposals (P), giving examples of each. He pointed out that S conflicts can be resolved by gathering data because they are conflicts of facts. He also showed how P conflicts might be resolved through experiments and action research since they are conflicts over the best way to accomplish something. Mostly, he spent time on T conflicts that are conflicts over goals and values. He argued that we can resolve value conflicts only by negotiating, bargaining, and, finally, by agreeing to disagree. The class analyzed several examples of interpersonal, intergroup, and international conflicts from the point of view of the S-T-P model and used those three concepts throughout the course as analytic categories.

Documenting Conflict in the World

Students were asked to make a bulletin board of conflict situations they found reported in newspapers or magazines. The bulletin board categories were—conflicts between individuals, conflicts between groups, and conflicts between countries. For each category, the teacher raised three questions:

1. What were the sources of the conflict?

2. Could the conflicting parties have solved the issue in another way?

3. Does this kind of conflict appear in our classroom? How? When?

The Robbers' Cave Experiment: A Lesson About Conflict

This lesson on conflict has three parts: (1) the student reader, (2) the student worksheet, and (3) the teacher worksheet. It is reprinted from Lippitt, Fox, and Schaible's *Social Science Laboratory Units* (1969).

Part 1: The Student Reader

Robbers' Cave Experiment

The experiment began in eastern Oklahoma, in a place where the hills are steep and the rivers swift, where the woods are thick and the trees are tall, where there are caves and crags and cliffs. Here, Indians once roamed and robbers hid in caves to split their loot and plan more raids on banks and trains. Here, too, is Robbers' Cave where one summer not very long ago, two groups of boys called the Rattlers and the Eagles camped, and hiked, and swam, and played games—and *fought*.

None of the eleven Rattlers had known one another until they boarded the bus that took them to Robbers' Cave State Park. Upon arriving, they organized their cabin, had supper, then built a roaring campfire. The next day they hiked to Robbers' Cave to explore the Stone Corral and later discover a swimming hole. After a swim, they decided to improve the place. Working together, they built a path of rocks to the hole and erected a diving board. They stayed there that night for supper.

The following day the Rattlers found a canoe near their cabin. Again working together, they carried it to their swimming hole. One Rattler hurt his toe, but he said nothing about it until someone saw the wound at bedtime. The other Rattlers admired him, and after that, Rattlers did not complain or cry when they were hurt.

On the third day the Rattlers took an overnight hike to a reservoir north of their camp. Because a storm was approaching and because someone had spotted a rattlesnake, all members of the group slept together in the same tent at night. The next day the Rattlers proved their toughness by hiking back to camp with only one stop for rest.

During the remainder of the week the Rattlers swam, played baseball, practiced pitching tents, had a treasure hunt, and sang songs around the campfire. Two Rattlers couldn't swim at first, but with help and encouragement from the others, they learned. Soon no Rattler was afraid to go off the diving board.

By now the Rattlers knew each other well. Each had a cap and T-shirt with RATTLERS and a rattler design stenciled on them. They had a flag. They had a swimming hole, a hideout, and hiking trails. They had worked on the park baseball diamond to make it smoother and they called it *our* diamond.

Then one day at the hideout, three Rattlers discovered some paper cups. The group discussed the matter. They wondered what outsiders had been there. Who were they?

The Eagles first met one another on their bus. The first night in camp they had a campfire after supper and roasted marshmallows. They discovered a canoe near their cabin and carried it down to a stream they named Moccasin Creek. They built a rope bridge across the creek, killed a copperhead snake, and later cooked their supper.

On another day the Eagles took an overnight hike to the reservoir, working together to carry the packs and equipment. The reservoir didn't appeal to them, so the Eagles voted to return and go to Moccasin Creek for a swim.

The Eagles played baseball, had a treasure hunt, took turns fixing food for lunch and supper, chose a song they called *our* song, and practiced pitching tents. They stenciled EAGLES on their T-shirts and a large E on their caps. They made a flag. They knew each other well.

Then two Eagles became so homesick that they had to leave camp. "Things are going to be a lot better around here now," said one of the nine Eagles who remained. "They chickened out," said another. "They are the only ones who will," added a third camper.

During a baseball practice at the end of the week, the Eagles heard the distant sounds of another group of boys.

"Ask those campers to play with us," one Eagle said to a member of the group.

The Rattlers had heard the other group playing ball on the park diamond. "Run them off! Challenge them!" several yelled. Then they learned that the other group wanted to challenge them to a baseball game. "They can't," the Rattlers responded. "We'll challenge them first. They've got a nerve!"

The Eagles and the Rattlers were about to meet for the first time.

Of course, the adults who acted as counselors for the Eagles and Rattlers had known each other for quite some time. They were social scientists from the University of Oklahoma under the direction of Dr. Muzafer Sherif. Camping out at Robbers' Cave State Park with two groups of eleven-year-old boys was their plan. Keeping the Eagles and Rattlers in separate groups and in separate camps was part of the experiment they were conducting in group behavior.

Arranging a series of games in which Rattlers and Eagles would compete was also part of the experiment. There was to be a four-day tournament of contests. These would include baseball, tug-of-war, touch football, tent pitching, skits and songs, and a treasure hunt. The group winning the most points would receive a trophy and each member of the winning group would receive a four-bladed knife.

The Rattlers hung their flag on the diamond backstop in preparation for the first game. The Eagles marched to the diamond with their flag on a pole, singing a song to challenge the Rattlers.

They looked each other over carefully, sizing up the situation. Then one Eagle called a Rattler "Dirty Shirt." A Rattler gave a catcall, and the razzing and name-calling began. As the game got under way, the Rattlers sang, "The first Eagle hit the deck, parley-voo. The second Eagle hit the deck, parley-voo. The third Eagle . . ." The Eagles yelled back, "Our pitcher's better'n yours!" And the Rattlers responded, "You're not Eagles, you're pigeons!"

The Rattlers won the game and they gave three cheers for the losing team. One Eagle found a Rattler glove left on the field after the game. He dropped it into the creek near the Eagle cabin.

That night after supper, the Eagles lost the first tug-of-war. On the way back to their cabin, they tore down the Rattler flag from the backstop and burned it.

The next day the Rattlers were furious. They grabbed the Eagle flag and destroyed it. The second game finally got started amid much jeering and catcalling, and the Eagles won. They won the second tug-of-war, too.

The contests seesawed back and forth. Good sports behavior went downhill, while name-calling and bragging increased. Finally, the Eagles won the tournament and all the prizes.

While the Eagles went swimming to celebrate their victory, the Rattlers raided the Eagle cabin. They scattered clothing and equipment all over. They took the trophy and some knives. When the Eagles returned and saw what had happened, they were boiling mad. The fighting that followed was serious and had to be stopped by the counselors.

Whenever the Eagles and Rattlers met, cries of "stinkers," "braggers," and "sissies" filled the air. Members of both groups held their noses when any of the other group were around. Neither group wanted anything to do with the other.

The social scientists who acted as camp counselors wanted to know what could be done to change unfriendly behavior to friendly behavior.

They had two ideas. The first was to plan activities that both groups liked and that could be done as one group. They hoped the boys would become more friendly if they had fun doing things together.

Attending a movie together in the mess hall didn't make the Eagles and the Rattlers like one another any better. Neither did shooting fireworks on the Fourth of July. Each group kept to itself. At some meals they got into "garbage fights" and littered the mess hall with food they had thrown at one another. The first idea was clearly a failure.

The second idea that the social scientists had was more successful. They arranged to have certain things break down so that the boys would have to work together to repair them. Neither group could do it alone. This is what happened:

One day, the boys in both groups discovered that the faucets in both camps were dry. Suddenly everyone began to feel very thirsty. Eagles and Rattlers both volunteered to help find the trouble.

The volunteers carefully combed the trails to the reservoir and to the water tank, looking for signs of trouble. None was found. Then one Rattler found a sack stuffed into a faucet at the tank. Without thinking who was a Rattler and who was an Eagle, all the volunteers got to work to remove the sack. After nearly an hour's work, the faucet was open. Then, without bothering to see whether Eagles or Rattlers went first, they lined up to take turns having drinks.

The last big event planned by the scientists was an overnight trip to Cedar Lake, sixty miles from Robbers' Cave State Park. All the boys were eager to go. They had their equipment ready and packed long before the time of departure. They were impatient to leave.

Each group traveled to Cedar Lake in its own truck. The Eagle truck was an old one, and later it became another reason why Rattlers and Eagles started to become friends.

Trouble arose at lunchtime after the arrival at Cedar Lake. The older truck, parked on a slight hill, would not start. Of course, the truck really was in good running order, but the boys believed that there was something wrong with it as one of the counselors strained and sweated to get it started. The truck was needed to get the food for lunch. The social scientists had deliberately left the food in a station wagon parked some distance away.

One of the tug-of-war ropes had been brought on the trip. When the boys saw that the truck would not start, someone suggested that they attach the rope and pull it up the hill. Perhaps as it rolled down the other side it would start.

Rattlers and Eagles alike pulled on the rope. The combined efforts of both groups were needed to get the truck started. Once the food was brought, both Rattlers and Eagles helped to get it ready. The boys took pride in what they had accomplished together, and some Rattlers sat with Eagles to eat lunch that day. "You never thought we'd be eating together, huh?" said a Rattler to an Eagle. And the Eagle laughed.

The next day at Cedar Lake, the counselors told the boys they would take a trip to the Arkansas border, a few miles away. On the ride to and from the border, the Rattlers and Eagles together discussed some of the experiences they had had in camp. They all sang songs together. At the border, members of both groups had their pictures taken.

Back at camp on the final night, all the boys had a campfire at the Stone Corral, which the Rattlers had always considered theirs alone, and which had been the site of their own campfires. There they entertained one another with skits, sang songs, and talked about the three weeks at camp.

Everyone returned to Oklahoma City the next day on one bus. Some of the boys exchanged addresses and many told their close companions that they would meet again. Some Eagles had discovered that the boys they liked best were Rattlers, and some Rattlers discovered that Eagles were their favorites. The Robbers' Cave Experiment was over.

Part 2: The Student Worksheet

Robbers' Cave Experiment

Directions: Answer the questions below after you have finished reading "Robbers' Cave Experiment" in your Resource Book.

1. The social scientists set up the experiment so that unfriendly behavior might result between the two groups. Put a check (✓) in the space in front of the sentences that tell something about the experiment.

_____ The two groups ate and slept together.

_____ The two groups ate and slept apart.

_____ The boys did not know each other before they came to camp.

_____ The boys knew each other well before they came to camp.

_____ The Eagles were always on one team, and the Rattlers were always on another team.

_____ Sometimes Eagles and Rattlers were on the same team.

2. Which phrases below describe the Rattlers and the Eagles during the first part of the experiment? Put a check (✓) in the space in front of the correct sentences.

_____ Eagles liked other Eagles.

_____ Eagles liked some Rattlers.

_____ Rattlers liked other Rattlers.

_____ Rattlers liked some Eagles.

3. Give three examples of unfriendly behavior between the Rattlers and the Eagles.

_____

_____

_____

4. The scientists had an idea that the boys would become more friendly if they did more things together as one group. What were two activities that the scientists planned?

_____

_____

5. The scientists arranged for both groups to have their meals together in the mess hall. How did the two groups behave when they had meals?

_____

_____

6. What was the second plan that the scientists used to make the two groups become more friendly toward one another?

_____

_____

_____

7. How did the two groups behave when they discovered that the faucets were dry? Put a check (✓) in the space in front of the sentence that correctly describes their behavior.

_____ Only Rattlers volunteered to find the trouble.

_____ Only Eagles volunteered to find the trouble.

_____ Some Eagles and some Rattlers volunteered to find the trouble.

8. How did the two groups act after they had worked together several times to solve common problems? Put a check (✓) in the space in front of the sentences that describe their behavior.

_____ Some Rattlers and Eagles became friends.

_____ Most Rattlers and Eagles became friends.

_____ The two groups stopped fighting entirely.

_____ The two groups discussed their experiences at camp.

_____ The two groups sang songs together.

_____ The groups entertained each other with skits.

_____ All the boys exchanged addresses.

9. Which phrases below describe the Rattlers and the Eagles at the end of the experiment? Put a check (✓) in the space in front of the sentences that describe the behavior of the boys.

_____ Eagles liked all other Eagles and some Rattlers.

_____ Eagles liked all other Eagles and most Rattlers.

_____ Rattlers liked all other Rattlers and some Eagles.

_____ Rattlers liked all other Rattlers and most Eagles.

_____ Most Rattlers and most Eagles liked each other.

10. During the experiment the two groups were kept in separate camps. They interacted only when there was a game or contest. Do you think they would have become more friendly toward each other if they had all been together in the same camp? Tell why you think the way you do.

_____

_____

Part 3: Teacher Worksheet

Robbers' Cave Experiment

This exercise underscores the major points of the experiment in group behavior conducted at Robbers' Cave State Park and is done in conjunction with the student worksheet.

Suggested Answers

1. *"The two groups ate and slept apart. The boys did not know each other before they came to camp. The Eagles were always on one team and the Rattlers always on another."*

2. During the first part of the experiment, each group was tightly knit. Eagles liked other Eagles and Rattlers liked other Rattlers.

3. Examples of unfriendly behavior between Rattlers and Eagles: they called each other names; one Eagle threw a Rattler mitt into the creek; Eagles burned the Rattler flag; Rattlers destroyed the Eagle flag; Rattlers raided the Eagle cabin and stole the prizes; Eagles raided the Rattler cabin.

4. Activities included a movie both groups watched in the mess hall; a fireworks display; having meals together.

5. They continued to behave in unfriendly ways. Each group kept to itself. The groups had "garbage" fights at mealtime.

FIGURE 9.1   Collaborate, Negotiate, Win–Lose

Strategy	Situation	Process
Collaborate	Common goals and differences	Cooperate
Negotiate	Joint outcomes, differences in goals	Bargain
Win–lose	Strong differences in goals	Compete, Coerce

A Role–Play Situation:

The girls' softball team was angry because the boys' basketball team got new uniforms and the girls' team did not. The girls believed they had been treated unfairly and talked to the coach. The coach reported the events leading up to the purchase of the boys' uniforms and said the administration did not believe the girls were treated unfairly. The girls were not convinced and made an appointment to see the principal.

Play out this situation so that it reflects all three conflict approaches: collaboration, negotiation, and win–lose.

6. This is the key to the experiment. The scientists arranged to have certain things break down (water supply, food truck) so that the boys would have to work together to repair them. Neither group could do it alone.

7. *Some Eagles and some Rattlers volunteered to find the trouble* when the groups discovered that the faucets were dry.

8. *Some Rattlers and Eagles became friends* after the two groups had worked together several times in solving important problems. *The two groups discussed their experiences at camp, the two groups sang songs together,* and *the two groups entertained each other with skits.*

9. At the end of the experiment, *Eagles liked all other Eagles and some*

Rattlers. Rattlers liked all other Rattlers and some Eagles.

10. Discuss this question in class or divide the class into groups and ask each group to discuss it. Assign one person in each group to make a report to the class later. It is likely that the two groups would have behaved in much the same way, even if they were all in the same camp.

Conflict Strategies: Collaborate, Negotiate, and Win–Lose

A high school social studies teacher presented Figure 9.1 and had students role play situations in which the parties behaved in the three different ways.

After the three role-plays, the students discussed the strengths and weaknesses of each strategy. They finished their discussion by talking about examples of the three strategies in our society today.

A School-Wide, Peer Conflict Managers Program

An K-5 elementary school decided to develop a school-wide program for solving student conflicts on the playground. The staff believed that children at an early age must develop the skills to resolve their own conflicts and urged a program using problem-solving strategies as an approach to discipline. The program contained the following elements:

A. Student conflict managers were selected from all third, fourth, and fifth graders. Selection was based on peer nomination and teacher recommendation. Parents were required to give permission. Twelve conflict managers were finally selected.

B. The counselor, using materials from various sources, developed a training program of about 15 hours in one week. Training included communication skills, problem solving, and team building, using strategies of role playing, interviewing, and games. The counselor used materials from the Oregon Law-Related Education Project (Coddington 1989) and Kreidler *Creative Conflict Resolution* (1984) in developing the training modules. Students met at lunch time and other released times for training.

C. Students were assigned a duty roster for the playground. When a conflict emerged, a conflict manager followed a series of steps. Basically the steps included:

1. Students reported what happened. (This was done by both conflicting parties and they were not allowed to interrupt each other.)

2. Each party paraphrased the other's report.

3. Students brainstormed to offer at least four different strategies for settling the conflict.

4. The students decided upon a resolution of the conflict.

D. A PCM (Peer Conflict Managers) form was filled out for each dispute, whether resolved or not resolved, and sent to the counselor's office. This enabled data to be collected about program effectiveness and supplied real-life examples to be used in ongoing meetings with peer conflict managers.

E. Regular meetings were held with peer conflict managers to discuss successful and unsuccessful cases of conflict resolution.

Debriefing Conflict in the Classroom

A kindergarten teacher spent the last part of each day asking students: (1) "What was one thing you liked about today?" and, (2) "What was a problem you had with another person?" Thus children had a chance to air any interpersonal conflicts that arose during the day and to find alternative strategies for resolving the conflict. As conflicts were reduced, the teacher used questions similar to those used in the cooperative circles described in chapter 8.

Debriefing in the classroom is not only a useful way to deal with conflict, but it is also an effective practice for general use. Teachers can encourage students to discuss their views of expectations, leadership, friendship and cohesiveness, norms, communication, and conflict, thus helping these students to understand the various concepts of classroom life that have been introduced in this book.

Students and Teachers as Organizational Participants

10

The primary building block of a school is its classroom groups. What takes place in class can be influenced by what is happening within other classes and by the culture of the school. Classes might be in the traditional style of self-contained rooms, or they might be organized into more fluid groupings where subgroups and individual memberships change regularly. No matter how the classes and teaching assignments are organized, the culture of the school can influence group processes in the classrooms.

In particular, social relationships among teachers can influence what takes place in classes. Teachers often bring into their classes some of the norms and expectations learned from colleagues about appropriate teacher-student behavior. For example, the seating arrangements, styles of instruction, and discipline techniques that are chosen by the teacher can each be influenced by faculty norms. Also, teachers establish self-esteem or self-doubt through relationships with colleagues and with the administration. In turn, teachers' self-concepts influence how they interact with students. And, students, on their part, are influenced by their teacher's reactions to them.

Objectives of this Chapter

This chapter addresses how organizational realities of schools influence teachers and students. After arguing for the importance of the school culture in classroom life, we present data on students' attitudes about school. We go on to address the special place of "at-risk" students. Next we summarize theories on how schools work as organizations and how school cultures might influence students, reviewing both external and internal organizational processes. Then we go on to discuss contemporary thoughts about "school restructuring" and curriculum innovation, focusing on how staff social structure and school innovation interact. Finally we show how organization-development strategies offer a method for grass-roots change in schools. We close by presenting many action ideas being used today to improve the organizational participation of students and teacher. This chapter is unique in its focus on students as organizational participants.

Importance of the School Culture for Classroom Life

The school as a formal organization is the arena in which various professional subgroups of faculty are expected to work together. It is the stage upon which various committees are formed, crucial problems are solved, and important, educational decisions are made. The school organization is composed of both formal and informal relationships among the faculty and between the faculty and the students. It also consists of the community and other important external forces and includes the curriculum and other academic resources. In short, the school organization is a living, complex, social system with multiple, interdependent parts. The classrooms constitute the key subsystems of the larger system. As an open system, a school and each of its classrooms must continually adapt to changes from within—from its teachers, committees, and students—respond to its teachers, committees, and students—and respond to forces from without such as budgets, parents, and boards.

Although the classroom group processes that we have described in the preceding chapters have the most significant and direct impact on student motivation and learning, it is relevant to consider how the school's adult culture can also influence students' attitudes and achievement. During the past thirty years, theory and research on the link between school organization and student psychology have been accumulating. We review a few of the more classical studies here.

Dreeben (1968) showed that through their structures of student management, schools teach the students "principles of conduct or social norms, and to act according to them." Sarason (1982) called what Dreeben saw "the culture of the school." According to Sarason, the school culture is a combination of its social structures and its social norms. Goodlad (1984) referred to such structures and norms as the school's "hidden curriculum."

In a famous field study, Menuchin and her colleagues (1969) demonstrated how the classroom group process and the material students learn can be influenced by the school organization. The researchers studied fourth graders in four, contrasting school cultures and found student differences in self-concept, cognitive skills, sex differentiation, group relations, and interactions with authority. In two schools, for example, there were differentiated norms guiding appropriate behaviors for boys and girls, whereas in the other two schools, boys and girls participated in similar activities and were not separated by sex in play or in work.

Research by Bigelow (1971) on twenty junior high classrooms showed that teachers who work cooperatively with colleagues to set instructional goals and to solve teaching problems also encourage more cooperation and give more social support to their students in the classroom. Bigelow compared schools with different amounts of staff collaboration, observing classroom interactions in all twenty classes. Using a slightly modified Flanders' Interaction Analysis (see chapter 8 for details), he found that classrooms within the more collaborative schools were characterized by teachers' initiating broad questions, accepting student ideas, and accepting student feelings. Also, in the more collaborative schools, students were initiating talk with teachers much more than they were in the less collaborative schools.

Research by Seeman and Seeman (1976) supported Bigelow's findings. They collected data from 35 classrooms in 12 schools, all involved in Goodlad's "League of Cooperating Schools." The Seemans observed that in some schools the teachers were engaged in "dialogue, decision making and action taking" to change the curriculum. Some of the school staffs manifested high degrees of collaboration while others were very low. The research data showed that teachers involved in the dialogue-decision-action process had students with more favorable attitudes toward school, and that those same teachers felt they had a higher sense of influence over their professional lives than did the teachers with low participation in staff collaboration.

Rutter et al. (1979) studied relationships between staff culture and student behavior by collecting longitudinal data from 12 senior highs in London. The data showed that in schools where staffs planned collaboratively and where teachers encouraged and supported one another, students were in attendance more often and committed delinquent acts less frequently. Also, exam successes were more frequent in schools where discipline was based on general expectations set by teachers consensually as a group, rather than left to individual teachers to work out for themselves.

Johnson and Johnson (1988) have demonstrated how the school organization can be set up to support cooperative learning in classrooms. The school organization is constituted of three types of cooperative adult teams: (1) teacher support groups of 3 or 4 to learn about and to implement cooperative learning in their classes; (2) school-wide task forces to develop and evaluate solutions to school-wide problems, and (3) ad hoc problem solving groups at faculty meetings. Procedures for introducing such adult teams into the school will be discussed later in this chapter in the section on Organization Development.

Student Attitudes Toward School

In a tour of small town school districts, we interviewed a diverse sample of 212 working and middle class teenagers (104 girls and 108 boys) singly, in pairs, in small groups, and in classes (see Schmuck and Schmuck, 1991, for details). We interviewed college preparatory and vocationally oriented students, class officers, athletes, and informal leaders. We even interviewed a few high school students soon after they had received a paddling from the principal. We also made informal observations of student behavior in the community and formal observations of 50 minutes each in 30 secondary classrooms.

We started the interviews by asking for the best and worst things about the school. The rank order of the most frequently oc-

curring answers for the *best things* were: (1) lots of friends; (2) everybody knows everybody else; (3) small classes with individual attention; (4) sports, clubs, and other extracurricular activities; (5) no drugs, muggings, or weapons; and (6) caring attitudes of teachers and administrators.

The rank order of the most frequently occurring answers for the *worst things* were: (1) too few electives or advanced courses; (2) teachers who don't care and are not friendly; (3) alcohol abuse; (4) gossip and rumors about sexual behavior or drinking; (5) closed campus, particularly at lunch; and (6) restrictive dress code.

We went on to ask students how they felt about the school and the town. Although they frequently started by stating favorable sentiments, well over 50% quickly pointed out how boring school was. When we probed them about their boredom, they spoke frankly about particular teachers (totaling, we surmise, about 30% of each student's classroom experience). They seldom responded negatively, however, toward the school as a whole, nor were they frustrated with extracurricular activities. *Most student frustration had to do with negative group processes in particular classes.*

Next we asked for behavioral examples, not for names of teachers. The rank order of the most frequently occurring answers for *good teaching* were: (1) gives students respect, is patient, and easy to get along with; (2) makes the subject interesting and fun by involving students in activities and demonstrations; (3) tells jokes and smiles a lot—good sense of humor; and (4) listens to students questions and makes changes in class to help students learn.

The rank order of the most frequently occurring answers for *bad teaching* were (1) low respect for students, lacks patience, and treats you like you are stupid; (2) seldom smiles, very serious and stern, and issues either too harsh or too permissive discipline; (3) doesn't care about or pay attention to individuals; not helpful; (4) doesn't explain well, lazy, hands out work sheets and tests; you have to learn everything on your own; and (5) has favorites; favors the smart students or one sex over the other.

The students thought that about 30% of their teachers—and particularly those teachers who steered clear of taking part in extra-curricular activities—were making school boring and, at times, stressful for them. The students viewed those teachers as lacking *respect* for adolescents, unwilling to try to establish *rapport* with them, lacking a *sense of humor,* not *caring* much about teaching, and playing *favorites.*

After talking frankly with over 200 adolescents, we have concluded that their views have not been taken into consideration in the literature of the school reform movement of the 1980s. Those reform reports focused on the intellectual competence and the academic performance of teachers, not on their compassion, empathy, respect, and love of young people. The reports of the 80s emphasized teachers' intelligence, academic achievement, course work within the liberal arts, and years of college education. They did not focus on the social-emotional characteristics of teachers that the adolescents themselves emphasize. The adolescents we interviewed were not concerned with their teachers' subject-matter competence, breadth of knowledge, or ability to do well in college classrooms.

Rather, *they wanted teachers to be human beings who would show trust, respect, and understanding of youth.*

The "at-risk" student is, of course, particularly vulnerable to the ill effects of bad teaching. Depending upon how "at-risk students" are defined, we estimate that easily over 50% of the youngsters in American schools today need special attention and loving care to succeed academically. The primary person to give such loving care is the classroom teacher. The primary stage on which it is administered, or not administered, is the classroom. "At-risk" students typically have low self-esteem and do not receive strong emotional support for school from their families. It is teachers who will have to pick up the slack and give out high amounts of respect and loving care to these students. Whether we like it or not, teachers of the 90s will have to be just as concerned with their students' mental health as they are with their students' academic achievement.

Sociological Influences on Schools

Some sociological characteristics of the school organization—its size, socioeconomic character, and neighborhood culture—can have an important bearing on what happens within the daily life of the school. Each of those characteristics can influence what transpires in the classrooms, yet school staffs often do not take concerted action to cope effectively with "external givens" of these sorts. Staffs with vision and collaboration can alter the detrimental effects of these contextual factors. They can use them, in particular, to the educational advantage of the "at-risk" student.

Size

Barker and Gump (1964), Baird (1969), Sher and Tompkins (1977), and Schmuck and Schmuck (1990 and 1991) have presented empirical evidence on the relationship between school size and the behavior of students toward one another. In all studies, it was found that although small and large high schools had about the same number of "behavioral settings"—facilities and activities in which students interact with one another—a greater proportion of students in small schools participated in the activities offered by the school than did the students of large schools. Students of small schools also reported more personal kinds of satisfactions, e.g., developing new competencies, being challenged, participating in activities they considered important, and becoming clear about their values. On the other hand, students from large schools reported more impersonal satisfactions that were less goal-oriented. They pointed also to vicarious enjoyments, affiliation and identity with the large groups, learning about persons and affairs, and receiving external rewards, such as points, for participation.

Nevertheless, students in large schools become just as close with some peers as their small school counterparts; however, these friendships more often take place outside of the school's formal program. A student in a large school typically is faced with many more alternatives such as the kinds of persons he or she will choose for friends. Such diverse choice is not present in the relatively homogeneous group of small school students. Students in a large school may choose friends quite different from themselves, and the peer structures of small cliques and dating couples become impor-

tant factors in the student's developing personality. As a student chooses friends outside the school, the importance of school-related activities decreases.

In studies of college environments, Pace (1967) and Astin (1968) reported that size was negatively related to college students' perceptions of their campus's friendliness, cohesiveness, and emotional supportiveness. In the larger colleges, the researchers found less concern for the individual student, lack of psychological involvement in classes, little familiarity with the instructor, greater competitiveness, and lower cohesiveness. Exceptions were found, but in general, smaller colleges were more supportive environments for effective group processes.

The data run counter to the idea that large schools are better than small schools because they can concentrate resources, develop more impressive activities, and stimulate more learning. In theory, large high schools can engage in many different activities and provide a diversity of curricula and events which allow a heterogeneous student body to follow a course of study best suited for each individual student. However, research on school size suggests that the *quality* of the use that is made of facilities is more important than their magnitude or impressiveness. The data on size offer evidence that some of the very important ingredients for support of academic learning—involvement, participation, and commitment—are not enhanced by large, impersonal schools.

How Can Educators Cope with Size?

The "school within a school" design can be an effective way of promoting small groups within larger groups. Some urban schools, for example, have established "houses" within a building, each house acting as a mini-school with its own faculty, students, and administration. Several houses together use the facilities of the larger institution, such as language laboratories, movie equipment, and athletic playing areas. While lectures and assemblies can be given to large audiences, seminars about the lectures can take place in the house.

Some teachers in large schools have found that by combining activities with colleagues, they can cope with the limitations in their teaching all subjects to their students. The "unit" plan is one method to help solve the problems created by increasing numbers of students and by increasing amounts of knowledge in several disciplines. A unit is typically made up of a team of four or five teachers, some experienced, some neophytes. One member might be a paraprofessional. Usually, the unit is made up of 125 students and has an age span of from two to three years. In social studies, the students can move into small groups and might remain in those clusters for the whole year. In reading or math, the students might be arranged for short times according to performance, with individuals moving from group to group as they progress. In other learning activities, the entire unit can be brought together for a movie, play, concert, or science demonstration. Following the large group meeting, small discussion groups might be formed.

The middle school (usually grades 6, 7, 8) has changed the departmentalized junior high into units which include a homeroom or advisee group. Homerooms or advisee groups meet daily to accomplish several purposes: (1) to provide study skill training, (2) to discuss adolescent issues, (3) to enable one faculty member to serve as a monitor on students' academic progress, and (4) to establish a core group of peers in an identified group. Homerooms or advisee groups often compete in intramural athletics, participate as a group in school sponsored fund drives, and serve as a psychological support center in a large school. For more information about middle school organization and programs, see Whisler (1990).

Class size offers another challenge to creative teachers. Smith and Glass (1979) showed that reduced class size has positive effects on classroom group processes. These authors' meta-analysis of research by dozens of others also demonstrates a strong relationship between class size and achievement. As class size decreases, educational effectiveness increases, with the strongest gains coming below 15 students. Studies by Stallings et al. (1978) and Carrington et. al (1981) showed correlation between smaller classes and the development of reading and math skills in elementary schools. Their research supports the idea that intensive, small group instruction is especially valuable for young students in developing the basic skills of reading and math.

Van Horn (1980) gave the following sound advice to teachers: (1) If a classroom is crowded, consider the use of visual partitions or increase the amount of cooperative learning; (2) Remember that seating arrangements preferred by teachers might not be preferred by students; (3) Try to influence students' selection of group leaders by seating potential leaders at the end of rectangular tables. By rotating those who sit in such a position, the teacher can influence the emergence of more and more class leaders. In addition, group students flexibly in pairs, trios, etc., depending on the task and time allowed.

Socioeconomic Characteristics

The relationship between students' social class and the position they achieve in the social structure after schooling has been documented (Carnoy, 1975; Coleman et al., 1966, Jencks, 1972). The consensus of that research is the fact that schools do *not* facilitate economic success and that students' social class (which is associated with race and ethnicity) is a better predictor than both I.Q. and school quality for later achievement and economic status in the larger society.

In a classic study, Sexton (1961) illustrated how the resources of a district are allocated in relation to the socioeconomic environment of the school. She found that money spent for schools in one urban district varied in direct proportion to the incomes of families in the school's neighborhood. She documented inequalities in (1) quality of buildings and facilities; (2) ratio of students to school and classroom; (3) quality of teaching staff; (4) methods of testing and estimating student performance; (5) methods of grouping students; (6) quality of the secondary curriculum; (7) vocational and educational counseling of students; (8) opportunities for completion of high school and admission to college; (9) use of buildings by adults; (10) enrollment in preschool programs; (11) health, recreation, and food services facilities; and (12) total costs of educating students. All of these conditions were associated with the poorer performance of lower-income families. Although those data were collected 30 years ago, they still are relevant today. We include them here because the twelve conditions provide con-

crete benchmarks for investigating potential inequities in our schools due to social class differences of neighborhoods.

Of course, differences in resources across schools set the stage for differences in the psychology of classrooms. Herriott and St. John (1966) showed that teachers and principals of low socioeconomic status schools were less experienced and less satisfied in their jobs than those in high-status schools. Becker (1977) showed how teachers assigned to low-income schools considered a move to higher-income schools as a promotion, even though their titles, salaries, and benefits remained the same. Finn (1972) found that teachers in lower-income urban schools had lower expectations for student performance and paid more attention to I.Q. scores and achievement tests in evaluating student work than did teachers in middle-class suburban schools. Teachers in the suburban schools had smaller class loads, more teaching resources, and more support from psychologists than their urban counterparts. Teachers in lower-class schools, in contrast, did not have the resources, nor did they have the time to make adequate diagnoses of student problems. Consequently, the urban teachers used mental test scores primarily to measure the worth of a student's performance in the classroom.

Two interesting studies have questioned the relationship between social class and academic achievement. Both research by Gross (1966) and McDill et al. (1969) showed that parental support for academic success was very important for student achievement, regardless of the social class of the family. So, although the literature shows that the neighborhood's socioeconomic character *and* parental support of schooling have strong influence on a youngster's functioning in the classroom, the results are *not* so impressive that educators can justify failures to improve the quality of educational programs by "writing off" schools which are in low socioeconomic environments.

How Can Educators Cope With Socioeconomic Factors?

Important research by Edmonds (1979), Brookover (1978), Rutter (1979), and Goodlad (1984) have led to reconsidering how schools can cope with social class differences. Their work undergirds what has been called the "effective-schools movement." In a nutshell, their research showed that some particular schools are much more effective than others, even though all of them are in lower-class neighborhoods. The key factor in all studies was the staff's ability to work together on behalf of the students. Schools were most effective where staff members set goals together, where they decided on homework and grading policies together, and where they agreed on the rules for student discipline and were concerted and collaborative in their application.

The previously cited research of Gross (1966) and McDill et al. (1969) speaks strongly to bringing parents into the school as assistants for instruction. Frequently educators increase the division between school and neighborhood by adopting policies that separate the professionals from the parents and discourage, rather than encourage, parental visits to the school and parent participation in teaching and learning. There are many constructive steps that school faculties can take to use the resources of the

surrounding community. For example, in a recent article (Schmuck and Schmuck, 1990), we suggest some of the following: use of parents for tutoring or clerical work, special classes taught by parents with particular skills, cross-age tutoring programs using older students from the neighborhood, parent advisory boards with power to affect decisions in the school, and apprentice programs for students in the local business community.

Teachers, too, can do numerous things in their classes to overcome the undermining effects of problems due to social class. First, if teachers accept each student as a unique person—with special strengths and weaknesses—they have come a long way toward reducing social class biases. Second, if teachers are supportive and caring, students will follow in that same pattern, and a healthy and favorable climate for learning can be developed. Third, teachers must be careful to avoid the negative cycle of a self-fulfilling prophecy with students. They should call on students equally and give all students the same amount of time as the students search for answers.

There are also curriculum materials for students which focus on human problems in groups. The social psychology applications have been delineated in a series of units by the American Psychological Association, including Arends et al. (1981), who have published a high school course, *School Life and Organizational Psychology,* which has procedures that enable students to become change agents in their own schools. *Securing Every Learner's Future (SELF),* developed by the Orcutt, CA. School District (1977), applies concepts of group processes in the classroom to elementary and middle school classes. Ojemann (1958) created a curriculum focused on causes of individual behavior, while DeCharms (1968) offered a strategy to increase students' initiatory behaviors. Alschuler's program (1970) for training in achievement striving can be applied to helping students develop increased control over their own lives. And Stanford (1971) has shown how using popular books, movies, and magazines can be incorporated into a standard English curriculum with emphasis on human behavior. Most current documentation on "at-risk" students emphasizes the caring aspects of schooling. Caring is very important for "at-risk" students because they are often alienated from teachers, abused in their families, and experimenting with chemical substances to achieve self-esteem. Gardenas and McCarty (1985) and Mann (1985) have initiated successful programs for helping "at-risk" students do well in school.

Peer Group Norms

As Bain and Anderson (1974) surveyed the condition of adolescents in the 1970s, they concluded that young people were more likely to be influenced by their peers than a generation before. And, in the 1990s, with the decline of so many families in our society, that truism is even more correct today. Years ago, adolescents were in the formal work force and were strongly influenced by relationships at work. Now, with little teenage work and an absence of cohesive family life, there is a strong, informal, adolescent subculture which has high influence on students, and the direction of that influence can often be negative for academic life.

Wilson (1959) showed how norms of the peer group influence aspirations about higher education. He first pinpointed student aspirations in schools with three types of predominant populations as follows: school A—upper-middle-class, white collar, school B—lower-middle-class, white collar, and school C—industrial working class. Wilson found that in school A, 80 percent of students wanted to go to college; in school B, 57 percent wanted to go to college; and in school C, 38 percent wanted to attend college. Working class students who attended schools A and B were much more likely to want to attend college than working class students who attended school C. Similarly, upper-middle-class students in school C were much less likely to want to attend college compared with upper-middle-class students who attended schools A and B. The influences of peer norms altered the students' aspirations for college. Wilsons' findings have been replicated in four subsequent studies by Boyle (1966), Michael (1961), Sewell and Armer (1966), and Bridge (1979).

Indeed, peer norms can have a powerful influence on students in all social classes, even when families are cohesive and strong and regardless of personality differences. Mc Dill et al. (1969) showed that although the effects of social class tended to disappear when family and personality variables were held constant, various normative dimensions of the peer group still had significant influences, both on student aspirations and on academic performance.

In some schools, the faculty is continually embroiled in a battle with the student peer group, especially when the peer group norms are antagonistic to the achievement orientation of the teachers. Educators frequently find fault with parents, neighborhood, subgroup, or even the larger community for not socializing young people who have little conception of the "value of education." One target for educators to focus upon in trying to alter student attitude is the student peer group itself.

How Can Educators Cope With Peer Group Norms?

Educators need to develop plans for working collaboratively with their students. Initiatives for overcoming the "generation gap" should start with those in authority. Principals can establish advisory groups of students to listen to before making decisions. Teachers can use plans made by a student steering committee to guide the direction and activities of classroom learning.

Cooperation among teachers can go a long way toward making student cooperation in the school more likely. Students perceive teacher competition often as an indicator of the disorganized nature of the school environment. One teacher says one thing about discipline, etc., while another teacher says quite another thing. Is every person to be for himself or herself in the "organized anarchy" of the school? Teachers who collaborate with one another to establish priorities for goals, consistencies in grading, and group agreements about discipline will create a cooperative climate in the school that is conducive to student cooperation and to the strengthening of positive student attitudes toward school.

In an indepth study of boys' peer groups in two high schools, Kelly (1979) noted that peers can be socialized into feelings of competence and achievement motivation if the following criteria are met: (1) A diversity of formal and informal settings that encourages social interaction; (2) A variety of informal roles in the social environment that allows for spontaneous help giving and for personal interactions across divergent roles; (3) Varied competencies that are valued, and persons who contribute those competencies to the larger community; (4) Clearly recognized social norms for relating to the community; (5) A commitment on the part of faculty to examine the impact of the community environment on the students; and (6) An environment in the school where its dominant activities take into account the diverse cultural values of the students.

Internal Organizational Processes

> . . . schools do vary in effectiveness but the specific school characteristics that produce results are somewhat elusive . . . One of the crucial differences between an ineffective and an effective school may be something as vague as the school's atmosphere . . .

So wrote the authors in follow-up research on Project Talent (Shaycroft 1967)—and so write the authors of today (Johnson and Johnson 1990). By "school atmosphere" these writers are referring to the feeling tones as faculty actions are taking place. They are talking about the emotional vibrations, the faculty's procedures for working together, the norms that guide faculty behavior, and the way faculty members interact with one another. More specifically, they are referring to the methods faculties use to make decisions about school goals, how the curricula are planned and implemented, and how professionals, nonprofessionals and students interact with one another. In this section we will discuss aspects of the school's formal organizational structure and its informal organizational climate.

Formal Organizational Structure

Three formal aspects of schools that are influenced by size, socioeconomic factors, and peer group norms and that interact with the informal climate of the school are: complexity of educator roles, influence positions of teachers, and the leadership role of the principal. All three differentiate one school from another and can influence student behavior through the effect they have on the school's informal climate.

Complexity of Roles

Increased role complexity presents a mixed blessing to the participants of an organization. While the dysfunctions of bigness can be reduced by introducing small work groups such as departments or teams, the development of different interests between subsystems and intergroup competition and conflicts present new organizational problems. For example, role complexity can lead to conflicts between the *line* and the *staff* of an organization. Line people, such as the superintendent, principals, department heads, and teachers are focused on carrying out the core operations of the school. Those with staff positions, such as counselors, psychologists, curriculum specialists, and nurses, act more as specialists giving assistance to the line. Line people can become

frustrated when they are urged to accept advice from staffers who lack a comprehensive picture of how the school works. Staffers, for their part, feel frustration when they view themselves as expert, but lack influence over what goes on in the classroom and between teachers and administrators.

An example of line-staff conflict occurred while we were consulting in a school last year. For several months the teachers had been complaining that the counselor was not doing an adequate job. The problem, we thought, had less to do with the counselor's ability and more to do with a conflict of interest in the social structure of the school. The counselor spent most of her time working with parents and social agencies. The teachers saw only the problems of the students in their classes; they believed that the students were not being helped by the counselor. It was only after discussion facilitated by us that the teachers and counselor realized that their targets for the students were actually the same; it was their strategies that differed.

Lawrence and Lorsch (1967) found that achieving effective collaboration between line and staff is determined by the organization's procedures for dealing with conflict. When the organization does not have procedures for dealing with conflict, then the cleavages caused by line-staff differences can be destructive. On the other hand, when conflict is openly discussed, both role differences and collaboration can be simultaneously promoted. Bell (1977), for example, demonstrated how cooperative problem solving can enhance relationships between teachers and counselors in elementary schools. The researchers tend to suggest that flat organizations, such as elementary schools, need a well-articulated, overlapping structure for managing conflicts (e.g., a cross-grade-level committee), while large secondary schools should possess special structures for problem solving that cut across both line and staff (e.g., heterogeneous cross-school committees).

The multiunit, team-teaching structure can be a useful arrangement for managing conflicts in schools (see Schmuck et al., 1975, for details). The key is the link-pin role described by Likert (1961) which offers communication between each level of hierarchy and each team of administrators and teachers. For example, the school's leadership team links with the district office and the community, whereas team leaders communicate between the leadership team and the teachers. All staff members know someone who can communicate directly with the leadership, making for closeness, even in the face of the distance of hierarchy.

McPartland (1987) has shown how innovative middle schools can use simultaneously both the self-contained structure of the elementary school and the departmental structure of the secondary school for the benefit of students. The main advantage of the self-contained class is the fact that teachers can get to know the students well and therefore can respond effectively to their special needs. The main advantage of the departmentalized arrangement is that teachers can teach their specialty, thereby raising the quality of instruction and student achievement in that subject. The most innovative middle schools have tried to combine the self-contained and departmental structures into one. For example, semi-departmentalized, team-teaching arrangements are being used. One teacher offers instruction in science and math, while another teacher offers instruction in language arts and social studies. The two teachers work together as a team with about 50 students and run a home room and advisee groups together. Such a practice can offer high quality instruction from subject matter experts, while also addressing the individual needs of the students. Some more highly departmentalized middle schools have assigned a specific teacher or administrator to serve as an "advisor-advocate-mentor" to small groups of individual students.

Influence Positions of Teachers

Members of hierarchical organizations often feel powerless in relation to their authorities. In contrast, organizational members who become engaged in decision making can begin to feel more powerful and develop increased willingness to go along with organizational decisions. In many schools of a generation ago, the administrators made most organizational decisions. Now in the 1990s teacher empowerment has become an objective in many schools. The idea behind teacher empowerment is the concept that teachers will participate with the administrators in managing the school together. Research by Rosenholtz (1989) indicated that the satisfaction and effectiveness of teachers is associated with the teacher's perception of the extent to which he or she can influence the school's decision-making procedures.

In a classic study, prior to the excellent research by Rosenholtz, Hornstein et al. (1968) showed that teachers reported greatest satisfaction with their principal and the school district when they perceived that they and their principal were mutually influential and especially when their principal's influence was viewed as stemming from his or her expertise. As teachers feel more influential and begin to see their principal as an expert, they feel better about the school and manifest more emotional support in their contacts with students. As teachers become more engaged in school decision making, they take greater initiative in designing new programs for their own classrooms (particularly with "at-risk" students) and in getting feedback from other teachers before carrying their innovative plans to the principal.

As Rosenholtz showed, in schools with more equalized power relationships between administrators and teacher, the quality of teacher-student relationships in the classroom can also improve. And, as we summarized previously, Seeman and Seeman found that teachers' degree of dialogue, decision making, and action in school decisions were positively associated with the students' favorable attitudes. It appears as though, through participation in school affairs, teachers can exercise influence and in so doing are more likely to provide their own students with the positive feeling of power and responsibility.

Leadership Role of the Principal

The principal has the most potential influence in the school. Gross and Herriott (1965) in a nation-wide study of elementary principals, showed that principals' leadership influenced staff morale, innovativeness, professional performance, and student learning. They developed a concept to describe the principal's Leadership which they labeled Executive Professional Leadership (EPL). A principal's EPL score was determined by how much the teachers viewed their principal as being supportive, collaborative, and helpful to them.

Principals with high EPL scores: (1) had constructive suggestions for teachers about classroom problems; (2) displayed interest in improving quality of school programs; (3) gave teachers ideas about how to improve student achievement; and (4) made meetings a valuable educational event.

Although a national study on principal effectiveness has not been conducted recently, the role of the principal in leading faculties to maximize their effectiveness has captured center state. Principals are viewed as the single, most important element in the successful adoption of innovations, as instrumental in giving a school meaning and direction, and as providing continuous school improvement through staff development (see Leithwood and Montgomery, 1982, Blumberg and Greenfield, 1984, and Schmuck and Schmuck, 1990). In fact, the role of the principal has never before received so much attention as it has in the 1990s.

Contemporary ideas on the principal's role distinguish between leadership and management. The former is the principal bringing teachers, parents, and students into concerted and collaborative action to achieve increased student development. The latter is the principal seeing that the institutional standards set by boards and the law are carried out efficiently. Keirnes-Young (1986) found that principals who were effective leaders and managers executed four categories of activities: (1) *Action research*—the principals collecting evaluative data from teachers, parents, and students to study the outcomes of the school program; (2) *Social Architecture*—the principals communicating tactfully and effectively with teachers, parents, and students to bring all parties into collaboration and to help all parties to feel a part of the school; (3) *Staff Development*—the principals organizing programs through which teachers can develop new skills; and (4) *Political Strategy*—the principals bringing important, influential subgroups into collaboration and resolving conflicts that arise among them. Keirnes-Young's review explained that principals who can execute these four roles effectively are the leaders and managers of effective schools.

During the 1980s, there was considerable interest in how gender related to the principal's effective leadership. Previous research by Gross and Trask (1976) showed that female principals were more concerned than their male counterparts with curriculum, had staffs with higher morale, and tended to exert more influence in relation to their teachers. Later research by Shakeshaft (1987) also showed that women might be more effective school leaders than men. More research needs to be done in the 1990s on whether gender makes a significant difference in school leadership.

Although principals, whether female or male, have the single most powerful influence on a school's organizational processes, the teaching faculty as a collegial group also carries considerable influence. Chesler, Schmuck, and Lippitt (1963) found that while a teacher's willingness to try innovative practices depended on the principal's support of new projects, the support of the faculty was equally important. In schools where the principal was seen as supportive of innovation, but teachers were not, the influence of the principal was relatively unimportant. The faulty can and does undermine the principal's influence by dragging its heels and by sabotaging changes that do not meet with its approval.

Informal Organizational Climate

Climate refers to the affective states that pervade the group dynamics of the educators and students. It concerns how organizational participants relate to one another in terms of trust, openness, norms, social support, and cohesiveness. A school with a favorable climate has members who support one another in doing their best, share high amounts of influence, hold norms that are supportive of maximizing individual strengths, communicate openly and frequently, and consider developing together as growing professionals a cornerstone of their working as colleagues. Three important aspects of school climate are: (1) trust and openness of the staff; (2) norms held by staff members about the nature of human motivation; and (3) staff skills in communication and constructive openness.

Trust and Openness

If teachers possess feelings of comfort and rapport with colleagues, they also are supported in their feelings of self-worth and are better able to relate supportively to students. On the other hand, if teachers feel tense with other members of the faculty, they will tend to be "uptight" with their students. One good indicator of trust and openness is how often teachers ask one another to observe in their classrooms, as in peer coaching. Another is to watch for cues of teacher collaboration when they gather informally. Faculty lounges are settings that offer information about staff relationships. In some schools, there are taboos against discussing student related work, whereas in others, the faculty room may be the place teachers go to let off steam, get emotional support, or just to be let alone to unwind.

If fear, anxiety, and competition characterize staff relationships, creative teaching will not be encouraged, and constructive feedback among colleagues will not aim at collaborative efforts for improving classroom group processes. In schools where teachers compete or are antagonistic to one another, innovative classroom practices are the property of only one teacher, either because no one else knows about the ideas or because others are reluctant to "steal" the ideas for their own use. In schools where teachers trust and are open with one another, innovative ideas will be shared and teachers will support one another in their growth efforts. Trust and openness are the necessary underpinnings of peer coaching and collegial mentoring.

Norms About Human Motivation

McGregor (1967) distinguished between two conceptions of human motivation which he labeled "Theory X and Theory Y." Theory X stipulates that people are lazy and passive, and must be pushed and pulled to action. Theory Y argues that people are curious and active and should be allowed freedom to discover ways of doing things. Weisbord (1988) has described Theory X and Theory Y as an internal debate within a person or a group about human motivation. School staffs with Theory X orientations employ traditional leadership characterized by authoritarianism, one-way communication, and restrictive norms. Staffs with Theory Y orientations allow for more student freedom, are more collaborative, and employ more two-way communication. No matter how autonomous a classroom may be, it is part of a normative

context as well, and the teacher's classroom behavior will be influenced by the prevailing attitudes of the faculty.

Appleberry and Hoy (1969) have built on Willower's concepts of "humanistic" and "custodial" to describe educators' orientations to human motivation. Teachers who are custodial think of students as being in need of control and training because they lack responsibility and self-discipline. The school is seen by custodial teachers as being responsible for the students' actions and authority is seen as being appropriately hierarchical. In contrast, humanistic teachers view the school more like a community of human beings engaged in learning and development. They believe that power should be shared and that decisions should be made by those who are affected by them. In their research, Appleberry and Hoy found that faculties have high agreement about their custodial or humanistic assumptions and that these assumptions do influence how the school operates. "Open" schools have a prevailing humanistic norm, while "closed" schools are more custodial.

In related research, Swidler (1976) studied teachers' beliefs at two alternative high schools. She theorized that staffs of custodial schools would place high value on individualism and achievement; whereas, members of humanistic schools would place value on cooperative teaching and cooperative learning. The educators of the two humanistic schools Swidler studied valued egalitarian relationships with students, student autonomy, and self-direction. They resisted the traditional authority role of being the only evaluators of the students. As Goodlad (1984) emphasized, the "open," "free," or "alternative" schools of the 1980s have been formed out of humanistic assumptions about behavior, and those assumptions have resulted in some innovative organizational structures, particularly in middle schools.

Skills of Communication and Constructive Openness

Trust and openness will not by themselves guarantee that staff members will help one another become better teachers. Staff members must also be able to use the six communication skills presented in chapter 8. Teachers who are capable of carrying out such skills as paraphrasing with one another can more effectively do the same with their students.

Bigelow (1971), cited previously, showed that teachers who learned to use communication skills with one another during an organization development project also brought these skills into their classrooms. The teachers of the junior high that Bigelow studied transferred the collaborative teamwork they were experiencing with one another into cooperative learning in their classes. More recently, Johnson and Johnson (1990) have explained how cooperative activities among teachers can set the stage for teachers trying cooperative learning with their students.

Constructive openness, another important skill, is the art of giving feedback tactfully. One study looked at the effect of teacher feedback to the principal (Daw and Gage, 1967) and found favorable effects in changing the principal's behaviors when the feedback was given constructively and with the support of behavioral examples. Similar findings on feedback from student to teacher have also been obtained (see Gage,

Runkel, and Chatterjee, 1963, for data). Constructive openness carries the meaning of giving critical feedback to upgrade another person's role performance. It is best given by stressing both the strengths and the shortcomings of the other's performance. In a few schools where we have observed or worked, the use of constructive openness has become formalized. On a regular basis, the principal asks teachers for feedback, the teachers ask students for feedback, and the students ask their teachers for feedback. Each feedback exchange emphasizes both strengths and shortcomings.

Restructuring and Reform

A popular topic of the 1990s is restructuring the schools as part of a larger educational reform movement.

The reform reports (summarized by Lieberman, 1988) proclaim that we must restructure our schools by expanding teachers' participation in running the schools and by expecting decisions to be made more often at school sites rather than at the district office. Through empowering teachers, the reform reports argue, there will be a concomitant rise in teachers' professionalism. Such empowerment and professionalism will be fostered by enlightened school administrators who strive to encourage collegial problem solving and decision making among the teachers.

Eisner (1988) pointed to the barriers that keep teachers from collaborating with one another through collegial decision making. These barriers are not so much the authoritarianism of a traditional administration as they are the daily class schedule, the physical isolation of the classrooms, the structure of the curriculum, and the fragmentation of the school day. Tye (1987) referred to these common characteristics of the school as the "deep structure of schooling," and was not optimistic about changing them. Rosenholtz (1989), on the other hand, presented data to show that innovative and democratically oriented school principals can alter traditional teacher isolation by using techniques and practices of participatory management and organization development. She pointed out that collaborative relationships among teachers entail mutual goals among them, individuals caring for one another, helpful exchanges between them, and joint planning and evaluation of the curriculum. All of these processes can be created and facilitated by the principal.

Gladder (1990) intensively studied two senior high schools which were intentionally restructuring to achieve more collegial interaction among the teachers. Her results showed that seven conditions constrained teacher collaboration: (1) *The class schedule,* i.e., the teachers were organized by discrete, subject-matter disciplines and the day was divided into 50-minute segments; (2) *The physical facilities,* i.e, the teachers mostly saw and talked with their departmental colleagues; (3) *Too little time* for collaborative problem solving and decision making; (4) *Group norms of privacy and isolation,* a culture in which teachers believed that they alone were responsible for running their classes; (5) *The primary teacher rewards* came from students and administrators and not from colleagues; (6) *Teacher autonomy* to make decisions about how they would spend their planning periods was lacking; and (7) *Being congenial* meant to teachers *not interfering* with the work of a colleague.

In her conversations with the teachers, Gladder found that real teacher influence, and not just participation, was the key to the restructuring having a positive impact on the teachers. Gladder wrote, "Those teachers who collected and analyzed data about student achievement, selected the major problems, and then developed plans to tackle the problems appeared to be more committed to the school improvement plans than other teachers." Thus, teachers who felt *truly empowered* also took more workshops together, found more time to discuss new ideas with one another, and used more of their individual planning time to get together for group projects. In contrast, teachers who were asked to participate in discussions about school improvement but who did not really influence school goals and procedures did *not* feel committed to school improvement plans. Even though in large high schools it is difficult to engage 75–100 teachers in meaningful influence over school-wide decisions, there are some creative things that were being done in the two schools Gladder studied.

First, teachers from each department can be put on task forces to collect and analyze data about the students. The data are used by these teachers to pinpoint problems to work on for school improvement. The teachers themselves not only decide on the problem to solve but also come up with the solutions. Sometimes the teachers' solution might be to bring an expert to the school for a special training event. Under those circumstances, the participating teachers are much more likely to learn alternative practices than they would be if the administration had initiated the training without the teachers' influence.

Second, teachers can be paired off voluntarily to work together on improving their teaching. The key to success here is getting the teachers actually to observe each other teach. Once that happens, trust and support develops between them, and they will more openly discuss ways in which they would like to improve. Time for meeting in pairs or in task forces can be gleaned from creatively scheduling the traditional day. By working closely with their community, the principals of Gladder's two schools were able to change their schools' schedules one day a week so that teachers could meet together first thing in the morning for 45 minutes. Also, in one of the schools, the schedule could be arranged so that task forces and pairs had common planning periods or lunch periods when meeting time would be available.

Third, incentives can be given to teachers who will work collaboratively on school improvement. At one school, for example, small groups of teachers who would develop joint proposals for innovative curricula were granted money to attend workshops and to observe in schools where similar curriculum innovations were being tried. At another school, pairs of teachers who worked out a plan for regularly observing each other teach were granted extra time for planning and debriefing during the day. (It should be noted, however, that administrative rewards can backfire, particularly if the teachers who do *not* receive them think that they were unfairly distributed by the principal. Administrators can overcome that problem by having the teachers decide on how rewards will be distributed.)

Fourth, the teachers, themselves, can be given the responsibility for creating ways in which they can work together more collaboratively. Some possibilities are teachers agreeing to free up one of their colleagues by taking additional students for a period or two or teachers working together to design and implement a special workshop for their colleagues.

The School Organization and Student Reactions

Those who argue for school restructuring implicitly believe that there is a causal relationship between the quality of interpersonal relations among staff members and the ways teachers behave toward students in the classroom. A typical argument might go as follows:

When teachers collaborate with their principal and colleagues in setting goals and planning new actions, they begin to feel empowered as teachers, and their professional self-concepts and commitment become increasingly more favorable. Moreover, when teachers become more interdependent with one another, they can more effectively use the skill of constructive openness, thereby improving their teaching techniques through the giving and receiving of feedback. The prototype of such an exchange of feedback, nowadays, occurs in peer coaching. As teachers feel more self-worth and freedom to experiment with new classroom behaviors, they come to show more emotional support, understanding, and compassion for students. The students, in turn, feel better about themselves and put increased effort into learning.

Lewin's classical theory (1948) is useful for tracing the social-psychological link between school and student. He argued that behavior is caused by a concatenation of the person's perceptions of the environment and the person's personality structure. His theory was expressed as an equation:

Behavior = F(E and P), where F stood for function of, E stood for environment, and P stood for person. We see the school's structure and climate as offering stimuli for the E (environment), whereas the student's motives, attitudes, cognitions, and values constitute features of the P (personality).

Environmental Stimuli

The sociological and the internal organizational aspects of the school set the stage for the environment that the student experiences. Those distal stimuli combine to present several important proximal environmental stimuli that affect students' orientations to learning: *size of classes and the use of cooperative groups within them, consistency across classes, staff norms, and teacher expectations.*

Hare (1977) summarized a large number of studies, indicating that as group size decreases, the strength of friendship increases. His summary showed that teams of five or six members constitute the optimal number for getting tasks accomplished and for performing productively. Many classes are too large to be effectively supportive environments. That was shown clearly in the SAFE school study of the National Institute of Education (1977), which came up with the disturbing result that as class sizes rose, so did the risk of being attacked and robbed in the school. Small size alone, however, does not guarantee that friendly relationships will be pervasive in a class. In our study of classes in small town districts (see Schmuck and Schmuck, 1990, for data), we did not find many exemplary instances of emotional support in high

school classes, even among those as small as twelve students. It is really up to the teachers to build a positive classroom climate, regardless of its size.

As we have shown in the previous chapters of this text, teachers can create "smallness" out of "bigness" by either individualizing instruction so that students feel in tune with their cognitive development, or by establishing learning teams of two to six so that support for learning becomes possible. Moreover, through supporting cooperative behavior and through confronting subgroup and total class disruptions, teachers can establish a dispersed, informal support system within the peer group.

A problem that can arise as a result of a teacher's success in constructing a small group atmosphere in a large school is inconsistency across classrooms. This can be particularly troublesome in schools where students frequently move from one room to another. The inconsistencies of structure and procedures across classes, not to mention the differing leadership styles of teachers, can present a bewildering diversity for the adolescent. Psychological dissonance can be an outcome for the student, leading some students to feel mistrustful and alienated from certain teachers. In our recent study of small town schools (see Schmuck and Schmuck, 1991) high school students estimated that about 30% of their teachers were not trying to build emotionally supportive atmospheres in their classes.

Differences between classes can be understood also by the reinforcement patterns executed by the teacher and by the students' peers. Such differences can be more or less significant from one school to the others. As Dreeben (1968), Swidler

(1976), and Goodlad (1984) have shown, student behavior, reinforced by teachers and peers, can range from independence to collaboration and from rejection to acceptance. Moreover, as Seeman and Seeman (1976) indicated, teachers who are an integral part of the school's formal influence structure, as in contemporary attempts at restructuring, will tend to communicate more support for students than teachers who are removed from influence processes of the staff. Unfortunately, even the best of teacher intentions and the most skillful teaching might lead to a discouraging, overall situation for students when this occurs in a school where most of the teachers are performing differently. The impact of inconsistency and the attendant dissonance can, particularly for students who are insecure, discourage them from making an effort to learn.

The interpersonal aspects of staff norms and teacher expectations constitute another set of environmental stimuli for the students. Students who perceive their teachers cooperating will be more likely to want to cooperate with one another. And students are particularly sensitive to their teachers' expectations. Consider some of the following sample statements that we heard teachers express while we were touring schools in small towns in 1989:

"Don't start on your papers until I give instructions; many of you will do it wrong anyway," or, "I will have to watch the two of you very closely during the test," or, "This is a very difficult story; only a few of you will understand it. But let's try it anyway."

Of course, when teachers and peers come to share the same expectations for particular students, those expectations become very powerful indeed.

Personal Attributes

As the Lewinian theory states, behaviors are functions of environmental stimuli and personal attributes. About the latter, we find it useful to view students as possessing a master motive to strive for self-esteem and self-respect. Thus, we expect students either to seek a favorable perception of themselves as students or to devalue their role, making being a student an unimportant part of their self-concept.

We theorize from our experience and others' research that striving for self-esteem takes place in at least three motivational domains: *achievement and competence, power and influence,* and *affiliation and security.* Typical frustrations of these motives in school lead students to feelings of inferiority, powerlessness, and insecurity. These three negative conditions do not facilitate effective learning and achievement. Environmental stimuli that influence these three motives constitute ways in which the school organization can have direct impact on student academic performance.

Although the psychodynamics of student learning are very complex, it appears clear that organizational life and student learning are in some ways interrelated. Students perceive the conditions of their school organization as expectancies, incentives, reinforcement patterns, demands, and requests. Their responses to those influences depend on the congruence between their perceptions of the environmental stimuli and their needs for achievement, power, and affiliation. Wherever students can exercise initiative or have a choice in reorganizing teachers' behaviors to fit their own motives, the more likely it will be that the school environment becomes congruent with students' personal attributes, thereby facilitating learning.

The Innovativeness of the School

For schools and students to be in tune with one another, the schools must have the capacity to change themselves. A school's capacity for innovation is its ability to accept, adapt, restructure, and reject the new instructional ideas in education that are continually produced. The criterion used to judge the school's innovation is to ask, "To what extent do new instructional ideas facilitate student learning?" Contemporary interest in site-based management will result in more school innovation during the 1990s.

The roots of our concern today with site-based management go back 30 years. In the middle 1960s and soon after the classic publication of Halpin and Croft (1963) on school climate, R. Lippitt and colleagues at the University of Michigan carried out a large study of thirty schools to explore the relationships between organizational climate and school innovation. In one part of that study, Chesler, Schmuck, and Lippitt (1963) found that in schools where teachers competed with one another for the principal's favor, very little problem solving to improve instruction was being carried out. On the other hand, in schools where the teachers felt support from both the principal and from one another, teachers were more likely to share new ideas about instruction and to try out more creative classroom practices.

In another part of that study (Lippitt et al., 1967), the Michigan researchers noted that certain characteristics distinguished innovative schools from their less

innovative counterparts. The affective connections among teachers in innovative schools depended on (1) the teachers having sufficient time to meet together regularly, (2) cooperative work among all the staff, (3) group norms in support of teachers discussing instructional problems with one another, and (4) collaboration between the principal and groups of teachers in problem solving.

After the Michigan study, R. Schmuck and P. Runkel carried out a field experiment with a junior high school in Oregon to see if they could intervene to improve school climate and enhance teacher innovation. They spent twelve days over one school year training a staff of 60 to carry out cooperative problem solving about organizational and instructional concerns voted on by the staff. The training (see Schmuck and Runkel, 1970 and 1988) began with communication skills, moved through strengthening constructive-openness norms in teacher groups, emphasized problem solving to improve climate, and culminated with new organizational structures for staff communication about instruction. Evaluative data indicated that the school's climate did improve and that a number of innovations were tried by over half of the teachers. In particular, many new interdisciplinary projects with students were initiated by the teachers.

In a survey study, Hilfiker (1970) explored variables associated with district climate and how those variables related to teacher innovation. His statistical analyses showed that the most significant climatic conditions for innovation were not in the district at large, but in the individual school sites. The important variables were: (1) the social support provided by the principal, as perceived by the teachers; (2) the teachers' perceptions of the problem-solving adequacy of staff meetings; (3) the teachers' satisfaction with the time devoted to problem solving at staff meetings; and (4) the teachers' and principals' perceptions of openness, trust, and shared decision making as legitimate norms in the school.

Hilfiker's conclusions are just as appropriate today as they were over 20 years ago. He wrote that "the effectiveness of an organization is dependent on the ability of the members to solve problems together. If time spent in professional meetings is perceived by participants as a waste of time or if participants have a sense of 'going through the motions' or if people feel powerless to make adjustments in the system, then the problem-solving potential of professional meetings may be adversely affected." Hilfiker's data demonstrated the important role of the principal in initiating and maintaining a climate supportive of group problem solving, in running useful meetings, and in encouraging an atmosphere of trust.

Thomas (1973) came up with research results in Australia very similar to Hilfiker's. Thomas assessed school innovation by obtaining ratings from curricular experts, school administrators, and teachers; he used Halpin and Croft's "Organizational Climate Description Questionnaire" to assess school climate. His analyses revealed that the more innovative schools had: (1) staffs who perceived their principals to be supportive and accepting of individual variations among teachers; (2) staffs with high amounts of collegial trust and openness; and (3) principals who were not authoritarian and who did not supervise their teachers closely. Thomas concluded that authoritarian principals do not build collaborative

structures or faculty norms in support of schoolwide problem solving and instructional innovation. Our view of Thomas's findings today, seen in the light of current interest in site-based management, would also argue that authoritarian principals do not facilitate feelings of teacher empowerment; indeed, they work against them.

Throughout the 1970s and 1980s, Schmuck and Runkel (1988) worked on creating strategies for site-based management, democratic leadership, and teacher empowerment. The concepts and techniques that they created and tested are known as *organization development.*

Organization Development in Schools

Organization development (OD) is an intervention strategy to help school participants become more collaborative so that they can manage the school cooperatively. Its goal is to provide tools for teachers and administrators to improve their own school programs. Schmuck and Miles (1977) first defined OD in schools as " a planned and sustained effort to apply behavioral science for system improvement using self-analytic methods." The OD process engages the system members themselves in the active assessment, diagnosis, and transformation of their own group or organization.

Organization-Development Concepts

A school's effectiveness may be defined by how completely its resources are used for student learning. The typical strategy for promoting student learning has focused on improving curriculum and instruction within the classroom. A focus on the classroom can lose sight of the relevance of the school's culture as an important variable in student learning. A focus on classrooms accepts the culture of the staff as it presents itself, rather than seeing it, too, as a focus for improvement.

We have defined classroom climate as the many group processes working simultaneously to create a supportive or an unsupportive learning environment. Likewise, organizational climate denotes the interpersonal and group processes that facilitate or restrain academic productivity and supportive relationships among staff members for instructional innovation. OD offers a program of intervention into the whole social system of which administrators, teachers and students are a part. A supportive climate for the school's participants would include dispersed influence and friendship structures within the staff, supportive norms for trying new ideas, clear communication, workable goals, and agreed-upon strategies for cooperative problem solving and decision making.

Some critics of our schools have sought to emphasize the inferior nature of contemporary students and neophyte administrators and teachers in explaining the current weaknesses of our schools. In so doing, they have ignored the quality of the group dynamics and organizational climate of the school's participants. For instance, academically ill-equipped youngsters or poorly prepared teachers are often held responsible for the failings of our schools. Other inferior aspects focused upon are inadequate curriculum materials, poor teaching aids, and inadequate physical conditions of the classroom and school. All of these "incoming resources" are important to a school's success; however, improvements in

these items alone cannot solve the problems of our schools today. It is the social interaction of students, teachers, and administrators in all their various subgroups which determines how well the students will learn.

The energies of administrators are being spent inappropriately if they are focused primarily on improving the incoming resources to the school. Naturally, administrators must try to hire the best new teachers, but they should be even more concerned with how the teachers they now have work together.

Two examples of the inefficient use of a school's resources come to mind. Administrators often order curriculum materials that are stored in a closet or at the district office. Retrieval of these materials presents a difficult problem for teachers who lack time to browse through storerooms. Many expensive items go unused. This nonuse of curriculum resources might be altered, however, by collaborative staff planning and by administrator-teacher conferences focused on instructional improvement.

Another example of the inefficient use of school resources is the acollaborative norms often present in faculties. Teachers who are carrying out exciting and successful activities often are reluctant to tell their colleagues about their successes. Other teachers are reluctant to "steal" another's ideas. Still others are too busy to meet. In many schools we visited during the last few years, staff meetings typically did not provide time for teachers to discuss with one another their classroom practices. Such ineffective staff practices need not be inevitable by-products of school culture. The school culture itself can be a target of change. School faculties can alter their culture through organization-development techniques.

Organization-Development Strategy

OD, as delineated by Schmuck and Runkel (1988), aims at helping school participants to manage their school collaboratively. It focuses on improving the participants' communication and meeting skills and on their learning together to carry out goal setting, problem solving, action planning, and decision making. It strives to help school participants develop the shared skills, norms, roles, procedures, and structures that will enable them to change their modes of operating in order to enhance student learning.

There are five guiding principles in an OD strategy. First, the OD will be more effective if it is carried out with all members of a team, department, or school, rather than with individual educators who do not work together closely. By all members of a team, department, or school receiving the OD together, all key participants can see that their colleagues are accepting new group norms and new patterns of interaction and are truly acting upon them.

Second, OD should generate valid data for the members of the school about how their organization works. The data should deal with the staff's own internal organizational processes, thus offering the staff members a mirror for viewing themselves clearly as a functioning unit.

Third, discrepancies between the current achievement of the school and the school's performance goals are used as leverage points for change. The goals for a school are, of course, set by the school members themselves. The OD specialists do not determine the school's goals, but typically student learning is a central goal. By comparing goals to data on how things actually are in the school, dissonance is created which can motivate the participants to change their modes of operating.

Fourth, OD makes use of the available resources that already exist within a school to solve problems and develop new plans. The OD process does not offer ready-made solutions, but rather presents procedures for helping participants to think of a number of alternatives for their operations in the present and the future as well as helping people to develop plans of action to implement these alternatives.

Fifth, it is important that the OD include an outsider who facilitates the consultation. An outside person has a higher likelihood of being neutral and objective, while a subsystem participant already has been too involved in the ongoing group processes to offer a dispassionate point of view. Also, it is preferable for the OD outsider to work as part of an intervention team, rather than alone. An effective consulting team can be more accurate and creative in assessing problems and in helping participants develop alternative styles of operating than can any single individual. The OD outsiders take the role of organization development specialists.

The Organization Development Specialist

OD specialists, those who guide consultation in Organization Development, are typically found in industries, university settings, private consulting firms, and school districts. Counselors and school psychologists are often in key positions within school districts to act as OD specialists. Many counselors and psychologists have already developed the skills to facilitate groups and are often in a position to remain objective about the group processes of school organization. For these reasons, we will focus primarily on the counselor and the school psychologist as role-takers who can appropriately function as OD specialists within school districts.

Lighthall (1969) suggests that psychological specialists in schools should direct their energies toward defining and solving problems, "between people, between roles, and between pockets of friendship, familiarity, and high-frequency communication" rather than defining problems located solely *within* individuals. Lighthall outlines a matrix of nine elements of a school's social system which include staff, classroom, and school groups, and has developed a plan for training that he refers to as *social psychologists for school systems.*

Counselors and psychologists, however, are not the only people who can facilitate consultation in schools. Administrators and teachers have also worked successfully as OD specialists. Indeed, clusters of various types of professional educators can constitute a very strong OD team (for more details, see chapter 12 in Schmuck and Runkel, 1988).

OD Specialists as Internal Process Consultants

There are primarily three ways in which the counselor or psychologist of a particular school, performing as an OD specialist, can strengthen the organizational health of his or her school. All three of these types of consultation share some of the benefits of objectivity of the external consultant because they entail serving as a disinterested, third-party consultant.

1. Consulting with staff groups. The psychologist-counselor can serve as a process consultant during faculty meetings, observing the group in action, giving it feedback as to how it is functioning, helping the group to check out how the members feel, and leading the group in discussions about its norms and methods of operating.

Such consultants as the psychologist-counselor can encourage the airing of problems and conflicts which would probably remain hidden. These consultants can also help the group to discuss its communication patterns, problem-solving competencies, and decision-making procedures. Most important, process consultants teach members of a group to carry on their own diagnoses and to discuss their own processes of work, even when the consultants are not present.

In most schools, the principal serves as the convener of staff meetings. Although some principals can conduct group discussions effectively, we have found that a large number of principals do not have effective meeting skills. Group meetings can sometimes be improved by assigning the role of convener to other staff members on a rotational basis. Also, the group might ask for an OD specialist to serve for a short period as a process consultant to the group. The process consultant, in this case, might also serve once a week as a coach to the new convener. Counselors and school psychologists can serve as effective process consultants as long as they can remain detached from the major substantive concerns of the meeting. For elaboration on these points, see Schmuck and Runkel (1988).

2. Consulting with classroom groups. Another way that OD specialists can help to improve a school's interpersonal processes is by serving as process consultants to classroom groups. In this sort of consultation, the client is the entire learning group (not just the teacher), and the target is the improvement of the group climate by making use of many of the ideas and activities presented earlier in this book. Although we have aimed this book primarily at the classroom teacher, the counselor or school psychologist could use its contents with teachers—in workshops, for example—to improve their classroom group skills. The book could also serve as a basis for consulting with classroom groups.

By employing such consultative techniques as observation and feedback, communication skills, simulations, games, and innovative procedures, the consultant strives to help the class improve on group issues such as clarifying expectations, dispersing leadership, increasing attraction, establishing supportive norms, clarifying communications, and increasing cohesiveness. Vacha, McDonald, Coburn, and Black (1977) have developed an effective strategy, cluster of techniques, and instructional materials for consulting with classroom groups.

3. Consulting with school groups. More consultations to improve the systems functioning of schools have been aimed either at the staff or at the classroom. There is now considerable interest, however, in bringing students and teachers into more effective collaboration, especially concerning the development of educational alternatives and individualization of instruction.

Some staffs have tried to involve students in important decisions about how the school will operate, only to face frustration and disappointment with the low amount of interest shown by the students and the low amount of skill that both the teachers and

the students can muster in working together. We do not find this situation surprising. For students to become integrally engaged in a school's decision-making, it will take a considerable amount of planning, training, and relearning about the responsibility of a student in relation to faculty members.

To change a traditionally organized student government, for example, from a rubber-stamp council dealing with inconsequential matters to a fully functioning, interdependent body in relation to the faculty will take considerable time and know-how. In a like manner, teachers need to develop skills, norms, and structures to support new ways of interacting with students. The OD specialist can serve as a consultant to a staff-student group to help improve its communication skills, to develop diagnostic competencies, and to develop norms of constructive openness. The OD specialist might also serve as a process consultant in meetings to which students, teachers, and administrators are brought to work on real issues and concerns. We have written about engaging students in school-wide matters elsewhere (see Schmuck and Schmuck, 1991).

Counselors as Internal Process Consultants

The following is a case example of a counselor functioning as a process consultant inside the school. The sixth-grade teachers in an elementary school referred a few of their students to the counselor because of some acts of vandalism in the school. The amount of anger and irritation presented by the teachers over these acts and the counselor's suspicion that the problem involved more than merely a few random behaviors of vandalism prompted him to look further. He decided the issue entailed the sixth grades as classroom groups and their mode of operating as groups, rather than just a disciplinary issue concerning a handful of students.

In starting the consultation, the counselor interviewed the sixth-grade teachers, several students (some of those ostensibly involved in the vandalism), the principal, one cook, and the custodian to assess the nature and the magnitude of the problem. He organized a planning committee made up of some of the teachers, a few students, and the custodian (whom the counselor had discovered was involved in the problem). This committee met three times. At the first meeting, they discussed the vandalism, deciding, as they did so, that they did not have sufficient information about how the teachers, students, and principal viewed the locus of responsibility.

After the counselor collected more data, a second meeting was held to review the data and stake out action plans. The counselor discovered that almost everyone perceived the students as being responsible. He also found that the students felt that they acted out of frustration and on impulse and that they felt the teachers and principals were not listening to their concerns. The committee decided to try a two-day conference for the sixth-grade classes in order to arrive at some solutions. The committee met with the sixth grades to outline their findings and their recommendations.

The two-day conference included the teachers, students, the custodian, and, at times, the principal. The counselor served as convener and process consultant. The workshop involved learning about communication skills, cooperation in groups, and group discussion skills. Next, the counselor presented the data he had collected during the sessions. The data were used on the last day of the conference as part of a problem-solving sequence. The problem solving dealt specifically with vandalism. As a result, some minor punishment was suggested for the offenders, objectives and procedures were set up to prevent future problems of vandalism, and several plans of action involving communications among the principal, custodian, and students were decided upon.

The planning committee met one more time to design a half-day, follow-up session to determine if the action plans were being executed and how they were working out. Before the half-day session, the committee members interviewed students, teachers, the principal, and the custodian. Data from the interviews were presented to the entire body at the session. Toward the end of that session, it was decided to institute a full time planning group which would meet once a month to determine whether other problems were arising and to develop ways of working on such problems before they became too difficult to manage.

OD Specialist as Member of an External Team

Another way in which a psychologist or counselor can perform as an OD specialist is as the member of an intervention team which consults with another school in the district or in a nearby district. Cadres of OD specialists can be constituted not only of school psychologists and counselors but also of teachers, principals, curriculum specialists, and assistant superintendents. Each cadre member receives training in such substantive topics as communication, effective meetings, conflict and interdependence, problem solving, and decision making, as well as receiving a supervised practicum and lengthy education in the theory and research on organizations. Counselors and psychologists can be invaluable members of cadres, bringing to the discussions their knowledge of social psychology and group dynamics, previous roles as third-party members between teachers and students, and skills in interpersonal communication and conflict. For a detailed overview of how counselors, teachers, and administrators can work together successfully in an OD cadre, see Schmuck (1990).

Principals as External Process Consultants

Eileen Breckenridge (1976), an elementary level teacher, provides an exciting and detailed description of her school's attempt to improve climate. She describes her school:

> We had a fine reputation springing from an open building design and the innovative ways teachers were using space and materials. Our principal had many years of experience in guiding the educational process. Families moved into our neighborhood because of the school. Teachers from other schools came to observe our program.

Yet she noted that underneath the facade of excellence, something was seriously wrong. Rumor mongering among the staff, poor student attitudes, fights on the playground, and a principal who ran a tight ship that everyone secretly complained about were among the realities of this seemingly "outstanding" school.

The yearly inservice workshop was to feature the topic of "Climate Control." Ms. Breckenridge approached it with some dubiousness:

> Here, I thought, would be another so-called 'inspirational session' which would cost me a precious weekend, earn a unit of in-service credit I didn't need, and accomplish nothing. I didn't believe a problem in interpersonal relations such as existed in such complexity at my school could or would be solved in a weekend. I went to the Friday evening session because Mr. Jefferson had told us he expected all of his 'crew' would be 'on board' for the workshop.

Bill Maynard, a principal in another state, was the workshop convener and opened the meeting by discussing his own school and showing "before and after" slides of the changes. Then he guided the workshop through a modified brainstorming procedure, asking every participant to list privately all of his or her concerns about the school. People met in small groups to combine lists which were then read out loud and recorded.

Thirty-two items of staff concern were read and posted. Some examples of items included: (1) Tension exists between teachers and the principal: (a) problems are dismissed as indicating a "negative attitude"; (b) people are not free to express their opinions; (c) the organization of the school is top-heavy; the principal exercises too much authority. (2) Staff meetings are too long and accomplish little; there is need for a problem-solving orientation in these meetings. (3) There is too much competition, backbiting, and lack of self-evaluation among teachers. (4) Special education teachers need a classroom instead of a closet. (5) Unqualified people are making decisions about purchases and schedules. (6) There is too much hostility, alienation, and violence among the students. (7) Hot lunches are often cold and unnutritious. (8) Washrooms are dirty.

Then the staff members rank-ordered their concerns and ten items were selected for problem solving. Ms. Breckenridge describes the tenor of that process:

> I looked around the room as the final tallies were being called off. It had become very quiet. All the bustle of counting little slips of paper, all the casual chatter at each table had ended. It was a moment of truth. Mr. Jefferson was pale. He was fingering his mustache nervously. Clearly, in setting up a workshop to get at school problems he had not anticipated that *he* would turn out to be the number one problem.

Ten groups were assigned, each to deal with one problem. These groups used a problem-solving procedure requiring each of them to clarify the problem, list indicators that the problem existed, rewrite and refine the problem, develop an action plan to change the negative conditions, and make provisions for evaluation and feedback. Later, all the groups reported back with recommendations for the specific steps to be taken in the future. One very significant action plan called for a commitment by the principal to be more approachable and to set a daily time for teachers to talk with him.

> The workshop ended and the school week began. We had made a beginning, but I wondered if anything would come

of it. What if no one approached Mr. Jefferson during his new open hours? What if he didn't listen to someone who did? There were many ways this grand sounding program could fail in its birth struggles. . . . Back at school the following week, we planned a teacher-initiated staff meeting devoted to clarifying the continuation of our climate-control commitment. We began by electing Eric chairman. He had a few suggestions. 'Now is the time it can all die,' he warned. 'We have to be dedicated—now—to be sure it doesn't.'

It didn't die and kept growing and growing, and small changes occurred.

> One afternoon the PE teacher dropped by my classroom on an errand. 'I always like to visit your room,' she remarked. 'It seems like such an exciting place for kids.' I treasured those words of praise for a long time and tried to return the favor. I began to take time to notice and praise the efforts of my co-teachers. It was a contagious idea. Gradually, but definitely, such actions became a way of life for our staff.

In May a potluck dinner was arranged to assess "climate control" efforts. One parent commented, "It's the best school year we've ever had. What made it so?"

Ms. Breckenridge concludes:

> Only a few of the original thirty-two items remain as goals for next year. . . . We do not feel that we will ever reach a point where we can claim an atmosphere of openness and trust will not require constant attention. We will need to pass on to new staff members the strength and direction of our commitments. We have changed from a fragmented society to a

close-knit, family-like group—and we intend to make sure that the change is permanent.

It is important to note that the process consultant for this project was also an experienced site administrator. As a school principal, he had empathy for Mr. Jefferson and was able to build good rapport with him. This was a significant key to the success of the project.

School Psychologists as Members of an External OD Team

The coordinator of a cadre of OD specialists in a school district was asked by the principal and the cabinet of a junior high school to carry out an OD project with the entire faculty. The coordinator asked two teachers, a principal, and a school psychologist to constitute the external consultant team. The team designed and implemented the following three major training events.

The First Event

Training began with a six-day laboratory in late August. Almost the entire building staff was present to participate. The fifty-four trainees included all the administrators, all but two of the faculty, the head cook, head custodian, and head secretary. During the first two days, time was spent in group and intergroup exercises designed to increase awareness of interpersonal and organizational processes, e.g., the NASA trip-to-the-moon exercise, the five square puzzle, and planners and operators (see Schmuck and Runkel 1988, for details). Although these exercises were like games, they demonstrated the importance of effective communication for accomplishing a task

collaboratively. After each exercise, the school psychologist and her consulting colleagues lead discussions in small faculty groups. They talked about ways in which the experience was similar, or not similar, to what usually happened in their relations with one another in the school. All staff members then pooled their experiences and analyzed their relationships as a faculty. The OD specialists supported openness in giving and receiving feedback about perceptions of real organizational processes in the school.

During the last four days of the six-day laboratory, the faculty went through a problem-solving sequence, working on real issues that were thwarting the school's organizational functioning. After a morning of discussion and decisions (on the third day) which also served as practice in decision-making skills, three significant problems emerged. Each of three problems was assigned to one group, who followed a five-step procedure: (1) specifying the problem through behavioral description; (2) further defining the problem by diagnostic force-field analysis; (3) brainstorming to find actions likely to reduce restraining forces; (4) designing a concrete plan of action; and (5) trying out the plan behaviorally through a simulation with the entire staff. Each group worked on its own for the most part. The OD specialists served as group facilitators, rarely providing substantive suggestions and never pressing for results.

This first training event culminated with a discussion to highlight the resources of the staff. Members described their own strengths and those of their colleagues. Finally, they discussed what their school could be like if all the faculty's strengths were actually being used.

The Second Event

Early in the fall, the school psychologist and her consultant-colleagues interviewed all faculty members and observed several committees and subject-area groups to determine what uses they were making of the initial training. The data indicated that problems which remained unresolved were closely related to misunderstandings in communication, the overload of duties in some jobs, and difficulties that the work groups were having in using the problem-solving procedures effectively.

During the second intervention—held for one-and-a-half days several weeks before Christmas—the OD specialists focused on those three problems. They also explored additional ways for department heads to serve as communication links between the teachers and the administrators, to increase problem-solving skills of the departmental groups, to help the faculty explore ways of reducing the burden of duties on some staff members, and to increase effective communication between the service personnel and the rest of the staff.

The Third Event

This training event also lasted one-and-a-half days and took place several weeks before spring vacation. The main objective was to evaluate staff progress in solving the problems of resource use, role clarity, and staff participation. Another objective was to revivify any lagging group skills. Faculty members tried to devise ways to halt the cases of "backsliding" by modifying the school's procedures. They continued with those activities in departmental groups during the remainder of the spring term without the OD specialists.

Students as Organizational Participants

OD consultants have been shortsighted in not treating students as organizational participants during OD. Indeed, the theory and practice of OD only rarely has given weight to students as part of the client group. OD consultants, along with adult clients, typically have regarded students as products of the educational system to be acted upon and shaped as juveniles (not yet responsible citizens) who need to be controlled or protected, or as consumers who occasionally wish to express their reactions and preferences. Seldom have consultants, educators, or parents viewed students as full-fledged, organizational members who do, can, or should participate in school planning, problem solving, or decision making.

There are at least five advantages to student leaders participating with teachers in problem solving and decision making in a school: (1) Overcoming the generation-gap between adolescents and adults; (2) Improving the climate of relationships in the hallways, lunchroom, and playground; (3) Helping to resolve conflicts between students and between students and the adult educators; (4) Enhancing the self-esteem and self-confidence of the student leaders themselves; and (5) Creating a democratic and human school community in which the school becomes everybody's house.

It is important, too, to point out that adult efforts at school change can falter when students intentionally or unconsciously sabotage attempts by the professionals to work in new ways together. For example, we have consulted with elementary staffs that were attempting to move from a self-contained structure to team teaching. In a few of these schools, the students' expectations to have their own homeroom teacher were so strong that they resisted going along with the teachers' efforts at individualizing instruction and platooning the students into various groups. In another instance, we worked in secondary schools in which the staff's plans for student government went awry because of student apathy.

An explanation for students' sabotaging school improvement efforts might be the failure to adhere to a fundamental tenet of OD, which argues that consultation should be provided to important, intact subsystems of the school—to groups of role-takers who perform important tasks or sets of related, interdependent tasks. Since students outnumber adults by a substantial margin, many of the most important subsystems—classrooms, for example—have mostly student members. By virtue of excluding students from the set of organizational participants, consultants and their adult clients can have difficulties uncovering and managing important problems with the way work gets accomplished in the school. OD consultants have been unable to gain access to students' views about how the school functions and affects them, while teachers and administrators have been unable to predict how students will react to their plans.

What can go wrong? Teachers and administrators can become so preoccupied with their own work and responsibilities that they begin to exhibit insensitivity to students' preferences and experiences. Consultants, too, can concentrate so much on the adults that they get sidetracked from improving the quality of education for students. Teachers also can feel powerless to discipline students and burdened by the extent of the responsibilities they have assumed. Students can feel put down by imposed rules and become alienated when their ideas and energies have not been used.

In some schools, particularly in urban schools, alienation of adults from other adults and from students can be very high and can hinder learning. Moreover, within and across the different age groups that participate in schools, we have noted a correlation between alienation and mediocre performance. Even in rural schools, teachers, administrators, students, and consultants alike have sought the lowest common denominator to avoid debilitating and unproductive disagreement over different values.

We are not suggesting that obstacles to school improvement can be solved easily by bringing students in as full-fledged, organizational participants. We have to admit that student involvement in OD is largely untried, and that consultants, teachers, and administrators lack experiences upon which to ground collaborative work with students. We offer these comments on students as organizational participants, along with the action ideas delineated below, to raise a challenge for our schools. We look forward to a time when working to improve group processes in the classroom and in the school will receive equal billing from educators.

Implications for Teachers

The following statements summarize the most important implications in this chapter for teachers.

Classroom group processes can be influenced by aspects of the school organization. These are the factors of size, socio-economic character, and peer group norms, along with the internal organizational processes entailing both formal and informal aspects of group life in the school.

The formal variables that influence what transpires in classrooms are the complexity of roles, the influence positions of teachers, and the leadership role of the principal; while aspects of the informal organizational climate that influence classrooms are trust and openness, norms about human motivation, and skills in communication and constructive openness.

Teachers who seek to ameliorate problems in the group processes of their classrooms may face obstacles because of the strength of many of these organizational variables, but collaborative action on the part of teachers and administrators can lead to change in the variables.

Students are influenced by the school organization through ways in which their perceptions of bigness, consistency across classes, staff norms, and teacher expectations dovetail with their personal needs for achievement, affiliation, and power.

Aspects of the school organization also influence students by either supporting or inhibiting innovative programs of instruction. When the informal organization of the school does not encourage curricular innovation, the students' learning and school experience is likely to be negative, and that is particularly true for at-risk students.

Attempts to improve classroom group processes often should be either accompanied or preceded by attempts to improve the organizational processes of the staff. Consultation in Organization Development offers a strategy for helping staff members to become more aware of their own organizational processes and for facilitating problem solving together to improve their school program.

Organization Development entails an entire faculty improving its own group processes. It can be carried out by specially trained teachers, administrators, counselors, and school psychologists who are themselves members of the same district.

Adult professionals who model effective organizational development procedures will also foster a supportive social environment for the emergence of supportive classroom climates.

Attempts at school improvement should focus more on bringing students into interaction with teachers to collaborate on improving the group processes of the school and the classrooms.

Action Ideas for Improving Climate

Student Diagnosis of the Organizational Climate of the School

The questionnaire on school climate (see Instrument 10.1) has been used in several schools. It is a simple instrument to administer and to tabulate and can be given to

INSTRUMENT 10.1
Student Questionnaire on School Climate

Please think about what happens in your school. Some things that might happen in your school are listed below. We want to know how often you think these things happen. Fill in the blank next to each item with either a letter or a face to show the answers:

A = This *almost never* happens or

B = This *sometimes* happens or

C = This *often* happens or

D = This *almost always* happens

1. In this school people notice when things go wrong. _____

2. When things go wrong, someone tries to make them right. _____

3. I get to help decide what to do. _____

4. Other students get to help decide what to do. _____

5. Teachers listen to me in this school. _____

6. Other students listen to me here. _____

7. Teachers are easy to talk to. _____

8. Teachers can talk to the principal almost any time. _____

9. Teachers try "new" things here. _____

10. This school is a good one for someone with a new idea. _____

students of all ages. (It may also be read to the younger ones.) Its purpose is to provide feedback from students to a school faculty and can be administered to the whole student body or to a sample of respondents. When it is given to a sample, the students should be selected from all classrooms to ensure a representative group. The questionnaire should be given when the faculty has a plan for working on the school climate. Upon completion, the information could be used for improvement of school climate. Other instruments to assess the organizational climate of secondary schools can be found in Fox et al. (1973); in Schmuck and Runkel (1985); and as part of the action idea that follows. Also, in 1988, the National Study of School Evaluation (5201 Leesbury Pike, Falls Church, Virginia 22041) produced a revision of its *Student Opinion Inventory*. That questionnaire

accomplishes two goals: (1) to assess student attitudes toward the school, and (2) to provide students the chance to recommend improvements in the school.

Survey Data Feedback in Secondary Schools

A useful questionnaire to ascertain the functioning of the school organization from the point of view of students was developed collaboratively by teachers and researchers at the University of Oregon. This questionnaire, presented as Instrument 10.2, has been used in over forty junior and senior high schools. A typical procedure is to ask a committee of teachers and students to collect and to analyze the data, feed the results back to teachers and students, and then chair small groups of teachers and students in discussions about how to improve the organizational functioning of the school.

INSTRUMENT 10.2
Student Questionnaire on Organizational Functioning

This is not a test. We want to find out about how it feels to be in your school. If the words seem to be true about your school, circle "Yes"; if they don't, circle "No." If you don't know what the sentence is about, circle "I DK" (I don't know).

	Circle your answer		
People notice when something goes wrong; they try to make it right.	Yes	No	I DK
There is no one here who will help me when I have a problem.	Yes	No	I DK
Teachers plan a lot together when a change needs to be made.	Yes	No	I DK
People here are interested in ideas from everyone.	Yes	No	I DK
Teachers don't solve problems; they just talk about them.	Yes	No	I DK

INSTRUMENT 10.2 (Continued)
Student Questionnaire on Organizational Functioning

Goals

	Yes	No	I DK
People talk about the way they want the school to be.	Yes	No	I DK
I have certain things I want to do in school this year and I have told someone else about them.	Yes	No	I DK
Parents were not asked to help set school goals.	Yes	No	I DK
What we do here is because of "goals."	Yes	No	I DK
This school does not try to get better.	Yes	No	I DK

Conflict and Variety

People listen to each other, even if they are not friends.	Yes	No	I DK
No one else will help me if a teacher is unfair to me.	Yes	No	I DK
Most people here believe there is more than one way to take care of problems.	Yes	No	I DK
The principal will not listen to our "side" of an argument.	Yes	No	I DK
When we disagree here, we learn from each other.	Yes	No	I DK

Open Communication Up and Down

Teachers find it easy to talk to the principal.	Yes	No	I DK
I find it easy to talk to the teachers.	Yes	No	I DK
The principal talks with us frankly and openly.	Yes	No	I DK
I can easily get help from teachers if I want it.	Yes	No	I DK
People do not talk to each other here if they are from different parts of the school.	Yes	No	I DK
Teachers say mean things about each other.	Yes	No	I DK

Decision Making

Teachers help decide which adults will work at this school.	Yes	No	I DK
Parents do not help decide about new school programs.	Yes	No	I DK
People from this school give advice to the superintendent and his staff before things are decided about the school.	Yes	No	I DK

INSTRUMENT 10.2 (Continued)
Student Questionnaire on Organizational Functioning

I do not get to help decide what to do here in school.	Yes	No	I DK
None of the students gets to help decide what to do.	Yes	No	I DK

Responsiveness

In this school, it is OK to have a problem.	Yes	No	I DK
Teachers don't try "new" things here.	Yes	No	I DK
Students with special problems get help.	Yes	No	I DK
Students with new ideas get ignored.	Yes	No	I DK
The new things we do at this school are just what we need.	Yes	No	I DK

Attractiveness of the School

I would rather go to school here than in most other schools in this city.	Yes	No	I DK
Students here have a good feeling about each other.	Yes	No	I DK
New students and new teachers are ignored or "put down."	Yes	No	I DK
Teachers and students feel good about each other.	Yes	No	I DK
People here do not care about one another.	Yes	No	I DK

Two other surveys have been developed for assessing school climate. One by Kelley et al. (1986) measures climate comprehensively across ten categories: (1) Teacher-student relationships, (2) Security and Maintenance, (3) Administration, (4) Student academic orientation, (5) Student values, (6) Guidance, (7) Student-peer relationships, (8) Parent and community-school relationships, (9) Instructional activities, and (10) Student activities. It is distributed by the National Association of Secondary School Principals, 1904 Association Drive, Reston, Virginia 22091. The second by Sweeney (1988) is titled, "The School Climate Inventory" and also addresses ten factors of climate: (1) Supportive and stimulating environment, (2) Student-centeredness, (3) Expectations, (4) Feedback, (5) Rewards, (6) Sense of family, (7) Closeness to parents and community, (8) Communication, (9) Achievement, and (10) Trust. For more information, get in touch with Jim Sweeney in the College of Education at Iowa State University in Ames, Iowa 50011.

The High School Renewal Committee

An attempt to improve organizational life in New York high schools has been going on for the past twenty-five years under the title of "School Renewal." The core of this effort is a renewal committee in each participating school that is made up of selected teachers and students. The committee carries out an assessment of the school's achievements and its weaknesses. The assessment is done partly through discussion and partly through a formal instrument such as Instrument 10.2 on the previous page. After the diagnoses are amassed and analyzed, the committee discusses and plans actions for school improvement. Details of the process, along with examples of results, are presented in Bassin and Gross (1979).

Teacher-Student Cadre within the School

Another example of an effort to improve organizational processes in schools is the internal cadre of OD consultants. Teachers and students form a group called a "cadre" to facilitate problem-solving discussions within the school. Cadre members usually work in pairs to convene group discussions involving teachers and students, to carry out diagnoses of the school climate, to brainstorm about new ideas, and to organize and monitor action-planning. Models and procedures for such cadres can be found in Leatt and Schmuck (1988).

Leadership Training for Student Teachers

In this activity, the elected student leaders of junior and senior high schools receive special training in leadership skills. Typically the training takes place over several weekends away from the school. The leaders are helped in analyzing alternative leadership styles, given practice in the communication skills of paraphrasing, behavior description, feeling description, impression checking, survey taking, and gatekeeping, and helped in practicing how to convene student groups for effective discussions. There are many possible designs for such training; for several examples, see Medina (1979).

High School Course in Organizational Psychology

An instructional module, lasting from between four to fifteen weeks, has been published by Teachers College Press in collaboration with the American Psychological Association. The module, entitled *School Life and Organizational Psychology,* includes a text for students and a teacher handbook with duplicating masters. The units include topics such as the self and the organization, living in organizations, human motives and organizations, groups in organizations, roles in groups, and norms in groups. Students keep a log throughout the course, relating what they study to themselves as individuals and to their school as the "organization" under study.

We worked with a school where the elected leaders of the student government took this course together during the fall term and used the concepts and procedures of the course to help in their governing roles. The class satisfied their social science requirement and helped them perform more effectively as student leaders. The materials, published in 1981, can be ordered from Teachers College Press, 1234 Amsterdam Avenue, New York, N.Y. 10027.

Counselors as Facilitators of Climate Improvement

At the close of chapter 3, we described a strategy entitled *Improving Classroom Social Climate*. This curriculum package aims to help classroom teachers improve the group processes of their classrooms. In a number of schools where we have worked, counselors have brought teachers who are interested in trying that curriculum together for discussion. By working in collaboration with several teachers, the counselor strives to facilitate both increased commitment to the program and greater consistency across classrooms in the school. We believe that counselors can be effective by pursuing this approach to changing the informal climate of the school while also facilitating effective changes within classes.

A Student Council in Elementary School

Webb (1987) described how an elementary teacher became the sponsor of a school-wide student council in a K–6 school in California. The purpose of the council was to develop leadership, pride, and responsibility among council members. It would also be of service to the school. The teacher decided to work only with 4th, 5th, and 6th graders so that council membership would be considered a privilege of the older, more mature, and presumably more responsible students. Eight classes were a part of the project; each class submitted two names for membership, one was elected by peers, the other was nominated by the teacher. In addition to the 16 members, other students were invited to observe council meetings.

The role of the student council was advisory to the teachers and administrators. The council raised questions and made recommendations to the faculty. The teacher, along with three elected officers (president, vice president, and recording secretary), served as communication links between the council and the principal. Webb found that this student council was very useful in bringing students of different racial and ethnic backgrounds together. It also gave the participating students a genuine sense of responsibility for the school and for their education.

At one meeting, observed by Webb, discussions had to do with organizing a school-wide spirit week, introducing a school beautification campaign by making and displaying posters around the halls, and planting trees and flowers for Arbor day. The students reported that they were happy with the council. Important factors in the success were an energetic and supportive teacher-sponsor, a supportive principal, and a few supportive parents to help out as aides and in fund raising for special events.

Student Government in a Middle School

A group of teachers in a newly-formed middle school (grades six–eight) decided to work collaboratively with the student government. Two students from each homeroom were selected by their peers to serve in the government. The teachers retreated with the whole student government on a weekend at a teacher's cottage to work on establishing procedures for how the government would function. A counselor from the school also trained the students in communication skills and in how to run meetings effectively. The students developed school-wide projects, a few of which were to welcome incoming students each year with a special fair to acquaint these new students with the school and to interview both students and teachers about the strengths and weaknesses of the school. On one occasion, leaders from the student government were invited to a graduate class for educational administrators at a local university. Their visit to the university strengthened the cohesiveness of the leaders and their commitment toward working for school improvement.

The House System in a Junior High

At a junior high, the principal decided to ask all of the teachers to act as counselors at least part time. She did this in the context of introducing a house system into the school. Each house was made up of eighteen students and one teacher. The teacher served as an advisor and counselor to the students in the house. Also, the house groups teamed up in sports to compete against one another, making a house unit more cohesive. Many teachers held discussions about issues, such as mainstreaming and desegregation. One teacher used parts of the curriculum previously described as *School Life and Organizational Psychology*. Important decisions about courses to take were also discussed in the houses.

Varieties of Student Government in High Schools

Some high schools have tried different types of governing structures involving students. The most successful one that we have observed entailed a bicameral structure in which the teachers' senate was independent of the student government. The student government was organized through a house or homeroom structure and integrated by a link-pin structure, that is, each house had two representatives in the government. At the apex of the structure for the whole school was the principal's cabinet, which was made up of four officers from the teacher government and four student officers. The cabinet sought to resolve differences that would arise between the two halves of the bicameral structure.

An Inventory of School–Community Relations

A survey questionnaire presented in the Winter, 1990, edition of the *Journal of Educational Public Relations* offers 80 questions organized into four categories to assess educators' and parents' views of the school. The inventory is offered as a means to carry out a self-analysis of the school focusing on public knowledge and support of the school. The four categories are: (1) School Climate, (2) Parent Involvement, (3) Community Involvement, and (4) Communication-Information Processes.

Bibliography

Adkison, Judith. "Women in School Administration: A Review of the Literature." *Review of Educational Research,* 1981 51(3), 311–43.

Adler, Mortimer. *The Paideia Proposal: An Educational Manifesto.* New York: Harper and Row, 1983.

Ahlbrand, W. P., and B. B. Hudgins. "Verbal Participation and Peer Status." *Psychology in the Schools* 7 (1979):247–49.

Alexander, C., and E. Campbell. "Peer Influences on Adolescent Aspirations and Attainments." *American Sociological Review* 29, no. 4 (1964):568–75.

Allen, Vernon L., ed. *Children as Teachers: Theory and Research in Tutoring.* New York: Academic Press, 1976.

Allport, F. *Social Psychology.* Boston: Houghton Mifflin Co., 1924.

Allport, Gordon W. *Personality: A Psychological Interpretation.* New York: Henry Holt, 1937.

Allport, Gordon W. *The Nature of Prejudice.* Boston: Beacon Press, 1954.

Allport, Gordon W. *Becoming: Basic Considerations for a Psychology of Personality.* New Haven: Yale University Press, 1955.

Alschuler, A. S., Diane Tabor, and J. McIntyre. *Teaching Achievement Motivation: Theory and Practice in Psychological Education.* Middletown, Conn.: Education Ventures, 1970.

Amidon, E., and E. Hunter. *Improving Teaching.* New York: Holt, Rinehart & Winston, 1966.

Amidon, E., and A. Simon. "Teacher-Pupil Interaction." *Review of Educational Research* 35, no. 2, April, 1965.

Anderson, G. "Effects of Classroom Social Climate on Individual Learning." *American Educational Research Journal* 7, no. 2 (1970):135–52.

Anderson, H. H. "The Measurement of Domination and of Socially Integrative Behaviors in Teachers' Contacts with Children." *Child Development,* 10, 1939, pp. 73–89.

Angell, R. C. *Free Society and Moral Crisis.* Ann Arbor: University of Michigan Press, 1958.

Apple, M. "Work, Gender and Teaching." *Teachers College Record.* Spring, 1983, pp. 611–28.

Appleberry, J. B., and W. K. Hoy. "The Pupil Control Ideology of Professional Personnel in Open and Closed Elementary Schools." *Educational Administration Quarterly* 3 (1969):74–85.

Archambault, R. D. (ed.) *John Dewey on Education: Selected Writings.* Chicago, Ill.: University of Chicago Press, 1964 (Phoenix paperback edition, 1974).

Arends, R., and R. Schmuck, et al. *School Life and Organizational Psychology,* an instructional unit produced by the Human Behavior Curriculum Project. American Psychological Association. New York: Teachers College Press, 1981.

Argyris, C. *Intervention Theory and Method: A Behavioral Science View.* Reading, Mass.: Addison-Wesley Publishing Co., 1972.

Argyris, C., and D. A. Schon. *Theory in Practice: Increasing Professional Effectiveness.* San Francisco: Jossey-Bass, 1974.

Aronson, Elliot. *The Jigsaw Classroom.* Beverly Hills, Calif.: Sage Publications, 1978.

Aronson, Elliot, Nancy Blaney, Jev Sikes, Cookie Stephan, and Matthew Snapp. "The Jigsaw Route of Learning and Liking." *Psychology Today,* February 1975, pp. 43–50.

Asch, S. E. *Social Psychology.* Englewood Cliffs, N.J.: Prentice-Hall, 1952.

Asher, S. R., and J. M. Gottman. *The Development of Children's Friendships.* Cambridge, Mass.: University Press, 1981.

Ashton-Warner, Sylvia. "Spearpoint." *Saturday Review,* 24 June 1972, pp. 33–39.

Astin, A. W. *The College Environment.* Washington, D.C.: American Council on Education, 1968.

Atkinson, J., and N. A. Feather. *Theory on Achievement Motivation.* New York: John Wiley & Sons, 1966.

Back, K. "Influence through Social Communication." *Journal of Abnormal and Social Psychology* 46 (1951):9–23.

Backman, E. W., and P. F. Secord. *A Social Psychological View of Education.* New York: Harcourt, Brace & World, 1968.

Bain, Robert, and James Anderson. "School Context and Peer Influences on Educational Plans of Adolescents." *Review of Educational Research* 44, no. 4 (1974):429–45.

Baird, L. L. "Big School, Small School: A Critical Examination of the Hypothesis." *Journal of Educational Psychology* 60 (1969):254–60.

Bales, R. and P. Slater. "Role Differentiation in Small Decision-Making Groups." In *Family Socialization and Interaction Processes,* edited by T. Parsons and R. Bales, pp. 259–306. New York: New York Free Press, 1955.

Bandler, Richard, and John Grinder. *The Structure of Magic.* Palo Alto, Calif.: Science and Behavior Books, 1975.

Bany, Mary, and L. Johnson. *Classroom Group Behavior.* New York: Macmillan Co., 1964.

Bany, Mary, and Lois V. Johnson. *Educational Social Psychology.* New York: Macmillan Co., 1975.

Barbieri, Richard. *Classroom Practices in Teaching English 1977–78: Teaching the Basics—Really!* Urbana, Ill.: National Council of Teachers of English, 1978.

Barker, R., and P. Gump. *Big School, Small School: High School Size and Student Behavior.* Stanford, Calif.: Stanford University Press, 1964.

Barth, R. S. *Open Education and the American School.* New York: Agathon Press, 1972.

Bass, B. *Leadership, Psychology and Organizational Behavior.* New York: Harper & Brothers, 1960.

Bassin, M., and T. Gross. "Renewal: A Problem-Solving Model." *NASSP Bulletin,* May 1979:43–48.

Battle, E. S. "Motivational Determinants of Academic Competence." *Journal of Personality and Social Psychology* 4 (1966):634–42.

Becker, Howard. "The Career of the School-teacher" in Nosow and Form (eds.). *Man, Work and Society,* 1962, N.Y. Basic Books, pp. 321–29.

Belenky, Mary, Blythe Clinchy, Nancy Goldberger, and Jill Tarule. *Women's Ways of Knowing.* New York: Basic Books, 1989.

Bell, W. *The Impact of Organization Development Conducted by an Internal Cadre of Specialists on the Organizational Processes in Elementary Schools.* Unpublished doctoral dissertation, University of Oregon, 1977.

Benham, B., P. Giesen, and J. Oakes. "A Study of Schooling: Students' Experience in Schools." *Phi Delta Kappan,* V. 61, No. 5, 1980, pp. 337–40.

Benjamin, J. "Changes in Relation to Influences upon Self-Conceptualization." *Journal of Abnormal and Social Psychology* 45 (1950):573–80.

Benne, Kenneth, L. Bradford, J. Gibb, and R. O. Lippitt. *The Laboratory Method of Changing and Learning.* Palo Alto, Calif.: Science and Behavior Books, 1975.

Bennis, W., N. Berkowitz, M. Affinito, and M. Malone. "Authority, Power and the Ability to Influence." *Human Relations* 11 (1958):143–55.

Benton, A. A. "Reactions to Demands to Win from an Opposite-Sex Opponent." *Journal of Personality* 41 (1973):430–42.

Berger, J., B. Cohen, and M. R. Zelditch. "Status Characteristics and Expectation States." In *Sociological Theories in Progress*, edited by J. Berger, M. Zelditch, Jr., and B. Anderson. Boston, Mass.: Houghton Mifflin Co., 1966, pp. 29–46.

Berkowitz, L. "Sharing Leadership in Small Decision-Making Groups." *Journal of Abnormal and Social Psychology* 48 (1953):231–38.

Berliner, David C. "Developing Conceptions of Classroom Environments: Some Light on the T in Classroom Studies of ATI." *Educational Psychologist*, Vol. 18, No. 1, 1983, pp. 1–13.

Berne, Eric. *What Do You Say after You Say Hello: The Psychology of Human Destiny.* New York: Grove Press, 1972.

Berscheid, E., and E. Walster. *Interpersonal Attraction.* Reading, Mass.: Addison-Wesley Publishing Co., 1969.

Bigelow, R. C. "Changing Classroom Interaction through Organization Development." In *Organization Development in Schools.* edited by R. A. Schmuck and M. Miles. Palo Alto, Calif.: National Press Books, 1971.

Bion, W. R. "Experiences in Groups, I." *Human Relations* 1 (1948):314–20.

Bloom, B., T. J. Hastings, and G. F. Madaus. *Handbook on Formative and Summative Evaluation of Student Learning.* New York: McGraw-Hill Book Co., 1971.

Bloom, Sophie. *Peer and Cross-Age Tutoring in the Schools.* Hawthorn, Australia: Australian Council for Educational Research, Limited, 1978.

Blum, Robert. "Effective Schooling Practices: A Research Synthesis." Portland, OR.: Northwest Regional Education Laboratory, April, 1984.

Blumberg, A., and R. Golembiewski. *Learning and Change in Groups.* Maryland: Penguin Books, 1976.

Blumberg, A., and W. Greenfield. *The Effective Principal.* 2nd edition. Boston: Allyn and Bacon, Inc., 1984.

Bogen, I. "Pupil-Teacher Rapport and the Teacher's Awareness of Structures within the Group." *Journal of Educational Sociology,* 1954, 28, 104–14.

Bonney, M. E. "Assessment of Efforts to Aid Socially Isolated Elementary School Pupils." *The Journal of Educational Research* 64 (1971):359–64.

Boocock, S. S. "The School as a Social Environment for Learning: Social Organization and Micro-Social Process in Education." *Sociology of Education* 46 (1973):15–50.

Bossert, Steven T. "Cooperative Activities in the Classroom." In E. Rothkopf (ed.) *Review of Research in Education.* Washington, D.C., AERA, 1988, p. 225–50.

Bovard, E. "Interaction and Attraction to the Group." *Human Relations* 9 (1966): 628–39.

Bowles, S., and H. Gintis. *Schooling in a Capitalist America.* New York: Basic Books, 1976.

Boyer, Ernest. *High School: A Report on Secondary Education in America.* New York: Harper & Row, 1983.

Boyle, R. P. "The Effect of High School on Student's Aspirations." *American Journal of Sociology* 71 (1966):628–39.

Bradford, L., J. Gibb, and K. Benne (eds.) *T-Group Theory and Laboratory Method.* New York: John Wiley & Sons, 1964.

Bradford, L. "Group Forces Affecting Learning." *Journal of the National Association of Women Deans and Counselors* 23 (1960a).

Bradford, L. "Development Potentialities Through Class Groups." *Teachers College Record* 61 (1960b).

Bradford, Leland P. (ed.) *Group Development.* San Diego, Calif.: University Associates, 1978.

Breckenridge, Eileen. "Improving School Climate." *Phi Delta Kappan,* December 1976, pp. 314–18.

Bridge, R. G., C. M. Judd, and P. R. Moock. *The Detriments of Educational Outcomes: The Impact of Families, Peers, Teachers and Schools.* Cambridge, MA.: Ballinger Press, 1979.

Britton, Gwyneth. "Sex Stereotyping and Career Roles." *Journal of Educational Psychology* 61 (1970):365–74.

Brookover, W. B. *Effective Secondary Schools.* Philadelphia: Research for Better Schools, 1981.

Brookover, W. B., and J. M. Schneider. "Academic Environments and Elementary School Achievement." *Journal of Research and Development in Education.* 9, 1, (1971):82–91.

Brophy, Jere., and Thomas Good. "Teacher Expectations: Beyond the Pygmalion Controversy." *Phi Delta Kappan* 54 (1972):267–78.

Brophy, Jere., and Thomas Good. *Teacher-Student Relationships: Causes and Consequences.* New York: Holt, Rinehart and Winston, 1974.

Brophy, Jere., and Thomas Good. *Looking in Classrooms.* 3rd edition, New York: Harper and Row, 1984.

Brown, M., and N. Precious. *The Integrated Day in the Primary School.* New York: Agathon Press, 1968.

Brown, R. *Social Psychology.* New York: Free Press, 1965.

Bugental, D., and G. Lehner. "Accuracy of Self-Perception and Group Perception as Related to Two Leadership Roles." *Journal of Abnormal and Social Psychology* 56 (1958):396–98.

Burns, James MacGregor. *Leadership.* New York: Harper & Row, 1978.

Burstyn, Joan. "Women in the History of Education." Paper presented at the American Educational Research Association Meeting, Montreal, 1983.

Buswell, M. *The Relationship between the Social Structure of the Classroom and the Academic Success of the Pupil.* Ph.D. dissertation, University of Minnesota, 1951.

Byers, Paul, and Happie Byers. "Nonverbal Communication and the Education of Children." In *Functions of Language in the Classroom,* edited by Cazden et al., New York: Teachers College Press, 1972, pp. 3–13.

Calonico, J., and B. Calonico. "Classroom Interaction: A Sociological Approach." *Journal of Educational Research* 66, no. 4 (1972):165–69.

Campbell, E. Q., and C. N. Alexander. "Structural Effects and Interpersonal Relations." *American Journal of Sociology* 71 (1965):284–89.

Carhuff, Robert B. *The Art of Helping.* Amherst, Mass.: Human Resources Development Press, 1972.

Carnoy, Martin (ed.) *Schooling in a Corporate Society.* New York: David McKay Co., 1975.

Carrington, Andrew T., and others. *Class Size Project, 1980–1981. Final Report.* Virginia Beach, Virginia: Virginia Beach City Public Schools, August 1981. Eric Clearning House, ed. 237–521.

Cartwright, D., and A. Zander. *Group Dynamics: Research and Theory.* Evanston, Ill.: Row, Peterson, 1953, 1960; New York: Harper & Row Publishers, 1969.

Chaires, M. C. *Improving the Social Acceptance of Educable Mentally Retarded Pupils in Special Classes.* Unpublished Ph.D. dissertation, Indiana University, 1966.

Charlesworth, R., and W. W. Hartup. "Positive Social Reinforcement in the Nursery School Peer Group." *Child Development* 38 (1967):993–1002.

Charters, W. W., Jr., and Tom Jovick. "Principal Sex and Sex Equity in Educational Policies and Practices." In P. A. Schmuck, W. W. Charters, Jr., and R. O.Carlson (eds.) *Educational Policy and Management: Sex Differentials.* New York: Academic Press, 1981, pp. 35–54.

Cheatham, Annie. *Directory of School Mediation and Conflict Resolution Programs.* 425 Amity Street, Amherst, MA. 01002. 1988. (413–545–2462).

Chesler, M., and R. Fox. *Role-Playing Methods in the Classroom.* Chicago: Science Research Associates, Inc., 1966.

Chesler, M., R. A. Schmuck, and R. Lippitt. "The Principal's Role in Facilitating Innovation." *Theory into Practice* 2, no. 5 (1963):269–77.

Chesler, M., and J. Lohman. "Changing Schools Through Student Advocacy." In Schmuck, R. A., and Miles, M. (ed.) *Organization Development in Schools.* Palo Alto, Calif.: National Press Books, 1971, pp. 185–211.

Clifford, M. W. "Motivational Effects of Competition and Goal-Setting in Reward and Nonreward Conditions." *Journal of Experimental Education* 39 (1971).

Clore, Gerald. "Interpersonal Attraction: An Overview." University Program Modular Studies. Morristown, N.J.: Silver Burdett Co., General Learning Press, 1975.

Coddington, B. *Peer Mediation Program*. Portland, OR.: Oregon Law-Related Education Project, 1989.

Cohen, A. K. *Delinquent Boys*. New York: Free Press, 1955.

Cohen, E. *Designing Groupwork. Strategies for the Heterogeneous Classroom*. New York: Teachers College Press, 1986.

Cohen, P. A., C. C. Kulik, and J. A. Kulik. "Educational Outcomes of Tutoring: A Meta-Analysis of Findings," *American Educational Research Journal,* 19, 2, 1982, 237–48.

Coleman, James, E. Campbell, C. Hobson, J. McPartland, A. Mood, F. Weinfeld, and R. York. *Equality of Educational Opportunity*. Washington, D.C.: United States Government Printing Office, 1966.

Colman, Arthur D., and W. Harold Bexton, (eds.) *Group Relations Reader*. Sausalito, Calif.: GREX, 1975.

Combs, A. W., and C. Taylor. "The Effect of the Perception of Mild Degrees of Threat on Performance." *Journal of Abnormal and Social Psychology* 47 (1952):420–24.

Cook, L. A. "An Experimental Sociographic Study of a Stratified Tenth-Grade Class." *American Sociological Review* 10 (1945):250–61.

Cooley, C. H. *Human Nature and the Social Order*. New York: Free Press, 1956.

Cooper, Harris M. "Pygmalian Grows Up: A Model for Teacher Expectation Communication and Performance Influence." *Review of Educational Research* 49 (1979):389–410.

Coopersmith, S. *The Antecedents of Self-Esteem*. San Francisco: W. H. Freeman & Co. Publishers, 1967.

Coughlan, Neil. *Young John Dewey: An Essay in American Intellectual History*. New York: Free Press, 1976.

Crist, Janet. *Group Dynamics and the Teacher-Student Relationship: A Review of Recent Innovations*. Stanford: Stanford Center for Research and Development in Teaching, Memorandum No. 81, January 1972.

Crushschon, Ilena J. *Peer Tutoring: A Strategy for Building on Cultural Strengths*. Chicago, Ill.: Center for New Schools, 1977.

Crutchfield, R. S. "Conformity and Character." *American Psychologist* 19 (1955):191–98.

Dale, R. R. *Mixed or Single Sex School?* London: Routledge and Kegan Paul, 1969.

Dashiell, F. F. "Experimental Studies of the Influence of Social Situations on the Behavior of Individual Human Adults." In *A Handbook of Social Psychology,* edited by C. Murchison. Worchester, Mass.: Clark University Press, 1935, pp. 1097–1158.

Daw, Robert, and Nate Gage. "Effects of Feedback from Teachers to Principals." *Journal of Educational Psychology* 58 (1967):181–88.

Deal, Terry, and A. A. Kennedy. *Corporate Cultures*. Reading, Mass.: Addison-Wesley, 1982.

DeCharms, Richard. *Personal Causation*. New York: Academic Press, 1968.

DeCharms, Richard. "From Pawns to Origins: Toward Self-Motivation." In *Psychology and Educational Practice,* edited by G. Lesser. Glenview, Ill.: Scott Foresman, Co., 1971, pp. 380–408.

DeCharms, Richard. "Personal Causation Training in the Schools." *Journal of Applied Social Psychology* 2, no. 2 (1972):95–113.

DeCharms, Richard. "Pawn or Origin—Enhancing Motivation in Disaffected Youth." *Educational Leadership,* March 1977.

Deci, E. L. "Effects of Externally Mediated Rewards on Intrinsic Motivation." *Journal of Personality and Social Psychology* 18 (1971):105–15.

Deci, E. L. *Intrinsic Motivation*. New York: Plenum, 1975.

Deutsch, Morton. "A Theory of Cooperation and Competition." *Human Relations* 2 (1949):129–52.

Deutsch, Morton. *The Resolution of Conflict*. New Haven, Conn.: Yale Press, 1973.

Deutsch, M., and Harvey A. Hornstein. "The Social Psychology of Education." In Davitz, J. R., and Samuel Ball (eds.) *Psychology of the Educational Process*. New York: McGraw-Hill, 1970, pp. 179–222.

Developing Character: Transmitting Knowledge: A Thanksgiving Day Statement by a Group of 27 Americans. ARL, 2605 W. 147th St., Posen, Ill. 60649, 1984.

DeVries, D., R. Slavin, G. Fennessey, K. Edwards, and M. Lombardo. *Teams—Games—Tournaments*. Englewood Cliffs, N.J.: Educational Technology Publications, 1981.

Dewey, John. *Human Nature and Conduct: An Introduction to Social Psychology.* New York: Modern Library, 1930.

Dishon, D., and P. W. O'Leary. *A Guidebook for Cooperative Learning: A Technique for Creating More Effective Schools.* Holmes Beach, Florida: Learning Publications, Inc., 1986.

Doyle, W., G. Hancock, and E. Kifer. "Teachers' Perceptions: Do They Make a Difference?" Paper presented at annual meeting of the American Educational Research Association, 1971.

Dreeben, Robert. *On What Is Learned in School.* Reading, Mass.: Addison-Wesley Publishing Co., 1968.

Dubin, R., G. Homans, F. Mann, and D. Miller. *Leadership and Productivity: Some Facts of Industrial Life.* San Francisco: Chandler Publishing Co., 1965.

Duke, D. *The Retransformation of the School: The Emergence of Contemporary Alternative Schools in the United States.* Nelson-Hall, 1978.

Dweck, C. S., and N. D. Rapucci. "Learned Helplessness and Reinforcement Responsibility in Children." *Journal of Personality and Social Psychology* 25, no. 1 (1973):109–16.

Dyer, W. G. *Modern Theory and Method in Group Training.* New York: Van Nostrand Reinhold Co., 1972.

Dyer, W. G. *Insight to Impact: Strategies for Interpersonal and Organizational Change.* La Jolla, Calif.: NTL/Learning Resources Corporation, 1976.

Dyer, W. G. *Team Building: Issues and Alternatives.* Reading, Mass.: Addison-Wesley, 1977.

Dykhuizen, G. *The Life and Work of John Dewey.* Carbondale: Southern Illinois University Press, 1973.

Eagly, A. W., and W. Wood. "Gender and Influenceability: Stereotype Versus Behavior." In O'Leary, V. E., Unger, R. K., and Wallston, B. S. (eds.) *Women, Gender, and Social Psychology.* Hillsdale, N.J.: Lawrence Erlbaum Associates, Publishers, 1985, pp. 225–56.

Eder, Donna, and Maureen Hallinan. "Sex Differences in Children's Friendships." *American Sociological Review* 43 (1978):237–50.

Edmonds, Ron. "Effective Schools for the Urban Poor." *Educational Leadership.* Vol. 37, no. 1 (1979):15–24.

Educational Committee Coordinating Council of Community Organization. (eds.) *Handbook of Chicago School Segregation.* Chicago: Education Committee Coordination Council of Community Organization, 1963.

Educational Development Center, Inc. *Man: A Course of Study.* Cambridge, Mass.: Educational Development Center, Inc., 1969.

Eichhorn, Donald, "The School." In Johnson, M. (ed.) *Toward Adolescence: The Middle School Years.* Chicago: University of Chicago Press, 1980, pp. 56–73.

Eisner, E. "The Ecology of School Improvement." *Educational Leadership* 45 (5), 1988, 24–29.

Emerson, John M. *Conflict Resolution for Students: A Study of Problem Solving and Peer Conflict Management,* University of Oregon, Eugene, Oregon. Unpublished dissertation, 1990.

Epstein, Joyce. "Selection of Friends in Differently Organized Schools and Classrooms." In Epstein, J., and Karweit, N. (eds.) *Friends in School.* New York: Academic Press, 1983.

Epstein, Joyce. "On Parents and Schools: A Conversation with Joyce Epstein." *Educational Leadership* 47, 2, Oct. 1989, pp. 24–27.

Epstein, Joyce, and Nancy Karweit. *Friends in School: Patterns of Selection and Influence in Secondary School.* New York: Academic Press, 1983.

Erikson, E. H. *Childhood and Society.* New York: W. W. Norton & Co., 1950.

Evans, G. W., and R. B. Howard. "Personal Space." *Psychological Bulletin* 80 (1973):334–44.

Fargo, George, Charlene Behrns, and Patricia Nolan. *Behavior Modification in the Classroom.* Belmont, Calif.: Wadsworth Publishing Co., Inc., 1970.

Faunce, W. *Social Problems of an Industrial Civilization.* New York: McGraw-Hill Book Co., 1968.

Feldman, David Henry. "Beyond Universals: Toward a Developmental Psychology of Education." *Educational Researcher* 10, no. 9, November 1981, pp. 21–26.

Felmlee, Diane, and Maureen Hallinan. "The Effect of Classroom Interaction on Children's Friendships." *The Journal of Classroom Interaction* 14 (1979):1–8.

Fiedler, Fred. *Leadership*. Morristown, N.J.: General Learning Press, 1971.

Finn, J. "Expectations and the Educational Environment." *Review of Educational Research* 42, no. 3 (1972):387–410.

Finn, J., E. L. Gaier, S. Peng, and R. E. Banks. "Teacher Expectations and Pupil Achievement; Naturalistic Study." *Urban Education* 10 (1975):195–97.

Fisher, Roger and William Ury. *Getting To Yes: Negotiating Agreement Without Giving In.* New York: Penguin, 1981.

Flanders, N. A. *Teacher Influence, Pupil Attitudes, and Achievement.* U.S. Office of Education Cooperative Research Project No. 397, Minneapolis: University of Minnesota Press, 1960.

Flanders, N. A. *Analyzing Teaching Behavior.* Reading, Mass.: Addison-Wesley Publishing Co., 1970.

Flanders, N. A., and S. Havumaki. "The Effect of Teacher-Pupil Contacts Involving Praise on the Sociometric Choices of Students." *Journal of Educational Psychology* 51 (1960):65–68.

Flanders, Ned. "Some Relationships Among Teacher Influence, Pupil Attitudes and Achievement." In B. Biddle, W. Ellena (eds.) *Contemporary Research on Teacher Effectiveness.* New York: Holt, Rinehart and Winston, 1964.

Flanders, Ned. "Teacher Influence in the Classroom." In Bellack (ed.) *In Theory and Research in Teaching.* New York: Bureau of Publications, Teachers College, Columbia University, 1963, pp. 37–53.

Folberg, J., and A. Taylor. *Mediation: A Comprehensive Guide to Resolving Conflicts Without Litigation.* San Francisco: Jossey-Bass, 1984.

Ford, Donald H., and Hugh B. Urban. *Systems of Psychotherapy.* New York: John Wiley and Sons, 1965.

Fox, R., M. Luszki, and R. Schmuck. *Diagnosing Classroom Learning Environments.* Chicago; Science Research Associates, 1966.

Fox, R., R. A. Schmuck, E. Van Egmond, M. Ritvo, and C. Jung. *Diagnosing Professional Climate of Schools.* Fairfax, Va.: NTL Learning Resources, 1973.

Franke, R. H., and J. D. Kaul. "The Hawthorne Experiment. First Statistical Interpretation." *American Sociological Review* 43 (5):623–43.

Fraser, Barry, and Darrell Fisher. "Predicting Students' Outcomes from their Perceptions of Classroom Psychosocial Environment." *American Educational Research Journal,* 19 (4), 1982, pp. 498–518.

French, J., Jr., and B. Raven. "The Bases of Social Power." In *Studies in Social Power,* edited by D. Cartwright. Ann Arbor, Mich.: Institute for Social Research, 1959.

Friere, P. *Pedagogy of the Oppressed.* New York: Herder & Herder, 1970.

Furst, N., and E. Amidon. "Teacher-Pupil Interaction Patterns in the Teaching of Reading in the Elementary School." *The Reading Teacher,* January, 1965.

Fyans, Leslie J. (ed.) *Achievement Motivation.* New York: Plenum Press, 1980.

Gage, Nate L., Philip J. Runkel, and Bishwa B. Chatterjee. "Changing Teacher Behavior through Feedback from Pupils: An Application of Equilibrium Theory." In *Readings in the Social Psychology of Education,* edited by W. W. Charters, Jr. and N. Gage. Boston: Allyn & Bacon, 1963, pp. 173–80.

Gardenas, Jose, and Joan McCarty First. "Children At Risk." *Educational Leadership.* 43, 1, Sept. 1985, pp. 4–8.

Gardner, Alan, Mary Kohler, and Frank Riessman. *Children Teach Children.* New York: Harper & Row Publishers, 1971.

Gardner, J. *Self-Renewal: The Individual and the Innovative Society.* New York: Harper & Row Publishers, 1971.

Garrett, S. S., M. Sadker, and D. Sadker. "Interpersonal Communication Skills." In J. Cooper (ed.) *Classroom Teaching Skills.* 3rd. ed. Lexington, MA.: Heath, 1986.

Gathercoal, Forrest. *Judicious Discipline.* Ann Arbor, Michigan: 2nd ed. Caddo Gap Press, 1990.

Gazda, G., F. Asbury, F. Balzer, W. Childers, and R. P. Walters. *Human Relations Development: A Manual for Educators.* 2nd ed. Boston: Allyn & Bacon, 1977.

Gemmet, R. *A Monograph on Interpersonal Communications.* Redwood City, Calif.: San Mateo County Office of Education, October 1977.

Gersick, Connie J. G. "Time and Transition in Work Teams: Toward A New Model of Group Development." *Academy of Management Journal* 31, 1988, pp. 9–41.

Getzels, J. W. "A Social Psychology of Education." In *The Handbook of Social Psychology,* edited by G. Lindzey and E. Aronson. Reading, Mass.: Addison-Wesley Publishing Co., 1969, pp. 459–537.

Gibb, Jack. "Defensive Communication." *Journal of Communication* 11, no. 3 (1961).

Gibb, Jack. "Climate for Trust Formation." In *T-Group Theory and Laboratory Method,* edited by L. Bradford, J. Gibb, and K. Benne. New York: John Wiley & Sons, 1964, pp. 279–309.

Gilbertson, Marilyn. "The Influence of Gender on the Verbal Interactions among Principals and Staff Members: An Exploratory Study." In Schmuck, P. A. *Educational Policy and Management: Sex Differentials.* New York: Academic Press, 1981.

Gilligan, Carol. *In a Different Voice.* Cambridge; Harvard University Press, 1982.

Gladder, B. *Collaborative Relationships in High Schools: Implications for School Reform.* Unpublished doctoral dissertation, University of Oregon, December, 1990.

Glass, Gene V., and Mary Lee Smith. *Meta-Analysis of Research on the Relationship of Class Size and Achievement. The Class Size and Instruction Project.* September 1978. ED 268 129. And *Relationship of Class Size to Classroom Processes, Teacher Satisfaction and Pupil Affect, A Meta-Analysis.* San Francisco: Far West Lab. for Educ. Research and Dev., 1979. Ed 190–698.

Glasser, W. *Schools Without Failure.* New York: Harper and Row, 1969.

Glick, O. "Sixth Graders' Attitudes Toward School and Interpersonal Conditions in the Classroom." *Journal of Experimental Education* 38, 1970, pp. 17–20.

Glidewell, John C. "Unpublished data, reference file #884." Clayton, Mo.: St. Louis County Health Department, 1964.

Glidewell, John C. (ed.) *The Social Context of Learning and Development.* New York: John Wiley & Sons, 1976.

Glidewell, John C., M. Kantor, L. M. Smith, and L. Stringer. "Classroom Socialization and Social Structure." In *Review of Child Development Research* edited by M. Hoffman and L. Hoffman. New York: Russell Sage Foundation, 1966, pp. 221–57.

Goffman, E. *The Presentation of Self in Everyday Life.* Garden City, New York: Anchor Books, 1959.

Gold, M. "Power in the Classroom." *Sociometry* 21 (1958):50–60.

Golembiewski, R. *The Small Group.* Chicago: University of Chicago Press, 1961.

Golembiewski, R., and A. Blumberg. *Sensitivity Training and the Laboratory Approach.* Itasca, Ill.: Peacock, 1970, 1977.

Good, T. L., B. Biddle, and J. Brophy. *Teachers Make a Difference.* New York: Holt, Rinehart & Winston, 1975.

Goodacre, D. M. "Group Characteristics of Good and Poor Performing Combat Units." *Sociometry* 16 (1953):168–78.

Goodlad, John. *A Place Called School: Prospects for the Future.* New York: Macmillan, 1984.

Goodman, Norman. "Adolescent Norms and Behavior." *Merrill–Palmer Quarterly* 15, 1969, pp. 199–211.

Gouldner, A. W. "The Norm of Reciprocity: A Preliminary Statement." *American Sociological Review* 25 (1960):161–78.

Graham, S. *College of One.* New York: Bantam Books, 1967.

Gronlund, Norman E. *Sociometry in the Classroom.* New York: Harper and Brothers, 1959.

Gronlund, N. E., and L. Anderson, "Personality Characteristics of Socially Accepted, Socially Neglected, and Socially Rejected Junior High School Pupils." *Educational Administration and Supervision* 43 (1957):329–38.

Gross, Neal. "Some Sociological Correlates of the 'Academic Productivity' of Urban Elementary Schools with Pupils of Low Socio-Economic Status." Paper presented at the American Sociological Association meeting, Miami Beach, Florida, August, 1966.

Gross, Neal, and R. Herriott. *Staff Leadership in Public Schools.* New York: John Wiley & Sons, 1965.

Gross, Neal, and Ann Trask. *The Sex Factor in the Management of Schools.* New York: John Wiley & Sons, 1976.

Gross, Neal, J. B. Giacquinta, and M. Bernstein. *The Implementation of Educational Innovations.* New York: Basic Books, 1971.

Groth, Gretchen, John Lohman, Jean Butman, and Gary Milczarck. *Social Conflict and Negotiative Problem Solving.* Portland, Oregon: Northwest Regional Educational Laboratory, 1977.

Guskin, A. E., and S. L. Guskin. *A Social Psychology of Education.* Reading, Mass.: Addison-Wesley Publishing Co., 1970.

Guttentag, M., and H. Bray. *Undoing Sex Stereotypes: Research and Resources for Educators.* New York: McGraw-Hill, 1976.

Hall, E. T. "Environmental Communication." In *Behavior and Environment: The Use of Space by Animals and Men,* edited by A. H. Essen. New York: Plenum, 1971, pp. 247–56.

Haller, Emil J. "Pupil Race and Elementary School Ability Grouping: Are Teachers Biased Against Black Children?" *American Educational Research Journal* 22, no. 4 (Winter, 1985).

Hallinan, Maureen T. "Friendship Patterns in Open and Traditional Classrooms." *Sociology of Education* 49 (1976):254–65.

Hallinan, M. "Recent Advances in Sociometry." In S. R. Asher and J. M. Gallman (eds.) *The Development of Children's Friendships.* Cambridge, MA.: Cambridge University Press, pp. 91–115.

Hallinan, Maureen. "Structural Effects on Children's Friendships and Cliques." *Social Psychological Quarterly* 42 (1979):43–54.

Hallinan, Maureen, and A. Sorensen. "Ability Grouping and Student Friendships." *American Educational Research Journal.* (Winter, 1985) vol. 22, no. 4, pp. 485–99.

Hallinan, Maureen, and Nancy Tuma. "Classroom Effects on Change in Children's Friendships." *Sociology of Education* 51 (1978):270–82.

Halpin, A., and D. Croft. *Organizational Climate of Schools.* Chicago: Midwest Administrative Center, University of Chicago, 1963.

Hamblin, R. "Leadership and Crises." *Sociometry* 21 (1958):322–35.

Harburg, E. "Research on the Communication of Emotions and Hypertension." (Personal communication, 1986.)

Hare, A. P. "Small Group Discussions with Participating and Supervision Leadership." *Journal of Abnormal and Social Psychology* 48 (1953):273–75.

Hare, A. P. *Handbook of Small Group Research.* New York: Free Press, 1962, 1977.

Hare, A. P., E. F. Borgatta, and R. F. Bales. *Small Groups: Studies in Social Interaction.* New York: Alfred A. Knopf, 1955, 1965.

Hargreaves, D. H. *Social Relations in a Secondary School.* New York: Humanities Press Inc., 1967.

Harris, Thomas A. *I'm OK, You're OK.* New York: Avon Books, 1967.

Hartup, W. W., J. Glazer, and R. Charlesworth. "Peer Reinforcement and Sociometric Status." *Child Development* 38 (1967): 1017–1024.

Heider, F. "Social Perception and Phenomenal Causality." *Psychological Review* 51 (1944):358–74.

Heinicke, C., and R. Bales. "Developmental Trends in the Structure of Small Groups." *Sociometry* 16 (1953):7–38.

Heiss, J., and S. Owens. "Self-Evaluation of Blacks and Whites." *American Journal of Sociology* 78 (1972):360–70.

Hemphill, J. "Why People Attempt to Lead." In *Leadership and Interpersonal Behavior,* edited by L. Petrullo and B. Bass. New York: Holt, Rinehart & Winston, 1961, pp. 201–15.

Henley, Nancy, and Barrie Thorne. "Womanspeak and Manspeak: Sex Differences and Sexism in Communication, Verbal and Nonverbal." In *Beyond Sex Roles,* edited by A. Sargent. San Francisco: West Publishing Co., 1977, pp. 201–27.

Henry, Nelson B. (ed.) *The Dynamics of Instructional Groups.* 59th Yearbook. Part 2. Chicago: National Society for the Study of Education, 1960.

Hentoff, Nat. *Our Children Are Dying.* New York: Viking, 1966.

Herndon, J. *The Way It Spozed to Be.* New York: Bantam Books, 1965.

Herndon, J. *How to Survive in Your Native Land.* New York: Simon and Schuster, 1971.

Herriott, R., and N. St. John. *Social Class and the Urban School.* New York: John Wiley & Sons, 1966.

Hersey, P. *The Situational Leader.* Center for Leadership Studies, Escondido, CA, 1984.

Hilfiker, L. R. "Factors Relating to the Innovativeness of School Systems." *The Journal of Educational Research* 64, No. 1 (1970):23–27.

Hill, K. T., and J. B. Dusek. "Children's Achievement Expectations as a Function of Social Reinforcement, Sex of Subject, and Test Anxiety." *Child Development* 40 (1969):547–57.

Hodgkinson, Harold. *All One System: Demographics of Education, Kindergarten Through Graduate School.* Washington, D.C.: Institute for Educational Leadership, Inc., 1985.

Hoffman, Lois W. "Early Childhood Experiences and Women's Achievement Motives." *Journal of Social Issues* 28, 2 (1972).

Hoffman, L. R. *Group Problem Solving.* New York: Prager, 1975.

Hoffman, M. L. "Conformity as a Defense Mechanism and a Form of Resistance to Genuine Group Influence." *Journal of Personality* 25 (1957):412–42.

Hollander, R. P. "Some Effects of Perceived Status on Responses to Innovative Behavior." *Social Psychology* 63 (1961):247–50.

Holmes, John Greenville, and Dale Miller. *Interpersonal Conflict.* University Programs Modular Studies. Morristown, N.J.: Silver Burdett Co., 1976.

Horner, Matina. "Toward an Understanding of Achievement Related Conflicts in Women." *Journal of Social Issues.* 28 (1972):157–76.

Hornstein, H., D. Callahan, E. Fisch, and B. Benedict. "Influence and Satisfaction in Organizations: A Replication." *Sociology of Education* 41, no. 4 (1968):380–89.

Horowitz, Frances Degen. "The First Two Years of Life: Factors Related to Thriving." S. G. Moore, and C. R. Cooper. (eds.) In *The Young Child. Reviews of Research.* Vol. 3, Washington, D.C.: National Association for the Education of Young Children, 1982.

Horowitz, M. "The Conceptual Status of Group Dynamics." *Review of Educational Research.* Vol. 23. Oct. 1953.

House, W. C. "Actual and Perceived Differences in Male and Female Expectancies and Minimal Goal Levels as a Function of Competition." *Journal of Personality* 42 (1974):493–509.

House, W. C., and V. Perney. "Valence of Expected and Unexpected Outcomes as a Function of Locus of Control and Type of Expectancy." *Journal of Personality and Social Psychology* 29 (1974):454–63.

Hurt, Thomas, Michael Scott, and James McCroskey. *Communications in the Classroom.* Menlo Park, Calif.: Addison Wesley Publishing Co., 1978.

Illich, Ivan. *Deschooling Society.* New York: Harper and Row, 1970.

Jackson, J. M. "Structural Characteristics of Norms." In *The Dynamics of Instructional Groups,* 59th Yearbook, part 2, edited by N. Henry. Chicago: National Society for the Study of Education, 1960.

Jackson, Philip. *Life in Classrooms.* New York: Holt, Rinehart & Winston, 1968.

Jacobson, L. I., S. E. Berger, and M. Millham. "Individual Differences in Cheating During a Temptation Period When Confronting Failure." *Journal of Personality and Social Psychology* 15 (1970):48–56.

Jacques, David. *Learning in Groups.* Dover, N.H.: Longwood, 1984.

Janis, Irving R. *Victims of Group Think.* Boston: Houghton Mifflin Company, 1972.

Jencks, Christopher, M. Smith, H. Acland, M. Bank, D. Cohen, H. Gintes, B. Hayhes, and F. Michelson. *Inequality: A Reassessment of the Effect of Family and Schooling in America.* New York: Basic Books, 1972.

Jenkins, David H. "Characteristics and Functions of Leadership in Instructional Groups." In *The Dynamics of Instructional Groups* edited by N. Henry. Chicago: National Society for the Study of Education, 1960.

Jensen, A. R. "Review of 'Pygmalion in the Classroom'." *American Scientist* 51 (1969):447–57.

Johnson, D. W. *The Social Psychology of Education.* New York: Holt, Rinehart & Winston, 1979.

Johnson, David, and Roger Johnson. *Joining Together: Group Theory and Group Skills.* Englewood Cliffs, N.J.: Prentice-Hall, 1982.

Johnson, David, and Roger Johnson. *Learning Together and Learning Alone, Cooperation, Competition and Individualization.* Englewood Cliffs, N.J.: Prentice-Hall, 1975, 1984.

Johnson, David, and Roger Johnson. *Cooperation and Competition: Theory and Research.* Edina, Minnesota: Interaction Book Company, 1989.

Johnson, D. W., et al. "Effects of Cooperative, Competitive, and Individualistic Goal Structures on Achievement: A Meta-Analysis." *Psychological Bulletin* 89 (1981): 47–62.

Johnson, David, Roger Johnson, Edythe Johnson Holubee, and Patricia Roy. *Circles of Learning: Cooperation in the Classroom.* Alexandria, Virginia: Association for Supervision and Curriculum Development, 1984.

Johnson, David, Roger Johnson, Edythe Johnson Holubee, and Patricia Roy. *Circles of Learning: Cooperation in the Classroom.* Revised Edition. Edina, MN.: Interaction Book Company, 1986.

Johnson, Paula. "Women and Power: Toward a Theory of Effectiveness." *Journal of Social Issues* 32, no. 3 (1976):99–109.

Jones, Effie, and Xenia Montenegro. "Recent Trends in the Representation of Women and Minorities in School Administration and Problems in Documentation." Arlington, Va.: American Association of School Administrators, 1982.

Jones, S. "Self and Interpersonal Evaluations: Esteem Theories Versus Consistency Theories." *Psychological Bulletin* 79, no. 3 (1973):185–99.

Jordon, J. B. *Intelligence as a Factor in Social Position: A Sociometric Study in Special Classes for the Mentally Handicapped.* Unpublished Ph.D. dissertation, University of Illinois, 1960.

Jordon, T. E. *The Mentally Retarded.* Columbus, Ohio: Charles E. Merrill Publishing Co., 1961.

Joyce, B., and M. Weil. *Models of Teaching.* Englewood Cliffs, N.J.: Prentice-Hall, 1972 and 1980.

Kafer, Norman. "Friendship Choice and Performance in Classroom Groups." *The Australian Journal of Education* 20 (1976):278–84.

Kafer, Norman. "Interpersonal Strategies of Unpopular Children: Some Implications for Social Skills Training." *Psychology in the Schools,* 19, 1982, pp. 255–59.

Kahl, J. A. "Educational and Occupational Aspirations of 'Common Man' Boys." *Harvard Educational Review* 23 (1953):186–203.

Kalvelage, Joan, and Patricia A. Schmuck. *The Language of Inequality: A Fact Sheet for Administrators.* Salem, Oregon: Oregon Department of Education, 1981.

Kanter, Rosabeth. *The Changemasters.* New York: Simon and Schuster, 1983.

Kanter, Rosabeth. *When Giants Learn to Dance.* New York: Basic Books, 1989.

Karweit, Nancy, and Stephen Hansell. "Sex Differences in Adolescent Relationships; Friendship and Status." In Epstein, J., and N. Karweit (eds.) *Friends in School.* New York: Academic Press, 1983.

Kasarda, J. "The Structural Implications of Social System Size: A Three-Level Analysis." *American Sociological Review* 39 (1975):19–28.

Katz, D., and R. Kahn. *The Social Psychology of Organizations.* New York: John Wiley & Sons, 1966.

Keirnes-Young, Barbara. *The Principal As A Change Agent.* Unpublished doctoral dissertation, University of Oregon, 1986.

Kelly, James G., ed. *Adolescent Boys in High School: A Psychological Study of Coping and Adaptation.* Hillsdale, New Jersey: Lawrence Erlbaum, 1979.

Kirscht, J. P., T. M. Lodahl, and M. Haire. "Some Factors in the Selection of Leaders by Members of Small Groups." *Journal of Abnormal and Social Psychology* 58 (1959):406–8.

Koenigs, S. S., M. L. Fiedler, and R. DeCharms. "Teacher Beliefs, Classroom Interaction and Personal Causation." *Journal of Applied Social Psychology* 7, no. 2 (1977):95–114.

Kohl, H. R. *36 Children.* New York: New American Library, 1967.

Kohl, H. R. *The Open Classroom: A Practical Guide to a New Way of Teaching.* New York: A New York Review Book, 1969.

Kohler, W. *Gestalt Psychology.* New York: Liveright, 1947.

Kounin, J. S. *Discipline and Group Management in Classrooms.* New York: Holt, Rinehart & Winston, 1970.

Kounin, J. S., and P. V. Gump. "The Ripple Effect in Discipline." *Elementary School Journal* 59 (1958):158–62.

Kounin, J. S., P. V. Gump, and J. J. Ryan. "Exploration in Classroom Management." *Journal of Teacher Education* 12 (1961):235–46.

Kozol, H.R. *Death at an Early Age.* Boston: Houghton Mifflin Co., 1967.

Kozol, H. R. *Free Schools.* New York: Houghton Mifflin Co., 1972.

Krauss, H. H., and L. L. Critchfield. "Contrasting Self-Esteem Theory and Consistency Theory in Predicting Interpersonal Attraction." *Sociometry* 38, no. 2 (1975):247–60.

Kreidler, William. *Creative Conflict Resolution.* Glenview, Ill.: Scott, Foresman and Company, 1984

Kurdek, L., and A. Siesky. "An Interview Study of Parents' Perceptions of Their Children's Reactions and Adjustments to Divorce." *Journal of Divorce,* 3, 1 (1979):5–17.

Kurdek, L., and A. Siesky. "Children's Perceptions of Their Parents' Divorce." *Journal of Divorce,* 1, 4 (1980):339–77.

Kuriloff, A., and S. Atkins. "T-Group for a Work Team." *Journal of Applied Behavioral Science* 2 (1966):63–94.

Lahaderme, H., and Philip Jackson. "Withdrawal in the Classroom." *Journal of Educational Psychology* 61, 1970, pp. 97–101.

Laing, R. D. *Knots.* New York: Pantheon, 1970.

Lam, J. A. (1989). *School Mediation Program Evaluation Kit.* Amherst, MA.: National Association for Mediation in Education.

Lawrence, P., and J. Lorsch. *Organization and Environment: Managing Differentiation and Integration.* Boston: Harvard Business School, Division of Research, 1967.

Leatt, Desmond, and R. A. Schmuck. "Cadres of Organization Development Consultants in Schools: A Progress Report." UCEA Center on Organizational Development in Schools, Eugene, OR.: University of Oregon, 1988.

Leavitt, H. J. "Some Effects of Certain Communication Patterns on Group Performance." *Journal of Abnormal and Social Psychology* 46 (1951):38–50.

Leithwood, Keith, and J. Montgomery. "The Role of the Elementary School Principal in Program Improvement." *Review of Educational Research* 52, 3 (1982):309–39.

Lenney, Ellen. "Women's Self-Confidence in Achievement Settings." *Psychological Bulletin* 84, no. 1 (1977).

Lesser, G. (ed.) *Psychology and Educational Practice.* Glenview, Ill.: Scott, Foresman & Co., 1971.

Levin, Henry M. "Cost Effectiveness for Four Educational Interventions." Stanford, CA.: Institute for Educational Finance and Governance, 1984.

Lewin, K. *Resolving Social Conflicts.* New York: Harper's, 1948.

Lewin, K., R. Lippitt, and R. White. "Patterns of Aggressive Behavior in Experimentally Created 'Social Climates'." *Journal of Social Psychology* 10 (1939):271–99.

Lewis, Michael, and Leanora Rosenblum. *Friendship and Peer Relations.* New York: John Wiley and Sons, 1975.

Lewis, R., and N. St. John. "Contribution of Cross-Racial Friendship to Minority Group Achievement in Desegregated Classrooms." *Sociometry* 37, no. 1 (1974):79–91.

Lieberman, A. "Expanding the Leadership Team." *Educational Leadership* 45 (5), 1988, pp. 4–8.

Lieberman, M. A., I. Yalom, and M. Miles. *Encounter Groups: First Facts.* New York: Basic Books, 1973.

Lightfoot, Sara Lawrence. *The Good High School.* New York: Basic Books, 1983.

Lighthall, Frederick. "A Social Psychologist for School Systems." *Psychology in the Schools.* January 1969, pp. 3–12.

Likert, R. *New Patterns of Management.* New York: McGraw-Hill Book Co., 1961.

Likert, R., and J. G. Likert. *New Ways of Managing Conflict.* La Jolla, Calif.: NTL/ Learning Resources Cooperation, 1976.

Lilly, M. S. "Improving Social Acceptance of Low Sociometric Status, Low Achieving Students." *Exceptional Children* (January 1971): pp. 341–47.

Lippitt, Peggy, and John Lohman. "Cross-Age Relationships: An Educational Resource." *Children* 12 (1965):113–17.

Lippitt, Peggy, Jeffrey Eisman, and Ronald Lippitt. *Cross-Age Helping Programs: Orientation, Training and Related Materials.* Ann Arbor: University of Michigan Center for Research on Utilization of Scientific Knowledge, Institute for Social Research, 1969.

Lippitt, Ronald. "An Experimental Study of the Effect of Democratic and Authoritarian Group Atmosphere." *University of Iowa Studies in Child Welfare* 16 (1940):43–165.

Lippitt, Ronald. "Kurt Lewin, 1890–1947: Adventures in the Exploration of Interdependence." *Sociometry* 10, 1 (1947).

Lippitt, Ronald. "Unplanned Maintenance and Planned Change in the Group Work Process." *Social Work Practice.* New York: Columbia University Press, 1962.

Lippitt, Ronald, and M. Gold. "Classroom Social Structure as a Mental Health Problem." *Journal of Social Issues* 15 (1959):40–58.

Lippitt, Ronald, R. Fox, and L. Schaible. *Social Science Laboratory Units.* Chicago: Science Research Associates, 1969.

Lippitt, Ronald, N. Polansky, F. Redl, and S. Rosen. "The Dynamics of Power." *Human Relations* 5 (1952):37–64.

Lippitt, Ronald, et al. "The Teacher As Innovator, Seeker, and Sharer of New Practices." In *Perspectives on Educational Change,* edited by R. I. Miller. New York: Appleton-Century-Crofts, 1967, pp. 307–42.

Lipsitt, Lewis P. (ed.) *Advances in Infancy Research.* Norwood, N.J.: Ablex. 1 (1981).

Lockheed, Marlaine. *The Modification of Female Leadership Behavior in the Presence of Males.* Final Report, Educational Testing Service, Grant No. NE-G-00-3-0103.

Lockheed, Marlaine, and Katherin Patterson Hall. "Conceptualizing Sex as a Status Characteristic: Applications to Leadership Training Strategies." *Journal of Social Issues* 32, no. 3 (1976):111–23.

Long, L. D., and V. H. Frye. *Making It Till Friday.* Princeton, N.J.: Princeton Book Co., 1977.

Lord, Sharon. "Presentation to the Women's Educational Equity Act." National Directors Meeting, October 1976, Washington, D.C.

Lucker, G. W., D. Rosenfield, J. Siker, and E. Aronson. "Performance in the Interdependent Classroom: A Field Study." *American Educational Research Journal* 14, no. 2 (1976):115–23.

Luft, J. *Group Processes: An Introduction to Group Dynamics.* Palo Alto, Calif.: National Press Books, 1963, 1970.

Luft, J. *Of Human Interaction.* Palo Alto, Calif.: National Press Books, 1969.

Lynd, R. S., and H. M. Lynd. *Middletown in Transition.* New York: Harcourt, Brace & Co., 1937.

McCandless, Boyd R., Albert Roberts, and Thomas Starnes. "Teachers Marks, Achievement Test Scores and Aptitude Relations with Respect to Social Class, Race, and Sex." *Journal of Educational Psychology* 63 no. 2 (1971):153–59.

McClelland, C. *Power: The Inner Experience.* New York: Irvington Publishers Inc., 1975.

McClelland, D. D., J. W. Atkinson, R. A. Clark, and E. L. Lowell. *The Achievement Motive.* New York: Appleton-Century-Crofts, 1953.

McDill, Edward, Leo Rigsby, and Edmund Meyers, Jr. "Educational Climates of High Schools: Their Effect and Source." *American Journal of Sociology* 74, no. 6 (1969):567–86.

McGrath, J., and I. Altman. *Small Group Research.* New York: Holt, Rinehart & Winston, 1966.

McGrath, Joseph, and David A. Kravitz. "Group Research." *Annual Review of Psychology.* 32 (1982):195–230.

McGregor, D. *The Professional Manager.* New York: McGraw-Hill Book Co., 1967.

McKeachie, W. J. "Research on Teaching at the College and University Level." In *Handbook of Research and Teaching,* edited by N. L. Gage. Chicago: Rand McNally, 1963.

McMahon, I. D. "Relationships Between Causal Attributions and Expectancy of Success." *Journal of Personality and Social Psychology* 28 (1973):108–14.

McMillian, James H. *The Social Psychology of School Learning*. New York: Academic Press, 1980.

McPartland, James. "Balancing High-Quality, Subject-Matter Instruction with Positive Teacher-Student Relations in the Middle Grades." Center for Research on Elementary and Middle Schools, The Johns Hopkins University, Report 15, June, 1987.

Maccoby, E., and C. N. Jacklin. *The Psychology of Sex Differences*. Palo Alto, Calif.: Stanford University Press, 1976.

Mann, Dale. "Action on Dropouts." *Educational Leadership* 43, 1 Sept. 1985, pp. 16–17.

Mannheim, B. F. "An Investigation of the Interrelations of Reference Groups, Membership Groups, and the Self-Image: A Test of the Cooley-Mead Theory of the Self." *Dissertation Abstracts* 17 (1957):1616–1617.

March, J., and H. Simon. *Organizations*. New York: John Wiley & Sons, 1958.

Marrow, A. *The Practical Theorist*. New York: Basic Books, 1969.

Marshall, H. R., and B. R. McCandless. "A Study in Prediction of Social Behavior of Preschool Children." *Child Development* 28 (1957):149–59.

Marshall, Robert E. *The Effect of Classroom Organization and Teacher-Student Interaction on the Distribution of Status in the Classroom*. Unpublished dissertation. University of Chicago, Chicago, Ill., 1978.

Martell, G. "Class Bias in Toronto Schools: The Park School Community Council Brief." *This Magazine Is About Schools* 5, no. 4 (1971):7–35.

Martin, Jane Roland. "Excluding Women from the Educational Realm." *Harvard Educational Review* 52, no. 2, 1982, pp. 133–48.

Maykovich, M. K. "Reciprocity in Racial Stereotypes: White, Black, and Yellow." *American Journal of Sociology* 77 (1972):876–897.

Mayo, Elton. *The Human Problems of an Industrial Civilization*. New York: MacMillan, 1933.

Mead, G. H. *Mind, Self, and Society*. Chicago: University of Chicago Press, 1934.

Means, V., W. J. Moore, E. Gagne, and W. Hauch. "The Interactive Effect of Consonant and Dissonant Teacher Expectancy and Feedback Communication on Student Performance in a Natural School Setting." *American Educational Research Journal* 16 (1979):367–73.

Medina, G. *Student Leadership Skills: The Development and Testing of an Instructional Team*. Unpublished doctoral dissertation, University of Oregon, 1979.

Menlo, Allen. "Mental Health Within the Classroom Group." *The University of Michigan School of Education Bulletin*. Vol. 31 (May 1960): pp. 121–24.

Menuchin, Patricia, Barbara Biber, Edna Shapiro, and Herbert Zimiles. *The Psychological Impact of School Experience: A Comparative Study of Nine-Year-Old Children in Contrasting Schools*. New York; Basic Books, 1969.

Merriam, Mary Linda, and Bernard C. Guerney, Jr. "Creating a Democratic Elementary Classroom: A Pilot Training Program Involving Teachers, Administrators and Parents." *Contemporary Education* 45 (1973):34–41.

Merton, R. *Social Theory and Social Structure*. New York: Free Press, 1949.

Merton, R. *Social Theory and Social Structure*. Rev. ed. Glencoe: The Free Press, 1957.

Meskin, Joan. "The Performance of Women School Administrators—A Review of the Literature." *Administrator's Notebook* 23, no. 1 (1974).

Michael, J. A. "High School Climates and Plans for Entering College." *Public Opinion Quarterly* 25 (1961):585–95.

Miel, Alice, et al. *Cooperative Procedures in Learning*. New York: Teachers' College Press, 1952.

Miles, Matthew. *Learning to Work in Groups*. New York: Teachers' College, Columbia University, 1959 and 1981.

Miles, Matthew, and W. W. Charters, Jr. *Learning in Social Settings: New Readings in the Social Psychology of Education*. Boston: Allyn and Bacon, 1970.

Milgram, S. "Liberating Effects of Group Pressure." *Journal of Personality and Social Psychology* 18 (1965):73–81.

Miller, Casey, and Kate Swift. *Words and Women: New Language in New Times*. New York: Anchor Books, 1977.

Miller, J. G. "Living Systems: Basic Concepts, Structure, and Process." *Behavioral Science* 10 (1965).

Miller, Jean Baker. *Toward a New Psychology of Women.* Boston: Beacon Press, 1976.

Montanelli, D. S., and K. T. Hill. "Children's Achievement Expectations and Performance as a Function of Two Consecutive Reinforcement Experiences, Sex and Subject, and Sex of Experimenter." *Journal of Personality and Social Psychology* 13 (1969):115–28.

Moreland, Richard, and John Levine. "Role Transitions in Small Groups." V. L. Allen and E. VandeVliert. (eds.) *Role Transitions, Explorations and Explanations.* New York: Plenum Press, 1984.

Moreno, J. L. "Who Shall Survive?" Washington, D.C.: Nervous and Mental Diseases Publishing Co., 1934. Reprint. New York: Beacon House, 1953.

Mozdzierz, Gerald J., Maureen McConville, and Herbert Krauss. "Classroom Status and Perceived Performance in 6th Graders." *The Journal of Social Psychology* 75 (1968):185–90.

Muldoon, J. F. "The Concentration of Liked and Disliked Members in Groups and the Relationship of the Concentration to Group Cohesiveness." *Sociometry* 18 (1955):73–81.

Mulford, W. *Structured Experiences for Use in the Classroom.* Canberra, Australia: Centre for Continuing Education, Australian National University.

Murray, Henry A. *Explorations in Personality.* New York: Oxford University Press, 1938.

Napier, R. W., and M. Gershenfeld. *Groups: Theory and Experience.* Boston: Houghton Mifflin Co., 1973.

Nash, Roy. *Teacher Expectations and Pupil Learning.* Boston: Routledge & Kegan Paul, 1976.

National Study of School Evaluation. "Student Opinion Inventory." Falls Church, Virginia, 1988.

Nelson, J. F. "High School Context and College Plans—The Impact of Social Structure on Aspirations." *American Sociological Review* 37 (1972), pp. 143–48.

Nelson, Jeffrey. "Big Hit in the Inner City." *American Education,* December, 1978.

Nelson, Margaret. *Attitudes of Intermediate School Children Toward Substitute Teacher Who Received Feedback on Pupil-Desired Behavior.* Ph.D. dissertation, University of Oregon, 1972.

Newcomb, Theodore M. *Social Psychology.* New York: The Dryden Press, 1950.

Newcomb, Theodore. *The Acquaintance Process.* New York: Holt, Rinehart & Winston, 1961.

Newmann, Fred, and Judith Thompson. "Efforts of Cooperative Learning on Achievement in Secondary Schools: Summary of Research." National Center on Effective Secondary Schools, University of Wisconsin-Madison, Sept. 1987.

Nicholls, J. G. "Causal Attributions and Other Achievement-Related Cognitions: Effects of Task Outcome, Attainment Value, and Sex." *Journal of Personality and Social Psychology* 31 (1975):379–89.

Nixon, H. L. *The Small Group.* Englewood Cliffs, N.J.: Prentice-Hall, 1979.

Northway, Mary L. "The Stability of Young Children's Social Relations," *Journal of Educational Research* 11, 1968, pp. 54–57.

Northwest Regional Educational Laboratory. *Interpersonal Communications.* Tuxedo, N.Y.: Xicom, 1969.

Nyberg, D. *Tough and Tender Learning.* Palo Alto, Calif.: National Press Books, 1971.

Ojemann, R. "Basic Approaches to Mental Health: The Human Relations Program at the State University of Iowa." *Personnel and Guidance Journal* 36 (1958):198–206.

Olmstead, M. *The Small Group.* New York: Random House, 1959.

Pace, C. R. *Analyses of a National Sample of College Environments.* Final report, Cooperative Research Project No. 50764. Washington, D.C.: Office of Education, U.S. Department of Health, Education, and Welfare, 1967.

Palardy, J. M. "What Teachers Believe, What Children Achieve." *Elementary School Journal* (April 1969): pp. 370–74.

Parsons, T. *The Social System.* New York: Free Press, 1951.

Parsons, T., and R. Bales. *Family Socialization and Interaction Process.* New York: Free Press, 1955.

Pepitone, A. *Attraction and Hostility.* New York: Atherton Press, 1964.

Pepitone, Emmy. "Lessons From the History of Cooperative Learning: A Life Cycle Analysis." Paper presented at the International Association for the Study of Cooperation in Education, Regina, Saskatchewan, Canada, July, 1985.

Peters, Thomas, and T. Waterman. *In Search of Excellence.* Harper & Row, 1982.

Peterson, Penelope, Louise Cherry Wilkinson, and Maureen Hallinan (eds.) *The Social Context of Instruction: Group Organization and Group Processes.* New York: Academic Press, 1984.

Pett, M. "Correlates of Children's Social Adjustment Following Divorce." *Journal of Divorce* 5, 4 (1982):25–39.

Pettigrew, T. F. "Busing: A Review of the Evidence." *Public Interest* 30 (1973):88–118.

Poirier, G. *Students As Partners in Team Learning.* Berkeley, CA.: Center of Team Learning, 1970.

Polansky, N., R. Lippitt, and F. Redl. "An Investigation of Behavioral Contagion in Groups." *Human Relations* 3 (1950):319–48.

Pope, B. "Prestige Values in Contrasting Socio-Economic Groups of Children." *Psychiatry* 16 (1953):381–85.

Pope, B. "Socio-Economic Contrasts in Children's Peer Culture Prestige Values." *Genetic Psychology Monograph* 47 (1953):157–220.

Porter, Larry. "A Longer Look at Feedback: Skill Building for Senders and Receivers." *Social Change* 4, no. 3 (1974).

Postman, N., and C. Weingartener. *The Soft Revolution.* New York: Delacorte Press, 1971.

Potker, Janice, and Andrew Fischel (eds.) *Sex Bias in the Schools.* New Jersey: Fairleigh Dickinson University Press, 1977.

Price, K. *Intensity of Attraction as a Condition in a Social Psychological Balance Theory.* Ph.D. dissertation, University of Michigan, 1961.

Prutzman, Priscilla, Lee Stern, M. Leonard Burger, Gretchen Bodenhamer. *The Friendly Classroom for a Small Planet.* New Society Publishers, P.O. Box 582, Santa Cruz, CA. 95061, 1988.

Purkey, Stuart, and M. S. Smith. "Effective Schools—A Review." *Elementary School Journal* 83 (March 1983) pp. 427–52.

Rabbitt, Michael, Norman Kafer, and Jim Miles. "Non-Streaming and Classroom Sociometric Structure." *The Australian Journal of Education* 26, 1 (1982):99–101.

Raven, B. *Bibliography of Publications Relating to the Small Group.* Technical Report, No. 1, Office of Naval Research, Washington, D.C., 1959, 1969.

Raven, B. H., and W. Kruglanski. "Conflict and Power." In P. G. Swingle (ed.) *The Structure of Conflict.* New York: Academic Press, pp. 177–219.

Render, G., C. Moon, and D. Treffinger. "Directory of Organizations and Periodicals on Alternative Education." *Journal of Creative Behavior* 7 (1973):54–66.

Retish, P. M. "Changing the Status of Poorly Esteemed Students through Teacher Reinforcement." *Journal of Applied Science* 9 (1973):44–50.

Reynolds, Carol. "Buddy System Improves Attendance." *Elementary School Guidance and Counseling* 11 (4 April 1977):305–36.

Rice, A. K. *Learning for Leadership.* London: Tavistock Publications, 1965.

Richards, H. H. "Psychological Factors Associated with the Sociometric Status of Children Attending a Comprehensive School in Breconshire." *British Journal of Educational Psychology* 37 (1967):261–62.

Rioch, Margaret J. "The Work of Wilfred Bion on Groups." *Psychiatry* (February 1970):56–66.

Rioch, Margaret J. "Group Relations: Rationale and Technique." *International Journal of Group Psychotherapy* 20 (1970b):340–55.

Rist, R. "Student Social Class and Teacher Expectations: The Self-Fulfilling Prophecy in Ghetto Education." *Harvard Educational Review* 40 (1970):411–51.

Rivers, M. *Manipulating Freedom in Groups: Two Months Hell, Ten Months Heaven.* Adelaide: Education Department of South Australia, 1976.

Roderick, Tom. "Johnny Can Learn To Negotiate." *Educational Leadership.* (January 1988):87–90.

Roethlisberger, F. J. *The Elusive Phenomena.* Cambridge: Harvard University Press, 1977.

Roethlisberger, F. J., and W. J. Dickson. *Management and the Worker.* Cambridge, Mass.: Harvard University Press, 1939.

Rogacion, Sr. Mary Rebecca. "Training Youth Leaders Through Peer Counseling." In *Cooperation in Education,* edited by S. Sharon, et al., Provo, Utah: Brigham Young University, 1980.

Rogers, Carl. *Freedom to Learn.* Columbus, Ohio: Charles E. Merrill, 1969.

Rosenhan, D. L. "On Being Sane in Insane Places." *Science* 179 (1973):250–58.

Rosenholtz, Susan. *Teachers' Workplace: The Social Organization of Schools.* New York: Longman, 1989.

Rosenthal, R. "The Pygmalion Effect Lives." *Psychology Today* 7, Vol. 4 (April 1973):56–63.

Rosenthal, R., and L. Jacobson. *Pygmalion in the Classroom.* New York: Holt, Rinehart & Winston, 1968.

Rothbart, Myron, Swan Dalfen, and Robert Barrett. "Effects of Teachers' Expectancy on Student-Teacher Interaction." *Journal of Educational Psychology* 62 (1971):49–54.

Rothstein, P. *Educational Psychology.* New York: McGraw-Hill, 1990.

Rubin, L. *Children's Friendships.* Cambridge, Mass.: Harvard University Press, 1980.

Rubin, Z. *Liking and Loving: An Invitation to Social Psychology.* New York: Holt, Rinehart & Winston, 1973.

Rubovits, P. C., and M. L. Maehr. "Pygmalion Analyzed: Toward an Explanation of the Rosenthal-Jacobson Findings." *Journal of Personality and Social Psychology* 19 (1971):197–204.

Runkel, P. J., Marilyn Lawrence, Shirley Oldfield, Mimi Rider, and Candee Clark. "Stages of Group Development: An Empirical Test of Tuckman's Hypothesis." *Journal of Applied Behavioral Science* 7, no. 2 (1971):54–66.

Runkel, P., S. Wyant, W. Bell, and M. Runkel. *Organizational Renewal in a School District.* Eugene, Oregon: CEPM, University of Oregon, 1980.

Rutter, Michael, et al. *Fifteen Thousand Hours.* Cambridge, Mass.: Harvard University Press, 1979.

Ryans, D. G. *Characteristics of Teachers: Their Description, Comparison, and Appraisal.* Washington, D.C.: American Council on Education, 1960.

Sadker, Myra, and David Sadker (eds.) *Handbook for Sex Equity in Schools.* New York: Longmans, 1982.

SAFE School Study. Washington, D.C.: National Institute of Education, H.E.W., 1977.

Sagan, H. Andrew, and Janet Schofield. "Race and Gender Barriers: Pre-Adolescent Peer Behavior in Academic Classrooms." *Child Development* 54, (1983) pp. 1032–40.

Sandler, Bernice. *The Classroom Climate: A Chilly One for Women?* Project on the Status and Education of Women. Association of American College, Washington, D.C., 1982.

Saphier, Jonathon. "The Knowledge Base on Teaching: It's Here, Now!" In *Psychological Research in the Classroom.* Amabile and Stubbs (eds.) New York: Pergammon Press, 1982.

Sarason, Seymour B. *The Culture of the School and the Problem of Change.* 2nd edition, Boston: Allyn and Bacon, 1982.

Schachter, S. "Deviation, Rejection, and Communication." *Journal of Abnormal and Social Psychology* 46 (1951):190–207.

Schein, E. *Organizational Culture and Leadership.* San Francisco: Jossey-Bass, 1985.

Schein, E., and W. Bennis. *Personal and Organizational Change Through Group Methods.* New York: John Wiley & Sons, 1965.

Schmuck, P. "Administrative Strategies to Implement Sex Equity." In Klein, S. (ed.) *Handbook for Achieving Sex Equity Through Education.* Baltimore: Johns Hopkins Press, 1985.

Schmuck, P. *Sex Equity in Educational Leadership: The Oregon Story.* Newton, Mass.: The Education Development Corporation, 1982.

Schmuck, P. A. "Sex Differentiation in Public Schools Administration." Washington, D.C.: National Council of Administrative Women in Education, 1976.

Schmuck, P. A., and R. A. Schmuck. "Democratic Participation in Small Town Schools." *Educational Researcher,* 19, no. 8, (November 1990), pp. 14–20.

Schmuck, R. A. "Some Relationships of Peer Liking Patterns in the Classroom to Pupil Attitudes and Achievement." *School Review* 71 (1963):337–59.

Schmuck, R. A. "Some Aspects of Classroom Social Climate." *Psychology in the Schools* 3 (1966):59–65.

Schmuck, R. A. "Helping Teachers Improve Classroom Group Processes." *Journal of Applied Behavioral Science* 4 (1968):401–35.

Schmuck, R. A. "Influence of the Peer Group." In *Psychology and Educational Practice,* edited by G. Lesser. Glenview, Ill.: Scott, Foresman & Co., 1971, pp. 502–29.

Schmuck, R. A. "Peer Consultation for School Improvement." In *Advances in Experiential Social Processes,* edited by Cary L. Cooper, and Clayton P. Alderfer. Sussex, England: John Wiley & Sons Limited, 1978.

Schmuck, R. A. "Organization Development in the Schools." In *Handbook of School Psychology,* edited by Reynolds, C. R., and T. B. Guskin, New York: John Wiley, 1982.

Schmuck, R. A., and M. Miles (eds.) *Organization Development in Schools.* Palo Alto: Mayfield Press, 1971.

Schmuck, R. A., and P. Runkel. "Group Processes." In *Encyclopedia of Educational Research,* edited by J. Mitzel. New York: McMillian and Co., 1982.

Schmuck, R. A., and P. A. Schmuck. *A Humanistic Psychology of Education: Making the School Everybody's House.* Palo Alto, Calif.: National Press Books, 1974.

Schmuck, R. A., and P. A. Schmuck. "Humanistic Education: A Review of Books Since 1970." *The 1976 Annual Handbook for Group Facilitators.* La Jolla, Calif.: University Associates, 1976.

Schmuck, R. A., and P. A., Schmuck. "Adolescents' Attitudes Toward School and Teachers: From 1963 to 1989." *Bulletin of the National Association of Secondary School Principals,* Vol. 75, no. 533, March, 1991.

Schmuck, R. A., and E. Van Egmond. "Sex Differences in the Relationship of Interpersonal Perceptions to Academic Performance." *Psychology in the Schools* 2 (1965):32–40.

Schmuck, R. A., M. Chesler, and R. Lippitt. *Problem Solving to Improve Classroom Learning.* Chicago: Science Research Associates, 1966.

Schmuck, R. A., P. Runkel, J. Arends, and R. Arends. *The Second Handbook of Organization Development in Schools.* Palo Alto, Calif.: Mayfield Press, 1977.

Schmuck, R. A., and P. J. Runkel. *The Handbook of Organization Development in Schools.* Palo Alto, Calif.: Mayfield Press, Third ed., 1985.

Schmuck, R., D. Murray, M. Smith, M. Schwartz, and M. Runkel. *Consultation for Innovative Schools: OD for Multi-Unit Structures.* Eugene, Oregon: Center for Educational Policy and Management, 1975.

Schmuck, Richard. "Organization Development in Schools: Contemporary Concepts and Practices." In Reynolds, C. R., and T. B. Gutkin (eds.) *The Handbook of School Psychology.* New York: John Wiley, Second edition, 1990.

Schofield, Janet W. *Black and White in School: Trust, Tension or Tolerance?* New York: Prager, 1982.

Schofield, Janet. "School Desegregation and Intergroup Relations." In *Social Psychology of Education: Theory and Research,* edited by D. Bar Tal and I. Saxe. Washington, D.C.: Hemisphere Publishing Co., 1978.

Schofield, Janet W., and H. Andrew Sagar. "Peer Interactions in an Integrated Middle School." *Sociometry* 40, no. 2 (1977):130–38.

Schmidt, Fran, and Alice Friedman. *Fighting Fair: Dr. Martin Luther King, Jr. For Kids.* Miami Beach, Florida: Grace Contrino Abrams Peace Education Foundation Inc., 1986.

Schutz, W. *FIRO: A Three Dimensional Theory of Interpersonal Behavior.* New York: Holt, Rinehart & Winston, 1958.

Schutz, W. *The Interpersonal Underworld.* Palo Alto, Calif.: Science and Behavior Books, 1966.

Sears, P. "Levels of Aspiration of Academically Successful and Unsuccessful Children." *Journal of Abnormal and Social Psychology* 35 (1940):498–536.

Seashore, S. *Group Cohesiveness in the Industrial Work Group*. Ann Arbor, Mich.: Institute for Social Research, 1954.

Seeman, Alice, and Melvin Seeman. "Staff Processes and Pupil Attitudes: A Study of Teacher Participation in Educational Change." *Human Relations* 21, no. 1 (1976):24–40.

Segal, Mady Wechsler. "Varieties of Interpersonal Attraction and Their Interrelationship in Natural Groups." *Social Psychological Quarterly* 42 (1979):252–53.

Sewell, W. H., and J. M. Armer "Neighborhood Context and College Plans." *American Sociological Review* (1966):159–68.

Sexton, P. C. *Education and Income, Inequality of Opportunity in Our Public Schools*. New York: Viking Press, 1961.

Shaftel, F., and G. Shaftel. *Role Playing for Social Values: Decision Making in the Social Studies*. Englewood Cliffs, N.J.: Prentice-Hall, 1967.

Shakeshaft, Charol. "Strategies for Overcoming the Barriers to Women in Educational Adminsitration." In Klein, S. (ed.) *Handbook for Achieving Sex Equity in Schools*. Baltimore, Johns Hopkins Press, 1985, pp. 124–44.

Shakeshaft, Charol. *Women in School Administration*. San Francisco: Sage Publishing, 1987.

Shambaugh, Phillip Wells. "The Development of the Small Group." *Human Relations* 31 (1978):283–95.

Sharon, Shlomo, ed. *Cooperative Learning*. New York: Preager, 1990 A.

Sharon, Shlomo. "Cooperative Learning and Helping Behavior in the Multi-Ethnic Classroom." In H. C. Foot, M. J. Morgan, and R. H. Shute (eds.) *Children Helping Children*. London, England: John Wiley and Sons, 1990 B.

Sharan, Shlomo, and Yael Sharan. *Small Group Teaching*. Englewood Cliffs, N.J.: Educational Technology Publications, 1976.

Sharan, Shlomo, and Rachel Hertz-Lazarowitz. "A Group-Investigation Method of Cooperative Learning in the Classroom." In *Cooperation in Education*, edited by S. Sharan, et al., Provo, Utah: Brigham Young University Press, 1981.

Sharan, Shlomo, et al. (eds.) *Cooperation in Education*. Provo, Utah: Brigham Young University Press, 1981.

Sharan, S., and H. Shachar. *Language and Learning in the Cooperative Classroom*. New York: Springer-Verlag, 1988.

Shaw, M. E. *Group Dynamics: The Psychology of Small Group Behavior*. La Jolla, Calif.: NTL/Learning Resources Corporation, 1971, 1976.

Shaw, J. S. "Students Evaluate Teachers and It Works." *Nation's Schools* 91, no. 4 (1973):49–53.

Shaw, M., and J. M. Blum. "Effects of Leadership Style upon Group Performance as a Function of Task Structure." *Journal of Personality and Social Psychology* 3 (1966):328–42.

Shaycroft, Marion F. *Project Talent, the High School Years: Growth in Cognitive Skills*. American Institute for Research and School of Education, University of Pittsburgh, 1967.

Shepherd, C. *Small Groups*. San Francisco: Chandler Publishing Co., 1964.

Sher, J., and R. Tomkins, "Research and Action Agenda for Rural Education." Education for Rural America. Boulder, CO: Westview Press, 1977.

Sherif, M. "A Study of Some Factors in Perception." *Archives of Psychology* 187 (1935).

Sherif, M., O. J. Harvey, B. J. White, W. R. Hood, and C. W. Sherif. *Intergroup Conflict and Cooperation: The Robbers' Cave Experiment*. Norman, Oklahoma: University of Oklahoma Press, 1961.

Sherman, Lawrence. "Social Distance Perceptions of Elementary School Children in Age-Heterogeneous and Homogeneous Classroom Settings." *Perceptual and Motor Skills*, 58 (1984) pp. 395–401.

Shils, E. A., and M. Janowitz. "Cohesion and Disintegration in the Wehrmacht in World War II." *Public Opinion Quarterly* 12, no. 1 (1948):280–315.

Silberman, C. *Crisis in the Classroom*. New York: Random House, 1970.

Simmel, Georg. *Soziologic Untersuchungen Uber Die Former Der Vergefellshaftung*. Lepzig, Duneker, Humblot, 1908.

Simon, A., and Ed. Boyer (eds.) *Mirrors for Behavior*. Title IV, ESEA of 1965 in cooperation with U.S. Office of Education, Research Contract #OEC, 1–7–062867–3053, A Regional Educational Laboratory. Philadelphia: Research for Better Schools, 1967.

Simon, A., T. Samph, R. S. Soar, and E. Amidon. "Programming Teacher-Pupil Interaction Patterns." Paper for AERA, Feb. 1966.

Sizer, Theodore. *Horace's Compromise*. Boston: Houghton-Mifflin, 1984.

Slavin, Robert E. "Synthesis of Research on Grouping in Elementary and Secondary Schools." *Educational Leadership* (Sept. 1988).

Slavin, R. E. "Student Team Learning: A Manual for Teachers." In Sharan, S., P. Hare, C. Webb, and R. Hertz-Lazarowitz, (eds.) *Cooperation in Education*. Provo, UT: Brigham Young University Press, 1981.

Slavin, Robert E. "Classroom Reward Structure: An Analytical and Practical Review." *Review of Educational Research* 47, no. 4 (1977):633–50.

Slavin, Robert E. *Cooperative Learning*. New York: Longman, 1983.

Slavin, Robert E. "Cooperative Learning." *Review of Educational Research* 50 (1980):315–42.

Slavin, Robert E., and Nancy Karweit. "Effects of Whole Class, Ability Grouped, and Individualized Instruction on Mathematics Achievement." *American Educational Research Journal* 22, no. 3 (Fall, 1985): pp. 351–67.

Slavin, Robert E., S. Sharan, S. Kagen, R. Hertz-Lazarowitz, C. Webb, and R. Schmuck (eds.) *Learning to Cooperate, Cooperating to Learn*. New York: Plenum, 1985.

Smith, L., and William Geoffrey. *Complexities of an Urban Classroom: An Analysis toward a General Theory of Teaching*. New York: Holt, Rinehart & Winston, 1971.

Smith, M., and G. Glass. *Relationship of Class-Size to Classroom Processes, Teacher Satisfaction, and Pupil Affect*. San Francisco: Farwest Educational Laboratory, 1979.

Smith, P. B. *Group Processes and Personal Change*. London: Harper and Row, 1980.

Smith, Roy. "A Teacher's Views on Cooperative Learning." *Phi Delta Kappan* (May, 1987) pp. 663–66.

Snow, R. E. "Unfinished Pygmalion." *Contemporary Psychology* 14 (1969):197–99.

Snygg, D., and A. W. Combs. *Individual Behavior: A New Frame of Reference for Psychology*. New York: Harper & Row Publishers, 1949.

Sommer, R. "Classroom Ecology." *Journal of Applied Behavioral Science* 3 (1967):328–42.

Spector, P., and B. J. Suttell. *An Experimental Comparison of the Effectiveness of Three Patterns of Leadership Behavior*. American Institute for Research, 1957.

Stallings, Jane, and others. *Early Childhood Education Classroom Evaluation*. Menlo Park, California: SRI International, 1978. Eric Clearinghouse ED 210–20.

Stanford, B. "How Innovators Fail: Teaching Human Development." *Media and Methods* (October 1971) pp. 26–35.

Stanford, G. *Developing Effective Classroom Groups*. New York: Hart, 1977.

Stavig, Gordon R., and Larry D. Barnett. "Group Size and Societal Conflict." *Human Relations* 30, no. 8 (1977):755–61.

Stein, A. H., S. R. Pohly, and E. Mueller. "The Influence of Masculine, Feminine, and Neutral Tasks on Children's Achievement Behavior, Expectancies of Success, and Attainment Values." *Child Development* 42 (1971):195–207.

Steinberg, Jane, and Warren C. Hall. "Effects of Social Behavior on Interracial Acceptance." Paper presented at the American Psychological Association, Montreal, Canada, 1980.

Steinzer, B. "The Spatial Factor in Face-to-Face Discussion Groups." *Journal of Abnormal and Social Psychology* 45 (1950):552–55.

Stensaasen, Svein. *Rejected Pupils in the School Class*. Pedagogisk Forskning. Nordisk Tidsskrift for Pedagogikk. Oslo, Norway: Universitelsforlaget, 1965.

Stensaasen, Svein. *Should Rejection Reports be Included in Sociometric Testing*. Pedagogisk Forskning. Nordisk Tidsskrift for Pedagogikk. Oslo, Norway: Universitelsforlaget, 1967.

Stensaasen, Svein. *Interstudent Attraction and Social Perception in the School Class*. Oslo, Norway: Universitelsforlaget, 1970.

Stern, G. G. "Environments for Learning." In *The American College,* edited by N. Stanford. New York: John Wiley & Sons, 1962.

Stockard, Jean, Patricia Schmuck, Ken Kempner, Peg Williams, Sakre Edson, Mary Ann Smith. *Sex Equity in Education.* New York: Academic Press, 1980.

Stodgill, R. M. "Group Productivity, Drive and Cohesiveness." *Organizational Behavior and Human Performance* 8, no. 1 (1972):26–43.

Stodgill, R. M. *Handbook of Leadership: A Survey of Theory and Research.* New York: The Free Press, 1974.

Sullivan, H. S. "The Meaning of Anxiety in Psychiatry and in Life." *Psychiatry* 3 (1948):1–17.

Sumner, W. *Folkways.* New York: Dover Publications, 1906.

Sutton-Smith, B., and B. G. Rosenberg. "Sixty Years of Historical Change in Game Preference of American Children." *Child's Play.* Edited by R. E. Herron and Brian Sutton-Smith. New York: John Wiley and Sons, 1971.

Sweeney, J. *School Climate Inventory.* Ames, Iowa: Iowa State University, 1988.

Swidler, Ann. "What Free Schools Teach." *Social Problems* 24, no. 2 (1976):214–27.

Tajfel, H. "Social Psychology of Intergroup Relations." *Annual Review of Psychology* 33 (1982):1–39.

Takanishi, Ruby, and Sue Spitzer. "Children's Perceptions of Human Resources in Team-Teaching Classrooms." *The Elementary School Journal* 8, 4 (1980):203–27.

Tesch, F., L. Lansky, and D. Lundgren. "The One-Way/Two-Way Communication Exercise: Some Ghosts Laid to Rest." *Journal of Applied Behavioral Science* 8, no. 6 (1972):664–73.

Thelen, H. A. *Dynamics of Groups at Work.* Chicago: University of Chicago Press, 1954.

Thelan, Herbert. *Education for the Human Quest.* New York: Harper & Row, 1960.

Thomas, A. R. "The Innovative School: Some Organizational Characteristics." *The Australian Journal of Education* 17, 2 (1973):113–30.

Thomas, A., S. Chess, H. Birch, M. Hetzig, and S. Korn. *Behavior Individuality in Early Childhood.* New York: New York University Press, 1963.

Thompson, J. D. *Organizations in Action.* New York: McGraw-Hill Book Co., 1967.

Thorndike, R. "Review of Rosenthal and Jacobson, Pygmalion in the Classroom." *American Educational Research Journal* 5 (1968):700–710.

Thorne, Barrie, and Nancy Henley (eds.) *Language and Sex Difference and Dominance.* Rowley, Massachusetts: Newbury House Publishers, 1975.

Thorne, Barrie, Cheris Kramarae, and Nancy Henley (eds.) *Language, Gender, and Society.* Rowley, Massachusetts: Newbury House Publishers, 1983.

Tjosvold, D. "The Issue of Student Control: A Critical Review of the Literature." Paper presented at the AERA Annual Convention, April 1976.

Torrance, E. P. *Education and the Creative Potential.* Minneapolis: University of Minnesota Press, 1963.

Torrance, E. P. *Rewarding Creative Behavior.* Englewood Cliffs, N.J.: Prentice-Hall, 1965.

Touhey, John. "Sex Role Stereotyping and Individual Differences in Liking for the Physically Attractive." *Social Psychological Quarterly* 42 (1979):285–89.

Trow, W., A. Zander, W. Morse, and D. Jenkins. "Psychology of Group Behaviors: The Class as a Group." *Journal of Educational Psychology* 41 (1950):322–28.

Tuckman, B. W. "Developmental Sequence in Small Groups." *Psychological Bulletin* 63 (1965):384–99.

Tuckman, B. W., and W. Oliver. "Effectiveness of Feedback to Teachers as a Function Source." *Journal of Educational Psychology* 59 (1968):297–30.

Turner, Marion E. *The Child within the Group: An Experiment in Self-Government.* Stanford, Calif: Stanford University Press, 1957.

Tye, B. B. "The Deep Structure of Schooling." *The Kappan,* 69, 4, December 1987, 281–84.

Uguroglu, M. E., and H. Walberg. "Motivation and Achievement: A Quantitative Synthesis." *American Educational Research Journal,* 16, 4, 1979, 375–89.

Vacha, Edward F., William A. McDonald, Joan M. Coburn, and Harold E. Black. *Improving Classroom Social Climate.* New York: Holt, Rinehart and Winston, 1979.

Van Horn, R. "Environmental Psychology: Hints of a New Technology." *Phi Delta Kappan* 61 (10) (June 1980) pp. 696–98.

Walberg, H. J. "Personality Correlates of Factored Teaching Attitudes." *Psychology in the Schools* 5 (1968):670–74.

Walberg, H. J. "Predicting Class Learning: An Approach to the Class as a Social System." *American Educational Research Journal* 6, no. 4 (1969):529–42.

Walberg, H. J., and G. S. Anderson. "The Achievement-Creativity Dimension and Classroom Climate." *Journal of Creative Behavior* 2, no. 4 (1968):281–92.

Walberg, Herbert J. (ed.) *Educational Environments and Effects: Evaluation, Policy and Productivity.* Berkeley, CA.: McCutchan, 1979.

Wallen, J. *Interpersonal Communications.* Northwest Regional Educational Laboratory. Tuxedo, N.Y.: Xicom, 1969.

Wallerstein, J., and J. Keely. *Surviving the Breakup.* New York: Basic Books, 1980.

Walster, E., V. Aronson, D. Abrahams, and L. Rottman. "Importance of Physical Attractiveness in Dating Behavior." *Journal of Personality and Social Psychology* 4 (1966):508–16.

Warner, W., and P. S. Lunt. *The Social Life of a Modern Community.* New Haven, Conn.: Yale University Press, 1941.

Wax, R. *Doing Fieldwork: Warning and Advice.* Chicago: University of Chicago Press, 1971.

Webb, Nancy. "Organizing A Student Council in the Elementary School." *Catalyst for Change* 17, no. 1 (Fall 1987), pp. 4–5.

Weick, Karl. "The Spines of Leaders." In *Leadership: Where Else Can We Go?* edited by McCall and Lombardo. Durham, N.C.: Duke University Press, 1978.

Weiner, B. "A Theory of Motivation for Some Classroom Experiences." *Journal of Educational Psychology,* 71, 1979, 3–25.

Weiner, B. "Spontaneous Causal Search." *Psychological Bulletin,* 97, 1985, 74–84.

Weinstein, Rhona. *Student Perceptions of Differential Teacher Treatment.* NIE Grant Number G-79–0078. Unpublished Paper. Berkeley, Calif.: University of California, 1980.

Weisbord, M. *Productive Workplaces.* San Francisco, CA: Jossey-Bass, 1988.

Wells, Theodora. "Woman—Which Includes Man, of Course." *Project Awareness.* Olympia, Wash.: State Superintendent of Public Instruction, 1976.

Whisler, J. S. *Young Adolescents and Middle Level Education: A Review of Current Issues, Concerns, and Recommendations.* Kansas City, MO: Mid-Continent Regional Educational Laboratory, 1990.

White, R. W. "Motivation Reconsidered: The Concept of Competence." *Psychological Review* 66 (1959):297–333.

White, R. W., and R. Lippitt. *Autocracy and Democracy.* New York: Harper & Brothers, 1960.

Whyte, W. F. *Street Corner Society.* Chicago: University of Chicago Press, 1943.

Willower, D., et al. *The School and Pupil Control Ideology.* University Park, Pennsylvania: Pennsylvania State Studies Monograph, no. 24, 1967.

Wilson, A. "Residential Segregation of Social Classes and Aspirations of High School Boys." *American Sociological Review* 24 (1959):836–45.

Wilson, Noel, Clay Lafleur, Robert Brodie, Margaret Cary, Alan Dale, Brian Johnston, and Tess Young. *Developing the Classroom Group: A Research Report.* South Australian Education Department of South Wales, 1979.

Wilson, Stephen. *Informal Groups: An Introduction.* Englewood Cliffs, N.J.: Prentice-Hall, 1978.

Winch, R., T. Ktanses, and V. Ktanses. "Empirical Elaboration of the Theory of Complementarity Needs in Mate Selection." *Journal of Abnormal and Social Psychology* 51 (1955):508–13.

Winter, D., R. Alpert, and D. McClelland. "The Classic Personal Style." *Journal of Abnormal and Social Psychology* 67 (1963):254–65.

Withall, J. "The Development of a Climate Index." *Journal of Educational Research* 45 (1951):93–99.

Withall, John. "The Development of a Technique for the Measurement of Social Emotional Climate in Classrooms." *Journal of Experimental Education* 18, no. 2 (1949).

Withall, John. "Democratic Leadership: A Function of the Instructional Process." *School Review* 57, no. 5 & 6, (May-June 1949).

Withall, John, Herb Thelan, et al. "Experimental Research Toward a Theory of Instruction." *Journal of Educational Research* 45, 2 October 1951.

Withall, John, and W. W. Lewis. "Social Interaction in the Classroom." In *Handbook of Research on Teaching*. Gage, N. (ed.) New York: Rand McNally Publishers, 1963.

Withall, John. "Classroom Learning: Group and Social Factors." *International Encyclopedia of Psychiatry, Psychology and Neurology*. Vol. 3, Van Nostrand Reinhold: Aesculapius Publishers, 1977.

Women on Words and Images. *Dick and Jane as Victims: Sex Stereotyping in Children's Readers*. Princeton, N.J.: Women on Words and Images, 1972.

Woodward, Joanne. "Peer Acceptance for the Handicapped: Myth or Reality." *Phi Delta Kappan* 61 (1980):715.

Wyant, S. "Power to the Pupil: An Annotated Bibliography of Student Involvement, Student Power, and Student Participation in Decision-Making in Public Secondary Schools." Eugene, Oregon: Center for Educational Policy and Management, 1973.

Yager, S., R. Johnson, D. Johnson, and B. Snider. "The Impact of Group Processing on Achievement in Cooperative Learning." *The Journal of Social Psychology,* 1986.

Yancy, W. L., T. Rigsby, and J. D. McCarthy. "Social Position and Self-Evaluation: The Relative Importance of Race." *American Journal of Sociology* 78 (1972):338–57.

Zajonc, R. "The Concepts of Balance, Congruity, and Dissonance." *Public Opinion Quarterly* 24 (1960):280–96.

Zander, A., and A. R. Cohen. "Attributed Social Power and Group Acceptance: A Classroom Experimental Demonstration." *Journal of Abnormal and Social Psychology* 51 (1955):490–92.

Index